The Book of Job in Medieval Jewish Philosophy

The Book of Job in Medieval Jewish Philosophy

ROBERT EISEN

OXFORD
UNIVERSITY PRESS
2004

OXFORD
UNIVERSITY PRESS

Oxford New York
Auckland Bangkok Buenos Aires Cape Town Chennai
Dar es Salaam Delhi Hong Kong Istanbul Karachi Kolkata
Kuala Lumpur Madrid Melbourne Mexico City Mumbai Nairobi
São Paulo Shanghai Taipei Tokyo Toronto

Published by Oxford University Press, Inc.
198 Madison Avenue, New York, New York 10016

www.oup.com

Library of Congress Cataloging-in-Publication Data

Eisen, Robert, 1960–
The Book of Job in medieval Jewish philosophy / Robert Eisen.
p. cm.
Includes bibliographical references and index.
ISBN 0-19-517153-5
1. Bible. O.T. Job—Criticism, interpretation, etc., Jewish—History—To 1500.
2. Providence and government of God—Judaism—History of doctrines—Middle Ages, 600–1500
3. Philosophy, Jewish. 4. Philosophy, Medieval. I. Title.

BS1415.52.E37 2004
223'.106—dc22 2004013618

9 8 7 6 5 4 3 2 1

Printed in the United States of America
on acid-free paper

To Naomi

Preface

In 1986, when I was a graduate student, I had the privilege of becoming acquainted with the late Professor Frank Talmage, the distinguished scholar of medieval Jewish exegesis. I vividly recall a conversation I had with him one evening in his apartment in Toronto in which he spoke excitedly about the abundance of material in medieval Jewish exegesis yet to be explored, and he illustrated his point by showing me a bibliography he had recently assembled on medieval Jewish commentaries on the Book of Job containing seventy-six references. Most of these works, he exclaimed, had never been examined by modern scholars. He went on to ponder the significance of this large body of material. Why did medieval Jews compose so many commentaries on Job? How did they understand this provocative book? What would the commentaries tell us about medieval Jewish attitudes toward suffering?

That conversation I never forgot, and it became significant years later. My research interests eventually came to focus on biblical exegesis in medieval Jewish philosophy. I was motivated by the conviction that the medieval Jewish philosophers were highly skilled and creative exegetes whose interpretations of the biblical text had not been properly appreciated by modern academic scholars. In recent years, I became particularly intrigued by the fact that in the course of my research I had come across a significant number of references to commentaries on Job written by medieval Jewish philosophers. Recalling my conversation with Talmage, I decided to delve into these commentaries, and I soon realized that they were a fascinating collection of texts that had received relatively little scholarly attention. I therefore resolved to write this study. It is my hope that it will prove both Talmage and me right, that Talmage was correct in his speculation that medieval Jewish commentaries on Job are very much worthy of exploration and that I have been correct in believing that the medieval Jewish philosophers were exegetes whose skills as biblical commentators have been greatly underestimated.

I would like to thank a number of institutions that provided generous support for this project. A grant from the Fulbright Foundation in 1999–2000 allowed me to spend a sabbatical year at the Hebrew University in Jerusalem, where the bulk of the research for this study was conducted. I also received grants from the Memorial Foundation for Jewish Culture in 1999–2000 and from George Washington University in the summer of 2001.

I must thank a number of colleagues whose assistance was instrumental in the completion of this study. Avi Ravitzky issued the formal invitation to come to the Hebrew University as a Fulbright fellow and was very generous in providing scholarly help and advice throughout my year in Israel. Daniel Lasker and David Berger provided critical advice and assistance in dealing with the lengthy process of applying for grants. A number of colleagues read the entire manuscript and offered insightful comments and criticisms that improved it immeasurably: Mordechai Cohen, Zev Harvey, Marc Saperstein, and Susan Schreiner. Susan Schreiner is also to be thanked for her encouragement and for connecting me with Oxford University Press. I must also mention my parents, who read the entire manuscript and corrected many errors. A number of colleagues read and commented on individual parts of the manuscript: Ari Ackerman, Jason Kalman, Lawrence Kaplan, Menachem Kellner, Howard Kreisel, and Roy Pinchot. I received excellent bibliographic assistance from Qadir Amiryar and his staff at George Washington University, Michael Grunberger and his staff at the Library of Congress, Binyamin Richler and Yael Okun of the Institute for Microfilmed Manuscripts at the National Library in Jerusalem, and Pat MacNicoll, my colleague at George Washington University. Barry Walfish succeeded in locating a copy of Frank Talmage's bibliography of medieval Jewish commentaries on Job, which he sent to me. It was extremely helpful in the early stages of my research. Cynthia Read and Christi Stanforth at Oxford University Press did a marvelous job overseeing the review and production process of this study. Finally, I would like to make mention of Marvin Fox and Alfred Ivry, the two scholars most influential on me as a graduate student at Brandeis University and whose influence is evident throughout this study. Marvin Fox passed from this world before this project began, and the absence of his wisdom, advice, and insight was felt at every stage of its completion.

Some of the chapters in this book are based on previous publications of mine, and I would like to thank a number of journals for permission to reproduce portions of those publications. Sections of chapter 2 were taken from "Job as a Symbol for Israel in the Thought of Saadiah Gaon," *Da'at* 41 (Summer 1998): v–xxv. Chapter 4 is a revised version of "Samuel ibn Tibbon on the Book of Job," *AJS Review* 24, no. 2 (Fall 2000): 263–300. Chapter 6 is a revised version of "Gersonides' *Commentary on the Book of Job*," *Journal of Jewish Thought and Philosophy* 10 (2001): 239–88.

I would like to say a word about my wife Naomi, to whom this book is dedicated. I do not imagine that it is easy being married to an academic, particularly one who is in the midst of a challenging book project such as this one. This study deals with difficult commentaries written on one of the most cryptic books in the Bible. Deciphering them and making sense of their contents involved years of research and writing—along with a good many mood swings. (A number of colleagues, who appreciated the challenge I had taken on, joked that the tribulations involved in writing such a study would allow me to identify with the central character of the biblical book upon which it focused.) Throughout the writing of this study, Naomi was the ideal companion. She celebrated my breakthroughs and successes as if they were her own, and she provided much-needed perspective and a sense of humor when the going was rough. The completion of this study would have been impossible without her unflagging support. Finally, I cannot fail to mention our children Adeena, Sarit, and Yoni. If there were ever an antidote to the heaviness of the subject-matter in the Book of Job, it is to be found in their luminescent faces.

Bibliographic Note

English translations of biblical passages in this study are from the New Jewish Publication Society edition, *Tanakh* (Philadelphia: Jewish Publication Society of America, 1988), henceforth NJPS. However, in a number of instances I have deviated from the NJPS in order to capture the meaning of the biblical text according to the understanding of the thinker under discussion. In such instances, I indicate in my notes that I have departed from NJPS. Talmudic citations are prefaced by *B.T.* for *Babylonian Talmud* and *J.T.* for *Jerusalem Talmud*. Hebrew transliterations follow that of *Encyclopedia Judaica*.

Contents

1. Introduction, 3

2. Saadiah Gaon, 17
   The Philosophical Background: *Beliefs and Opinions* 5:3, 18
   The Commentary on Job, 20
      Antecedents, 28
      Exegesis, 30
      Exegesis and Philosophy, 38
   Concluding Reflections: Saadiah and the Christian Reading of Job, 39

3. Maimonides, 43
   The Philosophical Background: *Guide* III:17–18, 51, 45
   Maimonides on Job: *Guide* III:22–23, 48
      Antecedents, 71
      Exegesis, 72
      Exegesis and Philosophy, 74

4. Samuel ibn Tibbon, 79
   Ibn Tibbon on Job: *Ma'amar Yikkavu ha-Mayim* 15–18, 81
      Antecedents, 97
      Exegesis, 104
      Exegesis and Philosophy, 105
   Tibbonian Readings of Job: Immanuel of Rome, Elijah ben Eliezer ha-Yerushalmi, and Isaac Arundi, 105

5. Zeraḥiah Ḥen, 111
The Commentary on Job, 113
Antecedents, 131
Exegesis, 137
Exegesis and Philosophy, 139

6. Gersonides, 143
The Philosophical Background: Book 4 of *The Wars of the Lord*, 145
The Commentary on Job, 147
Antecedents, 152
Exegesis, 159
Exegesis and Philosophy, 165

7. Simon ben Ẓemaḥ Duran, 175
The Commentary on Job, 177
Antecedents, 189
Exegesis, 195
Exegesis and Philosophy, 197
Duran's Job and Duran's Biography, 198

8. Medieval Jewish Philosophy and the Exegesis of Job, 203
A Tradition of Commentaries? 203
The Medieval Jewish Philosophers as Exegetes of Job, 206
The Exegesis of Job and Systematic Thought in Medieval Jewish Philosophy, 212
Implications for the Study of Medieval Jewish Philosophy, 217

9. Job Medieval, Job Modern, 221

Appendix: A Bibliography of Commentaries on Job in Medieval Jewish Philosophy, 231

Notes, 235

Works Cited, 305

Index, 319

The Book of Job in Medieval Jewish Philosophy

I

Introduction

Few texts have elicited as large and diverse a body of interpretation throughout the ages as the Book of Job. Religious thinkers in Judaism and Christianity from late antiquity onward have produced scores of commentaries on this work, while Islamic thinkers developed an extensive tradition of interpretation on the Job story from a handful of references to it in the Koran. Literary figures, playwrights, and poets in both the medieval and the modern periods have composed numerous works creatively reshaping—and in some cases entirely rewriting—the dialogue in Job in order to impart new meaning to the original story. Modern academic scholars have parsed the Book of Job in every which way and have utilized every conceivable methodology to make sense of its content. The accumulated literature on Job is so overwhelming that it is well beyond the ability of any individual to master it.[1]

The fascination with Job is attributable to numerous factors. First and foremost, it is part of the biblical canon and has therefore received a good deal of attention simply because of its affiliation with Western civilization's most influential and widely read book. But there is much more to the fascination with Job than this alone. Job has perpetually intrigued commentators because it stands out as a unique book in the Bible, with its rich combination of philosophical reflection, prose, and poetry. Job's popularity is also attributable to its subject matter: in grappling with the problem of the suffering of the righteous, it addresses one of humanity's deepest and most vexing problems. Another critical ingredient contributing to the mystique of Job is that it resists easy interpretation on account of its lengthy and meandering dialogue, its ambiguities, its inner inconsistencies, and its cryptic, though dramatic, finale. In fact, it is unlikely that Job would have enchanted thinkers as much as it has if it had given a clear-cut answer to its central question. It is the very ambiguity of God's address from the tempest that makes the reader return to this text again and again.

Jews have succumbed to the allure of Job no less than other groups. It is, after all, part of their very own Hebrew Bible, and with the emphasis that Jewish culture has consistently placed on biblical interpretation as a means of expressing its views, it is understandable that Jewish thinkers would pay a great deal of attention to this most provocative book. Thus, there is profound interest in Job in practically every genre of Jewish literature, including midrash, poetry, exegesis, philosophy, and Kabbalah. Moreover, Jews have often had an advantage over others in grappling with the Book of Job by virtue of their capacity to read the text in the original Hebrew, a skill that is highly significant for understanding this particular biblical book, given the unusual difficulty of its language.[2]

The Jewish interest in Job seems to have been particularly acute in the Middle Ages. The early rabbis who predate this period had certainly commented on Job, and discussions about it are scattered throughout Talmudic and midrashic literature. But these discussions are fragmentary at best.[3] It is only in the medieval period that Jews began to compose full commentaries devoted entirely to the explication of Job, and they produced them in significant numbers. A list of medieval Jewish commentaries on Job compiled by Frank Talmage attests to the existence of some seventy-six such works produced by Jews from the year 900 to 1500, and there are probably many more that have been lost.[4]

These commentaries can be divided into two groups. The majority interpreted the Book of Job according to *peshat*, or the plain meaning of the text, an established hermeneutic method among Jewish exegetes in the medieval period. In accordance with this approach, exegetes attempted to establish the plain sense of the text through a careful line-by-line exegesis based on philology, grammar, and context.[5] A characteristic feature of this group of commentaries is its relative lack of interest in the broad philosophical themes in Job. These commentators thus made little attempt to grapple with such issues as the reason for Job's suffering and the meaning of God's mysterious reply to Job from the tempest at the end of the story. Their focus was almost exclusively on making sense of words, phrases, and verses.[6]

There was, however, a second and smaller group of medieval Jewish commentaries on Job for which the philosophical themes were central. These works were written by medieval Jewish philosophers who attempted to read Job as a philosophical dialogue concerning God's providential relationship with human beings. Most of them read Job against the background of a philosophical system, and because the majority were influenced by Maimonides, who was heavily dependent on Aristotle, their system was most often Aristotelian philosophy. Many of these commentators also incorporated the methods of the first group and provided a line-by-line exegesis of the text in order to understand its meaning with the help of grammar, philology, and context, much as the *peshat*-oriented commentators did. However, the major concern of this group was the philosophical meaning of Job.[7]

These commentators were thus the first interpreters in Judaism to provide readings of Job that were both comprehensive and philosophical. While many of the discussions in early rabbinic literature dealt with the philosophical aspects of Job, their engagement with those issues was oblique and lacked a coherent philosophical framework of the kind that Aristotelianism provided.[8] Moreover, the early rabbis never provided a comprehensive reading of Job.[9] As for the *peshat*-oriented commentators in the medieval period, these thinkers provided comprehensive readings of Job but were, as I noted earlier, uninterested in its philosophical aspects.

It is the second group of medieval Jewish commentators on Job that is the focus of the present study. These figures were an exciting group of interpreters who, while functioning in a worldview very different from our own, produced a series of diverse, original, and sometimes surprisingly radical readings of the Book of Job. Yet, their commentaries have for the most part eluded the attention of scholars in both the field of medieval Jewish philosophy and the field of biblical exegesis.

To get a better of idea of who these interpreters were and why they are worthy of study, let me first say a few words about the philosophical school of which they were a part. Medieval Jewish philosophy actually encompassed a wide variety of thinkers who often differed significantly from one another in their intellectual orientations. The one feature that united them all and has prompted both medieval and modern scholars to see them as representing a single school is the belief that the rational human mind has access to truths in all areas of knowledge from natural science to metaphysics, and that all matters of religion—doctrines, practices, and sacred texts—are to be interpreted in accordance with those rationally determined truths. Like the philosophical schools in the other two Abrahamic faiths, medieval Jewish philosophers borrowed a great deal from Greek philosophy, but they were also very much dependent for their understanding of this tradition of thought on the great Islamic philosophers—most notably Alfarabi, Avicenna, and Averroes.

Medieval Jewish philosophy had its formal beginning with Saadiah Gaon in the tenth century. However, it was Maimonides (1135–1204) who became the central figure of this school and gave it an authority it had not previously had. Maimonides' synthesis of Judaism and Aristotelian thought would be the single greatest achievement in medieval Jewish philosophy, one that would have an impact on Jewish thought for centuries to come.

Medieval Jewish philosophy would also spawn a great deal of controversy. Jews were divided over whether a rational understanding of Judaism was possible or desirable. Even within the philosophical camp there were deep divisions over the extent to which rationalism could be used in dealing with matters pertaining to religion. At one end of the spectrum were conservative philosophers who believed that rational speculation on religion should be kept within strict limits. At the other end were radical philosophers who were willing to entirely reinterpret Judaism's most basic beliefs in light of a thoroughgoing Aristotelianism.[10]

Medieval Jewish philosophers of all stripes seem to have had a great deal of interest in the Book of Job. I have found no fewer than seventeen commentaries on Job written by these thinkers. Fifteen are extant; two are lost. Of those that are extant, nine have been published, while six are available only in manuscript.[11] They were written by thinkers in a wide range of locations both in Christian Europe and the Islamic countries, the majority in France, Spain, and Italy.[12]

It should be noted that not all of these works are "commentaries" in the strict sense of the term. Some are lengthy discussions of Job contained in larger treatises. In fact, two of the most important expositions on Job in medieval Jewish philosophy are in this category: Maimonides' discussion of Job in chapters 22 and 23 in the third part of the *Guide of the Perplexed* and Samuel ibn Tibbon's discussion in chapters 15–18 of *Ma'amar Yikkavu ha-Mayim*. Nonetheless, for the sake of convenience, I will use the term "commentary" loosely to refer to these works as well.

Also significant is the fact that all of the commentaries on Job in medieval Jewish philosophy were composed after Maimonides, with the exception of Saadiah, and all of them bear Maimonides' influence. Therefore, the history of the interpretation of Job in medieval Jewish philosophy is largely defined by Maimonides and the attempts of later philosophers to grapple with his reading. Nevertheless, as we shall later see, it is a mistake to assume that these philosophers merely reiterate Maimonides' views.

That medieval Jewish philosophers should have had an interest in the Book of Job comes as no surprise. In treating the question of the suffering of the righteous, it is perhaps the most philosophical book in the Bible. Moreover, medieval Jewish philosophers were intrigued as much by Job's method as they were by its content. That the discussion of Job's suffering should take the form of a dialogue seemed to be the best proof that Job was a serious work of philosophy.

The fact that the commentaries on Job in medieval Jewish philosophy have received so little attention by modern academic scholars deserves some discussion. Only the commentaries of Saadiah and Maimonides have attracted significant scholarly interest, and between these two, Maimonides' exposition has been studied far more than Saadiah's. Scholarly analyses of Joban commentaries by other medieval Jewish philosophers are few and far between, amounting to no more articles than can be counted on the fingers of one hand. This neglect includes a work no less significant than Gersonides' commentary on Job, which was one of the first Hebrew books to be printed in the medieval period, was widely read by medieval Jews and was included in all traditional rabbinic Bibles. Only one scholarly article—my own—has been written on this work.[13]

The lack of scholarly interest in these commentaries can best be understood as a reflection of a more general lack of interest in medieval Jewish philosophers as biblical interpreters. Since the field's inception in the nineteenth century, the academic study of medieval Jewish philosophy has tended to focus almost exclusively on its systematic thought. Scholars such as Isaac Husik, Harry Wolfson, Julius Guttmann, and Shlomo Pines have expended a great deal of energy analyzing the philosophical argumentation used by medieval Jewish philosophers to determine their positions on such issues as divine attributes, creation, and providence. This scholarship has also been almost exclusively historical, devoted both to tracing the development of philosophical ideas within medieval Jewish philosophy and to locating its sources in philosophical schools outside it, particularly in the Islamic and Greek philosophical traditions. Attention has therefore been given primarily to the major systematic treatises in medieval Jewish philosophy, which are arranged mostly around philosophical issues, such as Saadiah's *Book of Beliefs and Opinions*, Maimonides' *Guide of the Perplexed*, Gersonides' *Wars of the Lord*, and Ḥasdai Crescas's *Light of the Lord*.

What has often been overlooked is the degree to which much of the literature written by medieval Jewish philosophers was in fact exegetical. Medieval Jewish philosophers, particularly after Maimonides, produced an extensive body of commentaries on various parts of the Bible. The major philosophical exegetes include Saadiah Gaon, Samuel ibn Tibbon, Gersonides, Joseph ibn Kaspi, and Isaac 'Arama.[14] Moreover, there is a great deal of biblical exegesis even in the systematic treatises in medieval Jewish philosophy. Thus, Maimonides explicitly introduces his *Guide of the Perplexed* as an exegetical work concerned with anthropomorphisms and philosophical parables found in the biblical text. In such works as Saadiah's *Book of Beliefs and Opinions* and Gersonides' *Wars of the Lord*, interpretations of the biblical text are frequently interspersed with philosophical argumentation. Yet, because the scholarship on medieval Jewish philosophy has been so focused on the systematic aspects of the literature, its exegetical dimension has received relatively little attention.

In recent years, there has been a growing recognition of the need to study the medieval Jewish philosophers as exegetes.[15] However, the tendency has been to mine this literature only for the insights it provides into systematic thought in medieval Jewish philosophy. Little interest has been shown in its exegesis *as* exegesis. Thus, few studies have been done on the hermeneutic aspects of this literature. An issue as central as the use of allegory as a hermeneutic tool in medieval Jewish philosophy awaits thorough scholarly analysis despite its importance in the intellectual history of medieval Judaism.[16] There has also been little exploration of the relationship between exegesis and systematic philosophy. This lacuna is a serious one, because an understanding of that relationship is crucial for coming to terms with medieval Jewish philosophy as a whole. After all, reason and revelation were widely regarded by the thinkers in this school as the twin fonts of truth.

I would like to emphasize that I am in no way denigrating the value of the scholarship in medieval Jewish philosophy. There is no question that a proper understanding of this field requires an exploration of its systematic content. The scholarship of such intellectual giants as Husik, Wolfson, Guttmann, and

Pines remains standard for the field. I am arguing only that a full account of medieval Jewish philosophy must include a serious engagement with its exegetical dimension.

If scholars of medieval Jewish philosophy have given minimal attention to the exegetical literature in medieval Jewish philosophy, scholars who specialize in medieval Jewish exegesis have hardly turned in its direction. The scholarship in this field has been devoted primarily to exploring exegetes whose interests were in *peshat* and *derash*. Little attention has been given to the philosophers.[17] The prevailing view seems to be that the latter, by virtue of the foreign philosophical views they read into the text, were not true exegetes. Yet, the exegesis of the medieval Jewish philosophers has not been examined sufficiently to justify such a conclusion.

The purpose of the present study therefore goes beyond providing a description of how medieval Jewish philosophers read the Book of Job. I intend also to draw much-needed attention to the exegetical literature in medieval Jewish philosophy in general. By analyzing how medieval Jewish philosophers interpreted the Book of Job, I hope to bring the exegesis of these thinkers to light as an exciting chapter in the history of Jewish thought, which neither scholars of medieval Jewish philosophy nor scholars of medieval Jewish exegesis can afford to ignore.

This is certainly not the first study that has been written on how a particular biblical book was interpreted by medieval Jewish exegetes. Most notable are two fine works, Uriel Simon's *Four Approaches to the Book of Psalms* and Barry Walfish's *Esther in Medieval Garb*.[18] However, there has yet to be a book-length study on how a particular biblical book was interpreted in medieval Jewish philosophy. While the studies of Simon and Walfish deal with the medieval Jewish philosophers, their exegesis is not separated out from medieval Jewish exegesis in general, and therefore the unique perspective the philosophers bring to the biblical text is not dealt with by these scholars.

I could have chosen for my purposes a number of books in the Bible that were of interest to medieval Jewish philosophers. For instance, a great deal of exegetical material in medieval Jewish philosophy has been written on the Song of Songs, Ecclesiastes, and the book of Proverbs.[19] Yet, I have opted for Job because of the continuous fascination this book has held for Western thinkers. If the medieval Jewish philosophers are to prove their value as exegetes, it is likely to emerge in their speculations on this most provocative text.

I had originally intended to do a study discussing all the commentators on Job in medieval Jewish philosophy. However, as I came across more and more texts, it became clear to me that I could not possibly do justice to all of them. I have therefore chosen six commentators for analysis: Saadiah Gaon, Maimonides, Samuel ibn Tibbon, Zeraḥiah Ḥen, Gersonides, and Simon ben Ẓemaḥ Duran. These figures will be discussed in their historical order. My principle of selection was simple: I chose commentators who I felt were important figures in medieval Jewish philosophy in general and also had something significant to say about Job in particular. I also chose enough thinkers that my readers would get a sense of the variety and richness of the material on Job in medieval Jewish philosophy. In the course of my discussion, I have also attempted, whenever possible, to make reference to insights from the commentaries of medieval Jewish philosophers I have not analyzed. Most notably, I have included a section at the end of the chapter on Ibn Tibbon that presents a brief treatment of three commentators who were influenced by this important thinker but which the limits of this study did not allow me to discuss at greater length: Immanuel of Rome, Elijah ben Eliezer ha-Yerushalmi, and Isaac Arundi.

Readers familiar with medieval Jewish philosophy may be surprised by my omission of some thinkers. I have not included a chapter on Joseph ibn Kaspi, who composed two commentaries on Job. My reason for excluding these works is that, first, they present us with unique difficulties. As I have argued elsewhere, Kaspi's commentaries are a maze of hints, innuendos, and ambiguities that allude to esoteric doctrines but in the end make it very difficult, if not impossible, to figure out how he actually read the Book of Job. Those who are familiar with Kaspi should not be surprised by this observation. Kaspi's penchant for wit, sarcasm, and mischief are well known and come through in particular in his attempts to conceal his true views from the masses. In the Job commentaries, those qualities are evident in the extreme. In truth, many of the writers I have chosen to analyze engage in esoteric discourse as well, but they reveal just enough of their esoteric views to make it possible for us to discern their true opinions. I do not believe that this is the case with Kaspi. I have therefore chosen to pass over him in favor of other commentators. Second, as mentioned above, I very much wanted to display a variety of approaches to Job in medieval Jewish philosophy, and this required a balanced presentation of both conservative and radical readings of Job. That balance would have been compromised by including Kaspi, since Kaspi is in the radical school and that approach is well represented by Maimonides, Ibn Tibbon, Zeraḥiah Ḥen, and, to some extent, Gersonides—all of whom are treated in this study.[20]

Other notable omissions are Obadiah Seforno and Meir 'Arama, both of whom composed commentaries on Job. My reason for excluding these thinkers is that they take a relatively conservative approach to Job and their interpretations of the book are not nearly as interesting and original as those of the two representatives of the conservative approach chosen for this study: Saadiah Gaon and Simon ben Ẓemaḥ Duran.

A proper examination of the commentaries I have chosen and an assessment of their significance both as philosophical and exegetical works require that I discuss them on a number of levels. For each commentary, my discussion will therefore focus on three interfaces: between the commentaries and their antecedent sources, between the commentaries and the biblical text, and between the commentaries and the systematic thought of the medieval Jewish philosophers.

The first interface concerns the relationship between the commentaries and the sources that shaped them. While each of the commentaries displays influences from a wide range of sources, the most important question here is how earlier commentaries in this study influenced later ones. Were the expositions on Job in medieval Jewish philosophy written in isolation, or were the later expositions written in response to the earlier ones? This question is significant because if the later commentaries were in fact influenced by the earlier ones, we must then ask whether there is enough commonality and cohesion among the commentaries that they constitute what is, in effect, a tradition of interpretation on the Book of Job. By "tradition" I mean a series of texts that share certain critical features identifying them as belonging to a common school while exhibiting a gradual evolution of views as each one responds to the ideas of its predecessors. All traditions, after all, display this balance between commonality and difference as they evolve over time. That my study proceeds in historical order will facilitate our ability to see how each thinker relates to his predecessors.

The discovery of a tradition of interpretation on Job in medieval Jewish philosophy would be important because it would strengthen my claim that the exegetical literature of the medieval Jewish philosophers deserves serious study. It would show that what we have here is not just a haphazard collection of texts, but a cohesive unit of texts that are quite self-consciously engaged in dialogue over several centuries.

The second interface between the commentaries and the biblical text concerns the philosophers in this study as exegetes. The major question here is how they made sense of the actual text of Job. In particular, we will need to assess the extent to which they recognized and were sensitive to the formidable difficulties in Job and how effectively they responded to those difficulties.

It may be helpful here to review the major challenges that interpreters of Job have faced throughout the ages. First, a question that readers of Job have often raised about the book as a whole is whether the story is based on historical events or is mere fiction. The biblical text relays the story as if it were history in that the book never explicitly identifies itself as fiction. And yet, the book's fable-like qualities are hard to ignore—even for those who take the Bible as the word of God. In particular, the story that frames the dialogue—what modern academics refer to as the prologue and epilogue—has an air of unreality about it. In fact, as early as the rabbinic period, Jewish commentators were sensitive to this question, and a debate about it is found in a number of sources. The best known of these is a Talmudic passage in which R. Samuel bar Naḥmani argues for Job's historicity against an anonymous rabbi who claims that Job "never was, and never existed."[21] We must therefore explore whether the commentators in this study are sensitive to this issue as well.

There are also many questions that commentators both inside and outside Judaism have consistently asked about the figure of Job himself. First, there is the question of Job's national origin. The biblical text never specifies whether Job is a Jew, an observation that in the rabbinic period spawned debate about Job's provenance.[22] Perhaps the more important and perplexing ambiguity concerns Job's character. Job's goodness is underscored in the opening lines of the story, where he is described as "blameless and upright" and as one who "feared God and shunned evil." Moreover, toward the end of the book, God singles out Job for praise when He scolds Eliphaz, Bildad, and Zophar for not having "spoken the truth about Me as did My servant Job."[23] However, a more negative depiction of Job's character seems to be implied in his protests against God at various points of the dialogue. Furthermore, Job seems to admit his guilt in speaking out against his suffering when he recants his protests at the end of the book.[24] The ambiguity in Job's character has prompted interpreters to propose widely different assessments of him, some praising him as the paragon of righteousness and others judging him to be deeply flawed. We therefore need to examine how the thinkers in this study depict Job and how they handle the ambiguities in the biblical text regarding both his national identity and character.

The actual dialogue between the various figures in the story—a section which makes up most of the book—has also elicited much speculation among commentators because of the problems it presents. The difficult Hebrew that characterizes the dialogue makes it hard to discern at times what the figures are even saying. It is also hard to determine whether each offers a distinctive view. At times, the views of the figures appear to be different, while at other times they seem to overlap with one another. Most perplexing is the role of Elihu. His entrance into the dialogue after Eliphaz, Bildad, and Zophar have finished speaking to Job would suggest that he supplies the answer to Job's dilemma, or at least furnishes some valuable information about it. The uniqueness of his position also seems to be suggested by the fact that he escapes God's censure at the end of the story.[25] But it is not clear from the content of Elihu's speech that he has anything to add to that which has already been said. Moreover, God Himself addresses Job after Elihu, leaving us to wonder again whether Elihu has made any significant contribution to the discussion. We must therefore examine how the thinkers in this study deal with these difficulties.[26]

Perhaps the key question in the Book of Job is the meaning of God's speech from the tempest. Most commentators assume that understanding this portion of the book unlocks its meaning, for here, it would seem, should be the explanation for Job's troubles given that it is the Deity Himself who now addresses him. Yet, it is by no means clear how God's long series of rhetorical questions to Job furnishes an explanation for his difficulties, nor whether it is intended to furnish any explanation at all. We will therefore have to see how the interpreters in this study deal with this most important section of the story.[27]

An exegetical question of a broad nature is the intended audience of the Book of Job. Its inclusion in the Hebrew Bible gives us reason to believe that the canonizers intended it for Jews. However, there is also an argument that its message is for those outside the Jewish fold. As noted earlier, Job is never explicitly identified as a Jew, and his predicament is one that has perplexed thinkers in all cultures. Therefore, the claim could be made that the Book of Job was meant to have universal significance. In fact, patristic and medieval Christian commentators pressed this interpretation to the best of their advantage in an attempt to remove the Book of Job from a specifically Jewish context and read a more universal Christian message out of it. Of course, the same writers had to find a way to impart universal meaning to the overall message of Job as well. Yet, there is sufficient ambiguity regarding that message to open the way for such a reading. After all, there is nothing unequivocally "Jewish" about God's response from the tempest.

The important question for our purposes is whether the thinkers in this study had anything to say about this issue. Did they assume that Job was a Jewish book, or did they also entertain the possibility that it had applicability to humankind as a whole? The question becomes more intriguing when one considers that rational philosophy, by its nature, has always had a universalistic thrust to it—one that is evident in medieval Jewish philosophy in general, not to mention the medieval philosophical traditions of the other two Abrahamic faiths. We must therefore explore whether the philosophers in this study read the Book of Job as a text imparting a message of universal import.

Another question is connected to these observations. If some of the thinkers in this study emphasized the Jewishness of the Book of Job, did they entertain the possibility that the Book of Job addressed itself to the historical experience of the suffering of the Jewish people as a whole? The identity between Job and the Jewish people was, in fact, a natural one for Jewish thinkers to make. Jews throughout the ages probed the Bible in order to understand their history, and given that the Book of Job dealt with a righteous individual who suffers, one would expect that Jews would have seen resonance between its major theme and their own condition, which was often characterized by persecution and humiliation. Indeed, the connection between Job and Israel was made in early rabbinic sources.[28] We must therefore see whether any of our commentators developed this connection as well.

By examining this issue, we seem to have made a transition from exegesis to theology. However, we should note that with the type of thinkers we are analyzing, one cannot always separate biblical interpretation from theology. These thinkers could explore the biblical text only from the perspective of their intellectual historical context.

Because we will be interested in how these medieval interpreters dealt with the broad themes in the Book of Job, there are aspects of their exegesis that I will not be able to explore adequately. Ideally, I would show how the philosophers in this study read each and every one of their points out of the biblical text. However, if I were to consistently perform such an exercise, a much lengthier study would be required, and important insights would no doubt be lost in a sea of exegetical detail. My strategy will therefore be to give a detailed account of how these commentators read their views out of the biblical text for only those sections in Job that they regarded as key. I am greatly aided by the fact that these philosophers tended to be in general agreement about which portions of the book these are. Thus, for instance, all of the philosophers treated here regarded Job 33 as highly important. Therefore, as I move from one thinker to the next, I will keep coming back to the exegesis of the same texts for close analysis, so that as the study proceeds comparisons can be made regarding how the commentators approached those texts in different ways.

An exegetical facet of the commentaries that I have to pass over entirely is the linguistic explorations of the interpreters. A number of them—most notably Saadiah and Zeraḥiah Ḥen—wrote full-length commentaries in which they provided not only philosophical insights about the Book of Job but also detailed explanations about its grammar and philology, much as the purely *peshat*-oriented exegetes did. In fact, Saadiah was one of the great pioneers in this type of exegesis. While interesting, this material is not relevant to the questions I am asking in this study. Again, the focus here is on how the commentators approached the broad themes of Job rather than its minutiae.

The third interface I will explore is the relationship between the commentaries examined in this study and the systematic thought of the medieval Jewish philosophers. All the thinkers in this study read the Book of Job as a philosophical dialogue about either providence or the related issue of reward and punishment. In addition, many of them find in Job significant treatment of a host of other philosophical issues, such as divine knowledge, evil, prophecy, and immortality. We shall also see that these thinkers read the Book of Job in accordance with their overall philosophical orientation, with some deriving a conservative philosophical message from it and others interpreting it in a more radical fashion.

The major question is whether these thinkers saw their commentaries on Job as merely a reiteration of ideas already derived from systematic philosophical discourse or viewed them as actually contributing to the development of those ideas. This question is perhaps most appropriate for the thinkers who produced systematic discussions on the very same philosophical issues dealt with in their commentaries: Saadiah, Maimonides, Gersonides, and Duran. Thus, for instance, both Gersonides' commentary on Job and the fourth book of his major systematic treatise, *The Wars of the Lord*, take up the question of providence. The question then is whether his commentary on Job merely repeats the ideas on providence found in the *Wars* or offers new insight into that issue.

Some of our thinkers, however, produced no systematic discussion on the philosophical subject matter they read out of the Book of Job. Ibn Tibbon and Zeraḥiah Ḥen are in this category. Nonetheless, they composed commentaries on Job on the assumption that the reader was familiar with the systematic treatment of providence in Maimonides. The question of the relationship between exegesis and systematic philosophy is therefore relevant for these figures as well, except that here we will have to assume that the systematic component is provided by Maimonides—at least as they understood him.

A proper analysis of this third interface is important for assessing the place of the exegetical works of the philosophers in medieval Jewish philosophy. If the exegetical literature on Job in medieval Jewish philosophy merely repeats ideas found in the systematic works, then perhaps the lack of interest that scholars of medieval Jewish philosophy have shown in that literature is justified because the exercise of producing biblical commentaries by medieval Jewish philosophers would have little philosophical value. But if it can be shown that the commentaries on Job actually contributed new ideas and insights on the issues taken up in the systematic works, it would indicate that, as a rule, the exegetical literature of medieval Jewish philosophers should be consulted in order to gain a comprehensive understanding of their thinking on the major philosophical issues.

In the course of my analysis, I will try as much as possible to discuss the three interfaces separately so that a determination can be made as to how the thinkers in this study deal with each one. However, a clean separation between the interfaces will not always be possible, since they are tightly intertwined. This is especially the case with Ibn Tibbon and Zeraḥiah Ḥen, who assume the correctness of Maimonides' philosophy and see themselves primarily as exegetes expanding upon and refining his exegetical program, as laid out in the *Guide of the Perplexed*. For these figures, the three interfaces tend to collapse into one another. The first, which is concerned with the relationship between their commentaries and those of their predecessors, is difficult to separate from the second, which concerns the relationship between their commentaries on Job and the biblical text, since both interfaces are so strongly governed by the influence of Maimonides. The same goes for the first interface and the third. Given that Maimonides is almost exclusively the source of systematic philosophy for Ibn Tibbon and Zeraḥiah Ḥen, the question of how those same works relate to those of their predecessors is tied up with how their commentaries relate to systematic philosophy. Again, in both instances, Maimonides' influence is decisive.

Some readers may feel that this tripartite scheme is too ambitious and that each of the interfaces could be the subject of a separate study. There is some truth in this charge. Discussing all three interfaces undoubtedly costs this study some depth in favor of breadth. However, a prime goal of this study is to demonstrate the richness of the exegetical works of the medieval Jewish philosophers, and I know of no better way to do this than by engaging these works in the multitiered analysis attempted here. I certainly admit the limitations of this approach, and I hope that other scholars will fill in the gaps.

Besides the three interfaces, there is one more issue that I would like to explore, and that is whether any commonality exists between the readings of Job examined in this study and those of modern readers. There has been relatively little scholarly analysis comparing medieval and modern biblical exegesis, Christian or Jewish, owing perhaps to the prevailing assumption that they have little in common.[29] However, it would be a mistake to assume that the gap between the two is as wide as is often thought. Medieval commentators demonstrate a great deal of care and precision in reading the biblical text, which leads one to suspect that their insights have relevance beyond their time period. In the final chapter, I will therefore offer some thoughts about the relationship between the medieval readings of Job examined in this study and those in the modern period.

Finally, one more observation about the method of this study. Most of the commentaries I shall be examining require unusually detailed and laborious analysis just to clarify their content, particularly those that are composed in an esoteric style. It was common for medieval Jewish philosophers to hide their true views on philosophical matters when they perceived them to be radical and thus potentially injurious to the common reader. They therefore concealed their positions with a number of techniques, such as deliberately abbreviating their statements, couching their opinions in the form of innuendo, or even expressing views that were the opposite of what they believed. This method of writing was made famous in medieval Jewish philosophy by Maimonides and was adopted by many of his followers. The majority of the commentators in this study indulged in this style of writing.[30] Therefore, much effort will be required to get past the obfuscation of these authors and discern their true views. I point this out so that readers who are not familiar with this type of writing will not be frustrated if my examination of the commentaries resembles the same sort of meticulous analysis used to solve a murder mystery. The nature of these texts requires that we engage in this type of reading. Sometimes lengthy discussion is needed simply to figure out what a particular author is saying even before his views are analyzed. I hope that the results of this painstaking analysis will render the effort invested in it worthwhile.

2

Saadiah Gaon

I begin my study with Saadiah Gaon (882–942), the first major Jewish philosopher in the medieval period.[1] Saadiah spent the first half of his life in Egypt, then wandered through Syria and Palestine before settling in Babylonia. There he became head of the prestigious Sura rabbinical academy in 928, rising to prominence as perhaps the greatest figure of the Geonic period. Saadiah was a pioneer in any number of Jewish disciplines. His biography is filled with a series of "firsts" in areas as diverse as Halakhah, philosophy, exegesis, Hebrew grammar, liturgy, and poetry. He was also the great protagonist in his period of rabbinite Judaism in its battles against the Karaite threat.[2]

It is Saadiah's philosophical and exegetical talents that will be of greatest interest here. Saadiah was the first major Jewish thinker to compose a systematic and comprehensive philosophical treatise on Judaism: *The Book of Beliefs and Opinions* (*Al-Mukhtār fi 'l-Amānāt wa-al-I'tiqādāt*). The content of this treatise, as well as its structure, was heavily influenced by Islamic theology, in particular the Mu'tazilite school.[3] In the area of biblical interpretation, Saadiah provided one of the first translations of the Hebrew Bible into Arabic, a translation that is still in use among Arabic-speaking Jews. He also composed commentaries on a number of books of the Hebrew Bible that greatly influenced later medieval Jewish exegetes.[4]

It is Saadiah's commentary on Job that will be the focus of the present chapter. Like all of Saadiah's biblical commentaries, it is a hybrid of close linguistic analysis, on the one hand, and philosophical interpretation, on the other. It begins with an introduction that provides an overview of Saadiah's philosophical understanding of Job and then proceeds with a line-by-line commentary on the biblical text itself in which glosses concerning grammar and philology alternate with philosophical insights.[5]

As mentioned in chapter 1, Saadiah is the only figure in this study besides Maimonides whose commentary on Job has received significant attention from scholars. Most important is Lenn E. Goodman's English translation of Saadiah's commentary. Goodman not only provides an accurate rendering of the commentary into English, he also supplies extensive notes and a number of introductory essays that interpret Saadiah's reading of Job against the background of Islamic and Jewish sources. In addition, Goodman provides an English translation of Saadiah's Arabic translation of Job. This is critical for understanding Saadiah's commentary because many of his glosses are dependent on his Arabic translation of the biblical text. Goodman's edition is therefore an invaluable resource for the analysis of Saadiah's commentary.[6]

My analysis of Saadiah's reading of Job will begin with a brief summary of his discussion of the suffering of the righteous in *Beliefs and Opinions*, where he lays out the philosophical ideas that are critical for his interpretation of Job. I will then summarize the contents of his commentary on Job. The discussion will then proceed in the order of the three interfaces outlined in the introduction. I will first discuss the sources and antecedents of Saadiah's reading of the Book of Job, then analyze Saadiah's reading as an exegetical exercise grappling with the biblical text, and finally revisit Saadiah's discussion of the suffering of the righteous in *Beliefs and Opinions* to determine precisely how his systematic thinking on theodicy relates to his exegesis on Job.

The Philosophical Background: *Beliefs and Opinions* 5:3

I open my discussion with a treatment of *Beliefs and Opinions* not because of its chronological priority to the commentary on Job. The order of composition of the two works is, in fact, unclear and is a question that I will be taking up later. Rather, the advantage of beginning with *Beliefs and Opinions* is conceptual, for it is here that Saadiah describes succinctly and conveniently the key philosophical ideas utilized in his commentary on Job.

The section of *Beliefs and Opinions* that concerns us is the third chapter of the fifth book.[7] Here Saadiah provides two reasons for the suffering of the righteous. First, God may simply be punishing them for sins they have committed. Saadiah's statement here is connected to remarks in a previous section where he explains that God punishes the righteous for sins in this lifetime in order that they be rewarded in the fullest possible manner in the world to come.[8] Another reason they suffer is that God may be testing them. In the ensuing discussion, two reasons are given for such trials. They allow the righteous to demonstrate their devotion to God and thereby earn extra reward in both this lifetime and the next. They also provide an opportunity for righteous individuals who have been blessed by God to prove to their fellow human beings their worthiness in having been selected for divine favor. Saadiah concludes that it is because of this public dimension of divine trials that God tests only those who are able to endure them.[9]

According to Saadiah, this notion of trials helps explain why some righteous individuals ask God for an explanation for their suffering but receive no response from Him. When someone is being punished for sinful conduct, God may inform that person as to the cause of his suffering in order to encourage repentance. However, when an individual experiences suffering as a trial, God will offer him no explanation because it would spoil one of the purposes of the trial, which is to demonstrate his righteousness to others. Were such a person to be informed of the reason for his suffering, his contemporaries could attribute his forbearance to the promise of an anticipated reward.[10]

What is most important for our purposes is that in this discussion, Saadiah makes it clear that his conception of divine trials is key for understanding the Book of Job. Saadiah cites Job as an example of a righteous individual who experiences a trial of this sort. According to Saadiah, Job was tested with unmerited suffering in order that others should know that he was deserving of the favor shown to him by God: "the endurance of the pious serves a useful purpose in that it enables mankind to understand that God has not chosen them gratuitously, as you learn from Job and his endurance."[11] What Saadiah means here—and this is clarified fully only in the commentary on Job—is that Job is "chosen" by God in that he begins the story as a wealthy man whose good fortune is divine reward for his righteous conduct. He is subsequently tested by the loss of his family and possessions in order to demonstrate to his fellow countrymen that his material well-being was earned by merit.[12] Saadiah also points out that by interpreting Job's suffering as a trial, one can understand why God did not provide Job an explanation for his ordeal when He addressed him in the final chapters of the book. Any explanation would have spoiled the whole purpose of the trial.[13]

A good deal of work has been done by modern scholars to trace the Jewish and Islamic sources that underlie Saadiah's discussion of the suffering of the righteous in *Beliefs and Opinions*. The notion that the righteous are punished for their few misdeeds in this life so that they can be rewarded fully for their good deeds in the world to come is found in a number of rabbinic passages.[14] Scholars have been particularly interested in the sources of Saadiah's conception of divine trials. Saadiah's idea that God tests the righteous in order to compensate them afterward in this life and the next has been traced to Mu'tazilite sources.[15] It has also been connected to the rabbinic concept of "sufferings of love" (*yisurin shel ahavah*).[16] The other purpose of divine trials—to display the worthiness of the righteous to their contemporaries—appears to be based on rabbinic sources regarding the patriarch Abraham. This connection, to my knowledge, has not been noted by previous commentators, and since it will be important for us later on, let me say a brief word about it.

A number of midrashic passages interpret the binding of Isaac as a test designed to exhibit Abraham's righteousness to the world in order to preempt any speculation that God chose him on a mere whim as the forefather of the

Jewish people. According to this reading, Abraham's willingness to sacrifice his son demonstrates unequivocally that he is uniquely worthy of the honor bestowed upon him. For our purposes, the most significant of these sources is in *Bereshit Rabbah*:

> *Sometime afterward, God put Abraham to the test* (*nissah*) etc. (Gen. 22:1): It is written, "You have given a banner (*nes*) to them that fear You, [that it may be displayed (*le-hitnoses*) because of the truth. Selah]" (Psalms 60:6). [This means] trial upon trial, greatness after greatness, in order to test them (*le-nasot*) in the world and exalt them in the world like a ship's ensign (*nes*). And what is its purpose? "Because of the truth. Selah;" in order that the attribute of [divine] justice may be verified in the world. Thus, if one says, "Whom He wishes to enrich, He enriches; to impoverish, He impoverishes; whom He desires, He makes a king; when He wished, He made Abraham wealthy, and when He wished He made Him king," then you can answer him and say to him, "Can you do what Abraham did? Abraham was a hundred years old when his son Isaac was born to him. After all this pain, it was said to him, *take your son, your favored one* etc. (Gen. 22:2) yet he did not refuse." [Hence], "You have given a banner to them that fear You, that it may be displayed."[17]

Making use of a pun on the term *nissah*, this midrashic passage sees the command to sacrifice Isaac as an attempt on God's part to "display" Abraham to the world in order to quash any accusations that he was chosen arbitrarily, and Abraham's compliance successfully dispels any slander of this sort. Furthermore, the passage appears to establish the notion of public trials as a general principle for all righteous people, not just for Abraham, because the first half of the passage speaks of public trials as appropriate for all people "that fear You." This source therefore anticipates Saadiah's notion that divine trials serve the purpose of providing public proof that individuals chosen for divine favor are worthy of their distinction.[18]

For our purposes, the most important idea that emerges from Saadiah's discussion of the suffering of the righteous in *Beliefs and Opinions* is that God tests the righteous in order to reward them in this life and in the world to come, and to prove to their contemporaries that they are worthy of a special relationship with God. Saadiah has already informed us that this idea accounts for Job's suffering. However, it is only in his commentary on Job that Saadiah fully explains that connection.

The Commentary on Job

I begin my analysis of Saadiah's commentary on Job by summarizing its contents. Most important is Saadiah's introduction to the commentary, because it is here that he lays out the basic philosophical premises underlying his reading of Job and provides an overview of his understanding of its dialogue. Saadiah reviews many of the same concepts on the suffering of the righteous in *Beliefs and Opinions*—particularly his notion of divine trials—but they are analyzed in somewhat greater detail as he attempts to apply them to the Book of Job.

As is often the custom in medieval Arabic literature, Saadiah begins his introduction with a lengthy statement of praise for God that gradually turns toward the topic of the treatise. Saadiah lauds God's kindness, which manifests itself in three ways: the creation of the world, the giving of divine commandments, and suffering. The last one is, of course, the issue of interest here, and its inclusion in a list of God's beneficent activities demands explanation. Saadiah therefore goes on to tell us that suffering is a divine gift because it is ultimately for a person's own good. There are, in particular, three types of suffering, and all are for our benefit. The first is for the purpose of "discipline and instruction." This is analogous to the discipline that a father uses on his own child to inculcate proper behavior.[19] The second is punishment for sin, which is for the good in forcing human beings to obey God's will. The third consists of trials: God inflicts suffering as an opportunity for an individual to earn reward by accepting his afflictions with patience.[20]

In the next section, Saadiah expands on the notion of divine trials with the intention of preempting any suggestion that they are evidence of divine injustice. Saadiah argues that such trials could not possibly be unjust because the Torah has told us that God can do no wrong. Moreover, the Bible provides us with the record of Job, who experienced a divine trial and, because he bore his test with fortitude, was amply rewarded in both this lifetime and the next.[21]

Saadiah reinforces his point by claiming that none of the figures in the dialogue of Job attributes injustice to God. According to Saadiah, Job's position throughout the book is that God can bring affliction upon the righteous because it is God's right to do as He pleases. While Saadiah recognizes that this viewpoint seems to impugn God's justice, he argues that this is not at all the case, for Job believes that although God's actions may be arbitrary, they are beyond human reproach. Eliphaz, Bildad, and Zophar take the position that God causes suffering only to those who sin, and therefore Job must have committed some transgression warranting punishment. Thus, there is no suggestion of any injustice on God's part. Finally, Elihu's view is that God can cause the righteous to suffer in order to test them. According to this position, God brings suffering on the righteous, and if they endure it with patience, they will be rewarded. Here, too, God's justice is preserved.[22]

It is Elihu's position equating the suffering of the righteous with divine trials that Saadiah deems correct regarding Job's predicament. Saadiah points out that a number of clues in the biblical text point to the superiority of his view. First, Elihu is the only figure in the dialogue not rebuked by God by the end of the story. Moreover, Elihu prefaces his speech with the declaration that he will rebut all the other positions in the dialogue. Apparently, Saadiah's point is that no other figure in the dialogue makes such a sweeping claim about his position and that this therefore attests to the superiority of Elihu's view.[23]

Saadiah sums up his overview of the dialogue by saying that God caused the story to be written down so that when we suffer, we will know that it is either because of sin or because of a trial. We will therefore affirm that despite our suffering, God is just. It is for this reason that Saadiah renames the Book of Job *The Book of Theodicy*.[24]

At the end of his introduction, Saadiah discusses the exegetical challenges that confront the interpreter of Job. Saadiah provides about as good a description of those challenges as one will find in medieval Jewish philosophy:

> Many of our nation look upon this Book of Job as an enigma, difficult to interpret and construe in several respects. The first is the tale of *satan*. Who is he? What is it that he says? What is his role? Second, the suffering of the prophet Job, despite the book's testimony that he was a *blameless, upright, and godfearing man* (Job 1:1). Third is the course of the argument between him and his companions and Elihu: what did each of them claim? How did they answer one another, and where did they object to one another? Fourth is finding the gist of the verses, i.e., identifying the sentences that contain the point of each speech. This is obscured by the plethora of arguments and profusion of discourse. The counterpoint of statement and rejoinder, rhapsodic embellishment, padding and flourishes, often smothers the argument which is the point intended. Fifth are the benefactions tangled allusively in the coil of God's speech: what are they, and what is their bearing on the reply which Job receives when he stands before the Lord?[25]

Saadiah goes on to explain the method he will use to deal with these difficulties. First, he declares his intention to be guided by philosophical reason as well as by a detailed examination of the language of the text. Of particular concern to Saadiah is the method required to make sense of the dialogue between the participants. Saadiah declares his intention, first, to abstract the key point from each of the speeches of the participants; second, to show how each speech is saying something different; and third, to demonstrate how each speech is a response to ideas enunciated previously in the dialogue.[26]

I would like to conclude the discussion of Saadiah's introduction by highlighting two significant points that emerge there. First, for Saadiah the Book of Job really has two distinct purposes: a theological and an ethical one. Its theological purpose is to uphold the principle of divine justice. Somewhat less obvious is that Saadiah also sees the Book of Job as providing ethical guidance in that the figure of Job serves as a model for patience in the face of suffering. Job inspires us to "adapt ourselves to patient acceptance" when dealing with our own afflictions.[27]

The two purposes of the Book of Job in Saadiah's thinking need to be emphasized, since he tends not to differentiate clearly between them. It is perhaps in the very last passage of Saadiah's commentary that we find the most explicit reference to the two themes. There Saadiah sums up his interpretation of Job by claiming that God wanted the story of Job to be written down "so that we may bear sufferings with fortitude when they befall us and not hasten to impugn God's judgment but submit to God and accept His wisdom and direction."[28] Note how Saadiah sees the Book of Job as teaching us about both divine justice and the exercise of patience in the face of suffering.

However, it is clear that of the two foci the theological concern is primary for Saadiah. It is that concern that immediately engages Saadiah's attention in the introduction, after he has begun to deal with the question of suffering, and it is that same issue that occupies him most as his introduction proceeds. The emphasis on the theological dimension of Job is also evident in Saadiah's decision to rename the Book of Job *The Book of Theodicy*.[29]

Another point in Saadiah's introduction that can easily be missed is that while Saadiah believes that the Book of Job is meant primarily to teach us about divine trials, he also believes that it reinforces the traditional notion that suffering can be divine punishment for sin. Saadiah tells us quite explicitly that the story of Job was recorded "that we might know, when sufferings and calamities befall us, that they must be of one of two classes: either they occur on account of prior sins of ours. . . . Or they are a trial from the Allwise."[30] What Saadiah is referring to here is that in addition to Elihu's position, which teaches us about divine trials, there is also the collective position of Eliphaz, Bildad, and Zophar, which claims that suffering is punishment for sin. Saadiah's point is that this position must be taken seriously as part of the central message of the Book of Job. But Saadiah is also careful to add that Job is meant to correct the mistaken impression that all suffering is due to punishment for sin, a belief that, Saadiah claims, is common in his own time. The Book of Job therefore informs us that individuals can suffer even if they are blameless and that in such instances suffering can be explained as a divine trial.[31] In short, the Book of Job is meant to show us that suffering can be *either* punishment for sin *or* a divine trial, but its most important lesson concerns the latter conception, since many people are unaware of this explanation for suffering.

Saadiah's introduction provides a great deal of information about his reading of the Book of Job. In fact, it lays out the entire scheme of the dialogue, along with an explication of the book's central message. Nevertheless, Saadiah's line-by-line exegesis of the biblical text yields more information pertinent to our concerns, and it is to this section that I now turn.

In his commentary on the first chapter of Job, Saadiah offers his views regarding the background of the story. Job and his companions are gentiles who live during the period of the exodus from Egypt. They are all descended from the patriarchs or their relatives. Job and Elihu are traced to Abraham's nephew Nahor; Eliphaz, to Esau; and Bildad, to Abraham. (The lineage of Zophar is unclear.) Saadiah supports all these connections with clues from the biblical text. Saadiah also informs us that the author of the book is Moses.[32] None of these views is original to Saadiah; they all have precedence in rabbinic sources.[33]

Saadiah goes on to emphasize the goodness of Job and his family. Job's righteousness is made clear in the very first verse of the book, where he is described as "blameless and upright" and one who "feared God and shunned evil." That Job's family is also righteous is evident from the fact that Job brings sacrifices at regular intervals just in case his children "have sinned and blasphemed God in their thoughts" (Job 1:5). The fact that Job is concerned only about their sinful thoughts suggests that they are entirely righteous in their actions.[34]

Saadiah then provides a series of lengthy observations regarding Satan and the *beney elohim*—the "divine beings," or, more literally, "the children of God"—who appear in the first two chapters of the book. Saadiah offers a novel interpretation of these figures by suggesting that they are not angels, as is commonly understood, but human beings who live in the land of Uz along with Job. The *beney elohim* are rendered by Saadiah as "God's beloved" in accordance with the translation of the term *ben* as "beloved," even though it is usually understood as "child," and Saadiah finds ample support for his interpretation in the biblical text. These people are beloved by God because they gather at regular intervals to worship Him. Hence, the description of their coming "before the Lord" on two separate occasions in the first two chapters.[35]

Satan is the leader of this group. He is given his appellation by the biblical text because he is Job's enemy. Saadiah adduces a number of biblical instances in which the term *satan* can refer to a human adversary and need not have any reference to an angel. As Saadiah would have it, the group Satan leads expresses envy of Job on account of his wealth and righteousness. They also slander him with the claim that he is righteous only because God has provided him with great blessing, and that if he were to suffer, he would immediately become an apostate. God therefore addresses Satan and offers to bring afflictions upon Job in order to prove to the group that he is indeed worthy of the favor that has been shown to him.[36]

At this point, incidentally, we finally have clarification of the passage in *Beliefs and Opinions* in which Saadiah uses Job as an example of those who undergo trials in order to demonstrate to "mankind" that God has not chosen them gratuitously.[37] In this instance, "mankind" is more precisely the human Satan and his cohorts, who must be shown that Job is worthy of the blessings he has received from God.

Saadiah is well aware that his understanding of Satan is a novel one, and he therefore expends a good deal of energy justifying it. First, Saadiah points out, Satan could not be an angel because all monotheists believe that God made angels to serve God, not to disobey Him. Yet, here Satan seems to go against God's will by wanting to harm Job, for in opposing the righteous, Satan is in effect rebelling against God Himself. Second, angels cannot feel envy, since this sentiment is a function belonging to the appetitive faculty of the soul, which is responsible for bodily needs. Angels do not have bodies, and therefore they cannot have an appetitive faculty. Yet, in this case Satan seems to envy Job. Third, we can assume that when He created angels, God had foreknowledge that they would not rebel, and therefore it is impossible that Satan would be an angel who would oppose God's will by wanting to torment the righteous. Yet, here he does just that.[38]

Goodman argues that there is another underlying reason for Saadiah's interpretation of Satan, and that is his desire to oppose midrashic, Christian, and Muslim views that make Satan a rebel angel and therefore do violence to the principle of monotheism. According to Goodman, Saadiah's sensitivities on this issue are heightened by his awareness of Manichean dualist doctrines expressed in his period, doctrines he criticizes in a number of passages in *Beliefs and Opinions*. Such doctrines were also the very ones supported by Saadiah's contemporary and opponent Hiwi al-Balkhi.[39]

To continue with Saadiah's exposition, God afflicts Job with trials involving his property in response to Satan's challenge. Thus, Job loses his wealth, and his children are killed. However, he remains steadfast in his righteousness. Satan is unimpressed and claims that if Job were to suffer afflictions affecting his body, he would not remain righteous. God therefore afflicts Job in this manner as well. Yet, even with this torment, Job does not lose his faith.[40]

In explicating these events, Saadiah also mentions that there is one other type of trial that God can inflict upon the righteous, and that is by way of "the soul"—by putting someone to death. God may take a righteous individual's life so as to reward him in the afterlife. This trial was inflicted not upon Job, but upon his children, who were killed. Saadiah therefore answers a question that has often plagued interpreters of Job, which is why Job's children lost their lives.[41]

Saadiah's reading of the first two chapters of Job inevitably forces him to make a number of clever exegetical moves in order to square his interpretation with the biblical text. For instance, he must reinterpret all language suggesting that it is Satan who directly afflicts Job, because, in Saadiah's rendering, Satan is only a human being and has no power over Job, at least not in the manner that a plain reading of the text suggests. Saadiah therefore consistently reads the text to mean that it is actually God who torments Job. Thus, God's statement to Satan that all Job has "is in your power" (Job 1:12) is taken to mean that all that Job has is "subject to your purpose and intent."[42] According to this reading, Satan does not actually have the capacity to afflict Job directly; rather, it is God who will execute Satan's wishes. Another example is God's directive to Satan before the second round of afflictions specifying that he may do with Job as he pleases, "only spare his life" (Job 2:6). This command is a problem for Saadiah's reading because it again suggests that it is Satan who afflicts Job, not God, and that it is for this reason that God is instructing Satan to spare Job's life. Saadiah circumvents the problem by interpreting the command "only spare his life" to mean "be heedful of his soul." That is, God is not actually giving Satan power over Job's soul but is only telling him to be mindful of it, since He will not accede to any suggestion to test Job to the point of actually killing him.[43]

Saadiah's interpretation of the ensuing discussion between Job and his three companions—Eliphaz, Bildad, and Zophar—has already been dealt with in part in the introduction to the commentary. There, as we have seen, Saadiah provides the general outline of the argument between them: Job's friends argue that he must have sinned to have experienced his afflictions, while Job maintains his innocence but does not accuse God of injustice on the assumption that He can cause suffering at His whim. What Saadiah adds in his line-by-line explication of the dialogue is an extensive commentary on how each address by the various participants is a response to previous addresses. It will not profit us to recount in detail what Saadiah says about these exchanges, since his interpretation of them does not add much to his overall conception of the dialogue. Suffice it to say that Saadiah does his best to show that the dialogue flows coherently from one address to the next.

As we found out in the introduction to the commentary, the correct interpretation of Job's situation is given by Elihu, for it is only Elihu who understands that a righteous individual such as Job can be caused to suffer as a test. The crux of Elihu's speech, according to Saadiah's reading, is his address in chapter 33. Saadiah believes that Elihu describes three types of individuals who receive reward in the afterlife: one who repents of his sins after God chastises him with suffering, one who repents of his sins before he has been made to suffer, and one who has no sins whatsoever but has been tormented by afflictions as a test of his faith. It is the last category that is applicable to Job.

It is not entirely clear how Saadiah reads the conception of divine trials out of chapter 33. It would seem that he finds this notion in Elihu's cryptic description of the sick person whom God afflicts with terrible torment, a description that begins with Job 33:19. In Saadiah's translation, Job 33:19–21 are to be understood as follows: "He might recompense him, too, for torments upon his bed and in his many wracking bones, until his soul retcheth at food, even the choicest aliments, and the bulk of his flesh perisheth from sight, his bones ground until invisible."[44] According to Saadiah's rendering, God is depicted here as rewarding an individual who is tested for the afflictions He brings upon him.[45]

Saadiah seems to understand the next two verses, Job 33:22–23, as providing more information about divine trials. These verses contain a description of the aforementioned sick person being rescued from his afflictions: "but when his soul [i.e., the soul of the righteous] is close to perishing and his life is at the point of death, if he hath one upright deed (*mal'akh*), albeit in a thousand, it serveth as an angel to speak in his behalf and tell mankind of his uprightness."[46] Saadiah adopts a rabbinic interpretation according to which the term *mal'akh*—which literally means "messenger" or "angel"—is taken to refer to the righteous individual's good deeds, which stand to his merit and therefore function as a sort of angel or messenger on his behalf before God.[47] The point of the passage, according to Saadiah, is that God rewards a person who is tested even if he has only one righteous deed out of "a thousand" to his credit. How much more is this case when that person is wholly righteous.[48]

According to Saadiah, Elihu's thoughts on this matter reach their conclusion several verses later, where the biblical text says that God restores the well-being of the person tested and "illumineth him . . . with the light of life" (33:30).[49] For Saadiah, the biblical text is teaching us about the rewards of the afterlife that await the righteous who have passed their test.[50]

In his commentary on God's speech to Job, Saadiah reiterates the view already expressed in his introduction, that God does not provide Job with an answer to the question of why he has suffered so that the test will not lose its meaning. God therefore chooses to speak to Job about the glories of creation.[51] Saadiah goes on to explain that Job, overwhelmed by God's address, acknowledges that his former understanding of his suffering was in error, and he now professes his complete ignorance of God's ways. Saadiah closes his commentary by telling us that Job receives reward in this world and the next for the patience he exhibited throughout his ordeal. Saadiah adds that his companions receive similar reward as well.[52]

One difficulty in Saadiah's reading that needs to be addressed is that one wonders how Elihu could inform Job that he is being tested if, as Saadiah emphasizes, the person who undergoes a divine trial must remain ignorant of the reason for his suffering for the trial to have any meaning. Our perplexity on this point is only deepened by the fact that in Saadiah's view, God resists telling Job that he is being tested precisely because Job must be kept in the dark about his trial. What sense does it make then for God to withhold information that Job has already found out from Elihu?

This problem can be solved with a careful reading of Saadiah's remarks on Elihu's address. As noted above, Elihu presents the idea of divine trials in the context of a larger discussion in which he argues that three types of individuals receive reward in the afterlife: one who repents of his sins after God causes him to suffer, one who repents before he suffers, and one who has no sins whatsoever but is made to suffer as a test of his faith. We are informed by Saadiah that Job is indeed in the third category. However, there is no indication that Job himself is given this information. Elihu merely describes the three categories of individuals without indicating where Job belongs in this scheme. Therefore, Job has no way of being sure that he is in fact being tested, and for all he knows he may very well be an individual in one of the other two categories mentioned by Elihu. What this means is that when Job is addressed by God, he has been introduced to the concept of divine trials but still does not know that he is experiencing one himself. The test is therefore still in effect as Elihu finishes his remarks, and God continues to keep Job in the dark about the reason for his suffering so that his trial will have meaning.

To summarize Saadiah's understanding of the Book of Job, Job is a historical individual and a righteous non-Jew who lives during the period of the exodus from Egypt. Satan is a human being and an acquaintance of Job who leads a band of companions to slander Job with the accusation that his righteousness is the result of the great wealth and large family with which God has blessed him. God therefore tests Job in order to prove to his contemporaries that his piety is indeed genuine. The test is also for the purpose of giving Job the opportunity to earn reward in this life and the next. Saadiah explains the dialogue between Job, Eliphaz, Bildad, and Zophar as an argument between two viewpoints: that of Job, who is convinced that God is just but has caused him to suffer arbitrarily, and that of his friends, who argue that Job must be suffering as a result of divine punishment for his sins. Job's friends teach a valuable lesson, but it is only Elihu who provides the correct explanation for Job's suffering by suggesting that the righteous can be made to suffer as a test.

Yet, it would appear that Elihu does not explicitly inform Job that he himself is experiencing a test, and therefore his trial continues as God speaks to him in the final section of the book. That God speaks to Job about matters unrelated to his test is interpreted by Saadiah as a necessary component of the trial. Were God to inform Job that he is being tested, the purpose of the trial would be entirely negated. As for the overall character of the Book of Job, Saadiah sees it serving both a theological and an ethical purpose. Its lesson is both that God is just and that we must exercise patience when our suffering seems to indicate otherwise.

Antecedents

The first interface concerns the antecedent influences that shaped the commentaries on Job analyzed in this study. As I noted in chapter 1, with this interface I am mainly interested in the extent to which later medieval Jewish philosophers in this study were influenced by earlier ones in interpreting Job. Because Saadiah is the first Jewish philosopher to write a commentary on Job, there are no antecedent Jewish philosophers who could have influenced him in the composition of his work. Nonetheless, there are antecedent influences on Saadiah's commentary from Islamic theology and rabbinic thought, influences of which one must be aware to have a comprehensive understanding of Saadiah's reading of Job. It is these sources that I will explore.

Goodman has done much of the work tracing these sources. He argues that Saadiah's understanding of Job has affinity with Islamic thinkers in the Mu'tazilite school, which, as noted earlier, was influential on Saadiah's theodicy. Islamic thinkers generally did not refer to the original Book of Job, but rather to the references to Job in the Koran, which furnished them with enough information to spin a rich tradition of commentary on Job's ordeal. In particular, Goodman argues that there is an affinity between Saadiah's reading of Job and that found in the Mu'tazilite commentator al-Zamakhsharī (d. 1144), who lived two centuries after Saadiah but reported Mu'tazilite readings of Job that date to Saadiah's period. Like Saadiah, al-Zamakhsharī envisions Job's suffering as a test that, when passed, yields reward from God. Goodman also shows that the Ash'arite school was significant in shaping Saadiah's reading of Job. Job's initial view in the dialogue, which attributes his suffering to the whims of divine will but sees no injustice therein, reflects the position of the Ash'arites, who espoused that very position regarding the suffering of the righteous. Saadiah's interpretation of the dialogue in Job can therefore be understood as a battle between Ash'arite and Mu'tazilite positions. Saadiah's sympathies for the Mu'tazilite camp are reflected in the fact that it is their viewpoint, represented by Elihu, that comes out victorious.[53]

Goodman also argues that Saadiah's understanding of the whole dialogical format of the Book of Job is influenced by the Kalam. The Kalam thinkers utilized an idiosyncratic dialectical method in their discussion of theological matters, and it would seem that Saadiah approached the dialogue in Job with that method in mind. But Goodman adds that the methodology of the Greek sciences, which had already begun to make significant inroads into the Islamic culture of Saadiah's period, is also evident in Saadiah's reading of Job. This comes through in Saadiah's systematic introduction to the commentary on Job and in his determination to find an overall conceptual unity in the book.[54]

In addition to finding Islamic roots in Saadiah's reading of Job, Goodman demonstrates the important role rabbinic sources play in shaping Saadiah's understanding of the book. As noted earlier, the rabbinic doctrine of "sufferings of love" is no less important than the Mu'tazilite doctrine of divine trials in determining Saadiah's views on theodicy in *Beliefs and Opinions*. This rabbinic doctrine therefore underlies Saadiah's reading of the Book of Job as well, Job being the exemplar of this type of suffering.[55]

I would like to supplement Goodman's observations by examining the rabbinic antecedents of Saadiah's view that Job is the biblical model of divine trials. Saadiah's choice of Job for this honor is somewhat surprising, since that role is generally reserved throughout rabbinic tradition for Abraham, who is tested in the episode of the *'akeidah* or "binding" of Isaac. Given Saadiah's heavy dependence on rabbinic sources, one wonders why, in this instance, he would depart from them.

It is always possible that Saadiah was simply unaware of his differences with the rabbis. After all, he never explicitly opposes their view. Yet, there is reason to suspect that Saadiah's choice of Job over Abraham is quite deliberate. Not only does he deny Abraham the honor of being the model for divine trials, but nowhere in his discussion of that issue in *Beliefs and Opinions* nor in his commentary on Job is Abraham's name even mentioned. It is always perilous to draw conclusions from what an author does not say, but given the strength of the association between Abraham and divine trials in rabbinic tradition, Saadiah's omission can only give us pause.

Upon closer examination, it would appear that Saadiah has not so much excluded Abraham from his conception of trials as he has incorporated him into the figure of Job. As noted earlier, Saadiah's entire conception of trials is informed by the figure of Abraham as depicted in rabbinic sources. We saw that the public dimension of trials is modeled on the midrashic Abraham, whose worthiness of divine favor is exhibited to his doubters by his willingness to undergo the test of the *'akeidah*.[56] Furthermore, Saadiah goes to great lengths in his commentary on Job to demonstrate that Job experiences a trial of this very kind. Therefore, the figure of Abraham in his rabbinic form lurks in the background of Saadiah's reading of Job, even though he is not mentioned. Abraham has not been left out, only subsumed. Yet, even if these observations are correct, Job is still the exemplary figure for Saadiah's conception of trials, and the question remains why he favors Job so decisively over Abraham.

It is not difficult to see why Saadiah made this choice. First of all, a number of rabbinic sources see a close association between the two. In one series of sources, Abraham and Job are compared with respect to their piety. Most find Abraham superior to Job in this respect;[57] others express the view that Abraham and Job are equal;[58] and yet a third group finds Job superior to Abraham.[59] Some rabbinic sources also make a direct connection between Abraham's trials and the suffering Job experiences. This appears to be the intent of a Talmudic passage that suggests that the *'akeidah* episode is prompted by a challenge from Satan regarding Abraham's worthiness.[60] Here the plot of the Job story is clearly reflected back onto Abraham's trial. Most intriguing are sources that claim that Abraham's trials are transferred directly to Job after the *'akeidah.* According to these passages, Abraham pleads with God immediately after the *'akeidah* that God not subject him to any more trials. God responds by informing Abraham that all his future trials will be inflicted on Job.[61] Therefore, if Saadiah preferred Job over Abraham as the biblical exemplar of trials, he may have been encouraged by these rabbinic sources. First, he may have adopted the minority view that Job's piety was superior to that of Abraham. Second, the close association between the two figures in all the sources alluded to here may have inspired Saadiah to co-opt the midrashic Abraham into the figure of Job without feeling that he was doing any injury to the former. Thus, Saadiah's choice of Job over Abraham may reflect a creative use of rabbinic tradition rather than a total departure from it.

There are other reasons for Saadiah's preference for Job. First, Saadiah may have been impressed by the fact that the whole of the Book of Job is devoted to an examination of Job's suffering, and that this examination takes the form of a dialogue that can be read as a philosophical discussion. While Abraham's trial is certainly central to the development of his role in the biblical text and in rabbinic Judaism as forefather of the Jewish people, it is only one short episode. Job therefore provides a much better focus for the issue of trials and their philosophical justification. Second, Job's predicament is a much better model for the type of trial that most ordinary people undergo. Abraham's trial is a psychological test imposed by a command that comes directly from God, while that of Job involves actual physical suffering without any prior communication from God, and when that communication comes, it does not clearly explain Job's ordeal. Thus, Job is a much better representative of Everyman than Abraham, and given the pedagogic emphasis in Saadiah's reading of the Book of Job, it makes sense that he would choose Job over Abraham to serve as a model for trials.

To sum up this portion of the discussion, there is no need to question the assessment made by scholars that, in his reading of Job, Saadiah draws heavily from Mu'tazilite and rabbinic thought. At the same time, it is also important to recognize Saadiah's originality here. Saadiah strikes out in an innovative direction by making Job the biblical model of divine trials, a role that is usually assigned in rabbinic tradition to Abraham. Certainly, Saadiah's preference for Job may have been prompted by sources within the rabbinic tradition itself, but even if this is the case, Saadiah's originality still comes through in his creative use of that tradition for his own purposes.

Exegesis

Let us now move to the second interface and assess Saadiah's exegesis of Job. The important questions here are whether Saadiah is sensitive to the major exegetical difficulties in the book, and if so, how he responds to them. The first question can be answered confidently in the affirmative. As we have seen, Saadiah, in his introduction to his commentary, makes a clear statement expressing his awareness of the many problems the Book of Job presents, such as its meandering dialogue and the cryptic nature of God's answer at the end of the book.

How, then, does Saadiah respond to these difficulties? We can best answer this question by referring back to the series of difficulties in Job described in chapter 1 and examining how Saadiah deals with them. With respect to the question of the historicity of the book, Saadiah simply assumes that Job and his friends are historical individuals; the question is when they lived and the nature of their lineage. We do not yet find in Saadiah the kind of sensitivity to this issue that we will see in later thinkers. Only with Maimonides will doubt be cast on the notion that Job and his friends were historical individuals, a position that will spawn much discussion in subsequent philosophers.

More interesting is how Saadiah deals with the inconsistencies and ambiguities in the depiction of the figure of Job in the biblical text—an issue that, incidentally, he does not single out in his own list of the book's problems. As we have seen, Saadiah's portrayal of Job is highly positive: Job serves as the model of patience and forbearance in the face of suffering. However, there are difficulties with this description, for even a cursory reading of the dialogue between Job and his friends reveals that Job is far less accepting of his suffering than Saadiah's interpretation would suggest.

Saadiah makes no attempt to blunt Job's barbs and protests against God. In fact, at one point Saadiah explicitly acknowledges Job's impatience. In his commentary on Elihu's address in chapter 35, Saadiah says:

> Elihu speaks explicitly of recompense in this chapter when he says, *Now, because he doth not, he recounteth his grievance* (Job 35:15) meaning that Job had reckoned only his sufferings and injuries, and then turned to self-pity and cries for help, because he did not know that the outcome of these sufferings would be immense relief. Had he understood this, he would not have bewailed his fate but borne it patiently.
>
> In this Elihu is right. For Job would have preserved his equanimity had he known that his recompense for all that he had suffered would be unmitigated.[62]

Here, Saadiah admits that Job did not suffer patiently—a far cry from his earlier description of Job as one who "bore the test with fortitude."[63] This is a significant inconsistency in Saadiah's reading of the Book of Job.

Another difficulty for Saadiah's portrayal of Job is the critical passage that appears in the last chapter of the book, in which God addresses Eliphaz: "I am incensed at you and your two friends, for you have not spoken the truth about Me as did my servant Job" (Job 42:7). God's positive assessment of Job is certainly in line with Saadiah's own understanding of him. The problem here is that according to Saadiah's reading, Job has not "spoken the truth" about God throughout the dialogue any more than his friends have. His notion that God has caused him to suffer arbitrarily is just as erroneous as their view that Job's suffering is punishment for sin.

Saadiah handles the problem by reading the passage as follows: "My wrath hath waxed against thee and against thy fellows, for ye did not speak the truth in my presence about my servant Job."[64] According to this rendering, God is accusing Job's friends of speaking falsehood not about God, but about Job! What allows Saadiah to read the verse in this way is a matter of conjecture, since he provides no justification for it. There is evidence that Saadiah had a different reading of the biblical text here. Yosef Kafiḥ notes in his edition of Saadiah's Arabic translation of Job that in one of the manuscripts upon which the translation is based, the last phrase of the passage in the original biblical text reads *be-'avdi iyyov*, "to my servant Job," rather than *ke-'avdi iyyov*, "as my servant Job."[65] The change of one letter here in the Hebrew—from a *beit* to the orthographically similar *kaf*—transforms the meaning of the passage entirely and fully justifies Saadiah's reading.[66]

If Saadiah is only partially successful in dealing with the ambiguities and inconsistencies regarding Job's character, he has a good deal more success in making sense of the long and meandering dialogue between Job and his friends. Saadiah manages to read the dialogue as a well-organized philosophical debate that finds its resolution in the position of Elihu. Moreover, as we have seen, Saadiah views Eliphaz, Bildad, and Zophar as serving a valuable function in the dialogue by introducing the reader to one of the central messages of the book, which is that suffering is sometimes retribution for sin. For even though they are mistaken in applying this notion to Job's situation, their position is still one of which the reader needs to be reminded, since it is correct in other instances. Thus, even the errant opinions in the dialogue are of importance to the book, not just the opinion of Elihu.[67] I also noted that Saadiah goes to great lengths to show how each of the speeches of the participants is a response to previous speeches.

Saadiah is also able to make sense of God's address to Job, which has troubled biblical interpreters more than any other portion of the book because it is highly unclear how God's remarks connect to the rest of the dialogue. Saadiah argues that God speaks about matters unrelated to Job's situation in order to ensure that his test have meaning. Were God to explain to Job why he has suffered, others could accuse him of bearing his test with patience for the sake of his anticipated reward. If God's address seems not to fit with the rest of the dialogue, it is, in Saadiah's opinion, for a very deliberate purpose.

An issue critical for understanding Saadiah's overall conception of the Book of Job is the audience to which he believes it is directed. Goodman points out that Saadiah's Job is a symbol with both universal and particular significance. Job represents the unmerited suffering of the righteous in humanity at large, but at the same time he is a symbol of the suffering of Israel and the Jewish experience of exile.[68]

This issue needs to be explored in further detail. The universal tone of

Saadiah's reading of Job is evident in the following passage in his commentary in which he sums up his views on the story's purpose:

> Knowing that throughout the ages the thoughts which pass before men's minds when sufferings befall them are of four sorts, corresponding to those which arose in Job's day, God required all this to be set forth for us, so that we might learn from it, discover the proper view, see its cogency and discard the rest.[69]

Here it would appear that the Book of Job is for humanity as a whole. Saadiah's belief in the universality of the message of Job is perhaps best expressed in the final passage of the commentary where he refers to the book as "a lesson to all creation."[70] The universal bent of Saadiah's reading is also evident from the fact that he believes the characters in the story to be non-Jews. Thus, the suffering of the righteous is clearly not just a Jewish problem. The universal thrust in Saadiah's reading of Job is certainly not surprising given that Saadiah's environment was largely Muslim and that the story of Job was well known and discussed in that culture.[71] Saadiah therefore had firsthand evidence that the Book of Job was of significance outside the Jewish community.

Yet, there is evidence that Saadiah also views the Book of Job as a text addressing the specific concerns of the Jewish people. Saadiah alludes to the association between Job and the Jewish people in a passage at the end of *Beliefs and Opinions* 3:10, where he responds to a number of challenges regarding Israel's adherence to the divine commandments.[72] One such challenge concerns the suffering of the Jewish people: why should the Jews observe the divine commandments if their obedience has brought only humiliation and contempt from the other nations? Saadiah replies:

> We say that if the adherents of the Torah had been granted perpetual sovereignty the non-believers might have said about them that they serve their God in order to preserve their favorable position; *as you know they said [this] about Job*. Indeed, they [i.e., the non-believers] would have also said about themselves that they did not obey [God] and turned away [from Him] because they had been brought low and had been treated with contempt and had not been granted sovereignty. Therefore, the Allwise elevated the latter and [still] they did not believe in Him, and thus proof against them was established; He debased the former and they did not deny [Him] and thus they were vindicated.[73]

Saadiah argues that God has brought humiliation on the Jews in order that they not be accused of obeying Him for the wrong reasons. Had their adherence to the commandments resulted in immediate reward, the non-Jewish nations might have accused them of being devoted to God for ulterior motives. Since they obey God's commandments despite their lowly condition, their integrity is beyond reproach. Most important for our concerns, Saadiah draws an explicit comparison between Israel and Job. While Saadiah does not elaborate on this comparison, it is not difficult to see its meaning. According to Saadiah, Job was accused by his enemies of worshipping God for ulterior motives and was therefore tested to demonstrate that his piety was in fact genuine. Similarly, Israel is afflicted with suffering so that the non-Jewish nations cannot challenge its sincerity in following God's directives.[74]

Saadiah makes no mention of the Jewish people in his commentary on Job. Yet, a careful reading of the commentary will demonstrate that even here that concern was not far from his thinking. In a central passage in Saadiah's introduction to his commentary on Job, he sums up his thoughts on the Book of Job:

> Therefore the Allwise caused their accounts to be written for us and set out as paradigms for us to learn from and so adapt ourselves to patient acceptance, that we might know, when sufferings and calamities befall us, that they must be of one of two classes: either they occur on account of prior sins of ours, in which case they are to be called punishments, and we must search out the relevant shortcomings and remove them and improve our actions, as it says, "Let us search our ways and probe them, and return to the Lord" (Lam. 3:40). Or they are a trial from the Allwise, which we must bear steadfastly, after which He will reward us. Thus, if we have searched ourselves and found nothing requiring punishments, we know that they are unprovoked and we call them a test and bear them patiently, as the prophet has said, "Fortunate are all those who wait for Him" (Isaiah 30:18). In neither case, do we ascribe any injustice to the Creator. Rather, we confirm the description He gave of Himself in His Scripture, "The Lord is just in the midst thereof," etc. (Zeph. 3:5). And that is why the book is given the title *The Book of Theodicy*.[75]

What is striking about this passage is that the three prooftexts cited here are all drawn from biblical passages dealing with the experience of Jewish exile. The notion that suffering must first force us to examine our conduct in order to determine whether our sinful deeds are the cause is supported by Lamentations 3:40, "Let us search our ways." The relationship between this citation and Jewish suffering requires little comment. The Book of Lamentations, which was written in response to the destruction of the first Temple, is wholly devoted to the theme of exile, and the verse cited, which focuses on repentance, encapsulates one of its central themes.

More important are the other two verses cited in this passage that support Saadiah's conception of trials. Both prooftexts, Isaiah 30:18 and Zephaniah 3:5, are again drawn from portions of the biblical text that deal quite specifically with the experience of Jewish exile among the gentile nations. The verse from Zephaniah is particularly significant when one looks at its context. The crescendo of the passage is just a few verses ahead of the one cited by Saadiah:

But wait for Me—says the Lord—
For the day when I arise as an accuser;
When I decide to gather the nations,
To bring kingdoms together,
To pour out My indignation on them,
All My blazing anger.
Indeed, by the fire of My passion
All the earth shall be consumed.
For then I will make the peoples of pure speech,
So that they all invoke the Lord by name
And serve Him with one accord. (Zeph. 3:8–9)

This passage, with its strong images of redemption, was interpreted from the Talmudic period onward as a prophecy regarding the messianic period,[76] and it appears to have had the same meaning for Saadiah. The same passage is cited in *Beliefs and Opinions* in connection with a discussion about the final redemption of Israel.[77] Thus, in a key passage in his introductory discussion to the Book of Job, Saadiah sends a strong signal that the Book of Job deals with Jewish exile and the hoped-for reconciliation with God.

My observations here also suggest that, in Saadiah's thinking, both explanations for suffering in the Book of Job—suffering as punishment for sin, and suffering as divine trial—are directed to the Jewish people as whole. For in the passage just cited, Saadiah's choice of proof texts implies that on the national level suffering can be due to either of these two causes. The first verse from Lamentations deals with punishment for sin of the sort experienced in the destruction of the first Temple, while the verse from Isaiah addresses the issue of suffering experienced by Jews who are righteous and are being tested. Finally, in identifying Job's suffering with that of the Jewish people, Saadiah is not entirely original. He is following in the footsteps of a number of midrashic passages that make the same connection.[78]

Did Saadiah have any difficulty with the notion that Job is a symbol of Israel even though he is not a Jew? Saadiah never addresses this question; however, it is unlikely that this issue would have troubled him much. In his commentary on Genesis, Saadiah exhibits a tendency to read events in the early biblical history as prefigurative of later events in the history of Israel. This is evident in particular in Saadiah's interpretation of the stories of the Garden of Eden and the Flood. Saadiah considers both these stories as allegories for the events of later Jewish history. They provide valuable instruction about the importance of the commandments and the dire consequences that follow if the commandments are not followed. In the Garden of Eden story, for instance, the garden itself is a symbol of the Temple; the laws given to Adam represent those of the Torah;[79] the snake is symbolic of the false prophets; Eve is representative of the kings of Israel, who were easily swayed by these prophets to disobey God; and the exile from Eden prefigures the exile from the land of Israel.[80] A similar type of reading is given to the Flood story, the details of which are again read as a foreshadowing of the later exile of the Jewish people.[81] All this shows that there is an established pattern in Saadiah's thinking of reading pre-Sinaitic episodes as prefigurations of later events in Jewish history that therefore have valuable lessons to teach the Jews about their relationship with God. The Book of Job seems to have served the exact same purpose in Saadiah's mind, for it too is a story that Saadiah locates among pre-Sinaitic gentiles, and like the Garden of Eden and Flood stories, the purpose of Job is to provide insight into the suffering God inflicts on the people of Israel.

The connection between Job and Israel in Saadiah's thinking may also shed light on how Saadiah understands the dialogue between Job and his friends. We saw earlier that in his interpretation of the discussion, Saadiah appears to be reproducing the debate between schools in Islamic theology regarding theodicy. Yet, there may be another dimension here. It is noteworthy that the dialogue, as Saadiah reads it, also reproduces the lines of debate between the Jews, on the one hand, and Christians and Muslims, on the other, regarding the meaning of Jewish suffering. Job's friends accuse him of not acknowledging past misdeeds that are responsible for his suffering, while Job maintains his innocence. In a similar vein, Christians and Muslims argued that the Jews were in a state of humiliation because of their sins, while the Jews denied such accusations and maintained their belief in being God's chosen. Saadiah never explicitly connects the dialogue in Job with interfaith polemics; yet one wonders if this was a factor in his reading of the book, given the association he makes between Job and Israel.[82]

What emerges from my analysis of the second interface is that Saadiah very much appreciates the major exegetical difficulties in the Book of Job and that he displays considerable originality in his solutions to those difficulties. I do not want to overstate my case. It is obvious that Saadiah's systematic thought in large part dictates how he reads the biblical text. There are any number of instances in which the meaning of the text is stretched in order to accommodate the philosophical ideas he intends to find in it. Therefore, Saadiah is often the philosopher, reading ideas into the biblical text, rather than the exegete, reading them out of it. An excellent example of this tendency is his interpretation of the interaction between God and Satan. Saadiah goes to great lengths to reinterpret the text because of the philosophical problems it presents for him. Even more important, the views on suffering that Saadiah uses to make sense of the entire dialogue in Job are based on systematic speculations ultimately rooted in Islamic and rabbinic theology. Saadiah's philosophical agenda also explains the one major exegetical weakness that we detected in his reading of Job. When it comes to the character of Job, he falters because his highly positive view of Job as one who passes his test with patience makes it difficult for him to come to terms with Job's protests. Here it would seem that his determination to understand Job's suffering as a divine test in terms consistent with Mu'tazilite and rabbinic thought overwhelms his exegetical sensibilities, and thus Job's intransigence throughout the dialogue remains a loose end that Saadiah never successfully ties in with his overall understanding of the story.

However, what is most important to recognize is that more often than not philosophical considerations coalesce with exegetical factors in shaping Saadiah's reading of the biblical text. That is, when he interprets the biblical text philosophically, he is often simultaneously attempting to answer exegetical difficulties that the text presents. This is most evident in Saadiah's interpretation of the dialogue in Job. In his interpretation of the discussion between Job and his companions, Saadiah may be reading the biblical text against the backdrop of the debate between Mu'tazilites and Ash'arites regarding theodicy; but it is critical to note that Saadiah's reading of the dialogue is equally an attempt to grapple with a major exegetical question that many exegetes have pondered, which is to determine what purpose the various viewpoints of Job's friends serve in the overall scheme of the book. Saadiah's answer is that they are all part of a well-organized philosophical debate. Moreover, there is exegetical significance in Saadiah's view that even the positions of Eliphaz, Bildad, and Zophar are deemed valuable despite the fact that God rebukes them in the end. By claiming that these figures remind us that suffering is sometimes punishment for sin, Saadiah lends greater meaning and coherence to the dialogue than it would otherwise have, for even the losers in the debate have a valuable message to impart. Saadiah also expends significant effort attempting to show how each of the speeches of the various participants in the dialogue answers previous ones. Thus, in Saadiah's reading of Job, philosophy and exegesis support, rather than oppose, each other.

The same duality of purpose is perhaps even more evident in Saadiah's interpretation of God's final address to Job—perhaps the most perplexing portion of the Book of Job. That God does not tell Job he is being tested is certainly an opportunity for Saadiah to reinforce his philosophical position that the righteous person is never informed by God of his trial lest it become meaningless. However, what should not be overlooked is that here too there is an exegetical reason for Saadiah's reading: he is trying to explain the lack of connection between the content of God's dramatic address to Job and the rest of the book. The lack of connection, according to Saadiah, is quite deliberate in that it serves the purposes of Job's trial. Again, the point is that Saadiah is reading his philosophical ideas into the text while at the same time solving one of the text's exegetical difficulties.

My observations are perhaps not all that surprising. As I noted in the introduction to this chapter, Saadiah is celebrated by scholars as an exegete who pioneered the use of Hebrew philology and grammar in reading the biblical text, and those skills are evident in his commentary on Job, much more so in fact than is apparent from my analysis. One might therefore expect that Saadiah would display similar skill with respect to the broader exegetical issues in the Book of Job that are of concern to us in this study.[83] Yet, Saadiah's interest in these issues can easily be missed by the reader because he never discusses them explicitly as he proceeds with his commentary, and they therefore tend to be masked by philosophical concerns. One must therefore read Saadiah with care in order to see that the larger exegetical questions of Job are indeed important to him.

Exegesis and Philosophy

The third interface concerns the relationship between the commentaries on Job of the thinkers in this study and their systematic philosophical works. With Saadiah, this means that we must look at the relationship between his commentary on Job and his treatise *Beliefs and Opinions.* Earlier in this chapter, I examined Saadiah's discussion of the suffering of the righteous in *Beliefs and Opinions* because it provided a convenient summary of conceptions that were central to his commentary on Job. I did not investigate the precise nature of the relationship between the two works, and it is to that question that I now turn.

The first concern in dealing with this matter is to determine the order in which these works were written. *Beliefs and Opinions* appears to have been completed around 933,[84] but we have no indication as to when the commentary on Job was written. There is reason to believe that the latter was written first. While in the commentary on Job Saadiah at no point refers to *Beliefs and Opinions,* there is one place in *Beliefs and Opinions* in which he alludes to the commentary. In a passage in the introductory chapter of *Beliefs and Opinions,* Saadiah cites Job 15:17–19 to support the notion that received tradition is a reliable source of knowledge and then adds that "this [form of knowledge] has conditions which we have explained in the interpretation of these verses in their [respective] places"—an obvious reference to his commentary on Job.[85] Sure enough, in his interpretation of those verses in his commentary on Job, Saadiah provides a number of insights about the use of tradition as a source of knowledge, and thus it would seem that it is indeed to this passage in the commentary that the above citation from *Beliefs and Opinions* is referring.[86] Here, it would appear, is proof that the commentary on Job was written earlier than *Beliefs and Opinions.*

This explains why in two other passages of *Beliefs and Opinions* that I have previously cited, Saadiah appears to assume that his reader is familiar with his commentary on Job. The first was in *Beliefs and Opinions* 5:3, in which Saadiah deals with the question of theodicy: "the endurance of the pious serves a useful purpose in that it enables mankind to understand that God has not chosen them gratuitously, as you learn from Job and his endurance."[87] What is noteworthy here is that Saadiah makes reference to the notion that Job is tested in order to prove to other human beings his worthiness of receiving divine favor. That reference would be lost on a reader unfamiliar with his commentary on Job, for nowhere in *Beliefs and Opinions* does Saadiah explain his conception of the public nature of Job's trial, and it is an understanding of the text that is quite innovative. It would seem, therefore, that in *Beliefs and Opinions* Saadiah assumes his reader's familiarity with his commentary on Job.

The same is true for a second passage, cited earlier, from *Beliefs and Opinions* 3:10, in which Saadiah attempts to explain why the Jewish people suffer: "we say that if the adherents of the Torah had been granted perpetual sovereignty the nonbelievers might have said about them that they serve their God in order to preserve their favorable position; as you know they said [this] about

Job."[88] Here again Saadiah assumes that his reader is familiar with his interpretation of Job's trial, which, like that of Israel, is designed to impress other human beings about the worthiness of those God has chosen for divine favor.

The next question is whether *Beliefs and Opinions* and Saadiah's commentary on Job at any point differ from each other regarding the issue of theodicy. I have found no differences of this sort, though it seems that the commentary on Job provides a somewhat fuller treatment of theodicy. The introduction to the commentary is itself a small systematic discussion in its own right, and it is longer and more detailed than the corresponding discussion in *Beliefs and Opinions.* Moreover, the dialogue in Job allows Saadiah to make a case for his conception of theodicy more fully than in his philosophical work.

What all these observations suggest is that Saadiah's commentary on Job was written prior to his discussion of theodicy in *Beliefs and Opinions* and that he intended it to be his central statement on that issue. That Saadiah viewed his commentary on Job in this way makes sense in light of the fact that he renames the Book of Job *The Book of Theodicy*. What this title suggests is that Saadiah regarded the Book of Job as a comprehensive treatment of theodicy, and therefore the commentary he produced on this book would serve a similarly important role in his own corpus of writings.

I am not suggesting that Saadiah's exegesis of Job was the source of all his reflections on theodicy. Saadiah clearly composes his commentary on Job with a theodicy already worked out prior to that effort, as is evident from his introduction to that work. There Saadiah lays out the systematic philosophical considerations that inform his reading of Job, considerations that are similar to those found in *Beliefs and Opinions.* But my analysis does show that exegesis seems to have been Saadiah's first and preferred medium for presenting his views on theodicy. It appears that he saw the Book of Job as fully sufficient for a theory of theodicy, and that he therefore composed a commentary on it that he believed would bring the value of this book to light for this purpose. Later in his life Saadiah revisited the same issue in *Beliefs and Opinions*, but only in order to summarize what he had already presented in his commentary on Job.

Concluding Reflections: Saadiah and the Christian Reading of Job

Our first commentary on Job in medieval Jewish philosophy has proven to be a highly engaging one. Saadiah's originality, evident in so many of his pursuits, is seen in his reading of Job as well. In the exploration of the first interface, I endorsed the view that Saadiah's interpretation of Job is heavily dependent on Islamic and rabbinic theology, but I also argued that he strikes out in his own direction by choosing Job over Abraham as the biblical exemplar of divine trials. In the investigation of the second interface, I was able to show that Saadiah was a thinker who was sensitive to the major exegetical challenges of the Book of Job and that his solutions to those difficulties were often quite innovative.

My analysis also demonstrated the importance of Saadiah's commentary on Job in his corpus of writings. This came through in the exploration of the third interface, in which we saw that it is Saadiah's commentary on Job that represents his major statement on theodicy, not his discussion of that issue in *Beliefs and Opinions*.

I would like to conclude my discussion of Saadiah by making some observations about the central thesis of Saadiah's reading of Job in comparative perspective. As already noted, Saadiah's suggestion that Job is undergoing a test that if passed will lead to future reward is a natural move for Saadiah to make in light of the Mu'tazilite and rabbinic thinking that inform his whole thought system. However, in his approach toward Job, Saadiah has an affinity with another tradition of interpretation on Job—one with which he was most likely unfamiliar—and that is the tradition of Christian commentators on Job. The notion that Job is undergoing a test that will result in future reward is most prevalent among Christian thinkers in both the patristic and the medieval periods. Moreover, Christian commentators share with Saadiah the fact that many of them produced full-length commentaries on the Book of Job in order to sustain this reading. This is not the case with the two schools that directly influenced Saadiah. Rabbinic sources provide only fragmentary glosses on Job, and the Mu'tazilites did not read the original text so as to compose commentaries on it.

It is therefore instructive to take a brief look at the Christian readings of Job that resemble Saadiah's. As early as the patristic period, Christian thinkers saw the solution to the challenge presented by Job's suffering in the notion of the afterlife and resurrection. That direction of interpretation was taken by such figures as Ambrose, Cassiodorus, and Gregory. The same understanding was later upheld by Thomas Aquinas. According to many of these exegetes, it is Job himself who affirms his belief in this solution. The notion that Job is aware of the explanation of his predicament is based on a well-known but difficult passage he utters in Job 19:25–27:

> But I know that my Vindicator lives;
> In the end he will testify on earth—
> This, after my skin will have been peeled off.
> But I would behold God while still in my flesh,
> I myself, not another, would behold Him;
> Would see with my own eyes:
> My heart pines within me.

The cryptic and ambiguous Hebrew in this passage allowed Christian thinkers to understand it as an allusion to the afterlife. However, some Christian thinkers who believed that the solution to Job's challenge lay in the notion of the afterlife were reluctant to place that insight into Job's mouth. It would seem that they wanted to accentuate Job's patience in the face of his trial, and that virtue would be greatly compromised if Job were aware of his future reward. This was, for instance, the position of John Chrysostom.[89]

Saadiah seems to have made a judgment similar to this latter viewpoint, for while he agrees that Job's suffering is due to a test that will bring future reward, he has Job remain ignorant of that reward for the duration of the dialogue. Saadiah, however, differs with Christian exegetes in viewing Job's future recompense as consisting of the material rewards he receives at the end of the book in this life, in addition to reward in the afterlife.

In light of these observations, it is interesting to see how Saadiah deals with Job 19:25–27. In Saadiah's rendering, the verses read:

> I know that the favored of God will survive, and others after them will arise upon the soil; and after my skin is corrupted, they will gather around this story of mine, and from the ills of my body I shall show signs of God, just as I witness myself, and mine eyes see naught that is foreign, when my piercing glances pierce my breast.[90]

According to Saadiah's commentary on these verses, the passage represents Job's hope that his story will be passed on to future generations so they will know that God afflicts the righteous arbitrarily and will therefore be able to bear their suffering with fortitude.[91] Therefore, Saadiah's rendering has no eschatological overtones. This is to be expected given that for Saadiah, Job's test would be spoiled by looking forward to such future reward.

What becomes apparent from the analysis in this chapter is that the interpretation of Job's ordeal as a test is widespread among thinkers in all three Abrahamic faiths in the medieval period, and that Saadiah, in understanding Job's suffering in this way, is reading the text in a manner that was common to a variety of medieval religious thinkers. That, of course, should not surprise us given that Satan's wager in the opening chapters of the book is certainly suggestive of a test. However, not all medieval Jewish philosophers would be comfortable with the notion that God would take a perfectly innocent individual and afflict him with terrible suffering in order to test him. As we move on to our next thinker, we will see an approach to Job that moves in a completely different direction.

3

Maimonides

Rabbi Moses ben Maimon, or Maimonides (1138–1204), is perhaps the only thinker in this study who needs no introduction. Born in Spain, Maimonides moved as a young man to Egypt, where he spent the rest of his life, rising to prominence as one of the most significant figures in medieval Judaism. His halakhic work, *The Mishneh Torah*, is regarded as a monumental achievement in the history of Jewish law. More significant for our purposes, his *Guide of the Perplexed* became one of the major philosophical works in the history of Jewish thought, setting the agenda for all philosophical thinking in Judaism from his death until the end of the medieval period and also exerting a substantial influence on Jewish thought in the modern era.[1]

Two issues need to be highlighted about Maimonides' philosophy in order to situate his reading of Job in its proper intellectual context and to understand why it differs from that of Saadiah. First, the overall synthesis that Maimonides is trying to forge no longer concerns the relationship between Judaism and Islamic theology, as we find in Saadiah. The period in which Jewish philosophers interpreted Judaism in light of Islamic theology was in fact relatively short-lived. By the time we come to the period of Maimonides, some two hundred years after Saadiah, the major challenge for Jewish philosophers is the synthesis between Judaism and Aristotelian philosophy. Jews discovered Aristotle through the great Islamic philosophers, such as Alfarabi and Avicenna, who expended much effort in interpreting Aristotle's thought in their commentaries on his writings and in their own original philosophical works. Maimonides became the most prominent Jewish student of this school, and he took it upon himself to reinterpret Judaism in light of this newly discovered wisdom.[2]

The seeds of Maimonides' synthesis are evident in sections of his halakhic works: his *Commentary on the Mishnah* and *Mishneh Torah*. However, it is Maimonides' *Guide*, written at the end of his life, that is the crowning achievement of this enterprise. The *Guide* is introduced by Maimonides as an exegetical work attempting to interpret selected portions of the biblical text that are problematic from a philosophical standpoint. In particular, Maimonides is concerned with two types of difficulties: anthropomorphic terms that fly in the face of demonstrative philosophical proofs that God is incorporeal, and extended passages in the biblical text that for one reason or another are philosophically problematic and require allegorical interpretation in order to reveal their true inner philosophical meaning.[3]

A second issue in Maimonides' philosophy that should be highlighted here is that Maimonides writes the *Guide* in an esoteric style in order to conceal his true views from the masses. Debate has raged ever since Maimonides' lifetime over what secrets he was actually hiding. Some have claimed he was a traditional Jew who supported traditional Jewish doctrines but was wary of revealing philosophical truths to the masses, who might misinterpret them. Others have taken a more radical approach and have argued that Maimonides was a thoroughgoing Aristotelian who wrote in an esoteric style in order to conceal the fact that he had divorced himself from many of Judaism's most cherished dogmas. Still others have taken a middle position between the two views.[4] Whatever the case, what is important here is that Maimonides' esoteric style makes him far more difficult to read than a figure like Saadiah.

It is against the background of these observations that we can approach Maimonides' reading of the Book of Job. Maimonides composes two lengthy chapters on Job in the third part of the *Guide* as part of his program to wed Aristotelian thought with the Bible.[5] The Book of Job is a prime example of a philosophically problematic biblical text of the second type that the *Guide* is designed to interpret. That is, it is a book the plain sense of which presents philosophical difficulties, and it must therefore be read allegorically in order to be properly understood.

Yet, if Maimonides' *Guide* as a whole is a challenge to understand because of its esoteric style, that problem is greatly magnified in his exposition on Job; scholars have long recognized that this is one of the most difficult sections of the *Guide*. Its difficulty can be explained in part by its connection to Maimonides' discussion of providence, which is one of the most impenetrable areas of his thought. This issue involves an assessment of the entire relationship between God and the world, and thus it is no surprise that on this topic and everything connected with it Maimonides would be unusually evasive.[6]

But whatever the reason for the difficulty of Maimonides' reading of Job, it will certainly affect my discussion in this chapter. A great deal of effort will have to be spent simply discerning what Maimonides says about Job. In some passages, every line will have to be carefully scrutinized in order to get to Maimonides' true intention. Only toward the end of the chapter will it be possible to analyze Maimonides' reading with respect to the three interfaces that are the focus of this study.

I should add here that, as noted in chapter 1, Maimonides' treatment of Job has been extensively studied—far more so than any of the other treatments of Job analyzed in this study. Therefore, in many respects, my analysis is indebted to the work of previous scholars. Most important, the central message I see in Maimonides' reading of Job has been suggested by others. Even so, with all that scholars have contributed in penetrating the meaning of Maimonides' interpretation of Job, I believe that there are still elements of it that have not been fully understood. Moreover, the analysis of Maimonides' reading of Job in accordance with the three interfaces that are at the center of my study will bring out dimensions of that reading that have not been considered by others.

The Philosophical Background: *Guide* III:17–18, 51

As I did with Saadiah, I would like to begin my analysis of Maimonides by first summarizing his systematic treatment of the philosophical issues underlying his reading of Job, which in this case concerns the broad issue of divine providence. Such a summary is imperative here, since, as noted above, his reading of Job is part of a larger section of the *Guide* dealing with providence, and the former cannot be understand without the latter.

Maimonides' central discussion of providence is contained in *Guide* III:17–18. He begins his deliberations by recounting five theories of providence proposed by previous schools:

1. The view of Epicurus is that there simply *is* no providence because there is no God. The world is the product of mere chance.
2. Aristotle's view is that God exercises providence, but only over those things that are stable and permanent. Therefore, there is general providence over the various species, but not over their individual members who are unprotected from harmful chance events.
3. The Ash'arite school of Islamic theology believes that providence consists in the exercise of divine will, which one cannot understand or question. Therefore, God can cause the righteous to suffer and the wicked to prosper without our being able to discern any reason for such actions.
4. The Mu'tazilite school of Islamic theology believes that all of God's actions in the world are dictated by wisdom. Thus, if the righteous suffer, it is because God is testing them so as to afford them the opportunity to gain greater reward in the world-to-come.
5. The fifth opinion is that of "our Law," according to which the principle of God's relationship to the world is justice. Providence is therefore "consequent on the individual's deserts, according to his actions." The implication here is that the good fortune people experience is always reward for good deeds, while their suffering is always punishment for sin.[7]

Maimonides then offers his own view on providence, which combines the opinion of Aristotle with that of the Law. Aristotle is correct with respect to all species in the sublunar realm except for human beings, who are governed by providence as dictated by the Law. Thus, for all species other than human beings, providence protects only the species as a whole, while their individual members are vulnerable to the harmful effects of chance events. It is only in the human species that individuals experience providence, and for them, as the Law tells us, the principle of justice applies: good fortune is reward for good deeds, while bad fortune is punishment for sin. Maimonides adds, however, that the exact "rule" of how reward and punishment are meted out is beyond our understanding.[8]

In *Guide* III:17, Maimonides also gives insight into the metaphysical mechanism responsible for individual providence. Human beings alone experience this special type of providence because of their intellects, which distinguish them from all other species. It is through the intellect that human beings receive "divine overflow," the divine energy that spills over into the world via the chain of Separate Intellects.[9] In *Guide* III:18, Maimonides elaborates further on how individual providence is operative in human beings by informing us that providence is not the same for all people in that it is graded according to the perfection of one's intellect. The greater one's intellectual perfection, the greater the divine overflow one receives and therefore the greater one's providence.[10]

There is much that is unclear here. At first, Maimonides supports the traditional view of "the Law" that God simply rewards and punishes individual human beings according to their deeds. But once he begins to discuss the mechanism of providence and formulates the notion of providence as consequent upon the intellect, it would seem that he is proposing a more naturalistic conception. Maimonides never tells us precisely what that conception is, but commentators from the medieval period onward have repeatedly suggested a number of possibilities. One is that the more developed an intellect one has, the more developed one's practical intellect will be, which according to Aristotelian psychology is that portion of the intellect responsible for deliberations regarding future choices. Someone with a highly developed practical intellect will therefore be able to maximize his well-being by consistently making intelligent decisions regarding future action. A second possibility is that the more developed a person's intellect, the more he will be able to achieve moral virtue, which in Maimonides' thinking involves the regulation of one's habits according to the principle of the Aristotelian mean. Moral virtue, in turn, leads to better physical health, which again results in greater well-being.[11] A third possibility seems to emerge from Maimonides' discussion of Job in *Guide* III:22–23.[12] According to most commentators, the final lesson Job learns in Maimonides' reading is that intellectual perfection can safeguard a person from suffering because it allows one to develop the ability to engage in the constant contemplation of God and thereby confers an inner psychological resistance to suffering. One basks in the pleasure of contemplating the Deity, with the result that one becomes impervious to physical affliction. According to this alternative, one does not so much circumvent suffering as learn to manage its ill effects.

Some commentators entertain more than one of these theories in the belief that, according to Maimonides, providence can express itself in a number of different ways. But what is important to realize is that none of these manifestations of providence require a personal God who intervenes in human events. Divine providence is "divine" only in the tenuous sense that the human intellect is connected to God through the Active Intellect, and it is the human intellect that saves a person from harm. Nor does God really reward and punish. In some sense, one rewards and punishes one's own self according to the degree of effort invested in perfecting one's intellect, which determines one's level of providence according to each of the possibilities just described.[13]

We therefore have two difficulties here. First, Maimonides seems to contradict himself in that he first supports a traditional conception of providence but later on argues for a more naturalistic conception. Second, it is not at all clear what precisely that naturalistic conception is.

The first difficulty can be cleared up by assuming that Maimonides is concealing an esoteric doctrine. This would explain why, in *Guide* III:17–18, he begins with a traditional formulation of providence but ends up with a more naturalistic conception. The first is meant to appease the philosophically uneducated reader, while the second represents his true view.[14] Some have gone as far as to claim that this latter, esoteric position is, in fact, that of Aristotle, whose conception of providence with respect to human beings Maimonides had initially denied.[15]

The second problem is much harder to solve, since the ambiguities in Maimonides' presentation do not allow us to easily discern which of the possible natural mechanisms of providence is correct. Moreover, the whole issue is further complicated by a much-discussed passage in *Guide* III:51. In the middle of the chapter, Maimonides dramatically breaks off his train of thought and shares what he feels is "an extraordinary speculation" that has just occurred to him regarding providence, by which "doubts may be dispelled and divine secrets revealed." The central idea expressed here is that when a person has achieved intellectual perfection and is constantly contemplating God, he is entirely protected from physical harm. As Maimonides puts it, "that individual can never be afflicted with evil of any kind."[16] Here is a formulation that seems neither traditional nor esoteric. On the one hand, Maimonides continues to uphold a concept suggestive of a naturalistic approach to providence, according to which providence is consequent upon the intellect. On the other hand, Maimonides provides what appears to be an extreme description of the protective capacity of providence that is more consistent with direct divine intervention. He is proposing that providence is foolproof in guarding an individual from any and all harm that may come his way, a level of protection that seems impossible within a naturalistic framework. Even the most developed intellect, it would seem, cannot safeguard a person so completely from danger according to the suggested mechanisms outlined earlier.[17]

Maimonides' discussion of providence in *Guide* III:17–18 therefore leaves many unanswered questions. It seems likely that Maimonides' esoteric position on providence is naturalistic, but its precise mechanism is not entirely clear. However, a number of commentators have argued that Maimonides' reading of Job, a few chapters later on in the *Guide*, provides critical insight into his views on providence, for there the entire issue of providence is revisited within the context of an exegetical exposition. It is to that section of the *Guide* that I now turn.

Maimonides on Job: *Guide* III:22–23

Maimonides begins his commentary on Job in *Guide* III:22 by emphasizing that the book is "extraordinary and marvelous" in that it is designed to "set forth the opinions of people concerning providence."[18] Maimonides also deems the book to be "a parable" and supports his claim by citing the Talmudic view that the story is a fiction.[19] What this means is that the Book of Job is precisely one of those scriptural texts with inner philosophical meaning that the *Guide* is designed to decipher. According to Maimonides, the parabolic nature of the book is reflected in the name of the country that is identified as Job's home, the land of *'Uẓ*.[20] Maimonides understands this name as an equivocal term. It can be a proper name, as is the case in one passage in the Bible;[21] or it can be read as an imperative form of the verb *'uẓ*, "to reflect" or "to meditate." It is this second meaning that Maimonides prefers. As Maimonides tells us, "It is as if [scripture] said to you: Meditate and reflect on this parable, grasp its meaning and see what the true opinion is."[22]

Maimonides characterizes the initial Job whom we meet before his afflictions as a figure with moral but not intellectual perfection, and it was for this reason that he would later fail to understand his suffering:

> The most marvelous and extraordinary thing about this story is the fact that knowledge is not attributed in it to *Job*. He is not said to be a *wise* or *comprehending* or an *intelligent man*. Only moral virtue and righteousness in action are ascribed to him. For if he had been *wise*, his situation would not have been obscure to him, as will become clear.[23]

Maimonides appears to base his view on the fact that Job is described in the opening verse of the story as someone who "was blameless and upright" and who "feared God and shunned evil."[24] Here only moral virtues are attributed to him, not intellectual ones.

In another passage, Maimonides elaborates on Job's initial limitations:

> [Job] said all that he did say as long as he had no true knowledge and knew the deity only because of his acceptance of authority, just as the multitude adhering to the Law know it. But when he knew God with a certain knowledge, he admitted that true happiness, which is the knowledge of the deity, is guaranteed to all who know

> Him and that a human being cannot be troubled in any way by any of all the misfortunes in question. While he had known God only through traditional stories and not by way of speculation, Job imagined that the things thought to be happiness, such as health, wealth, and children, are the ultimate goal. For this reason he fell into such perplexity as he did.[25]

Here we learn that Job's intellectual deficiencies were responsible for his having an incorrect view of providence. Job knew God only by "authority" and "traditional stories," not through philosophical speculation. Therefore, Job thought that happiness consisted of "health, wealth, and children," and it was for this reason that he became perplexed and protested when he experienced suffering. Only when he gained true knowledge of God did he make peace with his misfortunes and experience true happiness.

The full meaning of this last statement will become clear only later on in this presentation. What is important to notice at this point is that we begin to see the emergence of a radical edge in Maimonides' reading of the story. The initial Job is clearly representative of the philosophically uneducated masses in Maimonides' own community, whom he criticizes throughout the *Guide*. Maimonides pretty much gives away this association when he characterizes Job as having views similar to those of "the multitude adhering to the Law." They, like Job, have only moral virtue in that they adhere to the commandments, but they lack intellectual virtue. In addition, through his depiction of the figure of Job, Maimonides expresses disdain for the views of the masses regarding providence when he states that Job knew God only through "authority" and "traditional stories" and therefore believed that ultimate happiness consists in "health, wealth, and children." With this statement, it would seem, Maimonides is making the point that the masses read scripture literally without appreciating its philosophical meaning and therefore place their faith in the plain meaning of the biblical doctrine of reward and punishment, which promises physical and material well-being for the observance of the commandments. While it is not entirely clear just yet what the correct alternative view is, this position on reward and punishment is undoubtedly in error, according to Maimonides' thinking, in that Job ultimately comes to a higher understanding of what true happiness is.

Yet, we are somewhat ahead of ourselves. We have seen that, according to Maimonides, Job is intellectually deficient and therefore does not understand his suffering, but we have still not discussed Maimonides' views on the cause of his suffering. For this we must turn to Maimonides' views on Satan. Maimonides has a good deal to say about this figure; he occupies almost half of Maimonides' discussion of the Book of Job, with nearly the entire first chapter of his exposition devoted to him.

Maimonides introduces his views on Satan by telling us that all intelligent people—even those who believe that Job was a historical individual—are in agreement that Satan is an allegorical figure. But Satan is no ordinary allegorical figure; he is one "to which extraordinary notions *and things that are the mystery of the universe* are attached." Through an understanding of Satan, "great enigmas are solved, and truths than which none is higher become clear."[26]

Yet, as is often his custom when dealing with exalted matters in scripture, Maimonides' comments about Satan amount to little more than a series of cryptic clues that the reader must decipher. The first set of comments is key. Maimonides notes that when Satan first appears in the biblical text, he presents himself before God *after* the arrival of the *beney elohim*, the divine beings: "One day the divine beings presented themselves before the Lord, and Satan came along with them" (Job 1:6).[27] Maimonides claims that Satan is mentioned separately in order to signify that he arrives "without having been for his own sake the object of an intention or having been sought for his own sake," while the divine beings are those "whose presence was the object of an intention."[28] Maimonides also comments on the ensuing exchange between God and Satan, in which God asks Satan where he has been. According to Maimonides, Satan's reply, "I have been roaming all over the earth" (Job 1:7, 2:1), means that "there is no relationship between him and the upper world, in which there is no road for him." That is, Satan's "roaming" takes place only on earth, not in the heavens.[29] Maimonides also notes that the second time the biblical text describes the arrival of the divine beings before God, the biblical text says that "Satan came along with them to present themselves before the Lord" (Job 2:1). Here, in contrast to the first passage describing the arrival of the divine beings, Satan is very much part of the entourage. Maimonides concludes from this second passage that while Satan is separate from the divine beings, he "also has a certain portion" below the divine beings "in what exists," though his status is not identical to theirs.[30]

Maimonides has more to say about Satan, but let me first decipher the comments I have just cited. Medieval and modern commentators are divided over their meaning. I will first look at Maimonides' views on the divine beings. According to the medieval commentators Efodi and Shem Tov, the divine beings represent all the forces of nature, including the Separate Intellects, the spheres, and the natural forms, all of which are responsible for generation in the world of nature.[31] The same view is supported by the modern commentator Solomon Munk.[32] However, Avraham Nuriel views them as representative of the actual natural events that are produced by the forces of nature.[33]

The crux of the disagreement appears to be the ambiguity in Maimonides' understanding of the term *elohim*. In the biblical Hebrew, the divine beings are literally "the sons of *elohim*," and for Maimonides the term *elohim* can allude to a number of referents. It is, of course, one of the names of God in the biblical text, but in Maimonides' lexicon, it can also refer to angels. To complicate matters further, for Maimonides the term "angel" is itself equivocal and, in turn, can refer either to any natural force in the world, or more specifically to the Separate Intellects.[34] Interpretations of who the divine beings are according to Maimonides, will therefore vary in accordance with how the term *elohim* is understood. Those commentators who see the "sons" of *elohim* as a collective reference to the generative forces of nature clearly understand *elohim* as a reference to God. Those forces are, in a figurative sense, God's "offspring."[35] However, Nuriel, who construes the "sons" of *elohim* as natural events, interprets the term *elohim* itself as a reference to natural forces. In this reading, natural events are, in a figurative sense, the "offspring" of those natural forces.[36]

I would like to leave the question of the identity of the divine beings open for the time being, since we will be able to make a better decision on which of these alternatives is correct later on in the analysis. For now it is sufficient for us to understand that the divine beings represent some positive element, or elements, of the natural order.

Let us move on to look at Maimonides' understanding of the term "Satan." All commentators are agreed that for Maimonides Satan represents a negative and harmful force in the natural world, but they are in disagreement as to what that force is. Medieval commentators on Maimonides are practically unanimous in the view that Satan is a representation of the principle of privation, which is the absence of a natural form in an object that might normally possess it and is therefore responsible for the process of decay and corruption in the physical world.[37] Some, however, also see him as representative of matter.[38]

Modern thinkers entertain a much wider range of possibilities. Munk and Nehoray follow the medieval commentators in identifying Satan with privation.[39] Jacob Levinger argues that Satan represents privation, but specifically the privation of Job's wisdom, which, as we shall soon see, is a critical factor in Maimonides' explanation for Job's suffering.[40] Leonard Kravitz supports a variation on this position, arguing that Satan represents the imagination, the psychic faculty whose influence over Job is the cause of his lack of wisdom.[41] Alvin Reines is inclined to the view that Satan is representative of a combination of matter and privation.[42] Some suggest that Maimonides sees Satan as representing two different types of evils, on account of the fact that Maimonides draws attention to the differences in the biblical text regarding the two descriptions of Satan's arrival with the divine beings. For Shalom Rosenberg, the first mention of Satan represents privation, or cosmic evil, while the second represents the imagination, or human evil.[43] Nuriel argues that the first Satan represents harmful chance occurrences, while the second represents privation.[44]

I need not elaborate on how each of these views is constructed from the various hints and clues in Maimonides' reading of the Job story in particular, and the *Guide* in general, except to say that all of them are based on credible evidence. My own view inclines toward the medieval and modern commentators who identify Satan with privation. In order to see the merit of this interpretation, we must go back to Maimonides' discussion of evil in *Guide* III: 8–12. There Maimonides identifies matter and privation as the causes of evil. He goes on to explain that evil is always the privation of some good. Thus, for example, darkness is the privation of light; poverty, the privation of wealth; death, the privation of a living being's form. Privations occur only because of the instability of matter, which is unable to hold fast to its form and must therefore perpetually replace one form with another.[45]

By this description, matter could just as easily be the cause of evil as privation.[46] Yet, there is ample evidence to suggest that in Maimonides' thinking, Satan is representative of privation. As we saw earlier, Satan's separate arrival from the divine beings signifies for Maimonides that he comes along with them "without having been for his own sake the object of an intention or having been sought for his own sake."[47] In his discussion of evil in the *Guide*, privation is described by Maimonides in strikingly similar terms, but without the personification that accompanies his description of Satan. There Maimonides argues that as a general principle, an agent does not produce a privation directly, only by accident, since an agent cannot be the essential cause of the absence of something. Thus, for instance, when one turns out a lamp, one is not the direct agent of the darkness that ensues, only its indirect accidental cause.[48] For this reason, Maimonides goes on to say, privation is not produced by God in an essential way, but only indirectly in that God has created matter that acquires forms but will then relinquish them. God is therefore not directly responsible for evil:

> After these premises, it will be known with certainty that it may in no way be said of God, may He be cherished and magnified, that He produces evil in an essential act; I mean that He, may He be exalted, has a primary intention to produce evil. Rather, all His acts, may He be exalted, are an absolute good; for He only produces being and all being is good. On the other hand, all the evils are privations with which an act is only connected in the way I have explained: namely, through the fact that God has brought matter into existence provided with the nature it has—namely, a nature that consists in matter always being a concomitant of privation, as is known. Hence, it is the cause of all passing-away and of all evil.[49]

Note how Maimonides' language here foreshadows his remarks about Satan. That evil caused by privation is not produced by God "in an essential act" or by "primary intention" adumbrates Maimonides' description of Satan, who is not "the object of an intention" and is not "sought for its own sake."[50]

The identity of privation and Satan also explains Maimonides' reading of the description of Satan's second arrival in which he comes along with the divine beings who present themselves before God. As we saw, Maimonides concludes from this second passage that Satan "also has a certain portion" below the divine beings "in what exists," though his status is not identical to theirs.[51] To make sense of this second gloss, one need only look a little further in Maimonides' discussion of privation, where he describes the latter's one redeeming feature:

> Accordingly the true reality of the act of God in its entirety is the good, for the good is being. . . . Even the existence of this inferior matter, whose manner of being it is to be a concomitant of privation entailing death and all evils, all this is also *good* in view of the perpetuity of generation and the permanence of being through succession.[52]

That matter is wedded to privation is on some level reflective of God's goodness, for without the continuous succession of forms this combination allows, there would be no generation in the natural world whatsoever. Thus, privation serves a positive function in fulfilling God's purpose for the perpetuation of being. Maimonides' remarks about Satan's second arrival now make sense. Satan has "a certain portion" beneath the divine beings "in what exists," for without privation there would be no existence.

We can also make sense of Maimonides' interpretation of Satan's statement, "I have been roaming all over the earth." Maimonides construes this to mean that "there is no relationship between him and the upper world, in which there is no road for him,"[53] because privation exists only in the sublunar world. It is only there that things are subject to generation and corruption.

We can also decipher other portions of Maimonides' discussion of Satan that have not yet been mentioned. A passage that will become important later on in my analysis is Maimonides' interpretation of God's instruction to Satan that he may do with Job as he pleases, "only spare his soul" (Job 2:6).[54] Maimonides informs us that the "soul" here refers to "the thing that remains after death," and that it is this entity over which Satan has no power.[55] Maimonides is obviously referring here to the perfected theoretical intellect, which, upon achieving perfection, is the only part of the soul that is immortal. Maimonides is informing us that privation has no power over the perfected intellect since, as an immaterial entity, it resists all decay and corruption.[56]

We should look at one other series of thoughts on Satan that Maimonides offers in the final section of *Guide* III:22. There Maimonides focuses his attention on a Talmudic dictum of Resh Lakish: "Satan, the evil inclination, and the angel of death are one and the same."[57] Maimonides sees this statement as containing great wisdom: "it clarifies all that is obscure, reveals all that is concealed, and renders manifest most of the *mysteries of the Torah*."[58] As is his custom, Maimonides goes on to explain the Talmudic dictum in oblique terms, but it is not too difficult to figure out what he is saying here now that we have some understanding of his views on the figure of Satan. Maimonides tells us that the central message of Resh Lakish's dictum is that Satan, the evil inclination, and the angel of death "designate one and the same notion and that all the actions attributed to each of these three are only the action of one and the same thing."[59] It would seem that the one "notion" or "thing" uniting all three in Maimonides' thinking is privation. Satan, as we have seen, represents that very idea. The angel of death is another figure symbolic of privation, since, as Maimonides himself notes in his discussion of privation earlier in the *Guide*, death occurs when the body is deprived of its form—that is, the soul.[60] The evil inclination can also be related to the notion of privation in Maimonides' thinking. Elsewhere in the *Guide*, Maimonides equates the evil inclination with the imagination, because the imagination is a source of evil if dependence is placed on it to the exclusion of the intellect, the faculty through which human perfection is achieved.[61] Therefore, the imagination, or the evil inclination, is a privation in that it represents the absence of wisdom.[62]

Maimonides' discussion of Resh Lakish's dictum is important because it contains a passage that will help us determine how he understands the "divine beings" or "sons of *elohim*" whom Satan accompanies in the first chapters of Job. As we saw earlier, most commentators on Maimonides see them as representing the generative forces of nature, while Nuriel sees them as representative of the natural events produced by those forces. We can discern which theory is correct with the help of the following passage:

> Now as they [i.e., the rabbis] have explained to us that *the evil inclination* is *Satan*, who indubitably is an *angel*—I mean that he too is called an *angel* inasmuch as he is found in the crowd of *the sons of God*—*good inclination* must consequently also be truly an *angel*. Consequently that well-known opinion figuring in the sayings of the *Sages, may their memory be blessed*, according to which every man is accompanied by *two angels*, one to his right and the other to his left, identifies these two with *good inclination* and *evil inclination*.[63]

Maimonides attempts to explain the rabbinic identification of the good and evil inclinations with two angels that accompany every individual. He reasons that since the evil inclination is identified with Satan, who is in turn an angel in that he is among "the sons of *elohim*," the good inclination must also be an angel. We have already seen that for Maimonides the evil inclination is the imagination. It therefore seems likely that its counterpart, the good inclination, is the intellect. What is significant for our purposes is that in this passage the sons of *elohim* seem to be understood as forces of nature rather than the natural events produced by them, for the two inclinations that belong to the sons of *elohim* are clearly in the first category, not in the second. It would seem therefore that Nuriel's theory must be ruled out, and that Maimonides identifies the sons of *elohim* with the generative forces of nature, not the events produced by them.

One element missing from Maimonides' account of Satan is that he never indicates how the specific evils that afflict Job are actually related to privation. Important information on this issue is provided in an earlier discussion in *Guide* III:12 where Maimonides divides all evils into three categories. Some commentators have noted a correspondence between these three categories and the types of afflictions Job experiences.[64] Such a correspondence should not surprise us. Maimonides states in his introduction to the *Guide* that the non-exegetical chapters in his treatise are "preparatory" for those that are.[65] Maimonides' discussion of evil that is non-exegetical thus appears to be preparatory for his reading of Job, which occurs several chapters later. Furthermore, the chapters in *Guide* III:8–24 appear to form a single unit concerned with the issue of providence.[66] Thus, Maimonides' discussion of the three categories of evil in *Guide* III:12 and his discussion of Job in *Guide* III:22–23 are part of the same sub-section of the *Guide* and could be closely linked.

An examination of the three categories of evil in *Guide* III:12 demonstrates that there is a case for a correspondence between these evils and those that afflict Job. Maimonides' first category of evil in *Guide* III:12 includes natural disasters and illnesses that are connected to "coming-to-be and passing-away" and "matter," a clear allusion to the matter-privation complex discussed earlier. Here Maimonides specifically mentions evils that come as a result of "changes occurring in the elements, such as corruption of the air or a fire from heaven and a landslide."[67] The references to the "corruption of air" and "fire from heaven" seem to be allusions to the sorts of meteorological disasters that wipe out a portion of Job's livestock and his entire family. The fire from heaven is mentioned explicitly in the biblical text as burning up Job's flock of sheep, while the corruption of air could easily be an allusion to the devastating wind that fells the house in which Job's sons and daughters are feasting, killing them.[68]

In Maimonides' second category of evil in *Guide* III:12 are acts of human violence.[69] Here, too, there is a correspondence with Job's experiences, since he is certainly the victim of violence at the hands of the Sabean and Chaldean marauders who carry off his oxen and camels.[70] And even though Maimonides makes human violence a separate category in its own right, here again the cause of evil is privation, for we are told in the previous chapter of the *Guide* that all harms individuals inflict on each other, including violence, "derive from ignorance, I mean from the privation of knowledge."[71] The connection between Job's suffering and privation is again evident.

In Maimonides' third category are evils that human beings inflict upon themselves. Under this rubric Maimonides includes diseases of the body and the soul, which, he claims, are almost always caused by immoderate indulgence in food, drink, and sexual activity.[72] Here again there seems to be a correspondence with Job's suffering, since the final afflictions Job experiences take the form of bodily illness. Moreover, here again privation seems to be involved, since indulgence in the appetites could be due to the privation of wisdom.

There is, however, one major difficulty with this third correspondence. We have already learned that Job is seen by Maimonides as possessing moral virtue, the hallmark of which is moderation regarding physical vices. It is therefore difficult to see how Job's illness could fit into a category of evil caused by excesses with respect to those very vices. I have no solution to this problem. On the one hand, the correspondence between the three categories of evil and Job's afflictions seems too strong to deny. On the other hand, the last correspondence is certainly problematic enough not to be ignored.[73]

My analysis of Maimonides' reading of the prologue of Job is now complete. According to Maimonides, the divine beings represent the generative forces of nature, Satan is symbolic of privation, and Job suffers because of privation but is unaware that this is the cause of his troubles because of his intellectual deficiencies.

We are now in a position to turn to the explication of the dialogue between Job and his friends that occupies most of *Guide* III:23. Maimonides immediately notes a difficulty that has plagued many other interpreters: all the participants seem to be saying similar things with no clear response to Job emerging by the end of the story. Maimonides is able to confront this problem by attributing it to the esoteric style of writing that characterizes scripture as a whole.

The repetition of views is only apparent. It is a technique employed by the biblical text to conceal the fact that the book is a high-level philosophical debate about providence. In truth, each of the participants is saying something quite different, with each representing one viewpoint from the list of positions on providence spelled out earlier in Maimonides' introductory discussion of that issue. The correspondence of views can be discerned only by knowing which verses reveal the true opinion of each participant. Moreover, a correct view does emerge from the discussion, and it is that expressed by Elihu and God.[74]

Maimonides goes on to reveal the identity of each view. Job represents the view of Aristotle, according to which there is only general providence over the species, but no individual providence. Job adopts this view because his suffering has caused him to lose faith in the traditional model of reward and punishment in which he had previously believed. The view of Eliphaz is the opinion of "our Law," according to which Job is being punished for his sins. Bildad represents the view of the Mu'tazilites and thus claims that Job is being afflicted with suffering as a test in order to afford him the opportunity to earn greater reward in the world to come. Zophar takes the position of the Ash'arites, according to which Job's suffering is due to God's arbitrary will and thus it is futile to inquire about its meaning.

The correct view on providence is provided by Elihu and God.[75] Yet, any hope we might have that Maimonides would use this as an opportunity to clarify his own position on providence is quickly dashed. In his explication of the views of Elihu and God, we come up against the most difficult part of Maimonides' exposition of Job and one of the most difficult sections in the entire *Guide*.

Let me begin my examination of this portion of Maimonides' discussion by briefly summarizing what he actually says about the speeches of Elihu and God and noting where the difficulties lie. Maimonides begins his summary of Elihu's views by claiming that he seems to add nothing to the other views but that upon careful examination one sees that this is not the case. The new notion that is added by Elihu is "the intercession of an angel," which can save a person from the brink of death. That intercession, however, takes place only "two or three times" in one's lifetime. Another insight Elihu adds is a description of the "how of prophecy."[76]

The problem is that Maimonides offers little help to explain these enigmatic references. Who or what is the "angel" that rescues us from harm? What is the meaning of the reference to "the how of prophecy?" Maimonides' interpretation of God's speech is only a little clearer. God's lengthy descriptions of the glories of nature, which fill His address to Job, are meant to teach him that such descriptions represent the limit of what we can understand about divine providence. Ultimately, we have no real comprehension of how God governs the world, since God's ways are entirely unlike ours. Maimonides goes on to explain that this lesson in the equivocality of divine attributes is the central message of the Book of Job.[77] When one comprehends the dissimilarity between ourselves and God regarding providence, one is then able to cope with suffering and bear misfortune with equanimity. Furthermore, in light of this realization, the experience of suffering will only add to one's love of God.[78]

Here too some points in Maimonides' presentation require clarification. How does the discovery of the equivocality of divine attributes allow Job to cope with his suffering? How does suffering itself lead to love of God? There is also the question of the relationship between Elihu's remarks and those of God: are they saying the same thing or something different?

I would like to initiate the analysis of this section of Maimonides' reading of Job by turning first to Maimonides' modern interpreters.[79] As I noted earlier, most interpreters seem to agree on Job's ultimate lesson.[80] Job learns that one can guard oneself from suffering; however, that protection is not physical, only psychological. This psychological immunity from suffering is achieved when Job perfects his intellect, contemplates God, and detaches himself from the material concerns of the world so that he is entirely caught up with the pleasure of focusing all his thoughts on the Deity.

There is much disagreement about the other details in Maimonides' presentation—particularly his interpretation of Elihu's address. Kravitz argues that Elihu's angel is representative of the Active Intellect, which intercedes and saves a person from harm in the figurative sense that it is through the Active Intellect that one is able to perfect one's intellect, learn how to contemplate God, and gain psychological immunity from suffering.[81] Levinger takes the position that the angel is simply the human intellect itself, which in a perfected state provides the very same psychological immunity from suffering. Moreover, Levinger argues, Maimonides tells us that one is saved by the angel only two or three times, since it is difficult to maintain the intellectual concentration necessary to sustain a psychological immunity from suffering.[82]

Touati comes at the whole matter from a somewhat different angle by maintaining that there are in fact two types of providence to which Maimonides is alluding here. Elihu's angel represents the first type. Like Levinger, Touati argues that the angel is a metaphor for the perfected human intellect. However, Touati maintains that it saves a person from harm *physically*, since a perfected intellect includes a highly developed practical intellect for making rational choices that allow for the maximizing of one's well-being.[83] This explains Maimonides' reference to the "how of prophecy," for even though prophecy is not really a factor here, it is mentioned because it represents the supreme degree of intellectual perfection that subsumes under it all other perfections of the intellect, including that of the practical intellect. This interpretation also connects Maimonides' reading of Elihu with his earlier discussion about providence, for Elihu is merely confirming the notion of providence according to the perfection of the intellect. Touati goes on to argue that, according to Maimonides, the perfected intellect can save an individual in this manner only two or three times, since no person, no matter how intellectually perfect, can circumvent death.

There is also a second, higher, level of providence, according to Touati, which comes with an unusually high degree of intellectual perfection. This type of providence results not in physical protection from danger, but rather in the sort of psychological immunity from suffering with which we are by now familiar. Job achieves this form of providence at the end of the story. Raffel adopts an interpretation similar to that of Touati, with the exception that Elihu's angel is representative of the Active Intellect, which plays a critical role in the perfection of the practical intellect.[84]

Thus, all agree that in Maimonides' reading Job learns a psychological immunity from suffering and that this is equated with providence. On other issues, there is much disagreement. We again encounter difficulties regarding the ambiguity of the term "angel" in Maimonides' lexicon, which in this instance invites two interpretations—either the Active Intellect or the human intellect. There are also disagreements over whether, in addition to a psychological immunity from suffering, Maimonides alludes to a second, less exalted, form of providence that involves the exercise of the practical intellect.[85]

In large measure, I support the approach of Touati and Raffel, but there are a number of points about which I find myself in disagreement. Moreover, their analyses seem to miss certain insights. I would therefore like to reopen the question of Maimonides' interpretation of the final chapters of Job, and I will do so by subjecting every section of it to a detailed examination. Only in this manner can one arrive at the best possible reading of this most difficult section of the *Guide*.

Let us begin with the first part of Maimonides' interpretation of Elihu's views, in which the notion of the angel is introduced:

> The notion added by *Elihu* and not mentioned by one of them is that which he expresses parabolically when he speaks of the intercession of an angel. For he says that it is an attested and well-known thing that when a man is ill to the point of death and when he is despaired of, if an angel intercedes for him—regardless of what angel—his intercession is accepted and he is raised from this fall. This invalid is accordingly saved and restored to the best of states. However, this does not continue always, there being no continuous intercession going on forever, for it takes place two or three times. He says, *if there be for him an angel, an intercessor, and so on* (Job 33:23). And, having described the various states of the convalescent and his joy at returning to the perfection of health, he says: *Lo, all these things doth God work, twice, yea thrice, with a man* (Job 33:29). This notion is made clear by *Elihu* alone.[86]

The interpreters I have summarized identify the angel either with the Active Intellect or with the human intellect. However, a close reading of the passage will show that neither of these interpretations can be sustained—or, more accurately, neither of them is complete. Note Maimonides' precise language: "it is an attested and well-known thing that when a man is ill to the point of death and when he is despaired of, if an angel intercedes for him—*regardless of what angel* (*ayy mal'ākh kāna*)—his intercession is accepted and he is raised from this fall."[87] The key phrase here is "regardless of what angel," which suggests that this angel has an indeterminate identity. In order to understand fully the meaning of this phrase, one must go to the biblical passage upon which Maimonides is commenting. In this passage, which we will recognize from my discussion of Saadiah, Elihu describes a man who has been stricken with illness that brings him to the brink of death but who is then saved from his affliction:

> He is reproved by pains on his bed,
> And the trembling in his bones is constant.
> He detests food;
> Fine food [is repulsive] to him.
> His flesh wastes away till it cannot be seen,
> And his bones are rubbed away till they are invisible.
> He comes close to the Pit,
> His life [verges] on death.
> If there be an angel,[88]
> An advocate, one among a thousand[89]
> To declare the man's uprightness,
> Then He has mercy on him and decrees,
> "Redeem him from descending to the Pit,
> For I have obtained his ransom." (Job 33:19–24)

Maimonides suggests that the angel has an indeterminate identity because, as the biblical text tells us, it is "one among a thousand." Now one may understand this phrase to mean that this angel is a special being and is therefore distinguished from the multitude of other like beings. But Maimonides is clearly not reading the text this way. For him the notion that the angel is "one among a thousand" means that there are many such angels and that as long as the person is saved, it does not matter which one intercedes; hence, the interjected phrase "regardless of what angel." It is therefore difficult to sustain the suggestions that the angel is either the Active Intellect or the human intellect, since these angels have very specific identities.

I would therefore like to propose an alternative reading, one put forward both by a number of medieval commentators and by the modern commentator Munk. For Maimonides the angel is representative of *any* natural force or cause that comes to the aid of an individual in grave danger.[90] Neither the medieval commentators who espouse this view nor Munk justifies this reading with explicit arguments, but it has much merit. As I noted earlier, the term "angel" for Maimonides can, according to one of its meanings, denote natural forces of any kind, and it is in this broad sense that Maimonides appears to be construing the term here. Thus, the angel may indeed be the person's intellect, since the practical intellect is certainly capable of circumventing danger in a natural manner by making deliberations about future events. It may also be the Active Intellect, which plays a role in inspiring the human intellect to find a way to escape harm. Alternatively, it may simply be a chance event from the general providential order that has come to the person's rescue and has nothing to do with his intellectual deliberations. The point that Elihu is making, according to Maimonides, is that a person in grave danger can be saved by a wide range of natural processes. Elihu's angel is therefore deliberately nonspecific. Efodi expresses the matter in succinct fashion: "it is a natural matter that man will become ill, and if he has any sort of celestial or sublunar force (*ko'aḥ shemeimi o tiv'i*) that intercedes on his behalf and comes to help him, its intercession is received; if not, he will die."[91]

In light of this interpretation, Maimonides' remarks can be explained. The phrase "regardless of what angel" fits perfectly here: this angel indeed has an indeterminate identity, since it refers to any natural force that saves an individual from danger. We can also make sense of Maimonides' suggestion that this angel intercedes at best two or three times. A person in his lifetime can be rescued from danger by natural causes in only so many instances, but eventually death will have its final say. As we have already learned, all things decay due to privation.

Let us move on to the next portion of Maimonides' interpretation of Elihu's remarks. In the lines that follow his reference to the angel, Maimonides invokes the issue of prophecy. Maimonides informs us that before speaking about the angel, Elihu "also makes an addition . . . by beginning to describe the how of prophecy in his dictum: *For God speaketh once, yea twice, yet* [*man*] *perceiveth not. In a dream in a night vision, when deep sleep falleth upon men* (Job 33:14–15)."[92] Touati and Raffel are the only modern interpreters who attempt to make sense of this remark. They suggest that Maimonides is alluding to providence provided by the practical intellect, which can help an individual avoid danger through its calculations and deliberations about future events. Although such providence is experienced by people who are not prophets, the prophet is mentioned here since his intellect is more developed than that of other human beings and is therefore most capable of experiencing this form of providence.

Touati and Raffel may be right here. However, to my mind a somewhat better reading is provided by the medieval commentator Efodi, who suggests that Maimonides is referring specifically to the faculty of divination. Efodi's reading is close to that of Touati and Raffel: divination is a talent that, in Maimonides' thinking, is merely a higher-order manifestation of the practical intellect. With divination the practical intellect is stimulated to make deliberations about the future that have a high degree of accuracy.[93] But an advantage of Efodi's reading over that of Touati and Raffel is that it makes better sense of Maimonides' specific focus on prophecy here, in that divination is concomitant with that capability. Another advantage of this reading is that it fits nicely with the biblical text upon which Maimonides is commenting:[94]

> For God speaks time and again
> —Though man does not perceive it—
> In a dream, a night vision,
> When deep sleep falls on men,
> While they slumber on their beds.
> Then He opens men's understanding,

And by disciplining them leaves His signature
To turn man away from an action,
To suppress pride in man.
He spares his soul from the Pit,
His person, from perishing by the sword. (Job 33:14–18)

We cannot be sure how Maimonides would have understood this passage, since he only cites the first lines, and he says little to explain that citation. Yet, the basic notion expressed here, which is that God gives individuals information in prophetic dreams that allows them "to turn away from an action" and spare them "from the Pit" and "perishing by the sword," seems to support Maimonides' notion of divination.[95]

One should not put inordinate emphasis on Maimonides' allusion to prophecy. The central issue for Maimonides seems to be Elihu's reference to the angel. My guess is that Maimonides highlights the issue of divination only because he views it as one type of angel that can rescue an individual from harm. After all, divination is a natural avenue—and a most effective one at that—for circumventing danger. It is therefore one of the natural providential processes represented by the angel.

In the conclusion of his exposition of Elihu's remarks, Maimonides explains the rest of Elihu's speech contained in chapters 34–37:

> Thereupon he begins to confirm this opinion and to make clear its method by describing many natural circumstances, such as his describing thunder, lightning, rain, and the blowing of the winds. He combines this with many subjects belonging to the circumstances of animals—I mean an outbreak of pestilence referred to in his dictum, *In a moment they die, even at midnight, and so on* (Job 34:20); the occurrence of great wars referred to in his dictum, *He breaketh in pieces mighty men without number, and setteth others in their stead* (Job 34:24); and many other circumstances.[96]

That Elihu in subsequent chapters "begins to confirm this opinion" and "make clear its method" indicates that Maimonides construes the remainder of Elihu's speech as a reinforcement of what he has already said. In fact, this seems very much the case, for here again, in Maimonides' reading, Elihu dwells primarily on "natural circumstances"—that is, natural processes he has already discussed in his remarks about the angel. The emphasis here, however, seems to be specifically on the destructive processes caused by privation, which limit the ability of the angel to bring salvation more than a handful of times. In Maimonides' reading, Elihu refers to violent meteorological phenomena, pestilence, and warfare—all of which, as we saw earlier, are related to privation.[97] It is also noteworthy that the destructive processes to which Elihu is referring are precisely those that have afflicted Job, as we noted earlier. That Maimonides reads Elihu's remarks as dealing with such evils is, of course, no surprise, since it makes sense that Elihu would explain those evils specifically affecting Job.[98]

What comes out of my analysis is that, according to Maimonides, Elihu tells Job the following: The natural order consists of benevolent and harmful processes. There are the "angels" or natural forces that can save an individual from the brink of death. These include a range of processes, such as beneficial events in the general providential order, or the advantages that come with a developed intellect such as the capacity for divination. But there are also forces of privation, which are destructive and are manifested in such phenomena as violent weather, pestilence, and warfare. Eventually, it is the latter that win out, since the intercession of the angels cannot go on forever, given that all human beings eventually die.

What is compelling about this interpretation is that it creates a correspondence between Maimonides' understanding of Elihu's remarks, on the one hand, and his interpretation of the divine beings and Satan who appear in the prologue, on the other. Elihu speaks of beneficial natural forces, or angels, which are synonymous with the divine beings of the prologue. He also refers to harmful natural forces caused by privation, which are identified with Satan. This correspondence is in fact necessary, since what Elihu is doing, according to Maimonides, is explaining to Job why he has suffered, and this means that he must inevitably tell Job about the natural forces which the divine beings and Satan represent and their role in his afflictions at the beginning of the story. These are figures with which the philosophically adept reader is already familiar by the time Elihu speaks, but Job himself is not.

In the next section, Maimonides explicates God's address to Job:

> Similarly you will find that in the prophetic revelation that came to *Job* and through which his error in everything that he imagined became clear to him, there is no going beyond the description of natural matters—namely, description of the elements or description of meteorological phenomena or description of the natures of the various species of animals, but of nothing else. For what is mentioned therein in the way of description of *firmaments* and the *heavens* and *Orion* and the *Pleiades* occur because of their influence upon the atmosphere; for He draws his attention only to what is beneath the sphere of the moon. *Elihu* too derives his warnings from the various species of animals. For he says: *He teacheth us from the beasts of the earth, and maketh us wise from the fowls of the heaven* (Job 35:11). The purpose of all these things is to show that our intellects do not reach the point of apprehending how these natural things that exist in the world of generation and corruption are produced in time and of conceiving how the existence of the natural force within them has originated in them. They are not things that resemble what we make. How then can we wish that His governance of, and providence for, them, may He be exalted, should resemble our governance of, and providence for, the things we do govern and provide for? Rather, it is obligatory to stop at this point and believe that nothing is hidden from Him, may He be exalted. As *Elihu* says: *For His eyes are upon*

> *the ways of man, and He seeth all his goings. There is no darkness, nor shadow of death, where the workers of iniquity may hide themselves* (Job 34:21–22). But the notion of His providence is not the same as the notion of our providence; nor is the notion of His governance of the things created by Him the same as the notion of our governance of that which we govern. The two notions are not comprised in one definition, contrary to what is thought by all those who are confused, and there is nothing in common with them except the name alone.[99]

The first thing to notice here is that, according to Maimonides, God reinforces what Elihu has just said. This is evident from the first words of the passage, in which Maimonides makes clear that God "similarly" teaches Job about "natural matters"—the "similarly" here referring back to Elihu's remarks, which Maimonides has just finished explicating. That is, God addresses Job about natural processes just as Elihu had.[100] However, God adds a new idea here, according to Maimonides. God teaches Job that the workings of divine providence are ultimately beyond our ken. We cannot possibly comprehend how things are "produced in time" and how the "natural force within them has originated in them." How, then, can we understand divine providence? In other words, Job gets a lesson in the equivocal nature of divine attributes, one focused specifically on the issue of divine providence.

Thus, God supplements Elihu's remarks by telling Job that what he has learned from Elihu is ultimately all that one can really know about providence. There are natural processes that are either beneficial or harmful, and the description of those processes is the limit of what human beings can fathom about how God governs the world. Maimonides is not denying that we can have any knowledge of providence whatsoever; it is just that our understanding of it is highly circumscribed.[101]

A number of observations will help us appreciate fully what Maimonides is saying here. First, one must be aware that Maimonides is, on one level, simply trying to make sense of the biblical text. A large portion of God's address to Job consists of a series of rhetorical questions meant to underscore his ignorance regarding the processes of nature. The following verses at the beginning of God's speech are typical:

> Where were you when I laid the earth's foundations?
> Speak if you have understanding.
> Do you know who fixed its dimensions
> Or who measured it with a line?
> Onto what were its bases sunk?
> Who set its cornerstone
> When the morning stars sang together
> And all the divine beings shouted with joy? (Job 38:4–7)

Maimonides interprets these sorts of questions to mean that God is teaching Job about the unfathomable nature of providence.

Second, Maimonides' train of thought becomes clearer when we are aware that he is also drawing from philosophical teachings found in other portions of the *Guide*. Most obvious in this regard is his reference to the equivocal nature of divine attributes, which is as basic a doctrine as any in his philosophical thought.[102] Maimonides also seems to be alluding to the notion that there are limitations to human knowledge regarding the celestial realm, a theme voiced in a number of passages in the *Guide*.[103] The knowledge imparted to Job pertains only to the sublunar realm, since "there is no going beyond the description of natural matters" when it comes to understanding divine providence. More specifically, Job's inability to understand how providence works is predicated on the fact that human beings cannot fathom "how these natural things that exist in the world of generation and corruption are produced in time and . . . how the existence of the natural force within them has originated in them." While it is not entirely clear what Maimonides is referring to here, my own guess is that he is alluding to the uncertain knowledge that human beings have about the Separate Intellects and the emanation scheme of which they are a part. One of the chief examples that Maimonides cites of human limitations in understanding the celestial realm is the lack of demonstrative proof for the existence of the Separate Intellects other than the Active Intellect.[104] This limitation has important implications for understanding providence, since the Separate Intellects make up the emanation scheme connecting God to the world below and play a key role in guiding natural processes. Maimonides seems to have had this difficulty in mind when he claims that Job learns from God of his inability to comprehend how "natural things . . . are produced in time" and how "the natural force within them has originated in them."[105]

At this point in his exposition, Maimonides has essentially finished his explication of the dialogue. Yet, it would seem that Job has learned precious little. He has been told by Elihu and by God that human fortune in this world—including Job's suffering—is tied to natural processes, and that one cannot comprehend God's role in determining such fortune since our knowledge of divine providence is limited to a description of those processes.

But Maimonides takes one more critical step in his reading of Job, which adds a whole new dimension to his interpretation of the story and his views on providence. In his concluding statement about Job, Maimonides says:

> This is the object of the *Book of Job* as a whole; I refer to the establishing of this foundation for the belief and the drawing attention to the inference to be drawn from natural matters, so that you should not fall into error and seek to affirm in your imagination that His knowledge is like our knowledge or that His purpose and His providence and His governance are like our purpose and our providence and our governance. If man knows this, every misfortune will be borne lightly by him. And misfortunes will not add to his doubts regarding the deity and whether He does or does not know and whether He exercises providence or manifests neglect, but will, on the contrary, add to his love, as is said in the conclusion of the pro-

> phetic revelation in question: *Wherefore I abhor myself, and repent of dust and ashes* (Job 42:6). As the [sages], may their memory be blessed, have said: *Those who do out of love and are joyful in their sufferings.*[106]

Maimonides declares that the notion God teaches Job regarding the limits of human knowledge concerning divine providence is, in fact, the point of the book. Once he is aware of this conception, Job learns to bear his suffering with equanimity. Moreover, Job learns that misfortune can actually inspire the individual to increase his love of God. It is for this reason that Job recants in the final chapter of the book. He is now at peace with his suffering and, having experienced it, has learned to love God all the more.

Medieval and modern commentators regard as key here the notion that Job learns to bear his misfortune with equanimity. As I pointed out earlier, commentators are practically unanimous in the belief that for Maimonides the ultimate message of the Book of Job is that Job learns what is, in effect, an inner psychological resistance or immunity to suffering. I would like to add my support for this view. Indeed, it seems clear from the passage just quoted that Job learns to divorce himself internally from his afflictions, and that this is the central theme that Maimonides draws out of the Book of Job. I would also accept the claim of Touati and Raffel that what we have here is effectively a separate and higher order of providence than that which Elihu had described, one that comes only with a high degree of intellectual perfection. Elihu referred to providential natural processes or angels that can save an individual from harm, but these processes are fallible and do not eliminate all suffering. The form of providence alluded to here does not protect the individual physically, but it is, in some sense, a more effective form of providence, in that it allows the individual to regard suffering as being of no consequence.

These ideas are confirmed in a passage that I have already cited in part:

> [Job] said all that he did say as long as he had no true knowledge and knew the deity only because of his acceptance of authority, just as the multitude adhering to the Law know it. But when he knew God with a certain knowledge, he admitted that true happiness, which is the knowledge of the deity, is guaranteed to all who know Him and that a human being cannot be troubled in any way by any of all the misfortunes in question. While he had known God only through traditional stories and not by way of speculation, Job imagined that the things thought to be happiness, such as health, wealth, and children, are the ultimate goal. For this reason he fell into such perplexity as he did. This is the meaning of the dictum: *I had heard of Thee by hearing of the ear; but now mine eye seeth Thee; wherefore I abhor myself and repent of dust and ashes* (Job 42:6). This dictum may be supposed to mean, *Wherefore I abhor all that I used to desire and repent of my being in dust and ashes*—this being the position he was supposed to be in: *And he sat among the ashes* (Job 2:8).[107]

According to this passage, Job is a figure who initially believes in a traditional view of providence, one that identifies reward and punishment with physical and material matters. But by the end of the story, when he has come to know God with "a certain knowledge," he discovers that "true happiness" consists of "the knowledge of the deity" and that one cannot be "troubled in any way by any of all the misfortunes" he has experienced. This is the ultimate meaning of Job's statement of contrition to God at the very end of the book: "wherefore I abhor myself and repent of dust and ashes."[108] According to Maimonides' reading, Job in this verse expresses regret for having attached himself to material things and for having mourned their loss.

I would like to dwell further on this second type of providence that Job achieves because of its importance in Maimonides' reading of Job and his theory of providence. Let me begin by characterizing the psychological immunity to suffering this form of providence entails. As Howard Kreisel has pointed out, the state of inner equanimity described here is best understood in light of a larger religious-ethical ideal that Maimonides spells out in *Guide* III:51.[109] There Maimonides delineates the highest form of devotion to God that one can achieve, in which a person's thoughts and emotions are constantly focused on Him.[110] It is accomplished only after one has mastered the sciences and has thus achieved the highest knowledge of God possible for human beings. It is then that one can cultivate an intellectual and emotional connection with God so as to reach a state of constant contemplation of Him. Maimonides indicates that devotion of this sort is exemplified by the prophets.[111] Maimonides also tells us that on its highest level, this form of devotion allows one to continue with mundane activities while being constantly connected to God in one's inner life. This capacity is apparently found only in the greatest of the prophets, such as Moses and the Patriarchs.[112]

Kreisel has also provided a fine analysis of the metaphysics that apparently underlies this most exalted way of life. The key concept is the notion of the acquired intellect, to which I alluded earlier. While Maimonides says relatively little about the acquired intellect in his writings, he provides a number of hints and clues regarding this idea in various works. There is also precedent for this concept among the Islamic thinkers with whom Maimonides was familiar. The acquired intellect is essentially a perfected intellect that, at an advanced stage of development, has the capability of achieving a semi-autonomous status similar to that of the Separate Intellects or even God Himself, in that the intellect is no longer dependent on the body but is still able to affect it. It would appear that in Maimonides' thinking, this stage of perfection is prerequisite for the highest form of religious devotion, in which one is in a constant state of contemplation of God. The acquired intellect also best accounts for the capacity of the greatest prophets to contemplate God while participating in the ordinary affairs of the world. Just as God or the Separate Intellects can emanate upon and affect the physical world below them while remaining undiminished, so can a person with an acquired intellect participate in the world while his contemplation of the divine is unaffected.[113]

What Job achieves at the end of the story, according to Maimonides' reading, perfectly matches the form of religious life described here. Job not only gains knowledge and love of God, he also seems to achieve a contemplative state that is consistent with an acquired intellect. Furthermore, it is this state that allows Job to detach himself internally from suffering, for with an acquired intellect one contemplates God while maintaining only tenuous ties to matters of the physical world. Touati and Raffel are therefore correct in seeing this state as a higher level of providence than that described by Elihu, for the achievement of an acquired intellect and the psychological resistance to suffering it confers are consequent upon only the highest form of intellectual perfection.

Our observations here shed new light on a passage examined earlier. We saw that Maimonides interprets God's command to spare Job's soul to mean that Satan has no power over the "thing that remains after death," an allusion to the perfected intellect, which gains immortality because it is not affected by privation. With this interpretation Maimonides seems to be referring to the concept of the acquired intellect, which is able to detach itself from material matters in order to become immune to privation and suffering.[114] Thus, the issue here is not so much immortality per se, but rather the capacity of the perfected intellect to resist the ravages of privation in this life en route to immortality in the next. Read in this way, Maimonides' brief comment on God's command to Satan to spare Job's soul is more than just an interesting bit of philosophical information that he adds to his discussion of the prologue; in effect, it encapsulates and anticipates the central idea that he later draws out of the Book of Job.

I should also add here that it is because Job achieves intellectual perfection and love of God at the end of the story that Maimonides is able to explain why he is singled out for praise by God in the final chapter of the book. According to Maimonides, God tells Eliphaz that he and his two friends "have not spoken the truth about Me as did My servant Job" (Job 42:7), because Job has just recognized in the preceding verse that physical and material well-being—"dust and ashes" (Job 42:6)—are of no importance compared to the contemplation of God that comes with the perfection of the intellect. Thus, God's praise for Job is prompted only by the latter's recantation at the end of the story.[115]

We now have some understanding of the exalted state that Job achieves, in Maimonides' thinking, but there are still important points about this issue that require clarification and, to my knowledge, have not been dealt with by other commentators. For instance, it is not entirely clear how an understanding of the equivocal nature of the language of divine providence leads Job to a psychological immunity to suffering. I would like to suggest two possible interpretations to explain this connection, interpretations that are perhaps complementary. First, by learning that there is no hope in having a complete understanding of the true nature of divine providence, Job recognizes the futility in striving for physical and material well-being. There is simply no point in chasing after these things, since there is no reliable way of knowing whether one's efforts will be rewarded. Job therefore comes to the realization that true happiness must be sought in a realm beyond the physical, and that it consists only in cultivating the intellect and the contemplation of God. A second possibility is that Job must learn about the equivocality of divine attributes in order to contemplate God, for in Maimonides' thinking this is the highest form of knowledge that one can have of God, and this comes only through appreciating that divine attributes are entirely unlike ours. Thus, if in the first explanation the lesson in divine attributes helps Job lose interest in material things so as to achieve the proper contemplation of God, we are arguing now that the same lesson plays a constitutive role in that contemplation.[116]

Another point that requires clarification is how, in light of the lesson in divine attributes, suffering leads Job to a greater love of God. In order to understand what Maimonides is saying here, we must first be aware that love of God for Maimonides is the emotional component that accompanies one's knowledge of Him. As one learns more, by studying natural science and metaphysics, about how God's ways are manifest in the world, not only does one's knowledge of God increase, so does one's love. Thus, love of God also becomes an important component of the highest level of religious devotion, characterized by the acquired intellect, which Job himself experiences. At this stage, one not only contemplates God intellectually, but is passionately attached to Him.[117] With this in mind, we can explain how the lesson in divine attributes inspires Job to regard suffering as a vehicle to achieve love of God. Suffering only confirms for the individual that divine providence in this-worldly affairs is indeed unfathomable. It therefore reinforces his sense of futility in being attached to physical and material well-being and encourages him to detach himself from those concerns. He is then able to cultivate an acquired intellect and develop a passionate emotional attachment to God. Suffering therefore strengthens Job in his attempt to distance himself from the affairs of this world and strengthen his ties with God both intellectually and emotionally.

It will perhaps clarify matters to recognize that what Maimonides is effectively telling us is that an understanding of the equivocality of divine attributes and the experience of suffering both lead an individual to the same place. Both bring one to the realization that there is no value in material and physical goods and that the only goal worth pursuing is the contemplation and love of God.[118]

I conclude my analysis of Maimonides' notion that providence consists of psychological immunity to suffering by focusing on the rabbinic source that he cites at the end of his exposition on Job to support this idea. The full text of the rabbinic source is as follows: "those who are insulted but do not insult, who hear themselves reviled but do not reply, who act out of love and rejoice in afflictions, of them Scripture says: 'And those who love Him are like the sun rising in its power' (Judges 5:31)."[119] Maimonides' use of this citation in this context has, to my knowledge, not been analyzed by other scholars. Yet, a close examination of its usage is instructive, since it both confirms my interpretation of Maimonides' reading of the final portion of Job and opens up a new dimension in it.

On a basic level, the rabbinic source supports Maimonides' point that those who have achieved love of God at its highest level are immune to suffering, because it suggests that those who love God bear insult and affliction with joy.

But there is more. It seems that the passage is meaningful to Maimonides not just because of its basic message, but because of the particular prooftext it cites. The verse from Judges 5:31—"And those who love Him are like the sun rising in its power"—has, in fact, been a source of perplexity for commentators on the Talmud because it is not entirely clear how it supports the point the rabbis are making.[120] Yet, in the context of Maimonides' thinking, the prooftext fits perfectly. In order to understand why, one must realize that in a number of places in Maimonides' writings, God is compared to the sun. This motif has antecedents in Islamic and Greek sources with a Neoplatonic bent, where it is most appropriate, given that God is envisioned as being connected to the world through a scheme of emanation that is often compared to the emanation of light. And since, as scholars have already pointed out, Maimonides draws from such sources in formulating his conception of God and emanation, the comparison between God and the sun is most appropriate for him too.[121] Thus, it is evident how Maimonides would have understood the prooftext in the above passage: the analogy between those who love God and the sun is an analogy between those who love God and God Himself! And, indeed, this confirms the metaphysical foundations of Maimonides' understanding of Job's final lesson. For as we have seen, Job is able to bear his suffering with equanimity because he has an acquired intellect, which is an intellect that, in its detachment from affairs of the world, is similar to one of the Separate Intellects or even God Himself.[122]

The rabbinic dictum Maimonides cites here can also help us uncover yet another aspect in his reading of Job when we look at the only other place he makes reference to this source. It appears in a well-known passage in *Laws of Character Traits* in the *Mishneh Torah*, Maimonides' halakhic exposition on ethics.[123] In that passage Maimonides makes the point that while it is imperative to follow the mean—in the Aristotelian sense of the term—when cultivating character traits, two traits are the exception to that rule: anger and pride. With these qualities the mean is not sufficient; we must go to the opposite extreme of inordinate humility and passivity. Why Maimonides singles out these two traits has been dealt with by others and is not a question that need concern us.[124] The important point is that at the very end of the passage Maimonides sums up his thoughts by citing the same rabbinic source under discussion here.

It takes little reflection to see how the discussion in this section of the *Mishneh Torah* is relevant to Maimonides' reading of Job. In the biblical text itself, Job exhibits the two undesirable character traits that must be avoided. Throughout the dialogue, Job expresses anger both at his friends and at God.[125] He is also chided for his haughtiness; God's lengthy descriptions of natural phenomena and His rhetorical questions to Job at the end of the story are clearly meant to humble him. While Maimonides does not dwell on Job's ethical failings, he does allude to them. Maimonides speaks of Job's impatience with God in the face of his suffering, which he claims is characteristic of most people who experience afflictions.[126] Maimonides alludes to the problem of Job's pride when he tells us that when Elihu first speaks to Job, he "started to reprove Job and to tax him with ignorance because of his having manifested self esteem."[127] The appearance of the rabbinic source at the end of Maimonides' exposition of Job therefore brings out an important dimension of his understanding of the book. It indicates that Job undergoes not just an intellectual transformation, but also an ethical one. A person who had reacted with pride and anger in the face of suffering now, after having achieved an acquired intellect, views his afflictions with total calm and equanimity.[128]

At this point, all the components of Maimonides' reading of Job can be put in place. What is key here is the recognition that Maimonides' reading of the prologue of Job effectively contains all the information needed for understanding his reading of its concluding chapters. This makes sense, since in Maimonides' reading, Elihu and God inform Job why he has suffered, and that information has already been revealed to the philosophically knowledgeable reader in the prologue.

In the prologue we learn of "divine beings" who represent benevolent generative forces in nature that are responsible for our physical and material well-being. Opposed to these forces is Satan, who represents privation and is responsible for our suffering. Job's suffering is therefore nothing other than a series of manifestations of privation. There is also a hint in the prologue about how one might escape the harmful effects of privation. God instructs Satan to spare Job's soul, which means in philosophical terms that there is one element in human beings that privation cannot touch, and that is the acquired intellect.

In the final chapters of the book, these truths are revealed to Job and elaborated upon. Elihu teaches Job that there are angels that correspond to the "divine beings" in the prologue. These are the benevolent natural processes in the world and can include either events in nature that work to our benefit or the operations of the practical intellect, which preserve an individual from harm through its deliberations about future events. Elihu specifically alludes to the prophetic capacity of divination, which is a high-level manifestation of the deliberative activity of the practical intellect. Elihu then goes on to mention destructive events, such as pestilence and war, that are due to privation and correspond to Satan. He also makes the point that eventually privation wins out over the angels, since no human being lives forever. Death is the ultimate form of privation, at least as far as human beings are concerned.

When God addresses Job, He has little to add to Elihu's remarks about the actual operations of providence, but the important lesson He teaches Job is that what Elihu has told him is all that one can really know about providence. We can describe natural processes, but how God governs the world is unfathomable, since our providence is not like His providence.

It is Job himself who draws out the most important insight regarding providence by proposing that there is a second and higher order of protection from privation than the natural processes represented by Elihu's angel. Job concludes that true happiness consists not in material things—"dust and ashes"—but in intellectual perfection, which leads to an acquired intellect and the perpetual contemplation of God. This realization allows Job to cultivate a psychological immunity to suffering, achieve love of God, and thus avoid the ravages of Satan, or privation. Another insight in the prologue has been confirmed: because Job has cultivated an acquired intellect, his soul has been "spared" from Satan.

One final observation. It is noteworthy that Maimonides does not deal with the happy ending to the Job story, according to which Job has his wealth returned to him and begins a new family. A plausible speculation on how Maimonides might have understood this conclusion is provided by Levinger, who argues that Maimonides would surely have seen this portion of the story as part of its exoteric layer. Job's family and wealth are restored only in order that the story make sense to the uneducated traditional reader, who believes that God gives us rewards in the physical and material realm. Yet, the philosopher will know that divine providence does not function in this manner.[129]

Antecedents

Now that we have an understanding of how Maimonides reads the Book of Job, let us analyze it in terms of the three interfaces. I begin with the first interface, which concerns the relationship between Maimonides' reading of Job and that of his predecessors. Commentators have in general failed to mention that Maimonides' reading of Job is, in important respects, indebted to that of Saadiah.[130] First, Maimonides seems to have followed Saadiah's lead in viewing the Book of Job as a debate between competing schools of thought. While Saadiah never identifies the schools, as Maimonides does, it is clear that for Saadiah the dialogue encapsulates the dispute between Mu'tazilites and Ash'arites on the suffering of the righteous. Maimonides has expanded that debate by having the participants in the dialogue represent a series of other viewpoints alongside those of the Mu'tazilites and Ash'arites. He also seems to have borrowed Saadiah's technique of making sense of the dialogue between Job and his friends by identifying specific verses in their addresses as the focal points of their respective positions. Saadiah tells us in the introduction to his commentary on Job that he "shall follow the course of the Book's words, introducing each speech in the discourse of Job and of his companions with the sentences that contain the point, elucidating their meaning, so that it may be discerned among the verbal and conceptual padding, rhapsodic and rhetorical."[131] Maimonides takes the same approach but adapts it to his esoteric agenda. Thus, according to his scheme, the verses isolated from the "verbal and conceptual padding" in the speeches of the participants key us in to esoteric positions deliberately hidden in the text.

Maimonides also seems to have followed Saadiah in identifying Elihu as the figure who provides Job with the correct understanding of divine providence. There is, to my knowledge, no other precedent for this choice in early rabbinic literature or in commentaries on Job that precede Maimonides. Most significant is that the section of Elihu's speech that Maimonides identifies as the one revealing his position is the very same section upon which Saadiah focuses for the same purpose. Both are intrigued by Job 33:14–30, and both hone in specifically on Elihu's allusion to the angel as key to the passage.[132]

It is also clear that Maimonides rejects central elements of Saadiah's reading of Job. This is evident not just from the fact that Maimonides is an Aristotelian, who reads Job against the backdrop of a thought system very different from Saadiah's. We have indications that Maimonides actively opposes Saadiah's reading of Job. In a well-known passage in his discussion of providence, Maimonides vehemently rejects the notion that God tests individuals in order to increase their reward, and while he never identifies Saadiah specifically as the author of this view, he attributes this position both to the "Mu'tazila" and "the latter-day Geonim," which commentators generally believe is a veiled reference to Saadiah.[133] Maimonides' opposition to Saadiah on this issue carries over into his reading of Job: he implicitly rejects Saadiah's attempt to apply his notion of divine trials to Job by attributing that conception to Bildad, who, like Eliphaz and Zophar, turns out to be incorrect in his view of providence. In short, while Maimonides is inspired by Saadiah in his technique of how to approach the Book of Job from a structural standpoint and in his identification of the section of the book holding its central message, he clearly breaks from Saadiah in his reading of the book's actual content.

Exegesis

The second interface is concerned with Maimonides as exegete, in particular how he confronts the major difficulties the Book of Job presents. With all that has been written on Maimonides' interpretation of Job, little has been said about this issue. Yet, at this point, it should be clear that in his exposition on Job, Maimonides is doing a good deal more than merely using the biblical text as a platform for his philosophical views; he is also attempting to bring coherence to it. First, Maimonides confronts the difficulty of the dialogue in Job, and, as I have noted, he does so in a manner that betrays the influence of Saadiah. Maimonides observes that the views of the participants seem to overlap with one another and that there is therefore no obvious direction to the discussion. He solves this problem by arguing that the text is muddled only according to its exoteric reading. When it is read on an esoteric level, the dialogue is actually a debate between different philosophical and theological schools.

A similar strategy is evident in Maimonides' handling of the ambiguities in the biblical text regarding the figure of Job. At the center of the solution to this problem is Maimonides' view that Job begins the story as a righteous individual only according to the exoteric reading of the text, and that in its esoteric reading Job is deeply flawed. Thus, the first verse of the story praises Job only for his moral virtue, in order to cue the reader that this is the only form of virtue he possesses and that Job lacks the higher virtue of intellectual perfection. This move allows Maimonides to then explain the inconsistencies regarding Job in the rest of the book as phases in his intellectual journey toward theoretical perfection. Thus, Maimonides is able to account for Job's protests against God throughout the dialogue. Not having a true understanding of God's ways because of his intellectual deficiencies, Job mourns the loss of his health, wealth, and children in the belief that the possession of these is true providence. His disillusionment eventually leads him to adopt the Aristotelian position according to which there is no divine providence over individuals whatsoever. But Elihu and God help Job eventually come to a higher understanding of the workings of providence, achieve intellectual perfection, and recognize that physical and material well-being are of little importance compared to rewards that come with the contemplation of God. Once Job comes to these realizations, he recants his earlier protests, and it is at this point that he earns praise from God as "My servant" who, in contradistinction to his friends, has "spoken the truth about Me."

What is perhaps most impressive about Maimonides' reading of the Book of Job from an exegetical standpoint is the way he brings coherence to it by establishing harmony between the prologue and the final chapters of the book. Medieval and modern commentators alike have fretted over the fact that the discussion between God and Satan is never referred to again in the ensuing dialogue. What is most disturbing is the lack of any mention of it in God's address to Job, where one would have hoped that an explanation would be forthcoming of why God acceded to Satan's request to make Job suffer. Maimonides solves the difficulty by reading the dialogue between God and Satan as an allegory for philosophical truths that are then revealed both by Elihu and God in the final chapters of the book. Thus, the first chapters and the last chapters of Job are, in fact, saying precisely the same thing; they both teach critical lessons about providence and explain why the righteous suffer. It is just that the first chapters reveal those truths in allegorical form and do so only to the philosophically educated reader, while in the last chapters those truths are revealed more explicitly and are imparted to Job as well.[134]

My observations about Maimonides' exegetical strategies lead us to an important conclusion. Scholars have generally understood Maimonides' esoteric and allegorical reading of the biblical text as serving a philosophical function in that its primary purpose is to read philosophical ideas into the biblical text. It becomes clear from my analysis that Maimonides' use of allegory serves an exegetical function as well. That is, allegory is not just a device for reading philosophical truths into the biblical text; it is also an exegetical tool for *making sense* of the biblical text. Thus, an allegorical reading of Job allows Maimonides to organize the dialogue between Job and his friends as a debate between different schools of thought regarding providence. It helps him deal with inconsistencies regarding the figure of Job. Above all, it allows him to smooth out the disharmony between the prologue and the last chapters of Job by making the prologue express in symbolic form the very same message that is expressed in the closing chapters.[135]

As part of my exploration of the exegetical dimension of Maimonides' reading of Job, I must also look at whether Maimonides had any thoughts about the audience to which the Book of Job was directed. Did Maimonides view it as a book with universal meaning? Or did he think that its message was specifically for the Jewish reader?

Maimonides never explicitly takes a position on this issue, but there is enough material in his reading of Job to construct his viewpoint on the matter. One can certainly detect a universalistic thrust in Maimonides' reading of Job. First, Maimonides treats the dialogue as an ecumenical discussion between representatives of different philosophical and religious viewpoints, with the viewpoint of the Torah being only one of the positions represented—a position that, in fact, turns out not to be correct.[136] Second, and perhaps more important, in Maimonides' reading, the central lesson of the Book of Job is theoretically applicable to all people, not just Jews, since any individual should be able to achieve intellectual perfection and experience providence in the manner Maimonides describes.[137]

Yet, there is also a particularistic element that enters into Maimonides' reading of Job. Maimonides strongly hints that the figure of Job as he begins the story is representative of the Jewish masses, who have an erroneous view of providence because they adhere to a literal reading of scripture. Maimonides' message is that they, like Job, should become philosophically educated so that they too can achieve intellectual perfection and the providence that goes with it. In this regard, Maimonides reads the Book of Job as a text addressed to his fellow Jews, but it is important to point out that there is no suggestion on his part that the figure of Job is symbolic of the collective nation of Israel. Instead, Job is representative of only those Jews who are not philosophically enlightened. Maimonides' message may therefore be relevant for Jews, but not for the Jewish people as a whole. Put another way, Maimonides' reading of the Book of Job does not really address the Jews *as* Jews but only as individuals. Therefore, even Maimonides' particularism has a universalistic edge.[138]

Exegesis and Philosophy

The third interface, which concerns the relationship between Maimonides' reading of the Book of Job and his systematic treatment of providence, is the most problematic of the three interfaces. In order to examine this relationship fully, I would have to give a more thorough account of Maimonides' views on providence than that which I have already provided, and that is a task beyond the scope of the present discussion. We already have an inkling of the challenge involved in making sense of Maimonides' views on providence, having encountered the enormous difficulty of interpreting his major treatment of that issue in *Guide* III:17–18. Yet, my analysis would be incomplete without saying something about the third interface, for as I have noted, Maimonides reads the dialogue in Job as a debate between the viewpoints on providence summarized in *Guide* III:17. The parallel between Maimonides' reading of Job and his discussion of providence therefore makes it imperative that I offer some thoughts about the relationship between them, even if the conclusions are tentative.[139]

The major question is whether Maimonides' exposition on Job can help us define his position on providence in *Guide* III:17–18 with greater clarity.[140] It seems that in important respects, it does. My reading of Maimonides' interpretation of Job lends support to the distinction commentators have drawn between an esoteric and an exoteric understanding of providence in Maimonides' thinking. We saw earlier that Maimonides appears to be presenting an exoteric conception of providence in *Guide* III:17–18 when he takes the initial position that the opinion of the Law is correct for human beings, while that of Aristotle is applicable to all other animal species. According to this conception, God rewards and punishes individual human beings for their actions, while in other species providence is exercised only over the species as a whole. We also saw that as his discussion proceeds Maimonides seems to reveal an esoteric understanding of providence when he argues that providence over human beings is graded in proportion to one's level of intellectual perfection. According to this view, providence appears to be entirely naturalistic.[141]

If Maimonides' initial position on providence were truly his own, one would have expected that in his exposition on the Book of Job the correct viewpoint emerging from the dialogue would be that of the Law. After all, the debate here is focused quite specifically on providence as it affects Job who is a human being, and thus, in this instance, the view of the Law should be the final and correct explanation for Job's ordeal. However, as Maimonides would have it, the view of the Law is not the correct view here at all. That view is represented by Eliphaz, and his opinion turns out to be erroneous. Therefore, it seems likely that Maimonides' initial view of providence in *Guide* III:17 is meant for the masses.[142]

We can also infer from Maimonides' exposition on Job that his conception of providence as consequent upon the intellect, which emerges as his discussion in *Guide* III:17–18 proceeds, is indeed an esoteric view. That position seems to be represented by Elihu and God. Elihu informs Job that providence—to the extent that we can understand it—is dictated by natural forces. Moreover, with his reference to the "angel," he seems to hint that one who has greater intellectual perfection experiences greater providence. That individual will have a greater number of "angels" or natural forces to rescue him from harm since, in addition to the beneficial forces of the general providential order, he will have a highly developed practical intellect that will help him circumvent danger. The second higher level of providence that Job discovers also fits with a naturalistic conception of providence graded according to the perfection of the intellect. The more perfected one's intellect, the better able an individual will be to achieve an acquired intellect and develop a psychological immunity to suffering.[143] The position of Elihu and God therefore seems to give greater definition to the notion of providence according to the intellect. In short, by placing the view of the Law in the mouth of Eliphaz and by having Elihu and God represent the notion of providence according to the intellect, Maimonides seems to be signaling us about a distinction between exoteric and esoteric understandings of providence.

As I noted earlier, some commentators have gone a step further and argued that Maimonides' true view on providence is not only esoteric, it is quite consciously identical to that of Aristotle.[144] This theory seems to gain support from the naturalistic conception of providence that emerges from Maimonides' reading of Job. The interpretation, however, runs into trouble on one point, and that is that the figure who represents Aristotle's view is in fact Job, who turns out to be incorrect.

Hannah Kasher provides a marvelous series of insights that not only solves this problem, but strengthens the possibility that Maimonides' position on providence is that of Aristotle. Kasher's argument is that if one reads Maimonides' depiction of Job's position carefully, it does not match his understanding of Aristotle as presented in other parts of the *Guide*. According to Maimonides, Job argues that he has suffered because "the righteous men and the wicked are regarded as equal by Him, may He be exalted, because of His contempt for the human species and abandonment of it."[145] Job therefore believes in a Deity who willfully perpetrates evil, a conception of providence that bears little relation to that of Aristotle, according to whom God is neither willful nor evil but is simply an impersonal Deity unconcerned with individuals in any species.[146] Kasher also points out that in Maimonides' view, Job does not adopt his position on providence as a result of philosophical reflection, as one might expect from a genuine Aristotelian. Instead, it is adopted out of impatience: "this view was such as arises at the first reflection and in the beginning thereof, especially in the case of one whom misfortunes have befallen, while he knows of himself that he had not sinned."[147] I should also add here that Job, as he begins the story, is in Maimonides' mind representative of the masses, who are uneducated in philosophical matters, which is why he values only material well-being. This bolsters Kasher's claim that Job is far too ignorant at the beginning of the story to adopt an Aristotelian position on providence. Kasher concludes that Maimonides deliberately misrepresents Job's opinion and that Job, in fact, does not represent Aristotle. Maimonides' intention here is to signal the astute reader that it is Elihu who represents Aristotle's view, and that Aristotle therefore provides the correct position on providence.[148]

Regardless of how we read Maimonides' discussion of providence in light of his interpretation of Job, one thing that clearly emerges from my treatment of the third interface is the importance of Maimonides' exegesis of Job in his treatment of providence.[149] Most commentators believe that what Maimonides means by the notion of providence according to the intellect can be properly understood only with a thorough reading of his interpretation of Job, and my own discussion has borne that out. Most significant, it is only in his reading of Job that Maimonides reveals his view that the highest form of providence consists of psychological immunity from suffering. One could argue, as I have, that this same notion is part and parcel of Maimonides' view that providence is consequent upon the intellect, a view already expressed in his systematic discussion of providence. However, that connection becomes clear only from a retrospective reading of Maimonides' systematic discussion in light of his interpretation of Job. We can therefore conclude that Maimonides sees his exegesis of Job as serving a critical role for expressing his views on providence.

In conclusion, the richness and originality of Maimonides' exegesis of Job is evident on every level of my analysis. We discovered in the exploration of the first interface that Maimonides borrows a good deal from Saadiah. Like Saadiah, he sees the dialogue in Job as a debate between competing philosophical schools and believes that Elihu's address holds the key to the book as a whole. He also focuses on the same aspects of Elihu's address as Saadiah does in interpreting his position. However, in applying the canons of Aristotelian thought to the biblical text, Maimonides constructs a highly innovative and creative interpretation of Job. It is a reading that also has a radical edge to it.

In the analysis of the second interface, we saw that Maimonides proved to be an original exegete as well. Like Saadiah, Maimonides interprets Job in a manner in which philosophical and exegetical considerations coalesce in the interpretation of the biblical text. However, Maimonides is more sophisticated than Saadiah in his synthesis. With the help of his esoteric reading of the biblical text, Maimonides skillfully handles the ambiguities in Job's character. We saw in chapter 2 that Saadiah's treatment of this problem was a weak point in his reading of Job. Particularly intriguing is the way Maimonides brings coherence to the book as a whole by reading the prologue in allegorical fashion so that it anticipates the message that emerges in the final chapters of the book.

We have also seen how important the Book of Job was for Maimonides. The examination of the third interface showed that Maimonides uses his exegesis of Job for expressing some of his most important philosophical insights on the nature of the relationship between God and human beings. In fact, it is only in his reading of Job that we learn about the highest form of providence, which consists of a psychological immunity to suffering.

As we move on to examine the rest of the thinkers in this study, we will see that Maimonides' reading of Job greatly influenced other medieval Jewish philosophers. In fact, there is no reading of Job in medieval Jewish philosophy after Maimonides that does not bear his imprint. The next thinker we will explore is a sterling example of this phenomenon.

4

Samuel ibn Tibbon

The first significant Jewish philosopher after Maimonides to grapple with the Book of Job is Samuel ibn Tibbon (c. 1160–c. 1232), Maimonides' acquaintance and younger contemporary. Ibn Tibbon lived in Provence when that region witnessed the development of one of the most vibrant Jewish cultures in the Middle Ages. In the twelfth and thirteenth centuries, Jewish thinkers in Provence displayed remarkable creativity in blending traditional learning in biblical and rabbinic literature with the more recently developed disciplines of science, philosophy, Hebrew grammar, and mysticism.[1]

Ibn Tibbon was himself a sterling representative of this culture. Until recently, he was known primarily by scholars as a translator from Arabic to Hebrew of Jewish and Islamic texts in philosophy and science. In fact, translation was something of a family business. Several generations of Tibbonids were famous for engaging in this pursuit, beginning with Samuel's father, Judah ibn Tibbon. The crown jewel of translations belonged to Samuel himself, who rendered Maimonides' *Guide* into Hebrew, a work that not only made the most important philosophical treatise in medieval Judaism available to the Jews in Christian Europe, but was instrumental in shaping both the vocabulary and style of medieval philosophical Hebrew.[2]

Yet, thanks to scholarship done in recent years, it is now apparent that Ibn Tibbon was much more than a translator. He was also an original thinker in his own right who made important contributions in the areas of philosophy and exegesis.[3] With respect to philosophy, Ibn Tibbon appears to have been one of the most influential interpreters of Maimonides' *Guide*. Even during Maimonides' lifetime it was suspected that he held radical esoteric philosophical views, but it was Ibn Tibbon who was the first to lend sophistication to that viewpoint by developing an elaborate system of interpretation for unlocking the *Guide*'s secrets. His approach had a significant impact on subsequent interpreters of Maimonides.[4]

Ibn Tibbon also initiated a school of philosophical exegesis that would develop in Provence and Italy in the thirteenth century and included such thinkers as his son Moses ibn Tibbon, Zeraḥiah Ḥen, and Moses of Salerno. Ibn Tibbon took up the challenge of developing the exegetical techniques in Maimonides' *Guide* and applying them more comprehensively and extensively to the Bible than did Maimonides himself. Ibn Tibbon's two most important works were dedicated to this project. His *Commentary on Ecclesiastes* was one of the first commentaries written on an entire biblical book in light of Maimonides' philosophical teachings, while his *Ma'amar Yikkavu ha-Mayim* provided a similar type of commentary on various portions of the biblical text.[5]

Yet, despite a growing body of scholarship on Ibn Tibbon, *Ma'amar Yikkavu ha-Mayim* is available only in an inadequately edited text published in the nineteenth century.[6] In addition, there continue to be large gaps in our understanding of Ibn Tibbon's philosophical views. My interest here is in filling one such gap. Ibn Tibbon's discussion of the Book of Job constitutes a relatively small section of *Ma'amar Yikkavu ha-Mayim*, a mere 17 pages in a treatise that extends to 170 in the printed editions.[7] It is, nonetheless, an important section of that treatise in that it tells us a good deal about Ibn Tibbon's views on the critical question of providence. As we shall later see, it also influenced a number of subsequent Jewish interpreters of Job.

Despite its brevity, Ibn Tibbon's exposition on Job will present us with a challenge almost as daunting as that encountered in dealing with Maimonides. In *Ma'amar Yikkavu ha-Mayim* as a whole, Ibn Tibbon deliberately imitates Maimonides' elusive form of writing in order to hide his true philosophical views, and therefore we will encounter obfuscation at every step of the way in explicating Ibn Tibbon's reading of Job.[8] It is difficult to figure out not just what Ibn Tibbon is saying about Job, but where his analysis of that book fits into the overall framework of *Ma'amar Yikkavu ha-Mayim*. Indeed, the whole organization of this work is something of a mystery. It is ostensibly an inquiry into a problem in physics: earth is heavier than water and therefore should be submerged by the latter, yet large portions of earth poke out above the water and are in direct contact with air. While this issue is the stated focus of *Ma'amar Yikkavu ha-Mayim*, the work is largely made up of a series of loosely connected sections that analyze biblical passages from a philosophical standpoint, including the Book of Job, and Ibn Tibbon says little to explain what the interpretation of these biblical texts has to do with the problem in physics posed at the beginning of the treatise.[9]

Another obstacle to our understanding of Ibn Tibbon's reading of Job is that there is significant ambiguity in *Ma'amar Yikkavu ha-Mayim* as a whole regarding Ibn Tibbon's relationship to Maimonides. Throughout the work, Ibn Tibbon provides a philosophical analysis of biblical passages, many of which had already been discussed by Maimonides, and in instances of this overlap,

Ibn Tibbon's esoteric style of writing does not always make it easy to determine when he sees himself as an original philosophical interpreter of the biblical text and when he acts as a commentator on Maimonides. Moreover, when Ibn Tibbon explicitly acknowledges his debt to Maimonides, he assumes that his reader's understanding of Maimonides is precisely the same as his own and therefore sees no need to explain how he has read his predecessor. Yet, often his understanding of Maimonides is not at all clear.

We will encounter these difficulties in Ibn Tibbon's reading of Job because in this instance Maimonides provides an extensive discussion of the biblical material under discussion, and it will be quite obvious that Ibn Tibbon's own interpretation of Job is very much dependent on it. At the same time, it will not be entirely clear what the relationship is between Ibn Tibbon's exposition and that of Maimonides.

The problems concerning Ibn Tibbon's relationship to Maimonides are somewhat mitigated in his discussion of Job on account of a letter that Ibn Tibbon wrote to Maimonides on the subject of providence well before composing *Ma'amar Yikkavu ha-Mayim*. While the letter is concerned mainly with Ibn Tibbon's difficulty with *Guide* III:51, he spells out his overall understanding of Maimonides' theory of providence and in doing so offers his interpretation of the latter's reading of Job. We therefore have an independent reference to help us determine when Ibn Tibbon's reading of Job in *Ma'amar Yikkavu ha-Mayim* draws from Maimonides—at least as Ibn Tibbon understands him—and when it diverges from him. However, the discussion of Job in Ibn Tibbon's letter to Maimonides is too brief to guide us through his entire treatment of the book in *Ma'amar Yikkavu ha-Mayim*.[10]

Despite the many difficulties presented by Ibn Tibbon's discussion of the Book of Job in *Ma'amar Yikkavu ha-Mayim*, it is my belief that with a close reading, his interpretation of Job can be deciphered. That will be the primary challenge of this chapter. As with the discussion of Maimonides, I will spend most of this chapter simply attempting to discern what Ibn Tibbon says about Job. Only when this is accomplished will it be possible to analyze his reading in accordance with the three interfaces that are the focus of this study.[11]

Ibn Tibbon on Job: *Ma'amar Yikkavu ha-Mayim* 15–18

Ibn Tibbon's discussion of Job is not presented as an exposition of the entire book, but only as an explication of Elihu's position. Ibn Tibbon follows in the footsteps of Maimonides and Saadiah in believing that Elihu's discourse holds the key to Job, and therefore it is not surprising that he devotes a discussion to this one section of the book. Ibn Tibbon also expresses a more immediate interest in Elihu's position, and that is that Elihu's viewpoint on providence is, in Ibn Tibbon's thinking, similar to that represented in Psalm 73, a chapter that Ibn Tibbon has just finished analyzing. An examination of Elihu's remarks therefore serves to reinforce that viewpoint.[12] Despite the narrow focus of Ibn Tibbon's discussion, we are still justified in thinking of it as a commentary on the Book of Job as a whole because in the course of treating Elihu's views Ibn Tibbon provides an interpretation of a significant portion of the rest of the book as well.

Ibn Tibbon assumes an understanding of the events in Job leading up to Elihu's address that is drawn primarily from Maimonides. Job is a person with moral but not intellectual perfection. He therefore has a mistaken conception of providence in believing that God rewards and punishes in the physical and material realm. Thus, when he experiences suffering, he rejects the notion that God exercises individual providence over human beings. Job's three friends—Eliphaz, Bildad, and Zophar—who argue with him about the causes of his suffering represent the theological and philosophical schools attributed to them by Maimonides. Only when Elihu comes along does Job learn about the true nature of providence.

Ibn Tibbon also appears to adopt Maimonides' conception of Satan. It is here that we run into some difficulty figuring out how Ibn Tibbon understands his predecessor. Ibn Tibbon, like Maimonides, views Satan as representative of a malevolent natural force or forces responsible for evil and suffering. But it is not at all clear whether Ibn Tibbon understands Satan as a symbol for matter or privation, the two possibilities entertained in the previous chapter. There are also passages in which Ibn Tibbon seems to understand Satan as representative of chance occurrence. Presumably, all these manifestations of Satan are connected in Ibn Tibbon's thinking, but he does not elaborate on how.[13]

There is one matter regarding Maimonides' views on Satan about which Ibn Tibbon is quite explicit, and that is a disagreement he has with Maimonides on an exegetical point. As we saw in the previous chapter, Maimonides attempts to explain why it is that initially Satan is depicted as presenting himself to God only after the divine beings have done so, while in his second arrival Satan is described as accompanying them. According to my interpretation, Maimonides attributes the different descriptions to the dual function of privation, which, on the one hand, does not have God as its agent but, on the other hand, plays an important role in the perpetuation of the natural world.[14] Ibn Tibbon finds numerous faults with Maimonides' reading and solves the problem in a different manner.

According to Ibn Tibbon, the difference between the two descriptions of Satan is meant to distinguish between those evils that afflict the righteous person's belongings and children, on the one hand, and those that afflict his own body, on the other. In Ibn Tibbon's thinking, the question of why the righteous suffer simply does not arise with the loss of children or belongings, for such losses can be accounted for by explanations having little to do with a righteous person's conduct. Thus, Job's children die because of their own sins, not his, while Job's livestock perish because of chance occurrence. And if Job suffered as result of these misfortunes, his suffering has no real meaning here. Where the suffering of the righteous does become a problem is when the righteous individual himself is afflicted with bodily illness, for here the evil affects his very person. Therefore, it is this latter sort of evil with which the

Book of Job is concerned. For this reason, according to Ibn Tibbon, Satan is described as arriving separately from the divine beings the first time he appears. At this point in the story, he afflicts only Job's children and possessions, and his separate arrival symbolizes that these sorts of evils are not the main concern of the book. However, in the second instance Satan brings illness upon Job himself, and therefore he is described as accompanying the divine beings in order to symbolize that the evil affecting Job's body is the prime concern of the story. In short, while Maimonides interprets the different descriptions of Satan's arrival as relating directly to philosophical matters, Ibn Tibbon sees it more as a literary device designed to alert the reader to that which constitutes the central problem of the story.[15]

With these premises in mind, we can now proceed to analyze Ibn Tibbon's reading of Elihu's remarks. Ibn Tibbon begins his discussion of Elihu's position by spelling out its central point: immortality is "the most important component of providence" (*'ikar ha-hashgaḥah*). It is a message that Job eventually accepts. Job initially complained about the loss of material things because he knew God only through tradition as a Deity who rewards and punishes in the material and physical realm. From Elihu he learns that there is no value in these, only in immortal life.[16]

We should clarify that Ibn Tibbon assumes a purely philosophical understanding of immortality here. He adopts the view argued by a long line of Greek and Islamic interpreters that immortality comes about as a result of intellectual perfection. The general idea is that the perfected human intellect gains immortality by virtue of its eternal ideas, which do not decay despite the demise of the body. This is the lesson that, in Ibn Tibbon's reading, Job learns from Elihu.[17]

Ibn Tibbon goes on to explain in detail the arguments Elihu presents in order to convince Job of his position. According to Ibn Tibbon, they are found in Job 33, the same chapter Saadiah and Maimonides had designated as holding the key to Elihu's position and the Book of Job as a whole. According to Ibn Tibbon, Elihu begins this chapter by rebutting Job's claim made in the earlier part of the dialogue that physical suffering without any prior sin is evidence of divine injustice:

> He said to him—that is, Elihu to Job—regarding this complaint of his [i.e., Job's] that it was not justified and that it was not correct. He gave an explanation [for Job's suffering] by hint (*be-remez*) in order to refute it [i.e., Job's complaint] by saying "God is greater than man" (Job 33:12). That is, God's ways are elevated above the ways of flesh and blood. If matters of this sort [i.e., unjust suffering] are [considered] a corruption [of justice] in the ways of flesh and blood, it is not a corruption [of justice] in the ways of God who is elevated above all elevated beings. For it is possible that suffering can come upon one who has not sinned against God, even if he acted according to His will. Do not understand from my words that God brings suffering essentially (*be-'eẓem*) upon him who has not sinned and

> has acted according to His will—like the opinion of the Ash'arites and the Mu'tazilites [who believe this]; this was the opinion of Bildad and Zophar. Rather, they come upon him because of Satan—that is, by reason of some of the intermediaries to whom He has surrendered man on account of his [being composed of] matter(*ḥomer*)—that is, his body, not his soul, if he should want to preserve it. But the body is generated from corrupt matter and [thus] one does not have the capacity to preserve it completely, not from complete dissolution, nor from partial dissolution—that is, from suffering. [Thus,] there is no corruption [of justice] before God when he does not preserve [the body].[18]

Elihu argues that Job was not correct in complaining to God about the injustice of his suffering because God's ways are unlike those of man. When human beings inflict undeserved suffering on each other, it is an injustice. But when God inflicts undeserved suffering, it is due to the fact that man is composed of matter that receives influences from God via natural forces in such a way that it constantly undergoes generation and corruption. Therefore, God's justice is vindicated, because suffering does not come from Him "essentially" or by "first intention." The key prooftext for these ideas is Elihu's statement that "God is greater than man" (Job 33:12), which is taken to mean that in a concrete physical sense God's ways are "elevated above" those of human beings insofar as He is detached from the negative effects He causes in the world below.

We may note incidentally that this passage highlights the ambiguity in Ibn Tibbon's understanding of Satan. Ibn Tibbon tells us that suffering comes upon man "because of Satan—that is, by reason of some of the intermediaries to whom He has surrendered man on account of his [being composed of] matter (*ḥomer*)." From Ibn Tibbon's language it is not at all clear whether Satan is equated with matter or with harmful chance occurrences caused by intermediary natural forces that interact with matter. Nor is there anything here to rule out the possibility that Satan is privation, since privation could easily be the source of the vulnerability of matter to the degenerative effects of natural forces acting upon it.

Ibn Tibbon continues his exposition by explaining that Elihu's next step is to demonstrate to Job that not only does undeserved suffering fail to impugn God's justice, it is even a form of providence in its own right. That is because suffering of this sort inspires one to recognize that there is no correlation whatsoever between one's moral virtue and physical welfare. It therefore causes one to reassess the entire question of providence and to come to the realization that the immortality of the intellect must be the only true reward. Thus, while Elihu's intent is to explain to Job that immortality is the primary manifestation of providence, he also informs him that suffering is a secondary form of providence in that it helps enlighten the individual that immortality is indeed the highest reward. Furthermore, the implication here is that it is precisely this lesson that best explains Job's own misfortunes. His suffering was, in fact, a manifestation of providence designed to inform him that his traditional conception of providence was incorrect and that the highest form of providence is the immortality of the intellect.

These ideas are drawn out from Elihu's remarks on Job 33:14–31, the section of chapter 33 that was also of great significance to Saadiah and Maimonides. An explanation of how Ibn Tibbon reads this passage will require a good deal of effort, for it is at this point in his discussion that his esoteric method of discourse becomes increasingly evident as he attempts to conceal his philosophical views.

According to Ibn Tibbon, the first verse of this passage, Job 33:14, encapsulates Elihu's main message: "For God speaks in one manner / And in a second manner—though God does not perceive it."[19] Ibn Tibbon sees in this statement a reference to two aspects of providence: one by which God speaks to man in a manner He "perceives," and another in a manner God does not "perceive."[20] It is the second type of providence that becomes most important here for Ibn Tibbon's reading of Job, but in order to understand how it operates, we must look at the first type of providence.

According to Ibn Tibbon, the type of providence by which God communicates with man in a manner that God Himself "perceives" is none other than prophecy. This idea is inspired by the verses in Elihu's speech that immediately follow those just cited:

> In a dream, a night vision,
> When deep sleep falls upon men,
> While they slumber on their beds,
> Then He opens men's understanding. (Job 33:15)

These verses appear to confirm the common medieval philosophical association of dreams and prophecy, and Ibn Tibbon takes advantage of that association in surmising that Elihu is referring here to three different levels of prophecy that accompany different gradations of intellectual perfection.[21]

Ibn Tibbon goes on to explain that Elihu is referring to a rather specific type of prophetic communication, one that God imparts to a person such as Job, who is righteous in deeds but who has not achieved intellectual perfection. God informs such a person through prophecy that suffering can strike even someone like himself who exhibits righteous behavior, and that he should not feel pride in his moral rectitude since it will not protect him from harm. This is the meaning of the verses that follow the last citation:

> Then He opens men's understanding
> And by disciplining them leaves His signature
> To turn man away from action[22]
> To suppress pride in man. (Job 33:16–17)

According to Ibn Tibbon's reading, God disciplines the morally righteous individual by informing him through prophetic communication that he should "turn away" from an exclusive emphasis on proper "action" as his source of "pride."

Ibn Tibbon concludes that this type of prophetic communication is providential because it is meant to inspire the individual to recognize that moral perfection alone does not lead to immortality, which is the highest form of providence, and that immortality can be achieved only by cultivating intellectual perfection. In Ibn Tibbon's reading, this idea is encapsulated in Job 33:18, which follows the previous citation: "He [i.e., God] spares his soul from destruction, / His life from perishing by the sword."[23] The notion that God spares from destruction the "soul" of one who has received prophetic communication is understood by Ibn Tibbon as a reference to the immortality of intellect.

But it is the second type of providential communication, the kind God does not "perceive," that is relevant to Job's situation. According to Ibn Tibbon, the explication of this second type of communication is elaborated upon in Job 33:19–22, verses that begin the description of the sick person and immediately follow those dealing with prophecy:

> He is reproved by pains on his bed,
> And the trembling in his bones is constant.
> He detests food;
> Fine food [is repulsive] to him.
> His flesh wastes away till it cannot be seen,
> And his bones are rubbed away till they are invisible.
> He comes close to destruction,
> His life [verges] on death.

Commenting on these verses, Ibn Tibbon says:

> After [Elihu] explained the first way by which God speaks to human beings essentially (*be-'eẓem*) [which is] through the Active Intellect which overflows from Him, may He be exalted, by means of the prophet and wisdom, he began to explain the second way by which He seemingly speaks with human beings through chance occurrence (*ki-mdaber 'im beney adam be-mikreh*), as he says, "[God] does not perceive it" (Job 33:14). That is what [Elihu meant] in his saying: "[He is reproved] by pains on his bed" (Job 33:19). Thus, the order [of ideas] is as follows: "For God speaks once / And a second time—though [God] does not perceive it / . . . In a dream, a night vision etc." (Job 33:14–15), and by painful chastisements. He speaks [in one way] to them by dream and night vision. The second [way]—by which He seemingly speaks, though He does not perceive it—is by means of painful chastisements which come upon man. The intent is that God seemingly speaks to human beings in this manner by chance occurrence; that is, suffering and pain come upon them by means of Satan.[24]

According to a plain reading of the biblical text, the sick person described in the biblical passage above appears to be the same individual who is disciplined by God through prophetic communication. However, in Ibn Tibbon's reading, the description of the sick person introduces the second form of providence, the kind with which Elihu is concerned. Ibn Tibbon explains that the allusion to reproval by "pains" is a reference to suffering, which occurs by means of Satan, who in this passage is equated with "chance occurrence." In such instances, God "seemingly speaks to man," but God "does not perceive it" in that He does not have cognizance of the evil effects that the goodness of the natural order has on the world below.

What Ibn Tibbon appears to be saying is that the suffering of the righteous is in fact providential in that it is a way by which God indirectly communicates with them. What is actually communicated is not yet made clear, but it is obvious from the context of the discussion and becomes clearer in the course of Ibn Tibbon's subsequent remarks. The recipient of undeserved suffering learns essentially the same lesson as the one who receives prophetic communication of the kind identified with the first type of providence. That is, he learns from his suffering that there is no necessary relationship between exemplary moral behavior and physical well-being, and that true providence is immortality, which is achieved through intellectual perfection.

In sum, there are two types of providential communications to which Elihu refers that both teach the lesson that immortality is true providence, not physical well-being. The first type is prophecy, by which God directly imparts this information. Hence Elihu's reference to God's "perceiving" this type of providence, for here prophetic communication comes "essentially" from God via the Active Intellect. The second is the experience of suffering; it teaches the same lesson, only more indirectly, by convincing the individual that attachment to physical and material things is futile and that he should pursue intellectual perfection so as to achieve immortality. Here God does not "perceive" the communication He imparts because He does not cause evil as a matter of first intention. Moreover, it is also clear that Job's suffering is best explained by the second type of providential communication. Not only is his suffering not an indictment against God; it is, in fact, an expression of divine providence in that it is meant to disabuse him of his traditional view of reward and punishment and convince him that the most exalted form of providence is immortality.

At this point in his exposition, Ibn Tibbon has presented the basic position represented in Elihu's viewpoint, but Ibn Tibbon has more to say about the notion that suffering is a form of providential communication in the following section, which is perhaps the most difficult of Ibn Tibbon's entire exposition.[25] Here Ibn Tibbon's commentary is devoted to explicating Elihu's remarks in Job 33:23–31, which describe how the sick person is saved from his afflictions:

> [23] If there be an angel,[26]
> An advocate, one among a thousand
> To declare a man's uprightness,
> [24] Then He has mercy on him and decrees,
> "Redeem him from descending to destruction,
> For I have obtained his ransom;
> [25] Let his flesh be healthier than in his youth;

Let him return to younger days."
26 He prays to God and is accepted by Him;
He enters His presence with shouts of joy,
For He requites a man for his righteousness.
27 He [i.e., the righteous man] declares to men,
"I have sinned; I have perverted what was right;
But I was not paid back for it."
28 He redeemed him from passing into destruction,
He will enjoy the light.
29 Truly God does all these things
Two or three times to man,
30 To bring him back from destruction,
That he may bask in the light of life.

Ibn Tibbon identifies three crucial factors in this section that are connected to the type of providential communication that manifests itself in suffering: the angel who saves the individual in verse 23; prayer to God, referred to in verse 26; and repentance, which involves confession of one's sins to other men, alluded to in verse 27. A discussion follows as to the nature of the exact relationship between the three factors, with Ibn Tibbon concluding that while the salvation of the angel is a prerequisite for the other two, the reverse is not the case.

It is not at all clear what Ibn Tibbon is saying here. We do not know how any of these factors are connected to the notion that the suffering of the righteous is an expression of providence. Particularly unclear is the identity of the angel, which Ibn Tibbon considers the central factor. Ibn Tibbon informs us that it refers to an esoteric doctrine that cannot be openly explained, and he therefore alludes to it in deliberately ambiguous terms. At one point, Ibn Tibbon points to a clue in Elihu's remarks that, he claims, helps reveal the angel's true identity, thus raising our hopes that the mystery will be dispelled. Commenting on Job 33:23, "If there be an angel, / An advocate, one among a thousand," Ibn Tibbon tells us: "after he [i.e., Elihu] concealed [the identity of] this one angel [in not telling us] from which species of [the many] species which are equivocally called angels [this angel] belongs—he pierced the settings and said '[one] among a thousand.' That is, this one [angel] is from the angels that are in the thousands."[27] The reference to "piercing the settings" is an allusion to Maimonides' well-known interpretation of Proverbs 25:11—"A word fitly spoken is like apples of gold in settings of silver"—which Maimonides sees as an allusion to the dual level of meaning in scripture, with the apples of gold and settings of silver representing, respectively, scripture's inner philosophical meaning and its plain outer meaning.[28] The notion that Elihu pierces the settings by identifying the angel as one "among a thousand" therefore means that this phrase offers significant clues regarding the inner philosophical meaning of the angel. However, Ibn Tibbon's brevity quickly dashes our hope that in this passage we will gain access to his esoteric interpretation of the angel. Moreover, as one reads further in Ibn Tibbon's commentary, he continues to conceal the identity of the angel through ambiguity. In various passages, it could easily be a reference to the Active Intellect, the human intellect, or some other cosmological force beneficial to the individual. This ambiguity is clearly inspired by Maimonides, who, as we saw, suggests several meanings for the term "angel," all of which match the possibilities raised here. Ibn Tibbon also follows Maimonides in his elusiveness regarding the identity of the particular angel under discussion.[29]

There is yet hope for revealing the meaning of Ibn Tibbon's understanding of Elihu's angel, and it is to be found in one crucial passage that I believe provides clues not only on this matter but on the entire direction of Ibn Tibbon's discussion. In a section that follows the one just examined, Ibn Tibbon shares a series of thoughts, beginning with a criticism of Maimonides:

> It would seem that the Rabbi, the true teacher [i.e., Maimonides], believed that the mercy and redemption in the salvation of the angel, the prayer of the one chastised, his entering God's presence with shouts of joy, his declaration to men [that he has sinned]—are all to be understood as one [matter], as in our first explication.[30] For he did not mention from that whole matter anything other than the salvation [of the angel]. [It was] as if he understood the other things [i.e., prayer and repentance] as only a "setting," not that one would truly need them.
>
> It is true that it [i.e., the salvation of the angel] is the essential thing because it is a hint regarding necessary individual providence which exists for the [physical] bodies of animals; it is this [providence] which is alluded to in chapter 15 of the third part [of the *Guide of the Perplexed*], as he says, "the individuals of every species are not neglected in every respect." But there is no doubt that the verses, "He prays to God" (Job 33:26) and "He declares to men[, / I have sinned]" (Job 33:27) are not for concealment alone, in that they are the central element of the second way by which God seemingly speaks to human beings, not by salvation [of the angel], as we have said; for in them [i.e., prayer and repentance] there appears to be some manner of guidance for the one chastised to explore the reasons for his pains, deficiencies, and sins, until he understands them. It is as if God spoke to him and informed him of them [i.e., the reasons]. It would appear that it was about this that the sage [i.e., Elihu] intended to inform Job. Sometimes, through chastisements, good things come upon the one chastised by chance occurrence. For on their account [i.e., chastisements] he will be guided to that of which he had been ignorant; they are like a spoken statement to him and are providential for him by chance occurrence. Therefore, one should not protest regarding them, given that they are the cause of something good.[31]

Ibn Tibbon claims that Maimonides also understood the importance of the three factors in Elihu's remarks—the angel, prayer, and repentance. But he takes issue with Maimonides for placing all the emphasis on the angel and not on the other two factors, prayer and repentance. Ibn Tibbon is referring to the fact that in Maimonides' exposition of Elihu's speech in the *Guide*, only the angel, not prayer or repentance, is mentioned as key to the latter's message. Ibn Tibbon assumes that Maimonides interprets Elihu's mention of prayer and repentance as a smokescreen to conceal an esoteric doctrine regarding the angel.

What Ibn Tibbon is saying here is not of great help until the next few lines, where he provides vital information not only about his differences with Maimonides, but about his own position as well. He states that the angel in Elihu's speech is a "hint regarding necessary individual providence which exists for the [physical] bodies of animals" that is alluded to in *Guide* III:15, where Maimonides notes that "the individuals of every species are not neglected in every respect." In fact, the reference is mistaken; the clause cited from Maimonides appears in chapter 17 of the third part of the *Guide*, and the wording of Ibn Tibbon's own translation of the *Guide* matches the citation given here.[32] What is most interesting is that the section from which this citation is taken is Maimonides' description of Aristotle's theory of providence, according to which all species are protected only by general providence, there being no special providence for man.

A key clue to Ibn Tibbon's views is thus revealed. What Ibn Tibbon is saying is that, according to Maimonides, Elihu's speech conceals an esoteric doctrine that the righteous man is saved from his suffering only by general providence, as defined by Aristotle, not by a personal God. Elihu's angel in Maimonides' exposition is therefore nothing other than the forces of nature that fall under the rubric of general providence. Moreover, as Ibn Tibbon would have it, Maimonides reads Elihu's remarks about prayer and repentance as references designed only to appease those who hold the traditional view that salvation comes from the response of a personal God. Maimonides, in fact, does not see any efficacy in either.

Ibn Tibbon's understanding of Maimonides comes as no surprise. The same conclusions are drawn in Ibn Tibbon's earlier letter to Maimonides regarding providence. There he also interprets Maimonides as upholding an esoteric Aristotelian position on providence and sees Maimonides' reading of Job as evidence for this conclusion.[33]

What is most important for our purposes is that in discussing Maimonides' position, Ibn Tibbon makes clear what his own view is. It is apparent that he too assumes that Elihu's angel represents general providence, but he disagrees with Maimonides about the role of prayer and repentance which are also mentioned by Elihu. For Ibn Tibbon, prayer and repentance do indeed serve a necessary function in that they provide inspiration for the one who experiences unjustified suffering "to explore the reasons for his pains, deficiencies, and sins until he understands them." As such, "they are the essence of the second way by which God seemingly speaks to human beings." Through prayer and repentance, "it is as if God spoke to him and informed him of them."[34]

We now have a fuller understanding of how Ibn Tibbon conceives of unjustified suffering as a pedagogic and providential force and how he explains Job's afflictions. According to Ibn Tibbon, when the righteous man experiences suffering, he is inspired to offer prayers to God and confessions to other human beings, both of which serve the purpose of causing him to explore the meaning of his suffering. What he discovers through such actions are the lessons that, as we have already delineated, come from suffering: evil is caused by natural forces and not by any direct intentional action on God's part; there is thus no value in material well-being; and one must cultivate intellectual perfection to achieve immortality which is the highest form of providence.

What may be confusing is that in Ibn Tibbon's reading, Elihu makes reference to three forms of providence that function in tandem with each other and are not clearly differentiated. Suffering is providential in that it prods the individual to turn away from material matters. This in turn leads the individual to recognize that the most exalted form of providence is the immortality of the perfected intellect. Yet, the individual who makes this discovery through his suffering also needs the help of beneficial forces from general providence, or an "angel," to ensure that his afflictions do not kill him so that he can indeed pursue this highest form of providence. To put the matter another way, a righteous person must suffer enough to learn his philosophical lesson about immortality, but not so much that he dies and is unable to benefit from this lesson. The evil forces of nature that bring suffering on a righteous individual must be balanced by those that save him from harm, so that he is inspired to cultivate intellectual perfection and experience immortality.

Ibn Tibbon provides other details that are worth mentioning regarding the notion of suffering as divine providence. In one passage, he informs us that the pedagogic process initiated by suffering can occur more than once in the lifetime of an individual, a point derived from Elihu's remarks in Job 33:29–30, in which he states that God "does all these things two or three times" so that an individual may "bask in the light of life." Commenting on this statement, Ibn Tibbon says:

> This chastisement and this causing of pain after which there is the salvation of the angel, as well as mercy and redemption—God enacts for man two or three times. That is, there are those for whom one [experience of suffering] is enough, and through it they recognize their deficiencies and corruptions. But there are those who do not recognize [this] with one [experience of this sort], and require two or three [experiences].[35]

Thus, someone may experience providential suffering and the salvation from it by general providence a number of times before gaining proper philosophical insight from his experiences.[36]

Here, incidentally, Ibn Tibbon explicitly disagrees with Maimonides on an exegetical point. In Ibn Tibbon's view, Maimonides reads the statement that God saves an individual two or three times as saying that the angel saves a man only three times in one's life, given that no human being escapes from death—an interpretation of Maimonides that agrees with my own.[37] Ibn Tibbon argues that Job, being well aware that all men die, did not need to learn such a lesson. Instead, Elihu is teaching Job that the angel can save a man any number of times, the number three having no particular significance here.[38]

In another passage Ibn Tibbon gives us a better understanding of the individual for whom the lessons of providential suffering are specifically intended. Ibn Tibbon states that the person who stands to benefit from unjustified suffering is the individual who, like Job, is righteous in his actions but has not yet achieved intellectual perfection. Ibn Tibbon goes on to explain that if such people were never to experience suffering, the following consequence would result:

> they would consider themselves perfect individuals because they had not sinned in their actions and had performed good deeds. They would know God and His ways according to tradition and would not be aroused [to knowledge] of anything beyond this. They would not achieve the perfection intended for them in knowing God and His ways according to the true knowledge that is possible for man to know. They would remain in their [state of] deficiency.[39]

Ibn Tibbon thus emphasizes that perfection in one's actions not only is inadequate for achieving true providence, but can even be a hindrance by giving one a false sense of security that God will reward such an individual for his righteous behavior. Ibn Tibbon goes on to explain that Job was such an individual before he experienced his suffering. While Ibn Tibbon has already implied that there is danger in taking too much pride in one's moral virtue, it is here that this point is made most explicit.

Cryptic references cited earlier can now be cleared up as well. We understand why Ibn Tibbon states that the salvation of the angel can occur without prayer and repentance, but not the reverse.[40] Salvation through general providence is possible regardless of whether one prays or repents, since the latter activities only provide the opportunity to explore the philosophical meaning of one's suffering. But without the salvation provided by general providence, the righteous man might not physically survive his suffering, and thus the philosophical insights gained from the introspection inspired by prayer and repentance would be of no value.

Another cryptic reference to the angel in this section now makes sense as well. I noted earlier that when Ibn Tibbon first speaks about the angel, he focuses on Elihu's description of this angel as one "among a thousand," stating that this phrase is a crucial clue to what the angel represents. Given that we now have good reason to think that the angel represents general providence, Ibn Tibbon's allusion is transparent. He is subscribing to Aristotle's views on general providence as described by Maimonides, and in the latter's description of Aristotle's position, general providence expresses itself in any number of ways in that all natural endowments in the various species are manifestations of it. Thus, general providence safeguards animals by providing the faculty of locomotion in order to seek out what is beneficial to them and flee from what is harmful. Human beings are protected by the intellect in that each person, with the help of the intellect, "governs, thinks, and reflects on what may render possible the durability of himself as individual and the preservation of his species."[41] Therefore, when an individual is saved by general providence in a given instance, he is rescued by one of a "thousand" natural capacities that the latter supplies to the many species.

There is one more loose end in Ibn Tibbon's explication of Elihu's position that should be addressed. In arguing for the notion that suffering can have providential benefits, both Maimonides and Ibn Tibbon seem to be supporting an idea that comes dangerously close to that of the Mu'tazilites, who claim that God inflicts undeserved suffering in order to increase one's reward in the hereafter. Yet, both Maimonides and Ibn Tibbon reject that view; the Mu'tazilite position is attributed to Bildad, who, along with Job's other friends, turns out to have an incorrect position on providence. I also noted in chapter 3 that Maimonides singles out the Mu'tazilite view for censure. Maimonides voices strong opposition to the Mu'tazilites as well as to some of the early rabbis who support the notion that God inflicts undeserved suffering in order to increase one's reward.[42]

It is likely that both Maimonides and Ibn Tibbon would respond to these observations by arguing that there is a real distinction between their views and those of the Mu'tazilites. The latter position is that God inflicts suffering deliberately as a means to grant future reward. In the thinking of Maimonides and Ibn Tibbon, the process connecting suffering and providence is entirely different. Suffering comes in an impersonal manner through the forces of nature. It is the individual experiencing suffering who then, in some sense, brings providential reward upon himself by drawing the proper conclusions from his suffering.

Ibn Tibbon appears to allude to this distinction in a passage we have already cited. At the beginning of his explication of Elihu's remarks, Ibn Tibbon adds:

> Do not understand from my words that God brings suffering essentially (*be-'eẓem*) upon him who has not sinned and has acted according to His will—like the opinion of the Ash'arites and the Mu'tazilites [who believe this]; this was the opinion of Bildad and Zophar. Rather, they come upon him because of Satan—that is, by reason of some of the [celestial] intermediaries to whom He has surrendered man on account of his [being composed of] matter (*ḥomer*)—that is, his body, not his soul, if he should want to preserve it.[43]

Ibn Tibbon seems eager to point out that his views differ from those of the Islamic theologians, Ash'arites and Mu'tazilites, because they believe that suffering comes "essentially" from God, while he does not. While this remark is brief, it encapsulates the key difference between Maimonides and Ibn Tibbon, on the one hand, and the Islamic theologians, on the other. While in the view of Maimonides and Ibn Tibbon suffering comes from God non-essentially and thus non-intentionally in being a by-product of benevolent natural forces, for the Islamic theologians it is very much the product of God's will and is inflicted with a specific purpose in mind.

We must now turn to God's revelation to Job. It is noteworthy how little Ibn Tibbon has to say about this portion of the Book of Job. Yet, what he does say is striking. In a brief and novel interpretation, Ibn Tibbon claims that God never actually spoke to Job—at least not directly. Instead, God spoke to Job indirectly in the sense that He caused him to suffer. As we have seen, Ibn Tibbon believes that suffering is a divine communication in that it teaches valuable philosophical lessons about the true nature of providence, and that it was this sort of communication that Job received from God. In other words, God's theophany to Job is merely a restatement of what has already happened earlier in the book. It does not represent a new event after Elihu's address.

Ibn Tibbon hinges his reading on an original understanding of the "tempest" (*se'arah*) out of which God addressed Job. For Ibn Tibbon, the tempest is a metaphor for Job's "many chastisements." It was through these afflictions that God "spoke." Ibn Tibbon bases his reading on the observation that in no other place in the Bible does God speak to someone in a prophecy described as a tempest, an indication that in this case there was some other form of communication. He also cites verses from Elihu's speech, which he believes make the point that God addresses the righteous through chastisements:

> [God] declares to men what they have done,
> And that their transgressions are excessive;
> He opens their understanding by discipline,
> And orders them back from mischief. (Job 36:9–10)

According to Ibn Tibbon, the second part of this citation explicates the first part. The notion that God opens the understanding of human beings through "discipline" explains the manner in which He "declares to men what they have done." The same notion is reinforced by Elihu a few verses later:

> [God] rescues the lowly through[44] their affliction,
> And opens their understanding through distress. (Job 36:15)[45]

Here again, affliction is a means by which God communicates with human beings.

An important observation is that none of the various providential processes described by Ibn Tibbon in his reading of Job requires a personal God. Human beings are guided toward the ultimate providential reward of immortality by two types of providential communications: prophecy and suffering. Prophecy consists of a communication from the Active Intellect, which warns the recipient about the consequences of his lack of perfection. Although I have not discussed this form of providential communication in detail, it is presented in naturalistic terms. If one looks carefully at Ibn Tibbon's wording in his description of this form of providence, he refers to prophecy and wisdom interchangeably, as if to suggest that prophecy provides the same message as philosophical wisdom attained without any communication from God.[46] The providential role of suffering is also understood in naturalistic terms. Ibn Tibbon is referring here to suffering that all human beings experience through the natural order and that comes as result of their material composition. It is just that some human beings learn valuable philosophical lessons from that suffering. Similar observations can be made about the role of prayer and repentance. These force the individual to contemplate why he has suffered and to come to the philosophical realization that physical well-being is of no value, but there is no suggestion on Ibn Tibbon's part that God responds personally to either. As for the "angel" that saves human beings from harm so that they can cultivate intellectual perfection despite their suffering, here Ibn Tibbon is referring again to events in the natural order, as is clear from his interpretation and adoption of Maimonides' understanding of the angel and his identification of the Maimonides' viewpoint with that of Aristotle.

Ibn Tibbon seems well aware of the controversial nature of his thinking on these issues, which is why he presents his ideas in such cryptic terms. There is also evidence to suggest that in doing so, Ibn Tibbon sees himself as merely following the lead of the Bible. Ibn Tibbon provides an instructive example of how the biblical text conceals its esoteric views in his discussion of Elihu's angel. As we have seen, the angel represents general providence or the natural order which saves the righteous person who suffers, and that is a view Ibn Tibbon knows full well is in conflict with the traditional notion that there is a personal God who cares for the righteous. According to Ibn Tibbon, Elihu conceals his true views on this matter in such a way that the philosophically unsophisticated reader will think that he is referring to the traditional position. The key passage is Job 33:23–24:

> 23 If there be an angel,
> An advocate, one among a thousand
> To declare a man's uprightness,
> 24 Then He has mercy on him and decrees,
> "Redeem him from descending to destruction,
> For I have obtained his ransom."

The exoteric reading is that an angel saves a man from destruction (verse 23), but God is the ultimate cause of his rescue (verse 24). This reading assumes that God has a personal role to play here. But Ibn Tibbon notes that the "He" in verse 24 is ambiguous and should be read according to the esoteric meaning as a reference to the angel, not God. That is, it is only the angel that saves man, not God. Translated into philosophical terms, this means that only general providence saves man, and that there is no divine intervention here.[47]

In his discussion of prayer and repentance and their role in providence, Ibn Tibbon at times appears to be speaking in traditional terms, but a close reading of key passages reveals that this is not the case, and that once again his esoteric style of discourse is meant to conceal his radical position. For instance, in the passage in which Ibn Tibbon deals most extensively with prayer and repentance, he says:

> He who is rescued by prayer [offered] to God after he has aroused himself to the [knowledge of the] first cause of his pains and all matters in the lowly world—his prayer will be considered as righteousness and will rise up as appeasement before God. . . . He who is saved after confession of his sins and recognition of his deficiencies and his corruption, has been aroused to [the knowledge of] more than that to which those [mentioned] above have been aroused.[48] For he has also been aroused to [the knowledge of] the intermediary causes and ultimate [causes]—that is, to all the elevated beings that are above him.[49] He has also been aroused to [the knowledge of] the deficiency of the recipient [i.e., man] and his corruption.[50]

Note how Ibn Tibbon avoids any clear reference to personal divine intervention here. He does state that prayer will "rise up as appeasement before God," but even here he shies away from speaking of God as actually listening or responding to prayer. The emphasis is on prayer and repentance as a means to teach human beings about philosophical truth regarding the corrupting influence of matter. For this reason, Ibn Tibbon goes on to say that repentance is more effective than prayer in leading one to true knowledge. It forces the individual to probe the issue of suffering and to come to an understanding of how his own deficiencies as a material being and the actions of the celestial world are the cause of his suffering. Prayer merely acquaints him with the "first cause"—God—who is responsible for all events in the world.[51]

Ravitzky has already expressed suspicion that Ibn Tibbon's God is impersonal,[52] and we seem to have confirmation of this view. Yet, we must resist drawing a firm conclusion about Ibn Tibbon's philosophical orientation. Ibn Tibbon did not consider his reading of the Book of Job to be a comprehensive assessment of providence, as is evident from a statement at the end of his discussion in which he makes note of other forms of providence in addition to those dealt with in Job. Some of these other types of providence are "natural" (*tiv'iyyot*) in that they "are the result of the different types of angels that God commands so as to preserve man"; some are "according to choice and free will" (*beḥiriyyot reẓoniyyot*); and finally, there are "miraculous" forms of providence (*moftiyyot*), which are only for select individuals.[53] What these forms of providence consist of is not explained by Ibn Tibbon. Nonetheless, the mention of them does not allow us to say conclusively that Ibn Tibbon believes that God acts in an impersonal manner in all His activity. Of especial interest is the question of miracles, which Ibn Tibbon mentions. Ibn Tibbon identifies this form of providence with that which Maimonides discusses in *Guide* III:51, but adds that he will address this issue in a later work—though there is no evidence that he ever did.[54] Still, even if firm conclusions cannot be drawn, the suspicion that Ibn Tibbon adhered to an impersonal conception of God is greatly strengthened by our exposition of his interpretation of Job.

To summarize Ibn Tibbon's reading of Job, the central point of the book is that the highest form of providence is immortality and that immortality is in turn consequent upon intellectual perfection. In the course of his commentary, Ibn Tibbon also finds in the Job story a rationale for the suffering of the righteous. Suffering is a secondary providential force that has the purpose of leading a righteous individual to recognize that immortality is indeed the highest reward. It accomplishes this purpose by causing the righteous person to realize that there is, in fact, no correlation between righteous behavior and physical well-being, on the one hand, and wickedness and suffering, on the other, and that physical affliction is entirely the result of natural forces interacting with matter. From this insight, the righteous individual understands that providence could not possibly be equated with physical well-being in this world and that true providence must be in the afterlife. He also begins to understand that it is intellectual perfection that is needed to achieve immortality, not just perfection in one's actions. In short, unjustified suffering teaches what true providence is and the means to achieve it.

It also becomes clear in the course of Ibn Tibbon's discussion that suffering benefits righteous individuals of a rather specific type, namely those who, having achieved perfection in their actions but not in their intellect, believe that their actions will bring divine reward. It is they who will be most disillusioned by suffering in seeing the disparity between their righteous action and physical affliction. As a consequence, they will seek a philosophical explanation for their situation and come to the conclusion that the highest form of providence is in the afterlife. Job is an individual who goes through this very process with Elihu's guidance. He begins the story as a man righteous in conduct but lacking in intellectual perfection and expecting physical rewards for his righteous behavior. But after he experiences suffering, he learns that there is no relationship between righteous action and physical well-being, and that true providence is immortality, which is achieved through intellectual perfection.

Ibn Tibbon goes in a direction similar to Saadiah's and a number of medieval Christian commentators who believed that the answer to the problem of Job and the challenge of the suffering of the righteous in general can be found in the afterlife. According to this view, Job and all righteous individuals who suffer receive ample reward for their ordeal in the hereafter. In this manner, divine justice is upheld, despite its apparent absence in this world.[55] However, Ibn Tibbon strikes out on an original path by placing this approach to Job in a philosophical framework in which providence is understood in entirely naturalistic terms, and the afterlife is equated with the immortality of the intellect. Absent is any notion that God is deliberately testing Job so as to reward him in the hereafter, as Saadiah and the Christians suggest. Instead, Job experiences suffering through the natural order, which is the only form of divine communication he gets, and it is from that suffering that he must learn the necessary lessons to merit the afterlife.

Antecedents

We are now in a position to evaluate Ibn Tibbon's reading of Job in terms of the three interfaces at the center of this study. Let us look at the first interface, which concerns the historical relationship between the readings of Job in our study. That Ibn Tibbon adopts a good deal from Maimonides in his reading of Job is beyond dispute. Ibn Tibbon takes for granted Maimonides' entire framework for understanding the Book of Job up to the point that Elihu appears. In his interpretation of Elihu's position, Ibn Tibbon's exposition is undergirded by the Maimonidean notion that providence is consequent on the intellect. With regard to the particulars of Elihu's view, Ibn Tibbon offers what is essentially a commentary on the cryptic clues Maimonides provides. Thus, Ibn Tibbon's notion that Elihu describes two types of providential communication, prophecy and suffering, can be traced to Maimonides. With respect to prophecy, Ibn Tibbon is clearly inspired by Maimonides' allusion to the "how of prophecy," which is based on Elihu's reference to prophetic dreams. The idea that suffering is providential because it forces the individual to recognize the futility of attachment to material things is a concept that we saw was also present in Maimonides' reading of the final chapters of Job. We have also seen that Ibn Tibbon openly adopts Maimonides' conception of Elihu's angel.

We should note that Ibn Tibbon's understanding of Maimonides is often not the same as our own. First, Ibn Tibbon understands Maimonides' reference to the "how of prophecy" as an allusion to prophetic dreams, which contain warnings about the limited benefits of moral virtue. We construed it as an allusion to the operations of the practical intellect—in particular, the power of divination. Second, Ibn Tibbon seems to read Maimonides to be saying that it is Elihu who introduces the notion that suffering can be providential. Our view was that Maimonides finds this notion in Job's words in the final chapter of the book. Third, Ibn Tibbon claims that for Maimonides Elihu's angel is a symbol for the operations of general providence. We argued that Maimonides regards the angel as a symbol for the operations of individual providence, though it is providence understood in entirely naturalistic terms. These differences are to be expected, given the murkiness of Maimonides' presentation and the many ways in which it can be interpreted. The important point is that in his exposition, Ibn Tibbon is in large part attempting to make sense of Maimonides.

Certainly, there are some points about which Ibn Tibbon openly disagrees with Maimonides. Thus, he offers an interpretation different from Maimonides' regarding Satan's two arrivals in the biblical text, the meaning of Elihu's mention of prayer and repentance when explaining to Job the truth about providence, and Elihu's statement that the angel rescues an individual only two or three times. However, it is important to note that these disagreements are all exegetical, not philosophical. Ibn Tibbon does not depart from the philosophical premises of Maimonides' interpretation of Job; he only disagrees with how those premises are to be read out of the biblical text. At the basis of Ibn Tibbon's reading of Job is Maimonides' philosophical concept that providence is consequent upon intellectual perfection. The only question is how that idea is expressed in the Book of Job.

But there is one key difference between Ibn Tibbon and Maimonides that appears to be both exegetical and philosophical. Ibn Tibbon seems to depart from Maimonides in equating the highest form of providence with the immortality of the intellect and in claiming that this is Job's ultimate lesson. Indeed, there is evidence that Maimonides accepts the philosophical concept of immortality. He certainly alludes to it in a number of passages in his work. However, immortality is not a factor in Maimonides' general discussion of providence in the *Guide*, nor does it figure prominently in his treatment of Job.[56] This may be an instance in which Ibn Tibbon disagrees with his predecessor not just from an exegetical standpoint but from a philosophical one as well.

There is, nonetheless, solid evidence to suggest that in giving prominence to the theme of immortality, Ibn Tibbon very much saw himself as a faithful student of Maimonides. This conclusion emerges from Ibn Tibbon's letter to Maimonides on providence, where he explicitly argues that immortality is central to Maimonides' reading of Job and his overall theory of providence. As mentioned earlier, the focus of the letter is Ibn Tibbon's perplexity with *Guide* III:51, but for the purpose of discussing this chapter, he delineates what he believes to be Maimonides' esoteric doctrine of providence as developed in earlier chapters of the *Guide*. Ibn Tibbon argues that it is Maimonides' discussion of Job that is key for gaining insight into that doctrine, and he offers the following paraphrase of Maimonides' understanding of the story:

> After Job knew the Creator with true knowledge, he was not concerned about those felicities which are imagined to be felicities, such as health, wealth, and children. The intent is that he was not concerned about what happened to him after he knew about immortality. It was only this matter over which Satan was not given dominion, as it says "only spare his soul" (Job 2:6). . . .
>
> After he knew the Creator, he did not value money and it was thought of lightly by him. Similarly, his illnesses and disease were thought of lightly by him after he verified for himself the existence of an ultimate perfection and the immortality of the soul on account of it. . . .
>
> It seems to me that Aristotle agrees with this view; indeed most philosophers do, especially those who believe in immortality.[57]

Ibn Tibbon claims that, according to Maimonides, what Job learned is that immortality of the intellect is true providence, and that one achieves psychological immunity to suffering in this lifetime once one is aware of this ultimate reward. Ibn Tibbon also surmises that Maimonides' esoteric position on providence is identical with that of Aristotle.

Ibn Tibbon goes on to say that Maimonides' interpretation of Job does not exhaust Maimonides' esoteric speculations about providence. Ibn Tibbon describes another facet of providence in Maimonides' thinking, one that is equated with the workings of nature. All events in the world are the product of natural laws implemented by God, including the actions of man, which are controlled by his intellect. Hence, providence over man also expresses itself in the very existence and activity of the human intellect, which helps protect man from harm.[58]

What is of interest to us is that from Ibn Tibbon's letter we can be sure that he considered himself to be very much in line with Maimonides' thinking with his belief that immortality is the central theme of Job and the highest form of providence. But this immediately raises a question: what prompts Ibn Tibbon to read Maimonides in this way? As I have noted, Maimonides does not discuss immortality in his treatment of Job, nor does he explicitly link immortality with providence in his general treatment of that issue.

Ibn Tibbon's reasoning is not difficult to figure out. First, the connection between Maimonides' reading of Job and his thoughts on immortality follows from philosophical considerations. According to Maimonides, Job's ultimate lesson is that he achieves knowledge of God and love of God, which allow him to experience providence. For Maimonides these are achievements that also lead to immortality, since it is clear from the little that he says about this issue that he, like Ibn Tibbon, is in agreement with the Greek and Islamic interpreters, who saw immortality as consequent upon perfection of the intellect.[59] Thus, even if immortality is not discussed by Maimonides in his reading of the Job story, presumably he believed that Job would merit such a reward after achieving intellectual perfection. Moreover, given the centrality of Maimonides' reading of Job in his treatment of providence, one need take only one short step further to conclude that what Maimonides says about Job applies to his views on providence in general and that immortality is the highest form of providence for all human beings. It was therefore not difficult for Ibn Tibbon to conclude that for Maimonides immortality is both the central concept in the Book of Job and the most exalted form of providence.

Second, there are clear indications that in Ibn Tibbon's thinking, the lesson of immortality is alluded to in Maimonides' discussion of Job itself even if it is not discussed at length. This comes through in the passage just cited from Ibn Tibbon's letter to Maimonides. There Ibn Tibbon supports his contention that immortality is the central theme in Maimonides' commentary on Job by citing the latter's reading of God's directive to Satan in Job 2:6 that he can do to Job as he pleases, "only spare his soul." Ibn Tibbon says little to explain his understanding of this reference, but little explanation is needed. If we will recall, Maimonides does in fact allude to immortality here. For Maimonides the meaning of God's imperative to Satan is that the "soul" refers to "the thing that remains after death" and that it is this entity over which Satan has no power. In my own reading of Maimonides, I understood this statement as a reference to the acquired intellect, the point being that when one develops such an intellect, one achieves a psychological immunity from suffering. Immortality is secondary to the main issue here, which is that psychological immunity from suffering takes place in this lifetime, even before the acquired intellect survives in the next.[60] However, one can easily see how Ibn Tibbon reads the same passage in Maimonides in a different manner. For him, the mention of immortality is the central point. Maimonides is hinting to us that this is truly the ultimate expression of providence and thus the main theme of the Book of Job.[61]

While Ibn Tibbon offers an intriguing reading of Maimonides by putting immortality in the center of the latter's reading of Job, it is doubtful that it is correct. As I have argued, the message of Job, according to Maimonides, is focused on how providence expresses itself in psychological immunity from suffering in this life. Even if Job achieves knowledge and love of God, which should, in Maimonides' thinking, lead to immortality, Maimonides never suggests that the equation of providence with immortality is a central concern here. Still, whatever disagreements we may have with Ibn Tibbon, the main point is that he does not see himself as departing from Maimonides in his focus on immortality both in his reading of Job and in his understanding of providence in general. Thus, my initial observation still holds: Ibn Tibbon believes his differences with Maimonides to be exegetical, not philosophical.

There is one more apparent difference between Maimonides and Ibn Tibbon that deserves discussion. We have seen that according to Ibn Tibbon's novel reading of the final chapters of the Job story, Job does not experience prophetic revelation. It would seem that on this point he differs with Maimonides as much as at any point of his exposition. As we saw in the previous chapter, Maimonides believes that Job achieves intellectual perfection by the end of the story and that it is for this reason that Job experiences prophecy precisely as the Bible tells us.

The only motivation Ibn Tibbon shares with us to explain why he reads the final chapters of Job in this manner is exegetical. We saw above how he derives his interpretation from a number of clues in the biblical text. But, to my mind, there is another factor operating here, and that is that Ibn Tibbon does not believe that by the end of the story Job achieves intellectual perfection, which is a necessary prerequisite for prophecy.

Why Ibn Tibbon would have drawn such a conclusion can be understood by pointing out a problem in Maimonides' reading of Job. Maimonides sees Job as a figure who initially possesses only moral perfection but by the end of the story achieves intellectual perfection as well. The question that seems to have plagued Ibn Tibbon is how Job achieves this latter perfection in such short order. Maimonides consistently depicts the process of philosophical education as a long and laborious one, and yet there is no indication on Maimonides' part as to how and when Job went through this process. In fact, if we take the story at face value, it would seem implausible that Job would have become intellectually perfect after a few—albeit lengthy—conversations with his friends. I would like to suggest, therefore, that Ibn Tibbon was moved by these considerations to posit a reading that is much more realistic from a philosophical standpoint. Job simply does not achieve intellectual perfection, only an appreciation of its value as a prerequisite for immortality. He therefore does not experience prophecy either.

Maimonides might have replied to these objections by saying that the Book of Job is merely an allegory that teaches us valuable philosophical lessons, and therefore it need not be entirely realistic. Thus, one should not be troubled if Job achieves intellectual perfection in an unusually short span of time. This appears not to have been Ibn Tibbon's view. It seems that, according to him, there should be a close relationship between the biblical allegory and that which is feasible in reality. Therefore, Job could not have achieved intellectual perfection or prophecy.[62]

How, then, does Ibn Tibbon deal with the actual content of the last chapters of Job, in which God describes to Job the wonders of nature in order to emphasize the mystery of His ways? Maimonides' notion that Job achieves prophecy may be problematic in terms of his educational philosophy, but at least it makes sense of the biblical text. Maimonides' idea that Job's revelation consists of a lesson about the equivocal nature of divine attributes fits well with the biblical text, for according to its plain reading, the main theme of God's message to Job is his ignorance of God's ways. With Ibn Tibbon's view, the biblical text cannot be so easily explained, for if, in his reading, Job received no prophetic communication at all in the literal sense, what then is the meaning of God's remarks to him?

The difficulty in answering this question is that Ibn Tibbon has little to say about the content of God's address to Job. With the exception of his brief remarks about the non-literal meaning of the tempest, he has virtually no comment on it. Yet, upon reflection, it becomes clear that Ibn Tibbon has already implied an interpretation of God's revelation to Job. For if, as Ibn Tibbon tells us, God's address to Job is equated with the lessons he has already learned from his suffering, then all we have to do is to identify an insight in those lessons that resonates with the content of God's address. That insight is not too difficult to find. As we have seen, according to Ibn Tibbon, Job learns from Elihu of the distinction between divine and human attributes in the course of his education about the meaning of his suffering: God's ways are not like ours because God, unlike human beings, can cause people to suffer without injustice being attributed to Him. Evil does not come from God by first intention. My guess is that it is this same lesson that Ibn Tibbon would see as the philosophical meaning of God's address to Job, for this address also emphasizes the gulf between God's ways and those of man and could easily be interpreted as a reinforcement of Elihu's point. Thus, Ibn Tibbon would read God's communication to Job as reiterating a point that Elihu has already made. If this interpretation is correct, it may explain why Ibn Tibbon does not explicate the divine revelation. Since it does not add anything to Job's philosophical education, it is assumed that its meaning is transparent from his exposition of Elihu's speech.[63]

We can therefore conclude that Ibn Tibbon does indeed depart from Maimonides in his reading of the final chapters of Job. While Maimonides believes that Job achieves intellectual perfection and prophecy, Ibn Tibbon believes that he achieves neither. It is important to emphasize again that the issues here are exegetical, not philosophical. In dispute is not the nature of intellectual perfection, nor whether it leads to prophecy; on these points we can assume that Ibn Tibbon is in agreement with Maimonides. The question is whether it is plausible according to the story to suggest that Job was qualified for these achievements. What also may have been at issue, as we have suggested, is the extent to which biblical allegory must be realistic. Maimonides' position is perhaps explained by his willingness to read the Book of Job as an allegory that need not strictly reflect what is possible in reality, a position that would allow Job to accomplish what he could not in real life. By contrast, Ibn Tibbon's view perhaps emanates from his insistence that allegory should closely reflect reality, in which case Job could not have achieved the impossible. And yet, interestingly enough, in his explication of the final chapters of Job, Ibn Tibbon does not make his important departure from Maimonides explicit, even though in other instances he shows no hesitation about expressing exegetical differences with his predecessor.

As I noted at the beginning of this chapter, an important question regarding *Ma'amar Yikkavu ha-Mayim* as a whole is whether Ibn Tibbon is a commentator on Maimonides or an original thinker in his own right. That question can now be answered with respect to Ibn Tibbon's reading of Job. What emerges from my analysis is that in this section of *Ma'amar Yikkavu ha-Mayim* there seems to be a division between Ibn Tibbon the philosopher and Ibn Tibbon the exegete. In the realm of philosophical ideas, it is clear that Ibn Tibbon consistently sees himself as a faithful follower of Maimonides. At no point does he attempt to challenge or overturn what he believes to be the philosophical premises underlying Maimonides' interpretation of Job. Even in the one instance in which Ibn Tibbon appears to depart from Maimonides philosophically—the issue of immortality—we found evidence to suggest that he is merely interpreting him. It would seem, however, that Ibn Tibbon's exegesis is another matter. Here he displays originality and creativity, and he does so quite consciously. His reading of the Book of Job takes the cryptic exegetical insights provided by Maimonides—particularly in the latter's reading of Job 33—and not only makes sense of them, but also extends them to verses in the biblical text upon which Maimonides had not commented. In this way, Ibn Tibbon fills in the gaps left by Maimonides in interpreting the biblical text, with the result that in a number of respects he provides a more comprehensive understanding of the Job story. As part of this exegetical exercise, there are also a number of points about which Ibn Tibbon disagrees with Maimonides, such as his departure from him regarding Satan's two arrivals. Most noteworthy is the disagreement Ibn Tibbon has with Maimonides about the final chapters of Job. Ibn Tibbon strikes out on a most original path in suggesting that Job never achieves intellectual perfection or prophecy.[64]

Ibn Tibbon's relationship to Maimonides is illuminated by a series of general assumptions underlying Ibn Tibbon's philosophical-exegetical enterprise. As Aviezer Ravitzky has already shown, Ibn Tibbon approaches the biblical text with an elaborate theory of Jewish intellectual history. He echoes the thoughts of previous Jewish philosophers in believing that philosophy was an esoteric tradition originating with the Jews. Then he takes this theory in an original direction by giving a detailed description of how the esoteric truths of this philosophical tradition had been gradually revealed from biblical times onward in response to the circumstances of various epochs in Jewish history. Ibn Tibbon sees Maimonides' *Guide* as one link in a series of attempts to bring this tradition to light, and his own writing is an attempt to further reveal that tradition.[65]

This explains Ibn Tibbon's relationship to Maimonides in his reading of Job. On the one hand, Ibn Tibbon sees himself as having the responsibility of furthering the process of revealing the true esoteric tradition on the biblical text. It is for this reason that he draws out the esoteric meaning of the philosophical lessons in Maimonides' exposition on Job and provides a more lengthy and detailed discussion of its critical section than Maimonides had offered. Ibn Tibbon also sees the need to correct whatever errors he believes he has found in Maimonides' understanding of the biblical text, for this too is a necessary component in the process of bringing out its secrets. On the other hand, the revelation of the esoteric tradition is a process that Ibn Tibbon firmly believes should occur gradually throughout history. It for this reason that Ibn Tibbon feels the need to couch his presentation in an esoteric style that does not reveal too much.

These observations also provide insight into how Ibn Tibbon views the relationship between the Book of Job and the Torah. In Ibn Tibbon's thinking, the revelation of the esoteric tradition unfolds within the biblical text itself, with the later books of the Bible bringing out philosophical secrets concealed in its earlier parts. This, in fact, is a key principle in *Ma'amar Yikkavu ha-Mayim.* Ibn Tibbon constantly refers to texts in the prophets and the writings in order to reveal esoteric truths in the Torah. We can surmise, therefore, that in Ibn Tibbon's thinking the Book of Job reveals the true esoteric meaning of the doctrine of reward and punishment expressed in exoteric form in the Torah. While the Torah speaks of material reward and punishment, the Book of Job reveals the esoteric understanding of that doctrine. According to Ibn Tibbon, it is not just the Book of Job that performs this service. He informs us that the esoteric understanding of providence is also found in the Book of Psalms and in Malachi.[66]

Exegesis

Ibn Tibbon's reading of Job is so dependent on that of Maimonides that my analysis of the relationship between them has, in large measure, implicitly addressed the other two interfaces that are at the center of this study. With respect to the second interface, which concerns Ibn Tibbon as exegete, it should be obvious at this point that Ibn Tibbon mostly follows Maimonides when it comes to dealing with the major exegetical difficulties that the Book of Job presents. Ibn Tibbon adopts Maimonides' overall framework for understanding Job, and therefore Maimonides' solutions for those difficulties are largely preserved either explicitly or implicitly in Ibn Tibbon's exposition.

Nonetheless, Ibn Tibbon does depart from Maimonides on a number of exegetical points. The most significant of these is that Ibn Tibbon differs with Maimonides with respect to the meaning of God's revelation in the final chapters of the book. According to Maimonides, God's address to Job is understood as a necessary complement to Elihu's remarks in that it provides Job with important information about the equivocal nature of divine attributes so that Job can achieve intellectual perfection and experience psychological immunity from suffering. By contrast, in Ibn Tibbon's reading, God's revelation does not really take place; or, more accurately, it has already taken place by the time we reach the end of the book, in that God has metaphorically revealed himself to Job through his suffering. The effect of Ibn Tibbon's approach is that it places all the emphasis on Elihu as the figure who provides us with an understanding of providence, while it renders God's revelation to Job as an event possessing only minor significance. Ibn Tibbon's differences with Maimonides regarding the final chapters of Job therefore points to an important difference between them in their overall conceptions of what constitutes the center of the book. For Maimonides, Elihu and God are equally important in explaining Job's suffering, while for Ibn Tibbon, it is Elihu alone who performs that function.

Exegesis and Philosophy

With regard to the third interface, which concerns the relationship between Ibn Tibbon's exegesis and systematic philosophy, my analysis of Ibn Tibbon's relationship to Maimonides has, once again, already provided essential information. We have seen that if Ibn Tibbon intended to contribute new exegetical insights with respect to the Book of Job, he had no such interest regarding philosophy. In his reading of Job, Ibn Tibbon takes Maimonides' views on providence as a given and assumes that his reader has the very same understanding of Maimonides as his own.

Yet, even if Ibn Tibbon has no desire to be innovative with respect to philosophical ideas, my analysis shows that he unwittingly imparts an important new spin to the notion of providence. As we have seen, Ibn Tibbon's idea that the highest form of providence is immortality is probably inferred from clues in Maimonides, but I also argued that on this point Ibn Tibbon is reading a good deal more into Maimonides than can be justified. Thus, while Ibn Tibbon does not intend to be innovative with respect to philosophical ideas, in an important respect he certainly is, in that he shifts away from Maimonides' conception of providence as a subject concerned with matters of this world and moves toward the view that the proper focus of providence is the afterlife.

Tibbonian Readings of Job: Immanuel of Rome, Elijah ben Eliezer ha-Yerushalmi, and Isaac Arundi

The importance of Ibn Tibbon's reading of Job becomes evident when one examines its influence on three fourteenth-century Jewish philosophical exegetes who composed full-length commentaries on Job: Immanuel of Rome, Elijah ben Eliezer ha-Yerushalmi, and Isaac Arundi. Their commentaries on Job exist only in manuscript, and none of these works has received scholarly attention.[67] A comprehensive examination of these works is beyond the scope of the discussion here. Nonetheless, my analysis of Ibn Tibbon would not be complete without saying something about the nature and extent of his influence on them. We are, after all, concerned with the question of whether there is a tradition of interpretation of Job in medieval Jewish philosophy, and thus the question of Ibn Tibbon's influence on subsequent interpreters of Job is important. I will therefore dwell primarily on what the three commentators draw from Ibn Tibbon and save a more extensive analysis of their works for another occasion.

Of the three figures, Immanuel of Rome is the earliest. We know little about his life, but we are certain that he lived in Italy in the late thirteenth and early fourteenth centuries, a mere half-century after Ibn Tibbon. He is also the only one of our three thinkers to whom scholars have paid any substantial attention. Yet, the interest in him has been focused almost exclusively on his poetry, which is in his monumental work the *Maḥbarot*. Very little has been written about his large corpus of philosophical commentaries on the Bible.[68]

Immanuel's commentary on Job is lengthy.[69] He is one of the first figures in the school of Maimonides to provide a line-by-line commentary on the book.[70] In his opening invocation to the commentary, Immanuel tells his reader that his interpretation of the text will be based on that of Maimonides.[71] And indeed there is much truth in this. As with Ibn Tibbon, Immanuel interprets the events in the early chapters of the book in a manner similar to Maimonides. Thus, Job has moral but not intellectual perfection; Satan is representative of matter—one of the possible interpretations of Maimonides' understanding of this figure; and the various opinions attributed to Job and the three friends with whom he argues correspond, for the most part, to the schools of thought attributed to them by Maimonides.[72]

When we get to Immanuel's reading of the final chapters of Job, the major influence is more Ibn Tibbon than Maimonides—even though Ibn Tibbon is never mentioned.[73] In his introduction to the commentary, Immanuel informs us that the central theme of Elihu's remarks to Job is that immortality is the ultimate form of providence. In his reading of Job 33, Immanuel elaborates on this idea. According to Immanuel, Elihu informs Job that God communicates with human beings either by way of prophetic communication, which warns of oncoming disaster, or by physical suffering itself. Both are designed to convince the recipient that true providence consists in immortality that is achieved by intellectual perfection. All of this appears to have been inspired by Ibn Tibbon.[74] However, Immanuel appears to deviate from Ibn Tibbon in suggesting that, according to Elihu, individual providence consists not only of immortality of the intellect, but also of protection from physical harm in this world. This dimension of providence comes through in Immanuel's interpretation of Job 33. Throughout his commentary on this chapter, Immanuel argues that prophetic warnings and suffering inspire repentance, which in turn results in divine providence, which protects the recipient from oncoming danger. We therefore see a traditional element in Immanuel that we do not see in Ibn Tibbon.[75]

The dual nature of Immanuel's reading of Elihu's address also comes through in other places. For instance, in commenting on the angel who saves the suffering individual from his afflictions, Immanuel proposes two different interpretations. One is that it represents a person's past good deeds, which mitigate the divine punishment he will experience for his sins, an interpretation found in the Talmud and in Saadiah.[76] The other is that the angel represents the human intellect that "saves" a person, since it becomes immortal once it is perfected.[77] The first interpretation is clearly a traditional one, while the second is philosophical. We see the same tendency in Immanuel's interpretation of God's speech. Here again, Immanuel entertains two alternatives, one traditional, the other philosophical. Either God actually addresses Job through prophecy, or the tempest is merely a metaphor for Job's suffering. The latter alternative, as we have seen, is suggested by Ibn Tibbon.[78]

It is not entirely clear what the status is of the traditional element that Immanuel injects into his reading of the final chapters of Job. It could be that Immanuel genuinely deviates from Ibn Tibbon because he could not accept the radicalism of the latter's position. The other possibility is that Immanuel inserts the traditional element only in order to help conceal his true philosophical views, which agree with Ibn Tibbon's, and that what we have here is another example of esoteric writing.[79]

Immanuel also seems to have been aware of the difficulty discussed earlier regarding the proximity between Elihu's view, as understood by Ibn Tibbon, and that of Bildad, which is identified with that of the Mu'tazilites. I noted that these views seem to overlap in the belief that undeserved suffering helps an individual achieve reward in the afterlife. I also argued that Ibn Tibbon seems to have been conscious of this problem and in one passage makes sure to point out a key difference between the two positions.[80] That Immanuel is both aware of the problem and attempts to solve it is evident from the fact that he makes a critical change in Bildad's position as it is depicted by Maimonides. In Immanuel's reading, Bildad, instead of believing that undeserved suffering leads to reward in the afterlife, believes that it leads to reward in *this* life.[81] This clears the way for Immanuel to assert with confidence in another passage that when Elihu brings the subject of the afterlife into the discussion, he is offering a view entirely different from any of those offered by Job and his friends.[82] Undoubtedly, Immanuel alters Bildad's view so as to highlight the distinction between the latter's position and that of Elihu.[83]

Elijah ben Eliezer ha-Yerushalmi is a figure about whom we know even less than we know about Immanuel of Rome. His dates are 1320–1401; he lived in Crete; and he produced a number of works, including a commentary on Job.[84] Elijah's commentary is more a paraphrase of the biblical text than a line-by-line exegesis.[85] In terms of content, it bears an uncanny resemblance to the commentary of Immanuel. Like Immanuel, Elijah follows Maimonides more or less faithfully in his interpretation of events leading up to Elihu's speech, but when he comes to Elihu's speech itself, he adopts key elements of Ibn Tibbon's position without citing him.[86] He too believes that the central message of Elihu's address, and of the Book of Job as a whole, is that true reward consists of the immortality of the intellect.[87] Elijah also seems to follow Immanuel's lead in proposing that Elihu speaks of individual providence in the material and physical realm in addition to immortality of the intellect. While Immanuel was unclear about the source of this form of providence, Elijah explicitly ties it to the perfection of the intellect.[88] This idea helps Elijah make sense of the ending in Job, where the latter gets his wealth back and starts a new family. Having achieved intellectual perfection, Job merits these material rewards. Yet, Elijah says little about the mechanism of this manifestation of providence.[89] We are therefore left guessing, as we were with Immanuel, about whether Elijah has supplemented Ibn Tibbon's reading in order to express his own traditional leanings or is trying to conceal his agreement with Ibn Tibbon's radical views.[90]

Elijah also tampers with Bildad's opinion in a manner reminiscent of Immanuel. Like Immanuel, Elijah attributes to Bildad the belief that God inflicts suffering so as to reward individuals in this life. However, Elijah also goes in a new direction by ascribing to Bildad the view that suffering is punishment for sin, a suggestion that makes Bildad's opinion overlap that of Eliphaz.[91]

Despite the commonalties between his reading of Job and the readings of Maimonides, Ibn Tibbon, and Immanuel, Elijah says little about his sources. These thinkers are not cited by him as inspirations for his views.[92]

Isaac Arundi is a Spanish thinker who was active in the fourteenth century. He is the most obscure of the three writers under discussion here.[93] Yet, his commentary on Job is highly interesting.[94] It is a lengthy work that, like Immanuel's, is a line-by-line commentary on the biblical text. It also contains numerous digressions dealing with philosophical matters of one sort or another and cites a wide range of philosophical sources. One of its most intriguing features is that Arundi frequently attacks Gersonides' commentary on Job. To my knowledge, an attack of this kind on Gersonides is found nowhere else in medieval Jewish philosophy.

Arundi is similar to Ibn Tibbon, Immanuel of Rome, and Elijah ben Eliezer ha-Yerushalmi in that he accepts much of Maimonides' understanding of events in the early part of the book. Thus, Job is a figure with moral, not intellectual, perfection who initially believes that reward and punishment are this-worldly in character but loses his faith in this belief once he experiences suffering. Satan is representative of matter.[95] However, Arundi departs from them in his understanding of the dialogue between Job and his three friends—Eliphaz, Bildad, and Zophar. He gives a lengthy critique of Maimonides and Gersonides, who attempt to attach a different school of thought to each of the participants in the dialogue. Arundi argues that the three friends of Job share a common opinion and all believe in exactly the same traditional view of providence that Job held before he experienced his suffering.[96]

When it comes to Elihu's position, Arundi goes in a direction similar to that taken by Immanuel of Rome and Elijah ben Eliezer ha-Yerushalmi by adopting an interpretation reminiscent of that offered by Ibn Tibbon but without mentioning him by name. According to Arundi, the main thrust of Elihu's speech is that immortality of the intellect is the only form of providence. Arundi also seems to follow Ibn Tibbon in interpreting Job 33 as dealing with two types of providential communication and in proposing that the second of these is suffering, which is providential in forcing one to recognize that immortality of the intellect is true providence.[97] Arundi sticks closer to Ibn Tibbon's reading than either Immanuel or Elijah in that nowhere does he propose that according to Elihu there is individual providence in the material or physical realm. However, Arundi does deviate from Ibn Tibbon in his understanding of the first type of providential communication, suggested in Elihu's remarks. While Ibn Tibbon identifies it with prophecy, Arundi appears to identify it with simple intellectual cognition. God "communicates" to human beings in the sense that He imparts to them philosophical truths as they become educated in philosophical wisdom. Arundi is clearly referring to the natural process of cognition as it was widely understood by medieval philosophers, in which human beings perceive intelligibles because they are provided by the Active Intellect, which in turn receives them from God.[98]

Arundi also seems to follow Ibn Tibbon in rejecting the notion that God actually spoke to Job through prophecy. However, instead of arguing, as Ibn Tibbon does, that God's communication to Job consisted of the suffering He caused him, Arundi identifies it with the other type of providential communication, which consists of simple intellectual cognition. That is, by the end of the story, Job's revelation was only in being sufficiently educated in philosophical matters as to understand intellectually how divine providence works.[99]

There are also indications that, like Ibn Tibbon's God, Arundi's God is impersonal. Arundi never openly declares a position on this issue, but when all is said and done, there is no need for a personal God to perform the providential functions that Arundi attributes to Him. Most telling is the absence of any suggestion that there is individual providence in this world.[100]

The three commentaries I have examined are united by a common pattern. Maimonides seems to have been the major influence on all three in the interpretation of the early and middle chapters of Job, though in the final chapters it is Ibn Tibbon's influence that seems to have been more decisive. Given that all the commentators are agreed that the final chapters contain the book's central message, Ibn Tibbon's influence here is highly significant. What is perhaps most important is that it seems to be Ibn Tibbon's influence that inspires the three commentators to make the issue of immortality of the intellect a focal point in the final message of Job and to view it as the highest expression of providence.

The three commentaries do not adopt the views of Maimonides and Ibn Tibbon without qualification, nor are they identical to each other. Each modifies and supplements the views of his predecessors with his own insights. More significant is that Immanuel and Elijah appear to inject a traditional element in their readings of the final chapters of Job, one not found in Ibn Tibbon's commentary, by proposing that there is physical providence in this world in addition to immortality—though it is not clear whether either thinker was sincere in making this suggestion. It is only Isaac Arundi who seems to accept the radicalism of Ibn Tibbon's reading in an unqualified manner. Nonetheless, in all three commentators, Ibn Tibbon's influence is unmistakable. My analysis therefore provides a convincing example of Ibn Tibbon's pivotal position as mediator between Maimonides and later philosophical interpreters, a position scholars of medieval Jewish philosophy have only begun to appreciate.

Ibn Tibbon has emerged here as an interpreter who sees himself primarily as a commentator on Maimonides, rather than as an independent thinker in his own right. It is also evident that despite his dependence on Maimonides, Ibn Tibbon sometimes comes up with insights that are very much his own. These include a host of ideas that supplement, but also at times overturn, Maimonides' understanding of the biblical text. Most significant is Ibn Tibbon's notion that the Book of Job is designed to teach us that providence is to be equated with immortality and that there is no individual providence in this world that guards our physical well-being. While Ibn Tibbon may have believed that this is how Maimonides interpreted Job, in truth what he has done is develop a new understanding of the book, one that would have a significant impact on a number of subsequent Jewish philosophers.

5

Zeraḥiah Ḥen

Zeraḥiah ben Isaac ben She'alti'el Ḥen is the first Jewish philosopher after Ibn Tibbon to produce an interpretation of Job. Of his life we know little. He was born in the early decades of the thirteenth century in Barcelona, but we have no precise date. At some point he relocated to Rome, where, in the last quarter of the century, he became a highly honored teacher of Maimonides' philosophical thought.[1] Zeraḥiah composed commentaries on Proverbs and Job and two commentaries on the *Guide*, only parts of which have survived. He also engaged in lengthy correspondences regarding philosophical matters with two Jewish philosophers, Hillel of Verona and Judah ben Solomon, and these correspondences have been preserved. A substantial portion of Zeraḥiah's writings has been published, but none in critical editions. These writings include the commentary on Job, the commentary on Proverbs, the correspondence with Hillel of Verona, and a section from the correspondence with Judah ben Solomon. The rest remains in manuscript.[2]

In his works, Zeraḥiah connects himself quite explicitly to the Maimonidean-Tibbonian school of philosophical exegesis. While Zeraḥiah cites a wide range of sources in his writings, he generally does not cite anyone favorably except for Maimonides and Ibn Tibbon.[3] As for his philosophical orientation, Zeraḥiah's thought is firmly rooted in the same Islamic philosophical thinkers who inspired Maimonides and Ibn Tibbon, thinkers whom Zeraḥiah was able to read in the original due to his familiarity with Arabic. His writings display little influence from Christian scholasticism, which had begun to penetrate Jewish intellectual circles in Italy during this period.[4]

Zeraḥiah excited interest in modern scholarship as early as the nineteenth century, attracting the attention of scholars of no less stature than Moritz Steinschneider and Abraham Geiger, among others. The scholars of this period tended to focus almost exclusively on the historical aspects of Zeraḥiah's life and writings.[5] It is only in recent times that there has been interest in Zeraḥiah as a philosopher and exegete. Groundbreaking in this regard is the scholarship of Aviezer Ravitzky, who has analyzed various aspects of Zeraḥiah's philosophical thought and has attempted to locate it within the Maimonidean-Tibbonian school.[6]

Zeraḥiah's *Commentary on the Book of Job*, which appeared a little more than fifty years after Samuel ibn Tibbon's death, is the first exposition on the entirety of Job written by a Jewish philosopher in the Maimonidean school, and it is the first such commentary in medieval Jewish philosophy since that of Saadiah. It was published over a century ago by Israel Schwartz in *Tikvat Enosh*, a two-volume collection of a number of medieval Jewish commentaries on Job.[7] Schwartz's edition was based on a manuscript found in the Bayerische Staatsbibliothek in Munich.[8] Shortly after its publication, questions were raised about the integrity of this edition. In a review of Schwartz's work, Steinschneider took note of the fact that it was incomplete. In comparing the printed text to the original manuscript, Steinschneider pointed out a number of places where Schwartz had left out phrases or entire sentences without any indication to the reader that material was being omitted, nor any explanation of why it had been excised. Steinschneider was at a loss to explain these omissions.[9]

A comparison between the printed edition and the original manuscript bears out Steinschneider's observations and shows the extent of the problem. On almost every page of the commentary, Schwartz appears to have edited out phrases and sentences from the original manuscript that seemed to him repetitive or superfluous. In most instances, this editorial activity is of little consequence to the meaning of the text. Schwartz often chose to omit introductory sentences at the beginning of paragraphs or concluding sentences at the end of paragraphs, but in a number of cases, he unwittingly omits portions of the commentary critical for our understanding of it.[10] It goes without saying that Schwartz's editorial activity greatly diminishes the utility of his edition for scholarly research. In this chapter all citations of Zeraḥiah's commentary will therefore be from the Munich manuscript.[11]

One other difficulty with the text of the commentary is that, as I have shown elsewhere, Zeraḥiah appears to have composed two versions of it, with the later version differing from the earlier one in revealing more of Zeraḥiah's esoteric views on philosophical matters.[12] This observation does not affect my discussion. It merely underscores the importance of basing any analysis on the later and more comprehensive version of the commentary, and that is what I have done. The Munich manuscript I will be using for the present discussion represents the later version.

My analysis of Zeraḥiah's commentary on Job will be greatly aided by his correspondence with Judah ben Solomon. This correspondence predates his Job commentary and devotes a lengthy discussion to the Book of Job.[13] Moreover, a number of key philosophical portions of the Job commentary are drawn verbatim from this correspondence.[14]

Zeraḥiah's exposition on Job is much easier to read than that of Maimonides or Ibn Tibbon. This is not to say that Zeraḥiah's commentary is free of esoteric discourse. As we shall see, Zeraḥiah conceals philosophical truths, as Maimonides and Ibn Tibbon did. However, most of Zeraḥiah's presentation is clear and straightforward in a way that the presentations of his two predecessors are not, and when he does indulge in esotericism, he is often considerate enough to alert his reader that he is doing so. Also, his esoteric discourse does not display the type of dense and difficult writing that we saw in Maimonides and Ibn Tibbon, writing in which practically every line must be closely scrutinized to decipher its meaning. While we will certainly have to read Zeraḥiah's commentary carefully in order to understand its concealed doctrines, its esoteric passages are easier to penetrate than those found in the commentaries of his predecessors.

The structure of my discussion of Zeraḥiah will be similar to that used in my previous analysis. I will begin by outlining the contents of Zeraḥiah's reading of Job, with special attention being given to deciphering its esoteric doctrines. I will then proceed to an examination of the three interfaces around which I have structured this study.

The Commentary on Job

Zeraḥiah opens the introductory portion of his commentary with several lines of poetic verse in which he places his composition in the context of a larger mission of enlightening his fellow Jews about philosophical wisdom. Comparing the children of Israel to sheep lost on the "hills of wisdom," Zeraḥiah sees himself as responsible for bringing the stray sheep back to their true home in philosophical learning. Having just composed a philosophical commentary on Proverbs for this purpose, Zeraḥiah declares that he will now write a similar commentary on the Book of Job.[15]

Later on in his introduction, Zeraḥiah further clarifies the nature of his mission. He tells us that he was compelled to write commentaries on Job and Proverbs because all previous expositions on these books were written according to the *peshat,* or plain sense, not according to philosophical wisdom. Zeraḥiah points out that he had no desire to compose a commentary on Ecclesiastes or the Song of Songs because other sages of his generation had already done so—an obvious reference to Samuel ibn Tibbon and his son Moses, who had, respectively, composed philosophical commentaries on these biblical books.[16]

Nevertheless, in his attempt to come up with a philosophical reading of Job, Zeraḥiah does not see himself starting from scratch. He declares his intention to rely heavily on Maimonides' discussion of Job in the *Guide.*[17] In his introduction, Zeraḥiah makes clear that he will not always cite Maimonides because he is writing for those who are already familiar with the *Guide*'s esoteric truths.[18] He also emphasizes that when he discusses Maimonides' views, he will refrain from revealing too much for fear that such wisdom will fall into the wrong hands. He therefore tells us that if he mentions "a secret or secrets, it will be by way of hint (*remez*) or allusion."[19] In short, Zeraḥiah intends to follow Maimonides both with respect to his ideas and his style of discourse.

Elsewhere in his introduction, Zeraḥiah elaborates on the failings of previous commentators on Job. Special censure is reserved for Ibn Ezra, David Kimḥi, and Naḥmanides, who are chided not only for their inability to provide a philosophical reading of the Book of Job in their commentaries, but also for misunderstanding its *peshat*, or plain meaning. Their interpretations are therefore frequently criticized by Zeraḥiah in the course of the commentary on the biblical text itself.[20] The harshest and most frequent condemnations are reserved for Naḥmanides, who is mercilessly scolded throughout the commentary for his ignorance of matters of philosophy and science and for his erroneous readings of the *peshat*.[21]

In sum, Zeraḥiah characterizes his commentary as a project intended to break new ground in the interpretation of Job. It is meant to further the enterprise set forth by members of the Tibbon family, who had used the exegetical techniques of Maimonides to compose full-length commentaries on books of the Bible but had yet to produce a commentary on Job.[22]

In his introduction, Zeraḥiah also lays out his views on the general features of the Book of Job. The most important discussion of these matters—and perhaps the most original contribution in Zeraḥiah's reading of Job as a whole—is his treatment of the question of whether the Book of Job is an allegory. This topic is discussed primarily in Zeraḥiah's introduction to his commentary, but it is also dealt with at numerous points in the commentary itself. As we have seen, in the opening lines of his discussion of Job in the *Guide*, Maimonides had expressed the view that the Book of Job was an allegory, but he said little to justify that position. Zeraḥiah, as a faithful follower of Maimonides, endorses this view but goes much further by providing a lengthy series of arguments to support it.

Zeraḥiah's proofs for the allegorical character of the story are not presented in systematic fashion but are scattered throughout the commentary. Yet, since the same type of reasoning often underlies a number of different proofs, they can be organized according to the following categories:

1. *Lack of historical detail.* According to Zeraḥiah, the allegorical nature of the Job story is indicated by the fact that key historical details are missing. Zeraḥiah points out that we are not told about who Job was or when he lived, oversights that suggest such a character never existed.[23] Similarly, when Satan inflicts calamities on Job, we are not told what day or year they occurred. This indicates that the author meant the story to be representative of events that occur at all times, in all places, and to all people.[24]
2. *Contrived names of places and persons.* Some names and places are

contrived in order to reflect back on one or another aspect of the story, a feature characteristic of allegories. Zeraḥiah adopts Maimonides' view that *'Uẓ*, the place where Job lived, is related to the Hebrew *'eẓah*, "idea" or "insight," since the Book of Job is supposed to prod the reader to reflect on the philosophical lessons underlying the story.[25] Zeraḥiah also adopts the view alluded to in rabbinic sources that Job's name, *Iyyov*, is related to the Hebrew *oyev*, or "enemy."[26] As Zeraḥiah argues, the name is reflective of Job's situation. He is despised by God; he is despised by the forces of nature and by human beings who do him and his loved ones harm; and he is despised by his friends, who criticize him rather than comfort him.[27]

3. *Unusual descriptions of persons, places, or animals.* There are several examples of this tendency in the Book of Job, which again provide evidence of its allegorical character. The numbers of Job's children and flocks of animals are all presented in pairs adding up to multiples of ten: seven sons and three daughters, seven thousand sheep and three thousand camels, and five hundred oxen and five hundred she-asses.[28] Zeraḥiah proposes that these numbers are contrived so as to be representative of the average numbers of children and possessions that a wealthy individual would have.

   Zeraḥiah also pays attention to the fact that Job is described by God at the beginning of the story in superlative terms: "there is no one like him on earth" (Job 1:8). Here, too, Zeraḥiah claims that the description is evidence of the story's allegorical character, for it is unlikely that there would be no other person in the world with Job's qualities. While Job has virtues, he is not so exceptional that he should merit such praise.[29] Here Zeraḥiah seems to be making the astute observation that allegories—as well as related genres such as parables, fables, and fairy tales—often have characters that are described in unrealistic and exaggerated terms. Finally, Zeraḥiah makes note of the exotic, fictional beasts mentioned in God's speech, such as the Leviathan. These creatures are also characteristic of allegories. Such animals, Zeraḥiah explains, are designed to capture the attention of the reader and inspire him to explore the inner meaning of the story.[30]

4. *Unusual events.* In addition to the unlikely descriptions of people and animals in the Book of Job, strange occurrences also attest to the allegorical quality of the story. Zeraḥiah specifically cites the destruction of Job's flock of seven thousand sheep by fire falling from the sky as an event too incredible to be an actual historical occurrence. Zeraḥiah adds that the other two disasters that befall Job are far more believable, and that the author placed the plausible and unlikely events side by side deliberately. The unusual events will inspire the philosophically sophisticated reader not to read the story as historical truth and to search for its esoteric message. The plausible events will convince the unsophisticated reader to accept the story at face value.[31] Zera-

ḥiah also points to the ending of the story as another unlikely series of events and thus further evidence of the book being an allegory. That Job should have his wealth restored to him and begin a new family stretches the credulity of the reader.[32]

5. *Literary structure.* Zeraḥiah cites one argument regarding the structure of the dialogue as evidence that the story is allegorical. The number of speeches in the Book of Job is precisely twenty-six, which corresponds to the number of premises required to prove God's existence, according to Maimonides. It is also the numerical equivalent of the Tetragrammaton. These correspondences, Zeraḥiah believes, could not be mere coincidence and again attest to the allegorical nature of the story.[33]
6. *The uniform style of the dialogue.* Zeraḥiah argues that the literary style of all the speakers in Job is the same. It is therefore unlikely that they were historical individuals, since one would expect their speaking styles to differ from one another. Zeraḥiah cites as proof of his point that each of the biblical books of the prophets is written in the distinctive style of its author. It is thus clear to Zeraḥiah that one author composed the speeches in the Book of Job, and that they are not the product of actual historical individuals.[34]
7. *Philosophical difficulties regarding God.* Finally, as evidence for the allegorical quality of the Job story, Zeraḥiah points out a number of philosophical difficulties, most of which revolve around the classic problem of anthropomorphic representations of God and His activity. Pretty much all of these difficulties are connected to the conversation between God and Satan. Zeraḥiah cites the implausibility of a number of features in the interaction between the two, in particular the notion that God asks Satan where he has been, as if He were ignorant of his whereabouts, and that God would allow Himself to be convinced by Satan to cause an innocent man to suffer. Such events are patently absurd from a philosophical standpoint and again indicate that the Job story is fiction and must contain a deeper meaning.[35]

In the introduction to his commentary, Zeraḥiah shares one other insight regarding the question of allegory that should be mentioned. He asks why the author of the Book of Job does not openly inform us that the story is an allegory. Two explanations are provided:

> The first reason is that it is very much the custom among all sages of the world from our nation and from other nations to hide divine secrets from the masses. . . . The second reason is that if the author revealed all the matters of this book with absolute clarity and said that it is in truth an allegory, most people, or all of them, would run away from it and would deride the message of the book and the rest of its content. This author would do himself evil instead of

> good, and harm would result in that the book would be forgotten and would not be found today among people.[36]

Zeraḥiah explains that first it is customary for all nations to use allegory as a means to hide philosophical secrets.[37] Second, if the author were to reveal that the story is allegory, people would deride it and attack its author, with the result that the story would soon be lost.

It is not entirely clear what Zeraḥiah is referring to with his second reason. Why would people have such a negative reaction to the story if they knew that it was an allegory? Zeraḥiah cannot be alluding to the prospect that the esoteric truths, once revealed, would offend the traditional sensibilities of the common reader. That fear is already addressed in Zeraḥiah's first explanation. Zeraḥiah must therefore be referring to something different here.

What Zeraḥiah means can be appreciated by looking at a passage that appears at the end of the commentary, in which he attempts to explain why the rewards that are given to Job at the very end of the book are described in such detail. Zeraḥiah provides two explanations, the second of which is of interest to us. According to that explanation, the details of Job's rewards are meant to ensure that the masses will believe the story actually occurred and not suspect that it is an allegory, for by describing the rewards that Job receives in great detail, the traditional reader will be convinced of their veracity. This ploy is needed because, as Zeraḥiah puts it, "the masses run away from allegories and only want that which is according to its literal meaning and plain sense in all matters."[38] What Zeraḥiah reveals here is that the masses have disdain for allegory as a genre. They are interested only in stories that can be read as literal truth and have no patience for exploring deeper layers of meaning that they might contain. It would seem that it is this point that explains Zeraḥiah's second reason for not telling us that it is an allegory. It is not just that the masses may have trouble understanding or accepting the inner message of Job; they are fundamentally uninterested in *any* inner message that lies beneath the plain sense of the text.

Another issue that occupies Zeraḥiah in the introduction to his commentary is the identity of the author of Job. He believes that the Book of Job, unlike most other books of the Bible, fails to identify its author for reasons similar to those that explain why the book does not identify itself as an allegory:

> For these reasons as well, it was agreed upon and recommended [that the Book of Job] not mention explicitly the name of its author. For it was right and fitting that the other books of the Bible written and spoken with the Divine Spirit (*ruaḥ ha-kodesh*) mention the name of their author in them and the time that those words were communicated . . . for no one is allowed to dispute the true words of God, may He be blessed, or His intention commanded by one of His servants and messengers. But it is not proper for one to write down the time or the name of the author for something which is said or composed in order to express a certain opinion or to set

> forth a certain intention, since the intention comes from human consensus alone, even though it [i.e., the writing of that intention] is favored by God, may He be blessed, as one of the good endeavors and human activities desired by God, may He be blessed. Therefore, since the Book of Job did not clarify to us that its content came from the Mighty One, the author was not permitted, nor did he agree, to mention the name of the author except[39] by way of a greatly hidden hint, for in this manner—that is, by way of concealment—it tells us who the author was even though it did not explain this openly.[40]

This is an intriguing passage, though some of its ideas are not entirely clear. Zeraḥiah claims that biblical books produced by prophetic communication will cite the name of their author because it lends authority to the communication in that "no one can dispute the true words of God" or "His servants and messengers." Zeraḥiah goes on to explain that those biblical books that are not the product of prophecy, but merely express a human viewpoint, do not report the name of the author or the time they were written because in such instances what the author is saying is not authoritative.

What Zeraḥiah seems to be telling us is that in instances in which the prophet imparts a message emanating only from his own intellect, he refrains from identifying himself in order to be protected from the attacks of those ignorant in matters of philosophical learning, who are liable to criticize him for not conveying a divinely given message. That this is Zeraḥiah's intention follows from the fact that these thoughts are presented as reflections continuous with his previous speculations about why the Book of Job does not identify itself as allegory. Zeraḥiah explains the latter phenomenon by arguing that the author is protecting himself from the attacks of those ignorant in philosophical learning. It would seem, therefore, that the same explanation accounts for the author not announcing his identity.

In the continuation of the passage just cited, Zeraḥiah claims that the author of Job can nonetheless be identified from certain hints within the text:

> Indeed, from what can be understood from the subject-matter of the book we must say and believe that Moses wrote his book [i.e., the Torah] and the Book of Job. You already know that our rabbis said explicitly that Moses wrote his book and the Book of Job.[41] . . . The difference between the two books is that the book of Moses our teacher [i.e., the Torah] was written and composed by the Divine Spirit and from the Mighty One while the Book of Job was written and composed[42] from Moses's mind and from the abundance of his wisdom. He intended to inform [us] in it [about] beliefs regarding providence. It is also possible that he composed it from the Divine Will which emanated from Him, may He be blessed, like the other[43] books of the Prophets that were written and composed with the Divine Spirit.[44]

Zeraḥiah adopts the rabbinic view that it was Moses who composed the Book of Job. He goes on to provide evidence for this position by pointing to parallels between the structure of Job and the Torah. He cites the view of Maimonides that one cannot achieve proper knowledge of ethics and metaphysics without first knowing natural science.[45] That is the reason that the Torah begins with the creation story and the story of the Garden of Eden, which teach all the basic lessons in natural science, while the rest of the Torah consists of historical narrative and legal prescriptions that address the areas of ethics and divine science. The Book of Job is built on the same pattern in that the inner philosophical meaning of the divine beings and Satan, who appear in the opening chapters, concerns matters of natural science, while the rest of the book deals with providence, the knowledge of which is necessary for a proper understanding of divine science and ethics.[46]

The most interesting point that emerges from Zeraḥiah's discussion of authorship is that he places the Book of Job in a category of works that are not the product of prophecy. Zeraḥiah never explains how he arrives at this conclusion, but it is most likely that he is simply responding to the dialogical format of Job, a quality that marks it off from all other books in the Bible. This seems to have convinced Zeraḥiah that the Book of Job was the product of human philosophical reasoning, as opposed to other biblical books, which are presented in more apodictic form.[47] But whatever the reasoning behind Zeraḥiah's view, the radicalness of his position should not be lost. He is stating quite clearly that the Book of Job is the product of human wisdom and not revelation.[48]

Let us now examine how Zeraḥiah deals with the story line and dialogue in Job. Zeraḥiah's assessment of the figure of Job as the story begins is very positive. He enthusiastically embraces the praise for Job's ethical and religious qualities presented in the opening verses of the book.[49] It is noteworthy that despite Zeraḥiah's strong ties to Maimonides, he says nothing here or elsewhere about Job having intellectual deficiencies. As we shall later see, Zeraḥiah does, in fact, support that view, though he does not say so explicitly.

Zeraḥiah has a good deal to say about Satan and the divine beings. The divine beings are representative of the natural forms, while Satan is representative of matter, which is responsible for all human suffering.[50] These associations should be familiar to us. That the divine beings represent the natural forms is a variation on the notion entertained by a number of commentators on Maimonides, according to which the divine beings symbolize generative forces of some kind—though Zeraḥiah does not explain why he has singled out only the natural forms here. That Satan is representative of matter is, as already noted, one of a number of possible readings of Maimonides' interpretation of this figure, even if it is one I did not accept.[51]

Zeraḥiah adds an interesting twist to these Maimonidean formulations in connecting them to Job's wife. She enters the story just after Job experiences his suffering and encourages him to "blaspheme God and die" (Job 2:9). Zeraḥiah comments on her advice to Job by claiming that she, like Satan, is an allegorical representation of matter, which is the cause of suffering and death.

Her negative role is symbolized by the fact that she is not mentioned at the beginning of the story when the text enumerates the members of Job's family and possessions, and that she enters the story only to convince him to curse God, an action which merits the death penalty. Thus, she is the symbol of matter, which causes affliction and is responsible for death. Moreover, Zeraḥiah gives us insight into the parallel between the Garden of Eden story and the Job story alluded to earlier.[52] Just as Eve tempts Adam to eat from the Tree of Knowledge, thereby causing him to be punished with mortality, so Job's wife tempts him to curse God so that he will die. In both instances, the female, representing matter, attempts to bring death on the male, who represents form.[53]

Zeraḥiah also informs us here that both Satan and Job's wife are metaphors for the evil inclination, a motif Zeraḥiah seems to identify with the imagination. Zeraḥiah bases his view on Resh Lakish's Talmudic dictum that Satan, the evil inclination, and the angel of death are all one and the same, a dictum that had been central in Maimonides' discussion of Satan as well. For Zeraḥiah, the identification of Satan with the imagination is a second and alternative layer of interpretation alongside the association of Satan with matter. Furthermore, Zeraḥiah indicates that the two readings are connected for "whether the wife of Job is a metaphor for the evil inclination and Satan is a metaphor for matter, or Satan is a metaphor for the evil inclination and Job's wife [a metaphor] for matter, it all amounts to the same thing."[54] Zeraḥiah seems to be arguing here that since the imagination is rooted in matter in that it is a physical faculty, both matter and the imagination can be symbolized by the same metaphor: woman or Satan.[55]

The association of Satan with the evil inclination is developed more extensively in Zeraḥiah's correspondence with Judah ben Solomon. There Zeraḥiah reiterates the view that the divine beings are representative of the natural forms and Satan is representative of matter. But in a later portion of his discussion, Zeraḥiah cites a lengthy passage from his commentary on the *Guide of the Perplexed* dealing with Maimonides' discussion of Job—a section not preserved in any of the manuscripts of that commentary—and in that discussion, Zeraḥiah interprets the entire portion of the prologue in Job dealing with the divine beings and Satan according to psychological processes. The divine beings represent the good inclination, or the intelligibles (*sikhliyyot*), while Satan represents the evil inclination, or conventional truths (*mefursamot*). It would appear that the intelligibles represent the content of the intellect, while the conventional truths are the content of the imagination. Thus, in this correspondence, not only do we get a better explanation of how the divine beings and Satan are related to psychological processes, but we also see more clearly that Zeraḥiah attaches two fully developed layers of allegory to these figures: the motifs of form and matter alongside those of intellect and imagination.[56]

There is little to say about Zeraḥiah's interpretation of the dialogue between Job and his three friends—Eliphaz, Bildad, and Zophar. Zeraḥiah closely follows Maimonides by attributing to the four figures precisely the same schools of thought that Maimonides did and interpreting their discussion as a debate between those viewpoints. Thus, Job represents Aristotle; Eliphaz, the view of the Torah; Bildad, the Mu'talizites; and Zophar, the Ash'arites. These correspondences are laid out in detail in Zeraḥiah's introduction to the commentary.[57]

What is noteworthy about Zeraḥiah's commentary on this portion of the book is that he maintains his highly positive assessment of Job. Zeraḥiah consistently praises Job for the patience he displays in the wake of his afflictions and goes so far as to say that Job's behavior serves as a model for the proper reaction to suffering. This high estimation of Job's conduct in the course of the dialogue is first expressed in a passage in Zeraḥiah's introduction to the commentary, where he asks why the Book of Job was named after Job. Zeraḥiah gives two explanations, the first of which is of interest to us. According to this explanation, the Book of Job was named after Job because of the remarkable patience he displayed in the face of his ordeal, a patience that should serve as inspiration to everyone who deals with suffering.[58]

Zeraḥiah is well aware that his positive image of Job is potentially tarnished by Job's expressions of anger and impatience toward his friends and toward God at various points of the dialogue. Yet, Zeraḥiah is steadfast in his positive portrayal of Job. In the passage just cited, Zeraḥiah softens Job's first expression of rage, in which he curses the day of his birth, by arguing that this imprecation is innocuous since it is a curse directed at a duration of time that has no real existence.[59] But an even more important statement about Job's anger is found in Zeraḥiah's commentary on the first verse of the book. There he asks why Job is described as one who "feared God" if he is so critical of God after experiencing suffering. Zeraḥiah answers with the claim that there is no inconsistency between the text's description of Job's good qualities and his later criticisms of God, because the latter do not emanate from anger or rebellion but from genuine simplicity and innocence. As one devoid of philosophical learning, Job simply does not understand why he has suffered and therefore protests against God.[60]

Zeraḥiah also defends Job against Eliphaz's accusations in chapter 22, which specify a number of serious crimes that Job has committed:

> You know that your wickedness is great,
> And your iniquities have no limit.
> You exact pledges from your fellows without reason,
> And leave them naked, stripped of their clothes;
> You do not give the thirsty water to drink;
> You deny bread to the hungry.
> The land belongs to the strong;
> The privileged occupy it.
> You have sent away widows empty-handed;
> The strength of the fatherless is broken. (Job 22:5–9)

Zeraḥiah complains that previous commentators have used this passage as proof that Job is indeed wicked and worthy of punishment. He understands Eliphaz quite differently. In Zeraḥiah's reading, what Eliphaz is arguing is that

Job is a sinner, but only in comparison to God, before whom all material beings are sinners. Job's virtues as described in the opening verses of the story therefore remain true relative to other human beings.[61]

Zeraḥiah must also deal with the fact that at various points in the dialogue Job appears to address God as a personal Being. In Zeraḥiah's reading, Job represents Aristotle, who does not believe in such a deity. Zeraḥiah meets this challenge by claiming that Job speaks of God as a personal Being only for the sake of argument with his friends. That is, Job temporarily adopts the position that God is involved in the world only for the sake of pointing out its inconsistencies.[62]

The most important philosophical remarks in Zeraḥiah's commentary on Job are to be found, not surprisingly, in his handling of Elihu's address. Zeraḥiah faithfully follows Maimonides in viewing Elihu as the figure holding the correct position on providence and in focusing on Job 33 as the key chapter in his address. It is here that Zeraḥiah's presentation also becomes more difficult to follow, because he adopts a more esoteric style of discourse in order to conceal the central message in Job.

Zeraḥiah gives a summary of his philosophical understanding of Elihu's address at the beginning of his commentary on chapter 32, the chapter in the story in which Elihu first appears. Zeraḥiah begins:

> The opinion of Elihu, which we said in our introduction we might possibly discuss here, is not an opinion familiar to all learned individuals, only the elite among them. For this reason the Rabbi [i.e., Maimonides] did not explain the opinion of Elihu as he explained the opinion of Job and the opinion of his friends.
>
> Listen to the explication of this matter. Know that without a doubt the subject-matter of [the speech of] Elihu has within it[63] an inner meaning and secret regarding the secrets of providence and that his opinion was the most excellent of the opinions [in the dialogue], for it is said of him that he was more perfect and more wise than his friends.[64] He inclined toward the opinion of the philosophers who believe in providence over the species, not providence over individuals, except in one respect.[65] That is, if a person was exceedingly perfect he would experience divine providence,[66] but not at all times; only three times, for instance. This was [the meaning of] the intercession of the angel. That is to say, by means of that Active Intellect which is called an angel which is [associated] with that perfect man, he will achieve the attainment of that prophecy which comes from divine providence over him. But this [does] not [continue] forever. Therefore, [Elihu] spoke about the subject of prophecy and its great preciousness, that it comes in a dream when sleep descends upon people, because the nature [of prophecy] is not commonplace (*mefursam*) as with other ongoing natural events that never cease to be so according to their custom and nature. He connected this opinion with a second matter and that is the continuousness[67] of na-

> ture.[68] That is, he spoke about natural matters such as earthquakes and thunder and rain and the blowing of winds and many other natural matters.[69] All of this was to reveal his opinion that everything goes according to the nature of existence and if there is anything that acts outside of its nature once or twice, it is not common[70] but [occurs] only infrequently and with great difficulty.[71]

Zeraḥiah opens his interpretation of Job 33 by informing us that Elihu essentially supports the view of the philosophers according to which there is providence over the species, not over individuals. However, Elihu goes on to say that there are human beings who can experience individual providence, which is identified with the capacity for prophecy, and that such providence comes to those with "perfection"—an obvious reference to perfection of the intellect. The angel in Elihu's speech, to which Maimonides and Ibn Tibbon had drawn attention, is interpreted here as a reference to the Active Intellect, through which prophetic communications are imparted. Elihu tells us that the intercession of this angel occurs only two or three times because prophecy is difficult to achieve. Elihu then provides descriptions of natural phenomena in order to drive home the point that most events in the world proceed in accordance with regular natural processes and prophecy, by contrast, is exceedingly rare.

In the continuation of the same passage, Zeraḥiah provides what appears to be another interpretation of chapter 33:

> It is also my opinion that the matter of the sick person which [Elihu] mentioned in this story is an allegory for the sick soul which for so long a time is lacking perfection in the intellectual and ethical virtues which are in general the two great virtues the content of which is known. But when a person is perfect, then he will cognize what he did not cognize before his soul was healed from its illness and he will cognize the truths in their degrees. . . . That cognition which is given providentially from Him, may He be blessed, is called the intercession of the angel by which a man is perfect and is saved from eternal death. This was the matter about which Elihu said it is not common and [does] not [occur] in all people except "one in a thousand" (Job 23:3) for example, since the nature of existence requires this.[72]

In this cryptic passage Zeraḥiah seems to be reading Job 33 in an entirely different manner. The focus here is the description of the "sick person." As we may recall, according to a plain reading of Elihu's remarks, the person who experiences prophetic communication from God in a dream is also "reproved by pains on his bed" (Job 33:15) and is afflicted to the point of death before the angel comes along and rescues him.[73] According to Zeraḥiah, the second portion of the passage describing the sick person is an allegory for the person who lacks ethical and intellectual perfection. Such an individual will be healed from his illness when "he will cognize what he did not cognize previously," an allusion to intellectual perfection. At this point, he will be "saved from eternal death"—that is, he will achieve immortality. The intercession of the angel refers to the receiving of intellectual cognitions that result in intellectual perfection. What Zeraḥiah seems to be saying is that the angel is again the Active Intellect, but here its providential activity involves the imparting of cognitions leading to immortality rather than prophecy. Moreover, the notion that the angel comes to the rescue two or three times seems now to be interpreted to mean that it is immortality, not prophecy, that is an exceedingly rare phenomenon.[74]

All of this is rather confusing. What seems reasonably certain is that in Zeraḥiah's reading there are two types of providence that Elihu introduces: prophecy and immortality. However, Zeraḥiah gives no insight into how they are connected. A possible interpretation is that they are simply different forms of individual providence. Prophecy provides providential protection in this life, while immortality guarantees perdurance in the next.

A difficulty in figuring out Zeraḥiah's overall direction here is that he never explains how prophecy is providential. Zeraḥiah's most explicit statement about this issue is found in his comments on Job 33:15–17, where Elihu refers to prophetic communication. The crux of Zeraḥiah's position is stated in the following formulation: "God, may He be blessed, reveals to those who achieve His providence over them what human beings do and what they think, and He negates what He desires [to negate] and turns away what He wants [to turn away]."[75] Zeraḥiah's formulation is not terribly clear. He never explains what purpose is served by God's revealing to prophets "what human beings do and what they think," nor what he means when he says that God "negates what He desires [to negate] and turns away what He wants [to turn away]."

There is another possible translation for this passage, one that gives it a different spin. The subject of the last clause in the passage just cited may be the prophet, not God. Hence, the passage would read, "God, may He be blessed, reveals to those who achieve His providence over them what human beings do and what they think, and he [i.e., the prophet] negates what he desires [to negate] and turns away what he wants [to turn away]."[76] According to this reading, Zeraḥiah is endorsing a naturalistic conception of providence in which prophecy informs an individual about future events and allows him to circumvent harm foreordained in the natural order—a view not uncommon in medieval Jewish philosophy. Unfortunately, Zeraḥiah's ambiguous wording does not allow us to discern which of the translations is correct.[77]

At the end of his commentary on Job 33, Zeraḥiah goes on to explain the rest of Elihu's remarks in Job 34–37:

> "Pay heed, Job, and hear me" (Job 33:31): [Elihu] said that he should listen to him with respect to the things that remained for him to tell Job. These are the matters contained in the other responses [of Elihu] in which he tells him about natural things and their activities in the world, after he mentioned the [divine] governance over men in the world, their events, and their different actions. All of these

> things come from the power of God and His wisdom over which no other being has power and [which no being] can comprehend in any respect. . . . Elihu wanted to say here that if Job would understand his words which he would speak regarding these matters . . . he would know the ways of God, His guidance, and His wisdom regarding His creatures, and it would become clear to him from them that all of his arguments with the Creator were vain arguments and that no human being should judge the ways of God or His governance and that he should not object to them, since His wisdom is not our wisdom, and His governance is not our governance. There is no relationship whatsoever between what exists in Him and anything that exists in us. . . . Elihu alluded to this whole matter in mentioning to him the things which come into existence in the atmosphere, meteorological phenomena, their activities and movements, and in teaching him that the transgression was Job's in voicing objection to God and in his consternation regarding His actions in this world and His governance over His creatures which does not proceed according to our order, and [in his consternation regarding] the success of the sinful person and the failure of the righteous person and many other matters in this world regarding which man has consternation since they proceed according to an order not customary for us.[78]

According to Zeraḥiah, the final portion of Elihu's speech to Job is devoted to informing him that all his arguments against God are without merit since there is no way for human beings to comprehend God's providence in this world or to know why the righteous suffer and the wicker prosper. Zeraḥiah explains that it is for this reason that Elihu describes natural phenomena and juxtaposes them with descriptions of God's governance of human beings. Zeraḥiah has in mind the fact that from Job 34 to the middle of Job 36, Elihu discusses divine providence over human events, but from Job 36:26 through Job 37 he rhapsodizes about the glories of nature. The juxtaposition teaches Job that we cannot understand how God guides human events any more than we can comprehend how the world of nature functions.[79]

As for God's revelation to Job, Zeraḥiah states quite explicitly that God adds nothing to Elihu's ideas. God emphasizes the wonders of nature as Elihu had in order to reinforce the point that the workings of providence are beyond human understanding. Why, then, does God speak? Zeraḥiah tells us that God's address is merely a literary device to bolster Elihu's message. The author of Job "intended to strengthen the opinion of Elihu with another opinion that was the most excellent of opinions," and there is, of course, no opinion more excellent than God's.[80]

Zeraḥiah also adds here that God's speech provides further evidence that the Book of Job is an allegory, for if one assumes a literal reading here and actually believes that God speaks to Job, there are serious difficulties. First, it is hard to believe that Job experiences prophecy because he does not have intellectual perfection and is therefore not worthy of it. Job's prophecy is even more improbable given the remarkable nature of the communication. It provides a lesson in natural science more detailed than any in all of scripture. If a prophecy of this sort did not come to the prophets who possessed the greatest intellectual perfection, it certainly did not come to Job. Second, there is a great deal of repetition in God's speeches, and we know that God does not waste His words. Thus, Zeraḥiah concludes, there is proof here that the Book of Job is an allegory. Zeraḥiah adds that the repetition in God's speech is merely a pedagogical device for making clear the lessons regarding natural science that the author wants to impart.[81]

In his interpretation of the closing chapter of Job, Zeraḥiah sees Job's recantation as further evidence of the good character he displays throughout the book. Job dutifully accepts the lesson taught to him by Elihu that human beings are unable to comprehend divine providence and the suffering of the righteous, and he therefore regrets having protested against God. Because he repents, Job is rewarded with a new family and the return of his wealth. As noted earlier, however, Zeraḥiah is of the opinion that the rewards accorded to Job at the end of the story are not credible and are therefore one more piece of evidence that the entire book is an allegory.[82]

Now that we have come to the end of Zeraḥiah's commentary, we must note a significant difficulty in his overall understanding of Job. It does not take much reflection to recognize that there are serious inconsistencies between Zeraḥiah's interpretation of the final chapters of Job and his understanding of the book prior to those chapters. In earlier portions of his commentary, Zeraḥiah makes clear that the workings of providence are indeed within the realm of human comprehension. That was the whole point of Elihu's remarks in Job 33. Suffering is due to matter, which is represented by Satan. One can escape its evil effects and experience individual providence by achieving intellectual perfection, which in turn leads to prophecy and immortality. These insights explain why Job himself has suffered; he did not achieve intellectual perfection and was therefore defenseless against the ravages of matter. However, in Zeraḥiah's commentary on Job 34 onward, a different picture emerges. According to Zeraḥiah's reading, Job is informed that human beings are entirely unable to comprehend God's providential activity, and this is a lesson that Job, to his credit, comes to accept. Thus, according to Zeraḥiah's reading here, it is as if Job never actually absorbs the philosophical teachings Elihu imparts, for even though Elihu has explained how providence works, Job finishes the story convinced that the nature of providence is beyond our understanding.

One could argue that this inconsistency is rooted in Maimonides, and that Zeraḥiah, as an avid student of Maimonides, is merely following the master's lead. After all, Maimonides also holds the view that Elihu's address equates providence with natural processes and that his address is followed by God's revelation, which emphasizes the ignorance of human beings regarding providence. Thus, even in Maimonides' reading of Job, a positive explanation of providence is followed by the assertion that we have no knowledge of its operations. However, upon closer examination, the inconsistency in Maimonides is only apparent—at least, according to my own understanding of him. For Maimonides, God's address complements that of Elihu. God accepts Elihu's position that providence consists of natural processes but emphasizes the equivocality of divine attributes in order to underscore the point that our understanding of providence does not go beyond the natural realm. By contrast, Zeraḥiah makes no attempt to tie the two positions together as Maimonides does. In Zeraḥiah's reading, Elihu gives Job the entire truth about the workings of providence, while God denies that any truth of this sort is comprehensible to human beings. Moreover, as Zeraḥiah would have it, toward the end of his address in Job 34–37, Elihu himself emphasizes the limitations of human knowledge regarding providence, a position that again clashes with his teachings on providence in Job 33. Thus, it would seem that if one follows Zeraḥiah's reading carefully, there is inconsistency even within Elihu's position.

An explanation of the difficulty is that Zeraḥiah is engaging in esoteric discourse and wants to convey two messages, one to the masses and another to the philosophers. The theory of providence mapped out by Zeraḥiah in his discussion of Job 33 is directed at the philosophers and represents his genuine view, according to which providence is something we can understand. Providence comes with intellectual perfection, which allows us to circumvent the influences of matter in this life and to achieve immortality in the next. The lesson Job learns from Job 34 onward is directed at the masses, who need to be taught that there is no way for human beings to comprehend divine providence and that one must be accepting of God's ways even in the face of the suffering of the righteous. This is an appropriate message for those untrained in philosophical wisdom, since they are able neither to understand nor to experience providence and must therefore learn to be satisfied with their limited comprehension of God's ways. Thus, according to this reading, Job never really absorbs the meaning of Elihu's message. His understanding of providence as the story finishes remains a popular one despite Elihu's efforts.

This interpretation of Zeraḥiah's reading is confirmed with a careful examination of his comments on the very last lines of Elihu's address to Job:

> *Shaddai, great in power, we cannot understand* . . . (Job 37:23):[83] After Elihu finished giving his address to Job and informed him that there is no way for any human being to know God's ways and His governance of the creatures in this lowly world, he ended his address with him by saying, "Shaddai, great in power, we cannot understand;" that is, He is great in power so that our intellects and wisdom cannot comprehend Him. . . .
>
> *Therefore men are in awe of Him / Whom all wise people cannot perceive*[84] (Job 37:24): this means that because He is "great in power," men are in awe of Him. "Whom all wise people cannot perceive": *all* wise people will not comprehend Him—but a small number of them [will], as Elihu said at the beginning of his address, "It is not the many who are wise" (Job 32:9).[85] There is no doubt that in this matter, he is alluding to what he said in his first response, "For God

> speaks time and again/—Though man does not perceive it" (Job 33:14). He [also] said, "If he has an angel / An advocate, one among a thousand" (Job 33:23). For all of this [i.e., the verse under discussion] is an allusion to the opinion of Elihu. It is for this reason that he ended his address with this verse and with what he intended to explain in it.[86]

The significance of these remarks can easily be missed, though they are critical to Zeraḥiah's reading of Job. In his interpretation of the first verse, "Shaddai, great in power, we cannot understand . . . ," Zeraḥiah finds confirmation of the message that Job learns toward the end of the story—namely, that human beings cannot understand God's ways. But Zeraḥiah's interpretation of Elihu's subsequent and final statement—"Therefore men are in awe of Him / Whom all wise people cannot perceive"—is read by Zeraḥiah to contain an important qualification of the preceding verse, one that alters not only the meaning of the passage, but Zeraḥiah's reading of the entire final portion of Job. Elihu reads this verse in accordance with a strict logic. The "all" in "all wise people" is taken emphatically so as to imply an exclusion. *All* wise people do not comprehend God's ways; yet *some* of them do. And what is it that those chosen few perceive? Precisely the lessons in providence that Elihu gave at the beginning of his address regarding such matters as the angel in Job 33. Zeraḥiah concludes that Elihu deliberately closes his address with this verse in order to allude to those doctrines, which are the true intent of his remarks to Job.

The message is clear. The stance that Job accepts in the last chapters is directed to the masses, who are without philosophical learning. It is they who must believe in the incomprehensibility of God's ways. The truths that Elihu imparts regarding providence in chapter 33 are for the elite, namely the philosophers, who understand how providence truly functions. Elihu carefully conceals the fact that there are two positions here by alluding to the distinction between them in a highly veiled manner and by doing so in the very last line of his address to Job.

The conclusion that must be drawn here is that Zeraḥiah does indeed interpret the final portion of Job in a manner significantly different from Maimonides—at least, as I understand him. In Maimonides' reading, the lengthy descriptions of the glories of nature that make up the last section of Elihu's address and constitute the bulk of God's revelation are meant to teach Job about the equivocality of divine attributes, one of the most exalted lessons in Maimonides' philosophy. For Zeraḥiah, those same descriptions do nothing of the sort; they are meant merely to mollify and appease Job, to make him feel comfortable with his ignorance of philosophical matters regarding providence.[87]

These observations regarding Zeraḥiah's reading of the final chapters of Job shed valuable light on earlier passages in his commentary by making us aware of the esoteric message he is trying to conceal. Most significant is a passage appearing in the introduction, to which I have already alluded, in which Zeraḥiah explains that the Book of Job was named after Job because he is the model of patience in the face of suffering:

> The first [reason] is that different types of those afflictions came upon him which are representative of all the types of chance occurrences[88] that can occur to human beings. It [i.e., the biblical text] also mentioned the severest types of loss from which a person will learn—those [types of loss] and those less severe than them. [The biblical text intended] that one should not be shocked by any of them or criticize how divine governance could be this way or [say] how it is that He has caused all this or what is the reason for this whole loss. Even if one finds himself innocent and faultless, he should not criticize God's intention because of this or [entertain] other thoughts or imaginings that a person thinks and imagines when he sees in himself or in another person the severest of illnesses and afflictions of the body, children, or money. In all these events and occurrences, we learn in the case of Job that we should not think what is not proper to think nor criticize what one should not criticize. Rather every person should be content with and cleave more to the love of God and attribute everything that occurred to him to ignorance of Him and lack of comprehension of Him with respect to His governance, may He be blessed, and His providence in the world. And if many bad things and troubles occur to him, he should receive them with love as the sages said regarding this sort of matter, "those who do out of love and are joyful in their sufferings,"[89] as you will see this whole matter is alluded to with respect to Job. For after all those afflictions came upon him, it said, "For all that, Job did not sin nor did he cast reproach on God" (Job 1:22). He also did not give to matter, to which Scripture alluded in calling it the wife of Job, the capacity to seduce him and to make him change his mind when she said to him, "blaspheme God and die" (Job 2:9). Job did not receive her advice and was not seduced by her words. He responded to her, "blessed be the name of the Lord" (Job 1:21). For even in his time of anger he did not say anything about which we could criticize him. For when a person curses something that has no existence, there is no sin for him in this. For the day which Job cursed was something that had already passed. Moreover, time does not have existence as other existent beings do. Furthermore, all of the other things which he said of himself in the first response were all things that had passed and have no enduring existence as if they did not exist. All of this is an allusion and a parable [for the notion] that a man should be careful with the most insignificant of matters so as not to unleash his tongue and his anger. Even more so, it is possible that God, may He be blessed, will reward him with good at the end of his life for what he has suffered and borne, and

> the end reserved for him will be for his good and for the sake of giving abundance to him more than he had previously, as was the case with Job. Or his reward will be reserved for the world to come as Eliphaz said to him, "He injures, but He binds up; / He wounds but His hands heal" (Job 5:18), and said "You will know that all is well in your tent; / When you visit your wife you will never fail" (Job 5:24). Bildad said, "If you are blameless and upright, / He will protect you, / And grant well-being to your righteous home / Though your beginning be small, / In the end you will grow very great" (Job 8:6).[90]

Most of this passage expresses in emphatic terms that we must recognize, as Job did, that divine providence is beyond human comprehension and that we should not criticize God in the face of suffering even if it seems unjust. Instead, we should cleave to God and love Him all the more. What is most significant is the conclusion of the passage, in which Zeraḥiah says that if we accept the incomprehensibility of providence and bear our suffering with equanimity, perhaps God will reward us with material goods as he did Job, or with reward in the world to come as suggested by Eliphaz and Bildad.

These latter remarks reveal that Zeraḥiah's whole discussion here is addressed only to the masses and does not represent his true views. First of all, as noted earlier, Zeraḥiah does not take the end of the Book of Job seriously. The restoration of Job's family and wealth is viewed by Zeraḥiah as so fantastic that it is evidence that the story could be nothing other than an allegory.[91] Therefore, Zeraḥiah cannot be expressing his genuine opinion when he points to Job's reward at the end of the story as the model of what we should hope for when accepting our suffering without protest. Even more significant, note whom Zeraḥiah cites as support for the notion that God will grant reward in the world to come to those who are patient with suffering. It is Eliphaz and Bildad, who in Zeraḥiah's reading represent incorrect positions. Zeraḥiah adopts the Maimonidean view that Eliphaz represents the traditional Jewish view, while Bildad represents the Mu'tazilites. Elihu, whose view of the afterlife is the correct philosophical one, is not cited here, and for good reason: Zeraḥiah does not want to draw attention to the fact that immortality is only for the philosophers and not for the masses. Thus, Zeraḥiah is strongly hinting that what he is saying does not represent his true views.

We can sum up Zeraḥiah's reading of Job by noting its heavy dependence on Maimonides. He mostly follows his predecessor in his conception of the overall structure of the book and in his interpretation of many of its details. We have seen that Zeraḥiah also deviates from Maimonides in some respects. Most important, he reads God's address at the end of the book as a communication directed to the masses, who lack philosophical wisdom and must be taught that the workings of divine providence are beyond their comprehension. Still, we have yet to examine the exact nature of the relationship between Zeraḥiah's reading of Job and that of Maimonides, since our goal up to now has mainly been to outline the content of Zeraḥiah's commentary. In the next section of our discussion, in which we explore the first interface, an investigation of that relationship will be the main focus.

Antecedents

In truth, an examination of antecedent influences on Zeraḥiah's reading of Job must include more than a discussion of Maimonides. As noted earlier, there is the question of Ibn Tibbon's role in shaping Zeraḥiah's reading, since Zeraḥiah sees himself as an interpreter within the Tibbonian tradition of philosophical exegesis. However, Maimonides' influence is clearly primary, and therefore it is with him that I begin.

Zeraḥiah's relationship to Maimonides in his commentary on Job has a number of different facets. There are instances in which Zeraḥiah adopts a position or insight from Maimonides without qualification. For example, Zeraḥiah's interpretation of the dialogue between Job and his three friends—Eliphaz, Bildad, and Zophar—is lifted directly from Maimonides. The schools of thought that Zeraḥiah assigns to these figures are precisely those that Maimonides attributes to them.

It is more common, however, for Zeraḥiah to adopt a position or insight from Maimonides and augment it with his own embellishments. The best example of this tendency is perhaps Zeraḥiah's discussion justifying his belief that the Book of Job is an allegory. Zeraḥiah is clearly inspired by Maimonides' position here, but he goes well beyond his mentor in providing extensive arguments in support of it. We also noted that Zeraḥiah builds his views on Satan and the divine beings on Maimonidean foundations. The notion that Satan is representative of matter while the divine beings are representative of the natural forms falls within the general purview of possible readings of Maimonides' interpretation of these figures. Here, too, Zeraḥiah significantly embellishes Maimonides' views by creating a second layer of allegory on the basis of Resh Lakish's dictum, a layer in which Satan is identified with the contents of the imagination and the divine beings are identified with the contents of the intellect. Zeraḥiah also adds a creative twist when he draws a parallel between the divine beings and Job, on the one hand, and Satan and Job's wife, on the other hand, and then relates this reading intertextually to the story of Adam and Eve.

Zeraḥiah also elaborates on Maimonides in his interpretation of Elihu's position. Zeraḥiah's notion that Elihu identifies prophecy as one of the primary manifestations of providence is clearly drawn from Maimonides, who cryptically mentions prophecy in his own reading of Elihu's remarks.[92] Zeraḥiah seems also to have been inspired by Maimonides in finding the theme of immortality in Elihu's address. The connection to Maimonides comes through in a passage earlier in the commentary in which Zeraḥiah discusses his philosophical interpretation of Satan and the divine beings:

> I will add a hint of an explanation so that you will understand the matter of the divine beings, Satan, and Job's soul, which is also part

> of this issue[93] in that God says to Satan at the end of the event[s] in the story [i.e., Job's suffering], "only spare his soul" (Job 2:6).[94] Know that the divine beings are a hint for the natural forms which belong to the individuals of natural species of beings. The meaning of Satan is matter.[95] Natural individual beings are composed of the two of them, that is matter and form. And what He said in the end, "only spare his soul" (Job 2:6), is something which teaches about the immortality of the soul, as the Rabbi [i.e., Maimonides] explained when he said in this matter, "it is the thing which remains from the soul and that over which Satan has no dominion."[96] In conclusion, if you want to understand these matters, look at each and every issue and steer it toward natural matters. Do not allow yourself to guide your intellect to anything outside natural matters, for you will be able to see and to know that all that the Rabbi said[97] at the beginning of this story, all of it, goes according to the statements mentioned in the books about nature.[98]

In this passage, Zeraḥiah highlights the subject of immortality as a major theme in Job, alongside the issue of Satan and the divine beings. But most important, Zeraḥiah links the theme of immortality to Maimonides' interpretation of God's command to Satan "only spare his soul."[99]

In sum, the impression one gets is that Zeraḥiah relates to Maimonides in much the same way that Ibn Tibbon did. Like Ibn Tibbon, Zeraḥiah adopts Maimonides' basic framework for understanding Job, but he also develops a number of elements in that framework and fills in some of its gaps. Yet, Zeraḥiah is more comprehensive than Ibn Tibbon in supplementing Maimonides' reading of Job because he writes a full-length commentary on it. As we saw in chapter 4, Ibn Tibbon's exposition was relatively brief, it was focused primarily on Elihu's position, and it was part of a larger treatise concerned with a host of other biblical texts.

In a number of instances Zeraḥiah does not embellish on Maimonides' insights but departs from them. The most important example is one I have already examined in my summary of Zeraḥiah's commentary. Maimonides reads the last chapters of the Book of Job, in which God extols the glories of nature and emphasize the lowliness of man, as a portion of the dialogue in which Job learns important philosophical lessons about the equivocality of divine attributes and the true meaning of providence. According to Zeraḥiah's reading, the final chapters of the book convey the message that Job must be satisfied with his ignorance regarding providence since an understanding of God's ways is beyond human comprehension.

Zeraḥiah's departure from Maimonides is connected with another significant difference that he has with his predecessor, one that I have not yet discussed: Zeraḥiah depicts the figure of Job in a manner that sharply contrasts with that of Maimonides. In Maimonides, Job undergoes a radical transformation from the beginning to the end of the story. As the story opens, Job has intellectual deficiencies that are responsible for his erroneous views on divine providence and cause him to abandon his belief in individual providence once he experiences his afflictions. Maimonides also tells us that Job begins the story with ethical virtue, but he goes on to imply that Job fails ethically in the face of his suffering because of his impatience and pride. Yet, Job is able to correct both his intellectual and ethical faults by the end of the book. Through his dialogue with Elihu and God, he achieves intellectual perfection and prophecy. Job also learns passivity and humility. For Zeraḥiah there is no such transformation. Indeed, Zeraḥiah's Job begins the story on a more positive footing than that of Maimonides in that he has excellent ethical qualities that carry him through his suffering and allow him to experience the tribulations with patience. But in the end, Job does not advance much beyond his initial position. He remains ethically virtuous as the story closes but just as ignorant as he was at the beginning about the true meaning of providence. He advances intellectually to the extent that he recognizes that he should not question God's providential activity, but he never becomes enlightened about the esoteric meaning of providence.[100]

The differences between Maimonides and Zeraḥiah with respect to the figure of Job are reflected in the way they interpret Job 42:6, the critical verse in which Job repents. According to Maimonides' understanding, the verse is rendered as follows: "I had heard of Thee by hearing of the ear; but now mine eye seeth Thee; wherefore I abhor myself and repent of dust and ashes."[101] Job's reference to "dust and ashes" is to the state of mourning he experienced after his afflictions. By repenting "of dust and ashes," Job regrets having mourned the loss of his material goods, for he now knows that ultimate felicity is to be in a state of intellectual perfection in which one is detached from material concerns.[102] Zeraḥiah reads the passage in an entirely different manner. According to his rendering, the verse would read: "wherefore I despise and feel regret, seeing as *I am* but dust and ashes."[103] As Zeraḥiah explains in his paraphrase, "I despise what I have chosen, and I take [upon myself] regret and repentance regarding what I was thinking about Your governance in Your world, and I know that I am dust and ashes before You which has no value or importance."[104] What Job comes to realize is that it is he who is but dust and ashes, and it is for this reason that he is unable to comprehend God's ways and therefore regrets his former protests against Him. Thus, according to Zeraḥiah's understanding, Job's repentance does not consist of coming to a new understanding of providence, as he does in Maimonides, but in coming to the realization that he can have no understanding of providence at all. He repents because he is nothing compared to God and therefore recognizes that he cannot comprehend His ways.[105]

Though it is not clear why Zeraḥiah departs from Maimonides in his depiction of Job or whether he is even conscious of his differences with him, there is room for speculation. It would seem that both thinkers have the common desire to use the figure of Job as a model for the masses, who are ignorant of philosophical learning, but that each has a very different conception of how Job should serve in that role. For Maimonides, the figure of Job is an inspiration for the masses to overcome their limitations and pursue intellectual perfection so that they can experience providence. In Zeraḥiah's thinking, Job is a model of a very different sort. Job teaches the masses that they should accept their intellectual limitations and eschew any attempt to penetrate the secrets of providence. They should greet unjust suffering with composure and patience and avoid expressing any anger toward God.

What may underlie the difference between Maimonides and Zeraḥiah in their respective depictions of Job is a dispute over educational philosophy. Each thinker, it would seem, has a different view on the potential of the masses for philosophical enlightenment. Maimonides takes a positive view on this matter, while Zeraḥiah takes a negative one. That difference is played out in their respective views of Job in that Maimonides depicts Job as a figure whose intellectual deficiencies are correctable, while Zeraḥiah views him as an individual who will never achieve philosophical enlightenment.[106] If this interpretation is correct, it would explain not just Zeraḥiah's differences with Maimonides regarding the depiction of Job, but also his differences with him regarding the final chapters of the book. For if Zeraḥiah feels that Job can never be properly enlightened in philosophical wisdom, then he would be unable to accept Maimonides' view that Job receives from God a sophisticated philosophical lesson regarding the equivocality of divine attributes, and it would make perfect sense for him to interpret God's address as an attempt to convince Job of his limitations.

As I noted at the beginning of this portion of my discussion, we must also investigate whether Zeraḥiah's reading of Job betrays the influence of Ibn Tibbon. My suspicion that there is such a connection is aroused by the fact that Zeraḥiah regards the equation of providence with the immortality of the intellect as an idea central to Elihu's message and thus, by implication, central to the Book of Job as a whole. As I have shown, the hallmark of Ibn Tibbon's reading of Job is the notion that the immortality of intellect is the highest form of providence. As mentioned earlier, there is reason to believe that Zeraḥiah attributes the identification of providence with the immortality of the intellect because he believes that this is Maimonides' position as well. The question is whether Zeraḥiah arrived at this view through the influence of Ibn Tibbon, who reads Maimonides in the same way. Another significant thought that Zeraḥiah appears to share with Ibn Tibbon is the notion that God does not speak to Job in the final chapters of the book because Job does not have the requisite level of intellectual perfection to achieve prophecy. Zeraḥiah appears to be departing from Maimonides' optimistic view that Job achieves prophecy in much the same way Ibn Tibbon did.

There is circumstantial evidence that Zeraḥiah is familiar with Ibn Tibbon's reading of Job. As I mentioned in the introduction to this chapter, Zeraḥiah cites Ibn Tibbon frequently in his other works, and given that Zeraḥiah's commentary on Job was written toward the end of his life, it is likely that when he composed this work, he was well acquainted with Ibn Tibbon's discussion of Job in *Ma'amar Yikkavu ha-Mayim*. There is also evidence that casts doubt on a connection between Zeraḥiah's reading of Job and that of Ibn Tibbon. In his discussion of previous interpreters of Job in the introduction to his commentary, Zeraḥiah makes no mention of Ibn Tibbon. In fact, at no point of his commentary does Zeraḥiah cite Ibn Tibbon's exposition even to disagree with it.

Moreover, when one carefully examines the points of commonality between Zeraḥiah and Ibn Tibbon, one discovers that those commonalities mask significant differences. While Zeraḥiah seems to follow Ibn Tibbon in attributing to Elihu the notion that providence is to be identified with the immortality of the intellect, the two thinkers read Elihu's address quite differently. For one, in Ibn Tibbon's reading, Elihu's entire speech is focused on immortality; even Elihu's references to prophecy are interpreted in light of this issue. Zeraḥiah, by contrast, seems to view prophecy and immortality as two alternative forms of individual providence.

There are also important differences between the two thinkers regarding Elihu's description of the sick person in Job 33. Ibn Tibbon takes these verses quite literally. For him, the biblical text is saying that human beings experience suffering in order to teach them that material well-being is of no value and that one should seek immortality via intellectual perfection.[107] For Zeraḥiah, the same verses are interpreted allegorically. The sick person is a metaphor for the soul that has not achieved intellectual perfection.

One more point that distinguishes Zeraḥiah's reading of Job 33 from that of Ibn Tibbon is that Zeraḥiah interprets Elihu to be saying that immortality is an exceedingly rare phenomenon because it is experienced only by those with a high degree of intellectual perfection. He interprets the notion that the angel comes to the rescue only "two or three times" as an indication that immortality is only for a highly select group of people—for "one in a thousand," as Zeraḥiah puts it with the help of a phrase from Job 33:23.[108] This idea is absent in Ibn Tibbon, who does not interpret the biblical text in this way and does not make an issue of the rarity of immortality.

Finally, we should note that in his reading of Job 33, Zeraḥiah is quite explicit in denying any influences from previous thinkers when he says toward the end of his commentary on that chapter: "With respect to these verses which I have now explicated regarding Elihu's additional view,[109] I have seen no commentator sensitive to those things which one should be sensitive to; rather, they explicated them in ways that are strange and distant from Elihu's opinion."[110] In this passage, Zeraḥiah seems to rule out any influence from Ibn Tibbon's reading of Elihu's address.

A careful examination of the views of Zeraḥiah and Ibn Tibbon regarding God's revelation to Job demonstrates that here as well the commonality between the two thinkers is somewhat superficial. First, Ibn Tibbon radically reinterprets the biblical text to say that there was, in fact, no revelation to Job. The tempest refers to the turmoil of Job's suffering, through which he learned valuable philosophical lessons. Zeraḥiah also denies that there was a revelation here, but in contrast to Ibn Tibbon he allows the text to stand as is, for, as Zeraḥiah reasons, the entire Book of Job is an allegory, and therefore one need not read it literally here. Zeraḥiah argues that the insertion of Job's implausible prophetic revelation was quite deliberate on the part of the author because he wanted to draw our attention to the story's allegorical character.[111] Second, in Ibn Tibbon's reading, Job absorbs a fair measure of philosophical learning by the end of the book in that he learns from Elihu a good deal about providence—even if he himself does not achieve intellectual perfection and does not merit providence. In Zeraḥiah's reading, Job absorbs no philosophical learning whatsoever. As the story ends, he remains as ignorant about the true meaning of providence as he was at its beginning.[112]

On balance, it would seem that Zeraḥiah's reading of Job is in fact influenced by Ibn Tibbon. Given that Zeraḥiah is very dependent on Ibn Tibbon in his other works, that he was almost certainly aware of Ibn Tibbon's reading of Job by the time he wrote his commentary, and that he appears to adopt key elements of Ibn Tibbon's reading of Job, even if only in a superficial manner—it is hard to imagine that there is no connection between the two thinkers here. The question, then, is why Zeraḥiah fails to mention Ibn Tibbon in his commentary, and why, in his interpretation of Job 33 in particular, Zeraḥiah appears to rule out any influence from him.

It is possible that Zeraḥiah absorbed elements of Ibn Tibbon's reading—particularly the notion that Elihu equates providence with immortality—but felt that his own exegesis of Job was sufficiently different from that of Ibn Tibbon that he had no obligation to cite him. This explanation would fit nicely with my analysis, for I have shown that on those points where there appears to be significant agreement between the two thinkers, the agreement is quite general, and differences emerge in the details of their exegesis of the biblical text. Thus, when Zeraḥiah notes in his commentary on Job 33 that none of his predecessors has explicated this chapter properly, he may very well have had Ibn Tibbon in mind as one such interpreter. And if Zeraḥiah refrains from openly criticizing Ibn Tibbon as he does other exegetes with whom he disagrees, that is to be expected, given the reverence he expresses toward him in his other works.

To sum up this portion of my discussion, Zeraḥiah is clearly influenced by Maimonides in his interpretation of Job. Zeraḥiah relates to Maimonides in much the same way Ibn Tibbon did in taking the clues that Maimonides provides in the *Guide* and using them to construct a comprehensive interpretation of the biblical text. Yet, Zeraḥiah also departs from Maimonides in significant ways, particularly in his interpretation of the final chapters of Job and his depiction of the actual figure of Job. What should also be noted here is that when Zeraḥiah departs from Maimonides, his differences with him are exegetical rather than philosophical. At no point does Zeraḥiah openly disagree with Maimonides' philosophical premises regarding providence; he disagrees only with how they are read out of the Book of Job. On this point, Zeraḥiah is like Ibn Tibbon, who had a similar relationship to Maimonides when it came to philosophical matters.

As for Zeraḥiah's relationship to Ibn Tibbon himself, my sense is that Zeraḥiah is influenced by him as well in his reading of Job. There seem to be telltale signs of Ibn Tibbon's impact on Zeraḥiah's reading of Job at certain points of his commentary, particularly Zeraḥiah's view that Elihu identifies providence with the immortality of the intellect. Certainly, Zeraḥiah's connection to Ibn Tibbon is far more ambiguous than his connection to Maimonides, because Zeraḥiah never explicitly mentions Ibn Tibbon in his commentary. Still, Zeraḥiah may have incorporated elements of Ibn Tibbon's reading into his own but chose not to cite him because of significant differences between the two in their interpretation of the details of the biblical text.

A key point that distinguishes Zeraḥiah's reading of Job from the readings of both Maimonides and Ibn Tibbon is that Zeraḥiah displays a far greater degree of elitism in his commentary than either of his predecessors. This comes through in two ways. First and foremost, Zeraḥiah's Job does not achieve prophecy, intellectual perfection, or even a proper understanding of providence by the end of the story—a far more limited depiction of Job than that found in Maimonides or Ibn Tibbon. As I have argued, Zeraḥiah's message seems to be that the masses can do no better than Job, and that they must therefore accept their intellectual limitations as Job does. Second, Zeraḥiah makes clear in his interpretation of Elihu's position that immortality is only for a small minority of individuals, in that the "angel" rescues only "one in a thousand" souls from eternal oblivion. Maimonides and Ibn Tibbon certainly restrict providence to a special group of individuals, but in their readings of Elihu's views, neither of them emphasizes this point to the extent that Zeraḥiah does.

It is my sense that it is this last issue that Zeraḥiah regards as the most esoteric aspect of the Book of Job. It is one thing for Zeraḥiah to interpret Elihu to be saying that prophecy is an exceedingly rare phenomenon. That position is confirmed by the biblical text itself, and thus it is unlikely that Zeraḥiah's common readers would feel bad about being bereft of such a capacity. But to interpret Elihu to be saying that immortality is exceedingly rare is a significant departure from the traditional perspective and robs the common reader of one of his most cherished hopes, which is salvation from death. It is perhaps for this reason that in Zeraḥiah's reading of Elihu's remarks in Job 33, the immortality theme is couched in allegory—that of the sick person—while the theme of prophecy is not. The allegory adds another layer of concealment to a passage that is already esoteric, in order to hide its most radical element from the common reader.

Exegesis

Let us now examine the second interface, which concerns Zeraḥiah's commentary as an exegetical work attempting to make sense of the biblical text. Here, Zeraḥiah is similar to Ibn Tibbon in that his adoption of the Maimonidean framework for interpreting Job brings with it most of Maimonides' solutions to the book's major exegetical difficulties. Thus, for instance, Zeraḥiah organizes the dialogue in Job precisely as Maimonides does in interpreting it as a debate between different schools of thought on the subject of providence.

Zeraḥiah, however, also has a number of highly original insights into exegetical matters. By far his most impressive contribution in this area is the arguments he provides for his position that the Book of Job is an allegory. Zeraḥiah's discussion appears to be the first of its kind among medieval Jewish commentators on Job. It may also be the first of its kind among medieval commentators in general; I know of no similar discussion of Job among medieval Christian exegetes. The first serious debate among Christian thinkers about whether Job is history or fiction takes place no earlier than the fifteenth century, a full two centuries after Zeraḥiah.[113]

What is remarkable about Zeraḥiah's discussion of allegory is not just that he raises the issue of whether or not Job is fiction, but the quality of the argumentation he provides to prove his position. Zeraḥiah supports his view not just on the basis of philosophical considerations, as one might expect, but from insights regarding the literary qualities of the story, arguments that often exhibit considerable literary sophistication and sensitivity to the biblical text.[114]

I had intended to leave for my concluding chapter all comparisons between the medieval readings of Job examined in our study and those of modern scholars. Yet, Zeraḥiah's analysis of the allegorical nature of Job is so striking that it is appropriate to make some comment here about how his insights compare with modern scholarly views. While there is much in Zeraḥiah's deliberations that separates him from modern interpreters, Zeraḥiah also furnishes insights that clearly resonate with them. Zeraḥiah's argument that the Book of Job is from the hand of one author because of its uniform style, is remarkable in that it takes literary qualities into account in determining authorship. In truth, most modern scholars of Job do not believe that the book is as uniform in style as Zeraḥiah thinks. In fact, there has been a bewildering variety of theories among modern scholars regarding the different sources that make up the Book of Job and the time and order of their composition, and the general consensus seems to be that the Book of Job was not composed by one author.[115] Nonetheless, that Zeraḥiah should be sensitive to the question of literary style as a means of determining authorship is striking.

Perhaps even more impressive is Zeraḥiah's sensitivity to the contrived nature of the story, particularly its descriptions of Job's character, family, and wealth, in the prologue. As we may recall, Zeraḥiah takes notice of the numbers of Job's children and livestock, which are in pairs adding up to multiples of ten. He also finds the descriptions of Job's character too idyllic to be true. Similar observations are offered by recent commentators who have dwelt on the literary qualities of the story. For instance, Norman Habel, in his commentary on Job, consistently argues that the description of the details of Job's life are deliberately meant to accentuate the fantastic nature of his story as a tale belonging to the realm of "mystery and antiquity."[116] Zeraḥiah's argument that the exaggerated descriptions of Job's religious and moral character are proof of the fictional nature of the story anticipates Habel's observation that "the goodness of Job is portrayed in terms so idealistic that they hardly seem believable."[117]

Another original contribution that Zeraḥiah makes to the medieval exegesis of Job is his view regarding its authorship. Zeraḥiah accepts the Talmudic position that the author of Job is Moses, but he also argues that Moses produced

Job entirely from his own wisdom, not from prophetic revelation, and that it is why he does not identify himself as author. The notion that the Book of Job is the product of human wisdom is, to my knowledge, unprecedented in medieval Jewish exegesis. At the very least, Zeraḥiah is breaking with Maimonides here. In his discussion of the various levels of prophecy in the *Guide*, Maimonides identifies the Book of Job as a text written through "the Divine Spirit" (*ruaḥ ha-kodesh*), which is the second level of prophetic communication, and even though Maimonides does not regard this level of revelation quite as prophecy proper, he thinks of it as being close.[118] Zeraḥiah excludes the Book of Job even from this lower level of divine inspiration. He explicitly contrasts Job with other books of the Bible that are "written and spoken with the Divine Spirit (*ruaḥ ha-kodesh*)," and strongly emphasizes its purely human provenance.[119]

Zeraḥiah also strikes out in an original direction in his handling of the ambiguities surrounding the figure of Job. Maimonides had dealt with this problem by proposing an esoteric reading of the text, according to which the inconsistent depictions of Job are explained as phases in his journey from ignorance to intellectual perfection. We have already discussed how Zeraḥiah's portrayal of Job departs significantly from that of Maimonides and that a possible reason for this disagreement is their differing views over educational philosophy. But what is important for us in the context of this portion of my discussion is to see how Zeraḥiah's differences with Maimonides here are related not just to philosophical matters, but to exegetical considerations as well. Zeraḥiah follows Maimonides in using an esoteric reading of the biblical text in order to deal with ambiguities regarding the figure of Job, but he does so in a manner entirely different from that of his predecessor. As we have already seen, Zeraḥiah expends great effort casting Job in a highly positive light. Job begins the story as a person of great virtue; in the wake of his suffering, he is the model of patience and composure; when he utters protests against God, it is only out of a genuine curiosity to know the truth; when he is deemed wicked by other participants in the dialogue, what is meant is that he is wicked only in comparison to God; and when finally he learns by the end of the story that an understanding of God's ways is beyond the capacity of human beings, he dutifully listens. At the same time, Zeraḥiah also hints that Job is a model only for the masses, not for the elite, who are fully capable of understanding the workings of providence. Zeraḥiah's strategy is clear: He deals with the inconsistencies regarding the figure of Job by smoothing them over in order to present as positive an image of him as possible. He also signals us that this positive image is meant only for the masses, and that the philosopher should look elsewhere to find a model to guide him in coping with suffering.

Exegesis and Philosophy

With respect to the third interface, we see once again that Zeraḥiah has much in common with Ibn Tibbon. Like Ibn Tibbon, Zeraḥiah seems to accept unquestioningly Maimonides' philosophical views regarding providence. Also like Ibn Tibbon, he unwittingly imparts a new spin to the issue of providence by highlighting immortality as its central manifestation. As I argued in my discussion of Ibn Tibbon, Maimonides certainly believed in immortality and saw it as consequent upon intellectual perfection, but nowhere does he suggest that it is the most important expression of providence. Zeraḥiah has therefore gone in a direction similar to Ibn Tibbon.

An important question pertaining to the third interface concerns Zeraḥiah's philosophical orientation. Although in his commentary on Job Zeraḥiah accepts Maimonides' philosophical views on providence, this in itself does not tell us very much about how Zeraḥiah understood providence. It is well known that by Zeraḥiah's time there were radical interpreters of Maimonides who identified his esoteric views on all philosophical matters with those of Aristotle and therefore interpreted his positions on such issues as providence in a thoroughly naturalistic fashion. As we have seen, Ibn Tibbon appears to have been in this camp. But there were also those who read Maimonides in more traditional fashion and believed that Maimonides never questioned the existence of a Deity who was personally involved in the affairs of the world. My question then is, to which camp does Zeraḥiah belong? Which version of Maimonides does Zeraḥiah follow when we say that he adopts Maimonides' philosophical views on providence? Does he believe in a providential God who functions in an entirely naturalistic fashion? Or did he conceive of providence in more traditional terms?

Zeraḥiah has generally been perceived as a moderate Maimonidean thinker. Aviezer Ravitzky, in particular, has argued this position, and there is good evidence to support it. There are any number of passages in Zeraḥiah's writings where he clearly endorses doctrines that assume a personal God, such as creation *ex nihilo* and miracles.[120] However, my discussion of Zeraḥiah's reading of Job shows there is evidence that Zeraḥiah may have been more radical than scholars have realized.

The extent of Zeraḥiah's naturalism is evident from a passage that I have already cited, in which he sums up his thoughts on his interpretation of Satan and the divine beings who appear in the prologue of Job:

> In conclusion, if you want to understand these matters, look at each and every issue and steer it toward natural matters. Do not allow yourself to guide your intellect to anything outside natural matters, for you will be able to see and to know that all that the Rabbi said[121] at the beginning of this story, all of it, goes according to the statements mentioned in the books about nature.[122]

Zeraḥiah is emphatic that Satan and the divine beings can be understood only by referring to "natural matters."

The same attitude is evident in Zeraḥiah's interpretation of the particular afflictions Job experiences. As we have seen, Zeraḥiah discounts the possibility that the fire that falls from the sky and kills seven thousand sheep and their shepherds could have been an actual historical event. Such events, Zeraḥiah tells us, are highly unlikely according to natural law. Moreover, Zeraḥiah says that the author of Job deliberately coupled this disaster with other, more believable calamities in order to appeal to two levels of readers. The masses will infer from the plausible events that the story actually occurred, while the philosophers will take the implausible occurrences as evidence that the story is a mere allegory.[123] What is striking here is that Zeraḥiah never entertains the possibility that the fire falling from the sky is simply an event willed by God, and it is ruled out by him as an actual historical occurrence because it does not conform to natural law. Zeraḥiah's line of reasoning suggests a strong naturalistic tendency in his thinking.

In his reading of Job 33, which reveals the true secrets of providence, Zeraḥiah's philosophical orientation is more difficult to figure out. Zeraḥiah suggests that providence manifests itself in two ways: through prophecy and through immortality. With respect to prophecy, Zeraḥiah seems to take a naturalistic approach when he interprets Elihu's angel as the Active Intellect, which imparts prophetic communication. However, the extent of Zeraḥiah's naturalism here is not clear. He also considers prophecy to be a rare event that in some sense functions outside the realm of nature, for, as he tells us, Elihu dwells on the glories of nature after discussing the truths of providence in order to emphasize the contrast between natural occurrences, which are characterized by regularity, and prophecy, which is not.[124] Zeraḥiah's allusions to immortality seem more unambiguous in their naturalism. Here Zeraḥiah takes the philosophical view that immortality is consequent upon the perfection of the intellect, a position that appears not to require a personal God.[125]

Another place where Zeraḥiah seems to be supporting a naturalistic conception of providence is in his attitude toward the rewards Job receives at the very end of the story. As we have seen, he claims that these rewards are evidence that the story is a mere allegory, since such an ideal ending stretches the credulity of the reader.[126] Only a thinker with a strong commitment to naturalism would be troubled by such an issue. If Zeraḥiah believes in a God who intervenes in human affairs, the rewards Job receives should not be so incredible.

The evidence adduced here does not amount to proof that Zeraḥiah believes in an impersonal Aristotelian God, but there is certainly enough to make us suspect that his traditional pronouncements in other works about God's personal involvement in the world may not represent his genuine view. We have also seen that in his commentary on Job Zeraḥiah will at times engage in esoteric writing, in which he says one thing but means another. This in itself allows us to cast suspicion on the traditional descriptions of God's activities in his writings and makes us wonder whether Zeraḥiah is closer to Ibn Tibbon in his philosophical orientation than scholars have claimed. Only a thorough and careful reading of Zeraḥiah's writings will allow for a firm determination on this issue.[127]

Zeraḥiah presents us with a reading of Job that is very much in the spirit of Ibn Tibbon's exegetical enterprise in that he uses Maimonides' *Guide* as a resource to produce a comprehensive commentary on the biblical text. Yet, there is also evidence to suggest that some of Zeraḥiah's key insights regarding Job are taken directly from Ibn Tibbon himself. I have also raised the possibility that Zeraḥiah may be closer to Ibn Tibbon in philosophical orientation than scholars up to now have appreciated.

However, in a number of ways Zeraḥiah goes beyond Ibn Tibbon. He composes an exposition on the entire Book of Job, and this allows him to develop elements of Maimonides' reading of Job to a much greater extent than Ibn Tibbon did. The most significant example of this tendency is his fascinating discussion of allegory. In addition, Zeraḥiah's commentary displays a greater independence from Maimonides than does that of Ibn Tibbon. Most important in this regard is its elitist emphasis. In his interpretation of the final chapters of the book, Zeraḥiah depicts Job as a figure who does not achieve even a modicum of understanding about the true nature of providence and by implication will never experience it. This message seems to reflect a highly negative view of the masses, who can hope to achieve no more than Job. Zeraḥiah's elitism can also be detected in his notion that immortality is only for the select few—the doctrine that he seems to have considered most esoteric in Job.

In his elitist emphasis, Zeraḥiah departs not just from Maimonides, but also from Ibn Tibbon. In their readings of Job, neither of them has nearly as limited a view of Job as Zeraḥiah, nor do they make a point of denying the masses immortality. The elitist element in Zeraḥiah's reading of Job is therefore one of its most distinctive features.

6

Gersonides

Rabbi Levi ben Gershom (1288–1344)—better known in contemporary scholarship by his Latinized name, Gersonides—was one of the most remarkable intellectual talents in medieval Judaism. He lived at the tail end of the same vibrant Provençal culture that produced Samuel ibn Tibbon several decades earlier, a culture that, as I have already noted, was marked by its capacity for integrating learning in classical Jewish texts with the more recently arrived disciplines of philosophy and science. Of all the Jewish intellectuals who emerged from this culture, Gersonides was perhaps the most accomplished. As a philosopher, he is widely regarded by modern scholars as second in stature only to Maimonides; he was a biblical exegete of considerable distinction, his many commentaries achieving wide circulation in the medieval Jewish community; he was a renowned astronomer and mathematician who made lasting contributions in these areas of learning; and there is also evidence that in his time he was a highly respected halakhic authority. He was appreciated not just by Jews, but non-Jews as well. Many of his works, most notably those in mathematics and astronomy, were translated from Hebrew into Latin. Few Jews in any period have mastered so many areas of knowledge.[1]

What is of interest to us here is that Gersonides had a good deal to say about the Book of Job. His major philosophical work, *The Wars of the Lord* (*Milḥamot ha-Shem*), devotes an entire section to the subject of divine providence in which there are frequent references to Job.[2] He also produced a commentary on Job. Completed in 1325, this work is perhaps a more lengthy and thorough reading of Job than any examined in this study.[3] It is also distinguished in its organization, which is different from any we will encounter. After an introduction to the book, Gersonides follows a scheme that he uses in many of his other commentaries, in which he breaks the biblical text into sections, with each section covering several chapters. Each section is then analyzed with three levels of exegesis. In the first, "explanation of terms" (*be'ur ha-millot*), Gersonides gives his analysis of selected words and expressions. In the second, "explanation of the content of the matter" (*be'ur divrey ha-ma'aneh*), he paraphrases the contents of the text. In the third, "the principle which arises from the content" (*ha-kelal ha-'oleh me-ha-dvarim*), he sums up his general conclusions about the text.[4] We should also mention that Gersonides' commentary on Job was widely read by Jews in the medieval period, its popularity reflected in the fact that it was one of the very first Hebrew books to be printed and that it would eventually be included in all rabbinic Bibles (*Mikra'ot Gedolot*).[5]

It is remarkable how little attention has been paid to Gersonides' commentary on Job in modern scholarship. As I mentioned in chapter 1, a recent article of mine seems to be the lone scholarly piece written on this work.[6] One finds some discussion of the commentary in treatments of the related issue of providence in Gersonides' thought, but such discussion is usually superficial and tends not to go much beyond what Gersonides says about Job in *The Wars of the Lord*. There is perhaps no better example of the modern scholarly neglect of medieval Jewish philosophical exegesis in general than the lack of interest shown in this important biblical commentary.[7]

Gersonides is similar to Ibn Tibbon and Zeraḥiah Ḥen in that he is a thinker who is, broadly speaking, an Aristotelian heavily influenced by Maimonides. Yet, Gersonides differs from them in that his is a far more original philosophical mind. He combines Maimonidean thinking with insights gleaned from Averroes to forge highly innovative positions on all the major philosophical issues that occupied medieval Jewish philosophers. At the same time, he is not hesitant about departing from Maimonides' philosophical views when he sees fit. Gersonides also differs from Maimonides and many of his followers in his style of writing. While he displays an elitism reminiscent of that of Maimonides, he does not engage in esoteric discourse in order to conceal his views from the masses.[8]

Gersonides' originality, combined with his eschewal of esoteric discourse, makes our task in this chapter more straightforward than it was in the cases of Maimonides, Ibn Tibbon, and Zeraḥiah Ḥen. Since Gersonides does not conceal his true views, we will have to expend less effort simply figuring out what he says. Moreover, his fresh approach toward the Book of Job will allow us to distinguish more easily between the three interfaces that are at the center of this study; for while Gersonides' reading of Job is influenced by Maimonides, it is not so dependent on him that the three interfaces will be dominated by the first, as was the case with Ibn Tibbon and Zeraḥiah Ḥen. But it would be a mistake to infer from what I have said that Gersonides' reading of Job will be less challenging than the readings of Maimonides and his followers. As we shall see, Gersonides' commentary displays a richness and subtlety unmatched by any of the other expositions on Job analyzed in this study. Considerable effort will therefore be required to fully appreciate its content and meaning.

Because Gersonides provides a systematic discussion of divine providence in the *Wars*, I will begin my analysis in the same way I began my treatments of Saadiah and Maimonides. I will first offer a synopsis of Gersonides' views on providence in his systematic work for the purpose of getting acquainted with the basic philosophical concepts that underlie his commentary on Job. At this point in the discussion I will resist making any judgments about the chronological or conceptual relationship between the two works. I will then proceed with an analysis of the commentary on Job in accordance with the three interfaces. In the discussion of the third interface I will return to the treatment of providence in the *Wars* and give an evaluation of its relationship to the commentary on Job.

The Philosophical Background: Book 4 of *The Wars of the Lord*

Gersonides' treatment of providence in the *Wars* takes up the entirety of book 4 of that work.[9] Throughout his discussion, Gersonides assumes agreement among philosophers that the various species in the sublunar realm—including human beings—are protected by general providence.[10] The central question, then, is whether humans experience individual providence as well. There are, according to Gersonides, three positions on this issue. The first is that of Aristotle, according to whom there is no individual providence whatsoever. Gersonides explains that this position is the one taken up by Job in the wake of his suffering.[11] The second position is that of the majority of the followers of the Torah, which claims that individual providence reaches each and every human being and that God rewards and punishes individuals in accordance with their level of righteousness or wickedness.[12] Gersonides explains that this position appears in three variations:

1. According to the first version, some good and bad events that occur to human beings are the result of divine reward and punishment, but some events are the result of other causes. Thus, when a righteous person suffers, it may simply be due to his own folly. Gersonides identifies this view with the position of Eliphaz.[13]
2. According to the second version, good and bad events that occur to human beings are *always* the result of divine reward and punishment. The difficulty with this view is that many events do not seem in accordance with divine justice, for it is often the case that the righteous suffer and the wicked prosper. The solution proposed by the proponents of this position is that these events appear unjust only because we do not know their eventual outcome. Events that appear good now will turn out for the worse later on, while events that ap-

pear bad now will turn out for the better. According to Gersonides, this is the position of Bildad.[14]

3. The third version agrees with the second one in the notion that all good and bad events that occur to human beings are the result of reward and punishment, but it differs in explaining events that do not seem in accord with divine justice. According to this version, such events appear unjust to us only because we, unlike God, have no knowledge of the natural capacities of individual human beings. If a righteous person experiences evil, it is because God knows he has not developed his natural capacity for goodness as much as he might have, and he is therefore punished for his shortcomings. Conversely, a wicked person may experience well-being because he has made the best of his limited natural capacity, and he is therefore rewarded for the little good that he has done. According to Gersonides, this is the position of Zophar.[15]

The final view is that of the outstanding scholars of the Torah such as Maimonides, and its claim is that some human beings experience individual providence while others do not. According to Gersonides, this view is held by Elihu.[16]

Gersonides provides detailed arguments both for and against each of the positions on providence. Eventually he declares his support for the third position, which he then explicates in greater detail. According to this view, individual providence is limited only to those human beings who have achieved some level of intellectual perfection, and it manifests itself in one of two ways: prophecy and providential suffering. Prophecy is experienced by people with a high degree of intellectual perfection, and it confers upon an individual the capacity to predict the future so that he can maximize his well-being and circumvent danger.[17] Those who have achieved a lesser degree of intellectual perfection experience providential suffering, which Gersonides identifies with the Talmudic doctrine of "sufferings of love" (*yisurin shel ahavah*). This manifestation of providence can take one of two forms. With the first type, an individual is saved from physical danger by a painful event, and even though the providential event itself causes suffering, it rescues him from even greater harm. Gersonides illustrates this form of providence with an example of a person who is unable to travel on a voyage because a thorn has become stuck in his foot and who later learns that the ship on which he was supposed to travel sank. Here the suffering caused by the thorn is providential in having saved the person from a much greater threat.[18] The second type of providential suffering saves an individual from spiritual injury. If a person with a high level of intellectual perfection has begun to pursue physical and material needs and neglects his intellect, he may experience providential suffering as a warning that he should return to the cultivation of his intellect.[19]

The major difficulty for Gersonides lies in explaining how these two forms of providence square with his Aristotelian-Averroist conception of God. For Gersonides, God is a Being who is perpetually engaged in the activity of self-contemplation, has limited knowledge of particulars in the world below, and cannot experience a change of will. He therefore cannot be personally involved in human affairs, nor can He respond to human needs. Gersonides must therefore find a way to explain how such a God can be providential in the two ways just outlined.[20]

With respect to prophecy, Gersonides solves the difficulty by arguing that the prophet receives information about the future from emanations that come from God via the Active Intellect. Those emanations are present at all times, and the prophet is able to tap into them because of his perfected intellect. Therefore, God does not personally impart information here; instead, the prophet's intellectual perfection allows him to "retrieve" information from God that is perpetually available from impersonal emanations. God neither knows nor cares that such information has been received by the prophet.[21]

Providential suffering is more difficult to explain, because here the person receiving providence does not merely receive information; the actual events around him are affected. Gersonides responds to this problem with a solution that is not entirely clear. His argument seems to be that here, too, providence is determined by impersonal emanations that are available at all times for an individual with intellectual perfection, but in this case those emanations instantiate a series of providential laws rather than impart information, and those laws cause suffering that saves an individual from even greater harm.[22]

In short, the operative principle underlying Gersonides' views on providence is that all instances in which God appears to participate personally in providential action are in reality instances in which human beings bring providence on themselves. They do so by tapping into ever-present impersonal emanations from God that become operative once they have perfected their intellects. Those emanations provide either valuable information or an actual change of events that is of benefit to the individual.[23]

While Gersonides does not discuss immortality in detail in his treatment of providence, he does say in one passage that it is the highest form of providential reward. As with Maimonides, Gersonides has in mind a purely philosophical conception of the afterlife according to which the intellect survives after the demise of the body because it is filled with intelligibles that do not decay. A detailed discussion of immortality is contained in the first book of the *Wars*.[24]

The Commentary on Job

I will begin my discussion of Gersonides' commentary on Job by summarizing its contents.[25] Gersonides opens his introduction to the commentary with the declaration that he has decided to write an exposition on Job because it is a book of great benefit for teaching us about human perfection in the realm of philosophy in general and political philosophy in particular. The full meaning of this statement does not become clear until later on in the commentary. Yet, even here Gersonides gives us some idea of the philosophical value of the book when he informs us that Job deals with the subject of individual providence, one of the "fundamental principles" upon which the Torah is predicated.[26] According to Gersonides, it is this commonality between the Torah and the Book of Job that prompted the rabbis to propose that Moses was author of both works, a position Gersonides endorses.[27]

Gersonides goes on to explain that the Book of Job deals with the most formidable challenge to the notion of individual providence: the suffering of the righteous and the prospering of the wicked. It is a problem that has preoccupied Jewish and non-Jewish thinkers alike. It caused some of the early philosophers to deny that God knows particulars.[28] It inspired prophets and rabbis throughout the ages to raise questions about God's providence. According to the rabbis, even Moses was perplexed by this issue.[29]

Gersonides then explains why he feels a need to write his own commentary on Job. Previous commentators have misunderstood the book because they have been concerned almost exclusively with the meaning of its words and have not understood the philosophical concepts upon which it is based, an approach bound to fail given that its words are often equivocal. The only analysis of Job that proceeds in the proper manner is that provided by Maimonides in his *Guide of the Perplexed*. Maimonides correctly believed that the Book of Job is constructed on the principle that in the investigation of any philosophical matter one can come to a proper conclusion only by looking at all the possible opinions regarding it and judging their strengths and weaknesses. It is for this reason that, in Maimonides' reading, the views in the dialogue represent all the possible philosophical opinions on providence.[30]

Gersonides goes on to deal with the question of whether the Book of Job reports true historical events or is only an allegory. The view that Job is an allegory is supported by the notion that it seems most improbable that there should be a discussion that would by chance encompass precisely all the possible opinions on providence. On the other hand, there is strong evidence to suggest that Job indeed existed. First, it is not entirely unprecedented to find discussions on a given subject in which all the possible views are represented. Aristotle reports discussions of this sort in his deliberations on physics and metaphysics.[31] Moreover, Job is explicitly mentioned by Ezekiel.[32] Finally, the Book of Job itself gives biographical details about its central character and the other figures in the dialogue, and such details are often given by an author in order to prove a story's historicity.[33] Gersonides therefore seems to lean toward the view that Job existed, though he does not explicitly say so.[34]

Gersonides concludes his introduction with a quick summary of the philosophical principles one must know for a proper understanding of the Book of Job, a discussion primarily concerned with the sources of evil in the world.[35] Evil has one of two causes. It can come from matter, which is responsible not only for ill health but bad conduct as well. It is also responsible for evil that comes from outside the recipient in the form of violence from others, since violent conduct is also rooted in one's material make-up.[36] A second source of evil is chance events, such as earthquakes and fire falling from the sky—an apparent reference to lightning—and human beings can be harmed by these events if they happen to be in the wrong location.[37] Yet, chance events are not evil in essence because no evil can come from God. Instead, these occurrences are tied to matter because they are the result of natural processes designed to rectify an imbalance between the four elements. Moreover, God has placed within us the capacity to circumvent these events—through prophecy and veridical dreams.

Gersonides ends his discussion with an important qualification. He concludes that all the evils described here are not properly "human" evils in that they are concerned only with material well-being. True human good and evil are, respectively, intellectual perfection and the lack thereof.[38]

One point worth noting is that despite Gersonides' assertion that there are two sources of evil, there is, in effect, only one. Gersonides explicitly identifies matter as the source of the first type of evil, and in his description of the second type of evil, it turns out that matter is the source of evil here as well. It would appear, therefore, that matter is, in one way or another, the underlying cause of all evil.

Let us now proceed to Gersonides' interpretation of the story of Job itself. Gersonides gives us little information about the period in which Job lived. He mentions in several passages only that Job predates the Torah.[39] He says a good deal more about Job's character. The initial Job whom we meet before his suffering is a man of many good qualities. His ethical perfection is attested to in the very first verse of the book, where he is described as "blameless and upright" and as one who "feared God and shunned evil." He also has a certain degree of intellectual perfection in that he is learned in the natural sciences, as is evident from his discussion of nature later on in the dialogue. Job's only flaw is that he is not versed in the subject matter of providence, and it is for this reason that the biblical text fails to describe him as a man possessing wisdom. More specifically, he is confused about whether or not there is individual providence.[40]

Gersonides makes clear throughout his commentary that Job does believe in immortality.[41] It is only providence in this world that is a source of perplexity for him. Interestingly, one of the key passages Gersonides uses to support this reading is Job's statement in Job 19:25–27, "But I know that my Vindicator lives; / In the end He will testify on earth." As I noted earlier, this passage was widely read by Christians as a reference to the coming of Christ. Gersonides reads it as a reference to God, who will "vindicate" Job through immortality.[42]

The dialogue between God and Satan in the first two chapters of Job is interpreted by Gersonides as an allegory, the only section of the story that Gersonides explicitly treats in this fashion. Satan represents all the evils that befall Job, and those afflictions are in turn representative of the entire range of evils described in Gersonides' introduction. The initial evils Job experiences, evils that decimate his family and livestock, are those emanating from outside the recipient and come from matter and chance events. Job is the victim of human violence manifested in the attacks of the Sabeans and Chaldeans, and of chance occurrences in the form of fire falling from the sky and strong winds. The second round of evils Job experiences consists of evils that come from within the recipient. Job is stricken with bodily illness, which is caused by either the material make-up of the individual or by poor ethical conduct.[43] Gersonides never specifies which of these is the source of Job's illness. However, given that Job is described as having ethical perfection at the beginning of the story, it is likely that Gersonides would attribute Job's suffering to the effect his material constitution had on his physical health.

After experiencing these afflictions, Job's position on individual providence goes from confusion to outright rejection. Job concludes that human affairs are entirely governed by the heavenly bodies, with no regard for the well-being of the individual. It is for this reason that Job curses the day of his birth.[44] He now believes that all events are determined by the position of the stars on that day, and therefore they are responsible for his misery.[45] Yet, despite Job's rejection of individual providence, he still believes in general providence over the human species.[46] He also continues to believe in the immortality of the soul.[47] As we have seen, in the *Wars* Gersonides identifies Job's view with that of Aristotle.[48]

Gersonides surmises that Eliphaz, Bildad, and Zophar were probably well-known philosophers in their day.[49] In his explication of their dialogue with Job, Gersonides has them take up precisely the same positions attributed to them in the *Wars*: they all believe that individual providence watches over each and every human being in that God rewards and punishes human beings for their actions, but each supports a somewhat different version of this viewpoint.[50] As I have already noted, Gersonides informs us in the *Wars* that this position is held by most followers of the Torah.[51]

In Gersonides' thinking, it is Elihu who provides the correct position on providence. As we have already seen, in the *Wars*, this viewpoint is supported by the elite among the scholars of the Torah.[52]

Gersonides goes to great lengths to demonstrate how the addresses of the various participants in the dialogue contain philosophical arguments supporting their respective viewpoints, but it is beyond the scope of this discussion to recount them all. I will just note that many of these arguments are identical with those found in the *Wars*—though, as we shall see in our discussion of the third interface, there are some significant differences between the two presentations.

I should also say something about how Gersonides reads Elihu's philosophical position out of the biblical text, given that his is the correct viewpoint. There is much here that is familiar to us from Maimonides and his followers. Gersonides locates the key section of Elihu's address in Job 33:14–30. Elihu's statement in verse 33:14 that "God speaks in one manner / And in a second manner—though man does not perceive it" is taken by Gersonides to refer to the two major manifestations of providence: prophecy and providential suffering.[53] The verses that follow describe these two forms of providence. Prophecy is dealt with in verses 15–18, which relate that God speaks to human beings "in a dream, a night vision." Verses 19–30, which deal with the sick person, describe providential suffering. The "angel" who rescues the sick person in verse 23 is, in Gersonides' reading, the Active Intellect, which is the source of providential suffering. When Elihu tells us in verse 29 that the sick person is rescued by the angel only "two or three times," he is specifically referring to a case in which providential suffering attempts to save an individual from spiritual injury by warning him that he has strayed from the path of intellectual perfection. The individual in this instance receives a warning only a limited number of times before he is no longer worthy of providence.[54]

According to Gersonides, once Elihu outlines his view on providence, he also explains to Job why he has suffered. Elihu tells Job that he experienced his afflictions because he lacked intellectual perfection, a defect manifested in his imperfect understanding of providence. This defect was serious not just because it affected Job's own well-being, but also because it was potentially deleterious to the political and theoretical well-being of others. With respect to the political realm, Elihu argues that Job's position could have harmed others because a lack of belief in individual providence implies that there is no benefit in worshipping God and would therefore only encourage the wicked to remain set in their evil ways. Job's views were also liable to cause harm to the theoretical perfection of others because without the hope of experiencing individual providence, people would fail to develop their intellects in order to gain protection from oncoming danger in this life and immortality in the next.[55]

Incidentally, this explains why Gersonides states in his introduction to the commentary that the Book of Job has value for perfecting us in the realm of political philosophy. It teaches the truth not only about providence, but also about the negative societal consequences that can result from an erroneous view of providence.

In his exposition of God's address, Gersonides informs us that God in many respects repeats points made by Elihu. God extols the glories of nature at great length in order to emphasize the notion that divine providence is indeed manifest in all levels of creation. According to Gersonides, however, God does provide one piece of information not given by Elihu. While Elihu had explained why the righteous suffer, he did not account adequately for the prospering of the wicked. God explains the latter phenomenon by arguing that the wicked prosper because general providence provides a measure of well-being for everyone. Therefore, if the wicked receive benefit from this form of providence as well, there is nothing inherently wrong with this. In Gersonides' reading, this argument is implied in God's lengthy descriptions of the wonders of nature, which are designed to bring maximum benefit to all His creatures.[56]

According to Gersonides, Job admits his error in the closing chapter of the book. Job's recantation in 42:6 is taken to mean that he "despises" (*em'as*) having believed the things he believed and "regrets" (*ve-niḥamti*) having sat in a state of mourning in "dust and ashes," knowing as he does now that his suffering was his own fault. He has come to understand that if he perfects his intellect, he will experience individual providence and will be able to circumvent any future evil. Gersonides also explains why God goes on to scold Job's friends for not having "spoken the truth about Me as did My servant Job."[57] Job's friends supported a view they knew was wrong only in order to vindicate God, while Job at least defended a view he sincerely believed was right. Job perceived that there was injustice in this world and therefore argued that God must be ignorant of particulars. It was from this line of reasoning that Job concluded there is no individual providence, only general providence. Moreover, Job's view was closer to the truth because it was based on sense perception, while that of his friends was based purely on speculation.[58] Therefore, even though Job's view ultimately turned out to be incorrect, at least it was built on true principles. In fact, Job's view was certainly on the right track with respect to those who do not experience individual providence at all, since such people are in fact guarded only by general providence, in which Job believed. Elihu disagreed with Job only with respect to those who have achieved intellectual perfection, for such people do experience individual providence.[59]

Antecedents

Given that Maimonides is clearly the primary influence on Gersonides' reading of Job, I will begin my examination of the first interface by looking more closely at the nature of this influence. Maimonides is, in fact, the only other Jewish philosopher whose reading of Job Gersonides explicitly acknowledges in the course of his commentary. In his introduction, Gersonides cites Maimonides as the one interpreter who has properly understood the Book of Job as a philosophical discussion in which all viewpoints on the question of providence are represented. All other interpreters have erred in focusing only on the meaning of its words—an obvious swipe at the schools of French and Spanish exegesis concerned exclusively with the *peshat*, or plain meaning, of the biblical text.[60] Thus, Gersonides declares his intention to approach Job in the same spirit as Maimonides, and indeed Gersonides follows through by trying to show how the various figures in the dialogue represent different philosophical viewpoints in a manner reminiscent of his predecessor.

After his introduction, Gersonides mentions Maimonides only twice more, and in relatively unimportant contexts.[61] Yet, Maimonides' influence goes well beyond these explicit references. It comes through particularly in Gersonides' interpretation of the figure of Satan and the divine beings whom he accompanies in the prologue.[62] The divine beings are construed by Gersonides as "the powers that govern existence as the messengers of God."[63] Gersonides does not clarify what these "powers" are precisely, and perhaps this is the point; the divine beings represent forces in nature of every variety. This interpretation echoes that of Maimonides, who, according to my reading, identifies the divine beings with natural forces of one sort or another.[64]

The influence of Maimonides is also evident in Gersonides' interpretation of Satan. As we have seen, Gersonides views Satan as an allegorical figure for all the afflictions that will befall Job, afflictions that are in turn representative of all the major categories of evil that afflict mankind as a whole. I also noted that in Gersonides' thinking all categories of evil are ultimately tied to matter, for while he distinguishes between those evils that come from matter and those that are due to chance occurrence, he tells us explicitly in the introduction to his commentary that even chance occurrences have their basis in matter.[65] Therefore, it is safe to assume that while Gersonides sees Satan as representative of a range of evils, he considers him ultimately to be representative of matter. Now, according to my reading of Maimonides, Satan is a symbol for privation. However, I noted that a number of other interpreters are of the opinion that Maimonides construes Satan to be representative of matter, and given the ambiguity of Maimonides' remarks on Satan, this viewpoint is certainly understandable.[66] Therefore, it is likely that Gersonides equated Satan with matter because he believed Maimonides had made that identification as well.

Gersonides follows Maimonides' interpretation of a number of specific biblical passages regarding Satan. He accepts Maimonides' understanding of the term "Satan" as deriving from the verb *satah,* to turn away, because he "leads people astray from the correct path."[67] Gersonides also co-opts Maimonides' reading of Job 1:6, where Satan is mentioned separately from the divine beings whom he accompanies. According to Gersonides, Satan's separateness from the other divine beings is meant to teach that Satan "is not intended essentially," meaning that evil is not the product of God's first intention. As we have seen, the same point is made by Maimonides.[68] Gersonides also adopts Maimonides' interpretation of the biblical passages that describe Satan as "roaming all over the earth" (Job 1:7, 2:2). In Gersonides' reading, this description teaches that only in the sublunar realm "are such evils found, not among beings in the celestial realm," since it is only in the sublunar realm that matter corrupts.[69] We find a similar interpretation in Maimonides.[70]

Most important is that Maimonides' influence is felt in Gersonides' reading of Elihu's remarks in Job 33:14–30. Gersonides follows Maimonides in viewing that section of the dialogue as key to the book as a whole. Moreover, there is reason to suspect that Gersonides is influenced by specific elements in Maimonides' interpretation of that chapter. Gersonides' notion that prophecy is one of two major forms of providence described by Elihu is an idea that may have roots in Maimonides, who, as we have seen, also alludes to prophecy as one of the central elements in Elihu's address.[71] Gersonides' identification of Elihu's angel as the Active Intellect, which saves an individual from harm by means of providential suffering, also seems to have its roots in Maimonides, who highlights the role of the angel as a providential force. As we have seen, some interpreters argue that Maimonides also understands the angel precisely this way.[72] Gersonides also appears to have gone in a direction similar to Maimonides in his belief that God's speech to Job emphasizes the limitations of human knowledge in fathoming divine providence.[73]

Maimonides may not have been the only philosopher who influenced Gersonides' reading of Job. There is reason to suspect that Ibn Tibbon was a factor here as well. Important features of Gersonides' reading of Job 33 bear a striking resemblance to those found in Ibn Tibbon's *Ma'amar Yikkavu ha-Mayim.* Both Gersonides and Ibn Tibbon see Elihu's remarks in Job 33:14–30 as teaching us about two forms of providence: prophecy and providential suffering. Both thinkers see verse 14 as introducing these forms of providence: "For God speaks in one manner / And in a second manner—though man does not perceive it." For both thinkers, God's first "speech" is synonymous with providence that comes through prophecy, while his second "speech" is providence manifested in suffering.[74] Both thinkers see verse 19, which introduces the description of the sick person—"He is reproved by pains on his bed"—as a critical point of transition, where Elihu goes from discussing the first form of providence to a description of the second.[75]

There is certainly much that separates Ibn Tibbon's reading from that of Gersonides. For instance, Ibn Tibbon effectively denies that there is individual providence and therefore identifies prophecy and providential suffering with the general providential order. For Gersonides, prophecy and providential suffering are both expressions of individual providence. Also, in Gersonides providential suffering takes two forms, while in Ibn Tibbon there is only one.[76] Nonetheless, the two expositions exhibit unmistakable similarities in both structure and content.

The major difficulty with proposing a connection between Gersonides and Ibn Tibbon is that Gersonides never mentions Ibn Tibbon in his commentary on Job, nor in any other of his works, for that matter.[77] Moreover, in his introduction to the commentary, he speaks as if Maimonides' reading of Job is the only other philosophical discussion of Job of which he is aware: "We have not found any earlier thinker who has set out to explore the opinions of these people that argued with Job in this book other than the little that was written by the Rabbi, the Guide, in his book *The Guide of the Perplexed*."[78] Nonetheless, we must not rule out a connection between Ibn Tibbon and Gersonides. First of all, in his reading of Job, Gersonides may not have acknowledged Ibn Tibbon because he did not see him as anything other than an interpreter of Maimonides. Thus, he may have seen no need to acknowledge Ibn Tibbon's exposition on Job as a contribution separate and distinct from that of Maimonides. Another factor is that Gersonides often does not acknowledge the Jewish sources that influence his biblical commentaries. The strongest evidence for this tendency is found in a recent dissertation on Gersonides' commentary on Ecclesiastes by Ruth Ben Me'ir, who demonstrates that Gersonides makes use of a whole slew of Jewish interpreters whom he never acknowledges. Ben Me'ir shows that among these influences, one of the most prominent is none other than Ibn Tibbon, who himself composed an important commentary of his own on Ecclesiastes.[79] Thus, Gersonides' failure to mention Ibn Tibbon in his commentary on Job does not rule out the possibility that he was influenced by him. Finally, I should mention that we are certain that at one point in his life Gersonides owned a copy of *Ma'amar Yikkavu Ha-Mayim*. It is mentioned in a manuscript containing a list of books in Gersonides' personal library. It is therefore likely that Gersonides was at least familiar with Ibn Tibbon's reading of Job.[80]

Gersonides' similarities to Maimonides and Ibn Tibbon tell only part of the story. We fail to fully appreciate the originality of Gersonides' interpretation of Job if we do not understand how he departs from them. In fact, Gersonides has a markedly different conception from Maimonides and Ibn Tibbon of the central message of the story.[81] For the latter two thinkers, the purpose of the Book of Job is to enlighten us about what we may call the spiritual dimension of providence. In Maimonides' reading, Job goes from a figure who equates providence with material and physical rewards at the beginning of the story to one who at its conclusion understands that true providence consists of a psychological immunity to suffering that is achieved through the cultivation of an acquired intellect.[82] For Ibn Tibbon, the message of Job is even more spiritual, for, according to his reading, what Job discovers by the end of the story is that true providence is not to be found in this world at all, only in the afterlife with the immortality of the intellect. For Gersonides, the central message of Job is in some sense precisely opposite that suggested by Maimonides and Ibn Tibbon. In Gersonides' reading, Job actually starts off with a highly spiritual notion of providence in that he believes in immortality. The spiritual dimension of providence is therefore taken for granted throughout the dialogue. What Job needs to be convinced of is that there is also individual providence in this world that will safeguard his physical and material well-being, and it is only when Elihu enters the dialogue that he finally believes that such a form of providence exists.

Gersonides does not value the spiritual dimension of providence any less than Maimonides or Ibn Tibbon. As noted earlier, he too regards the immortality of the intellect as the greatest reward that a human being can receive.[83] Where he does differ with them is on the question of where the focus of the Book of Job lies. Gersonides reads it as a text centered exclusively on the issue of providence as it pertains to our material and physical well-being in this world. In fact, one gets the sense that in his commentary Gersonides deliberately avoids any attempt to spiritualize the notion of providence. According to Gersonides, immortality is mentioned by Elihu on two occasions as the ultimate reward. In both instances, it is mentioned by Gersonides without any accompanying philosophical explanation.[84] Moreover, the subject of immortality is entirely absent from Gersonides' exegesis of the most critical portion of Elihu's speech to Job in chapter 33, where Elihu reviews all the various forms of individual providence that come with achieving intellectual perfection.

These observations highlight an important facet of Gersonides' philosophical thought that is often unappreciated, and that is its conservative dimension. Although Gersonides became one of the favorite targets of criticism of the Jewish traditionalists, who opposed a philosophical approach to Judaism, a careful reading of his thinking reveals that he was not as radical as many other philosophers in the Maimonidean school. Gersonides' conservatism seems most evident here. By reading the Book of Job as focused entirely on the question of providence over our physical and material well-being in this world, Gersonides seems to be making an effort to defend the traditional notion that there is material reward and punishment in this life as taught by the Bible and the rabbis.[85]

It must be asked whether Gersonides' differences with Maimonides and Ibn Tibbon regarding the central message of Job indicate that his reading of the book was formulated in conscious and deliberate opposition to theirs. One may be tempted to answer this question in the affirmative, but caution is in order, since a difference of views is not always polemical. Furthermore, there is no explicit engagement on Gersonides' part with the views of his two predecessors regarding the central message of Job. Yet my suspicion is that in formulating his understanding of Job in the way that he does, Gersonides is indeed reacting to their readings, in particular that of Ibn Tibbon.

I believe a case can be made for this conjecture by delving further into Gersonides' differences with Maimonides and Ibn Tibbon and examining their respective intellectual-historical environments. For Maimonides and Ibn Tibbon, the chief target of criticism in Job is the viewpoint of the masses, who adhere to a literal reading of the Law and therefore believe in a simplistic and materialistic conception of reward and punishment. That view is erroneous, and those who are philosophically enlightened must be brought to a higher understanding of providence. Job's intellectual journey throughout the dialogue serves as a model for that transformation. That Maimonides and Ibn Tibbon should read Job in this manner fits with their wider agenda. They were forging a new synthesis between Aristotle and Judaism, and therefore they were very much focused on the distinction between the religion of the masses and that of the philosophers, with the intent of demonstrating the validity of the latter. Job's transformation reflects this agenda in that Job moves from a conception of providence as understood by the masses to one that is philosophically enlightened.

For Gersonides, the picture is entirely different. In his reading, Job is a figure who begins the story already educated in philosophical truths. His only shortcoming is that he is unsure about whether there is individual providence in the physical and material realm. By the end of the story, he discovers that such providence does in fact exist. It would appear, therefore, that for Gersonides the target of the Book of Job is not the masses, but the philosophers and their followers! It is they who, like Job, must be enlightened about the nature of providence as it pertains to this world.

As with Maimonides and Ibn Tibbon, Gersonides' approach can be explained in light of his intellectual environment. By the time Gersonides composed his commentary on Job in 1325, philosophy was no longer a rare or novel discipline for Jews. Philosophical learning was widespread in many medieval Jewish communities, and Maimonides' *Guide* was well known—particularly in Gersonides' own Provence. At the same time, it had become controversial. For more than a century prior to the period in which Gersonides wrote his commentary, philosophical learning had brought with it great turmoil in the Jewish community as pro- and anti-Maimonidean forces did battle with each other over the legitimacy of this brand of learning. In the thick of this battle were the works of Ibn Tibbon. He was recognized as one of Maimonides' most prominent and radical interpreters and was therefore a particular object of scorn among the traditionalist opponents of philosophy. It would also appear that his thinking on providence was an important issue in this controversy.[86]

Gersonides' commentary on Job could be read as a response to these events. It may have been written as an attempt to oppose the radical understanding of providence spawned by Tibbonian thinking by presenting a more traditional, but philosophically grounded, notion of providence. Gersonides agreed with Ibn Tibbon that ultimate providence is the immortality of the intellect, but he departed from him in believing that one could also justify the biblical-rabbinic notion that there is individual providence in this world that protects us physically and materially. For this reason, Gersonides' commentary deliberately pushes the issue of immortality into the background and directs its attention exclusively to providence in this world, for it is the latter issue that becomes the battleground for Gersonides against the radical Tibbonian understanding of providence.

Gersonides' construction of the figure of Job appears to be specifically designed to serve the purposes of this polemic. What better way to illustrate his point than to depict Job as a figure who is philosophically educated, who is unsure as to whether or not there is individual providence in this world, but who eventually discovers that there is providence of this kind? It would seem that the initial Job is meant to mirror the uncertainties about providence among philosophers in Gersonides' own time as the result of Ibn Tibbon's influence and the Maimonidean controversy. Gersonides' message to such people is that the biblical-rabbinic notion of individual providence is philosophically sound, as Job himself discovers.[87]

If this interpretation of Gersonides is correct, it would shed light on his understanding of Elihu's criticisms of Job after Elihu has told him the truth about providence. We saw in our summary that Elihu scolds Job for supporting an Aristotelian position on providence because it is liable to harm others with respect to both their political and their theoretical well-being; it would encourage them to continue in their wicked ways and discourage them from seeking intellectual perfection and the rewards it brings. Gersonides' reading of Elihu's chastisement of Job may have been meant as a veiled criticism of Ibn Tibbon and other Jewish philosophers of his ilk who were radical Aristotelians. Gersonides may have been attempting to alert them that their views are of great danger both to themselves and others. It is fine to be a follower of Aristotle; after all, Job's viewpoint was closer to the truth than the views of Eliphaz, Bildad, and Zophar. But to reject individual providence in the physical and material realm is not only unjustified from a philosophical standpoint but perilous for our theoretical and political well-being.

There are other important differences between Gersonides, on the one hand, and Maimonides and his followers, on the other, that can be explained by their different intellectual environments. As we saw in our summary of Gersonides' commentary, Gersonides debates the question of whether or not Job existed, and while he does not provide a decisive answer to this question, he seems to lean toward the view that Job in fact existed.[88] Here again, Gersonides has departed from his Maimonidean predecessors, who were unequivocal in their support for the view that the Book of Job is entirely allegorical.

Gersonides' position should not surprise us, because it fits well with his thinking on allegory in general. He employs this method of biblical exegesis quite sparingly in the belief that it should be used only when it is absolutely necessary. One such instance is the dialogue between God and Satan in the Book of Job, where the strong anthropomorphic imagery leaves Gersonides no choice but to adopt an allegorical reading. However, Gersonides apparently sees no need to view the rest of the book as an allegory.[89]

We see here again the conservatism of Gersonides. One of the key points of contention in the controversy over Maimonides' works was the allegorical reading of the biblical text by the philosophers. Traditionalists were incensed by a method of interpretation that seemed to denude scripture of its literal meaning in favor of an inner philosophical understanding that from their perspective was entirely foreign to Judaism.[90] Gersonides seems to have bowed to these pressures by adopting a method of interpretation that restricted the allegorical method to a limited number of places in the biblical text. His approach to the Book of Job is a prime example of an exceptional case of this sort.

Another significant difference between Gersonides and his Maimonidean predecessors has to do with the philosophical positions that he attributes to the various participants in the dialogue in Job. Gersonides follows Maimonides, Ibn Tibbon, and Zeraḥiah Ḥen in including the viewpoints of Aristotle and the followers of the Torah in the dialogue, but he departs from them by eliminating the Muslim theologians. Maimonides, Ibn Tibbon, and Zeraḥiah interpret the opinions of Bildad and Zophar as representing the Mu'tazilite and Ash'arite schools, respectively. Both in the *Wars* and in his Job commentary, Gersonides explicitly rejects these positions as unworthy of consideration.[91] In his commentary on Job, Gersonides explicitly acknowledges that his differences with Maimonides on this point have to do with their different intellectual environments. Commenting specifically on Maimonides' identification of Bildad's viewpoint with that of the Mu'tazilites, Gersonides says:

> I think that what caused him [i.e., Maimonides] to identify Bildad's view in this manner was what he discovered about the well-known opinions in his period regarding providence. And because he saw some degree of relationship between the opinion of Bildad and the opinion of the Mu'tazilites, on account of this he attributed the opinion of the Mu'tazilites to Bildad.[92]

Gersonides is convinced that Maimonides identified Bildad's view with that of the Mu'tazilites simply because of his intellectual environment, where that view was well known.

Gersonides' elimination of the Muslim theologians changes the whole nature of the dialogue. In Maimonides and Ibn Tibbon, the dialogue between Job and his friends is very much an ecumenical affair, inclusive of various religious and philosophical viewpoints. In Gersonides' scheme, the dialogue is much more narrow. It is, in effect, a battle between Aristotle and rabbinic Judaism, with Job representing the former and his three friends representing the latter.

This rereading should not surprise us. After all, the conflict between Aristotle and rabbinic Judaism defined Gersonides' own intellectual environment more than it did that of Maimonides and Ibn Tibbon. While there were certainly tensions in the Jewish community in Maimonides' and Ibn Tibbon's day regarding the introduction of Aristotle into Judaism, the controversy over this issue did not gain full momentum until the middle of the thirteenth century, when the battle lines between pro- and anti-Maimonidean forces were firmly drawn. This was well after Maimonides' lifetime and at the end of Ibn Tibbon's, but well before that of Gersonides.[93] It therefore makes sense that in his reading of Job, Gersonides would see its dialogue sharply divided between the view of Aristotle and the views of the rabbis.

This is not to say that Gersonides denies the universal significance of the debate between Job and his friends. In his commentary he depicts these figures as non-Jewish philosophers—or perhaps, more accurately, "pre-Jewish" philosophers who lived before the revelation at Mount Sinai.[94] He also emphasizes that from a theoretical standpoint all of the opinions in Job represent all the possible viewpoints one can have regarding providence.[95] Therefore, like Maimonides and Ibn Tibbon, Gersonides clearly sees the dialogue as universal in meaning in that it includes all philosophical views. Nonetheless, once we become aware of the identity of the various figures, it becomes clear that on another level he conceives of the dialogue in more narrow terms than his predecessors.

To sum up this portion of the discussion, Gersonides is clearly indebted to Maimonides and Ibn Tibbon for his reading of Job. He borrowed a number of elements from them in his interpretation of the structure and content of the book. We have also seen that Gersonides departs from Maimonides and Ibn Tibbon in significant ways, especially in his understanding of the central message of Job. While he values the spiritual dimension of providence as much as Maimonides and Ibn Tibbon, he seems determined to read the Book of Job as a text defending the existence of individual providence in the material and physical realm. Gersonides' differences with his predecessors may reflect his conservative tendencies, which inspired him to place the biblical and rabbinic notion of providence on a firm philosophical footing. His reading of Job may have also been formulated specifically in reaction to the most radical type of philosophical thinking on providence, represented by Ibn Tibbon, whose writings on this issue had become one of the focal points of debate in the controversy over Maimonides.

Exegesis

Let us now look at the second interface, which raises the question of whether Gersonides recognized the major exegetical difficulties in Job and, if so, how he confronted them. One thing that is obvious from our discussion is that Gersonides adopts some of Maimonides' strategies in dealing with these problems. Thus, Gersonides, like Maimonides, makes sense of the long, rambling, and sometimes directionless dialogue between Job and his friends by arguing that each defends a distinct philosophical viewpoint. Gersonides also follows Maimonides in bringing unity to the book as a whole by interpreting the interaction between God and Satan in the prologue as an allegory concealing the central message of the book, which then emerges in the addresses of Elihu and God.

In a number of respects, though, Gersonides provides original solutions to the exegetical challenges presented by Job. First, as already noted, Gersonides takes up the question of whether or not Job is an allegory, and though his position is not entirely clear on this issue, he seems to lean toward the view that Job was a historical individual. Gersonides is therefore the first medieval Jewish philosopher since Saadiah who takes this approach to Job.

More interesting is how Gersonides deals with the dialogue in Job. I have already noted that while Gersonides adopts Maimonides' view that the dialogue in Job is a debate between different philosophical viewpoints, he attributes viewpoints to them that are different from those assigned to them by Maimonides. Yet, even more important, Gersonides departs from Maimonides in suggesting that Job, Eliphaz, Bildad, and Zophar present opinions that, despite being incorrect, all have some truth in them. In fact, as Gersonides would have it, all of their views are in some measure co-opted into the final position of Elihu. Thus, according to Gersonides, Job is praised by God in the final chapter because his viewpoint has an element of truth in it. The same goes for the other participants, for even though Gersonides states that their views are more off the mark than Job's, they too have valuable things to say. Thus, for instance, Eliphaz, according to Gersonides' reading, argues that there is individual providence over all human beings by adducing evidence from prophecy and veridical dreams, phenomena that seem to indicate that a caring God has imparted providential information. Gersonides points out that Eliphaz is correct, and indeed the existence of prophecy and veridical dreams becomes a crucial element in Elihu's explication of providence. Another example is Bildad's position, which states that when evil afflicts the righteous, some good always emerges from it. Gersonides informs us that this view also turns out to have some truth in it because Bildad foreshadows the notion of providential suffering, which is supported by Elihu.[96]

By interpreting the dialogue in this manner, Gersonides brings coherence to the discussion because he not only justifies why there are different positions in the dialogue, but also explains how they all contribute to the central message of the book. Moreover, Gersonides' conception of the dialogue lends a certain symmetry to the discussion. Job starts off as a figure unsure as to whether there is individual providence. Once he suffers, he takes one extreme view, stating that there is no individual providence whatsoever, while his friends take the other extreme view, according to which there is individual providence for all human beings without exception. It is only when Elihu comes along that a higher synthesis of all the views is created with the claim that there is individual providence for some individuals but not for others. However, the symmetry of the synthesis in Gersonides' reading of Job is by no means perfect. I have already noted that according to Gersonides Job's position is closer to the truth than the views of his three friends.[97]

As for God's role in the dialogue, all the interpreters in this study thus far have had to deal with this question because they all see Elihu as the figure who provides the correct view, and the question then is what God contributes to the discussion. Gersonides has to confront the same difficulty, since he too sees

Elihu as the individual who supplies the true position on providence. In fact, as we saw in my summary of his commentary, Gersonides openly acknowledges the problem when he claims that in many respects God's speech merely reviews what Elihu has said. I also noted that Gersonides solves the problem by proposing that there is one point that God addresses that Elihu fails to deal with adequately, namely why the wicked prosper.[98] Gersonides therefore takes an approach similar to Maimonides in seeing a complementarity between Elihu's position and that of God, though the actual content of that complementarity differs somewhat from that in Maimonides.

Gersonides displays considerable exegetical ingenuity in dealing with the ambiguities and inconsistencies in the depiction of the figure of Job in the biblical text. I have already speculated that Gersonides' portrayal of Job was shaped in part by his intellectual environment in that it reflects his conservative reaction to the Tibbonian reading of the Book of Job. Yet, even if my hypothesis is correct, Gersonides' depiction of Job is equally an attempt to grapple with the difficulties regarding Job in the biblical text itself. We hear echoes of Maimonides' reading in Gersonides' suggestion that Job is an individual who has ethical perfection but is intellectually deficient, and that it is for this reason that he suffers. However, Gersonides' portrait of Job is more complex and nuanced than that of Maimonides, and it allows him to steer skillfully through the minefield of contradictory signals in the biblical text regarding his character.

As we have seen in my summary of Gersonides' commentary, Gersonides' depiction of Job is very positive. While Job is not intellectually perfect, he is learned in the natural sciences—an achievement that Maimonides does not see in Job—and his only intellectual flaw is that he is confused on the subject of providence in being unsure as to whether or not there is individual providence over human beings. Furthermore, if Job begins the story confused about providence, he is, by Gersonides' own account, in very good company. As Gersonides points out in the introduction to his commentary, many of the great prophets were perplexed about providence because of the problem of the suffering of the righteous. Moses himself was confused about this issue.[99] Thus, Gersonides' highly positive image of Job is again in evidence, for by emphasizing that the prophets themselves—even Moses—were confused about providence, Gersonides contextualizes Job's one great flaw in a manner that makes it most respectable. The praise accorded Job in the opening verse of the story is therefore fully justified.

However, Job's flaw turns out to be a critical one, because he lacks the intellectual perfection required to experience individual providence and is therefore vulnerable to the ravages of matter and chance events. The same flaw also causes him to settle on an Aristotelian position, denying the existence of individual providence, once he experiences his suffering, and it is for this reason that Job curses the day of his birth and throughout the dialogue argues against the notion that God cares about his predicament.

And yet, even when Job takes this incorrect position, his sophistication continues to shine through in Gersonides' reading. Gone is any suggestion that Job lashed out at God from frustration with his situation, as we find in Maimonides. There is a certain dignity and sobriety to the Job we meet in Gersonides' commentary, qualities that remind us of Zeraḥiah's Job but supplemented with a good deal more sophistication. He is a person who, despite his suffering, calmly defends his position on providence with philosophical arguments. Throughout the dialogue, Job's friends accuse him of blasphemy in attributing evil to God, but Job consistently counters that this is not the case. His position is that God merely suffers from weakness and lack of power. A more powerful God, he claims, could have arranged the world such that people who would suffer would not be created at all.[100]

Job also argues against the accusation that his position will corrupt the faith of others and cause them to abandon a life of piety. To this charge, Job responds that he in no way denies the value of doing good deeds and the worship of God. These are in fact useful in achieving immortality, belief in which Job continues to uphold despite his suffering. Job even argues that his views will encourage righteousness. His position will convince people to perfect their deeds in order to achieve reward in the afterlife and to abandon their interest in material goods, on the premise that such things are of no use to their ultimate well-being. As we have seen, Elihu argues that Job's position is harmful to others,[101] but in Gersonides' exposition of Elihu's charges, it is clear that Elihu is concerned about the unintended effects of Job's views, and he acknowledges that Job has no deliberate desire to corrupt the masses.[102]

Once Job is educated by Elihu in the true position on providence, he comes to understand that there is individual providence and that he suffered because he was not worthy of it on account of his lack of understanding of that issue. Note here that Gersonides avoids the discomfort that Ibn Tibbon and Zeraḥiah Ḥen felt with the Maimonidean notion that Job gains intellectual perfection in what seems to be an unreasonably short period of time. Gersonides' Job is already well educated from the outset, so there is no reason he should not be able to quickly absorb the lessons Elihu teaches him. Job's sophistication throughout the story also helps explain why God is subsequently able to praise Job as His "servant" while He chides Job's friends. As Gersonides tells us, even though Job supported an incorrect position on providence, it was a position held out of sincerity and had significant philosophical depth—much more than the positions of his friends.

Gersonides' overall strategy is clear. The biblical text gives us mixed signals about Job because he is a genuinely complex individual. He has sufficient perfection to win praise from the narrator at the beginning of the book and from God at the end of it, but not quite enough to keep him out of trouble in the interim. His initial confusion on providence is his Achilles' heel that causes him to experience suffering. It also causes him to stray toward an Aristotelian position before he corrects that deficiency with Elihu's help. It is for this reason that he must repent at the end of the story. And yet Job's philosophical sophistication stays with him even as he defends an erroneous conception of providence, so that when Elihu appears, he is readily enlightened.

I might add here that Gersonides' understanding of providence is fully compatible with the conclusion of the story, in which Job is rewarded with a new family and his wealth restored—even though Gersonides does not explicitly comment on this portion of the text. In Gersonides' thinking individual providence allows one to experience physical and material well-being. Therefore, there is nothing unusual in the fact that Job is able to start a new family and regain his wealth, for he is by this point intellectually perfect and thus worthy of individual providence.

I turn now to Gersonides' thoughts on the intended audience of the Book of Job. Like the other philosophers I have examined, Gersonides never deals with this issue explicitly, though his position is implied. As I mentioned in my examination of the first interface, it would seem that on one level Gersonides conceives of the story as having universal meaning in that Job and his friends are all pre-Sinaitic non-Jews. On another level, Gersonides also sees the story as having great significance for the Jewish people as a whole. As we have seen, this association is not unprecedented in medieval Jewish philosophy in that Saadiah also identifies Job with the Jewish people. Saadiah, however, does not develop that association explicitly; we had to infer it from hints and clues found in *Beliefs and Opinions* and in his commentary on Job. Gersonides is the first medieval Jewish philosopher to speak about this connection openly. He does so in a remarkable passage at the end of his explication of Elihu's remarks in Job 33:

> You should know, you the inquirer, that in a similar manner the doubt is resolved about what has been mentioned in the Torah regarding the evils that occur to us when we do not walk in God's ways and the goods that occur to us when we do walk in them, as mentioned in the blessings and curses.[103] That is, the [Jewish] nation as a whole will experience providence when it walks in God's ways. But when it begins to stray from the good way, then evil will be designated to come upon it from the [celestial] system. That warning[104] will reach that collective in one of the two ways that have been mentioned. That is, if there is a prophet among them, the warning will reach him and he will impart it to the nation as a whole; and if there is no [prophet], then [the celestial system] will bring upon that collective some suffering and afflictions, either to save them from bodily evil designated to come upon them, or to save them from spiritual failing in which they have become mired. For this reason, the Torah has explained that when evils of this type come upon the collective, they [i.e. the Israelites] should not attribute it to chance. Rather they should believe that everything comes from God, may He be blessed, in order to chastise them and force them out of [their] evil, [as] it says, "And if you behave toward Me as if these misfortunes are by chance . . ." (Lev. 26:21).[105] In this manner, good things will come to us when we walk in God's ways and when we are attached to Him by means of providence, not by the [effects of the celestial] system alone; evils will come to us when we stray from

> them. The Torah has already explained that at the end of the matter there will be punishment by the hiding of God's countenance—that is, the withdrawal of divine providence [altogether]. Regarding evil occurring to us at that time—if it is not evil designated to come upon us by the [celestial] system[106]—the Torah says, "and I will . . . hide My countenance from them" (Deut. 31:17). That is, the occurrence of evils by way of providence to chastise people is not perpetual, as Elihu mentioned in this response.[107]

Gersonides informs us here that the review of all the various forms of providence given by Elihu explains God's covenantal relationship to the Jewish people, in particular the system of rewards and punishments upon which that relationship is based. If the Jews obey God's will—which in philosophical terms means achieving moral and intellectual perfection through observance of the commandments—they will be worthy of experiencing prophecy and providential suffering. If they fail to observe God's will, they will experience no providence whatsoever.

This citation is the lone discussion of the Jewish people in Gersonides' commentary, and one could therefore argue that it is no more than an aside to the central themes that occupy him throughout the commentary. Yet, Gersonides' remarks seem more than casual. They are a summary of most of the essential features of Gersonides' position on the special status of the Jewish people, which are developed more extensively elsewhere in his writings.[108] Moreover, these remarks appear in the most important section of the commentary. It is here that Gersonides summarizes the central portion of Elihu's speech, which reveals his doctrine on providence.

This observation sheds interesting light on the nature of Gersonides' commentary. As we have seen, the central message of Gersonides' reading of Job is that there is individual providence in this world and that it guards our physical and material well-being. If Gersonides sees the Book of Job as relevant to the Jewish people, may it be then that this message regarding providence is directed specifically at Gersonides' fellow Jews? Is he perhaps addressing his Jewish contemporaries, who, in light of the Jewish exile and its tribulations, have become disillusioned with the notion that there is divine providence watching over them? If this is the case, Gersonides would be saying to them, in effect, that they should not lose hope, that there is indeed divine providence that functions in this world, and that they will experience it if they pursue moral and intellectual perfection.

I am not arguing here that the Jewish message in Gersonides' commentary is its major focus. It is clear that he viewed the Book of Job primarily as a universal discussion about providence. It would seem, though, that on another level he also saw it as containing insights of importance to the Jewish people and their circumstances. We may also add that Gersonides was well aware of the persecution of Jews in his own period. He lived in close proximity to two expulsions of Jews from France, one in 1306 and another in 1322, and to the Crusade of the Pastoureaux in 1320, which destroyed a number of Jewish communities in France. These events are alluded to in a number of places in his writings, and they all occurred before he composed his commentary on Job.[109] Therefore, it should not surprise us if Gersonides drew upon the Book of Job in order to respond to Jewish suffering.

Gersonides may have felt the question of providence over the Jewish people to be all the more urgent if indeed he was conducting a polemic against the Tibbonian understanding of providence, as I surmised earlier. For the danger of Ibn Tibbon's view was not just that it denied providence in this world to the individual, but that it also implicitly denied it to the Jewish people as a corporate entity. Gersonides may have therefore sought to assure his fellow Jews that there was indeed providence over the Jewish people in this world and that this notion was philosophically defensible. In short, Gersonides' remarks about the Jewish people may have been part of his conservative reaction against the radical interpretation of Maimonidean thought as typified by Ibn Tibbon.

What emerges from this portion of the discussion is that like the other philosophers I have examined thus far, Gersonides is not merely a philosopher attempting to read his philosophical views into the biblical text; he is also a biblical commentator attempting to grapple with its exegetical challenges. We have discovered as well that he is a biblical interpreter of considerable originality. For while in some respects he follows Maimonides in his endeavor to bring coherence to the Book of Job, he is certainly not a commentator on Maimonides in the manner of Ibn Tibbon and Zeraḥiah Ḥen. On a number of central issues, Gersonides confronts the challenges presented by Job with solutions that are very much his own.

Exegesis and Philosophy

I now proceed to the third interface, which concerns the relationship between Gersonides' commentary on Job and his systematic discussion of providence in book 4 of *The Wars of the Lord*. The examination of this interface will require a good deal more effort than has been expended on the same interface in the other thinkers in this study because Gersonides produced more literature on providence than any of them in both the exegetical and systematic modes. His commentary on Job may be the most lengthy one composed by a medieval Jewish philosopher, and his discussion of providence in the *Wars* is one of the most thorough treatments of this subject in medieval Jewish philosophy. There is therefore a great deal to discuss in examining the nature of the relationship between these two works.

Before I begin my analysis of this relationship, two important caveats are in order. First, we must rule out any attempt to explain the relationship between the commentary on Job and the discussion of providence in the *Wars* on the basis of when the two works were written. We know that the commentary was composed toward the end of the period in which Gersonides wrote the *Wars*. The *Wars* was written between 1317 and 1329, and as I noted earlier, the commentary was completed in 1325.[110] However, the *Wars* often cites the commentary, and therefore it would appear that Gersonides continued to revise the

Wars in light of the commentary after the *Wars* was completed. We must therefore view the two works as effectively contemporaneous. Second, we must resist any temptation to treat the relationship between the two works in accordance with the distinction between esoteric and exoteric writing, wherein the *Wars* is viewed as a treatise written for the philosophers and the commentary is understood as one composed for the masses. As noted earlier, scholars are in agreement that Gersonides does not use esoteric discourse.[111]

The first thing I should point out about the relationship between Gersonides' commentary and book 4 of the *Wars* is that there is a great deal of overlap between them. Certainly, the commentary deals with a more specific issue than the discussion of providence in the *Wars*, since, as Gersonides tells us, the commentary focuses on the question of the suffering of the righteous, while book 4 of the *Wars* treats the issue of providence in general.[112] However, this difference is of little significance, because in order to deal with the suffering of the righteous in the Job commentary, Gersonides effectively spends most of his energy formulating his position on providence as explicated in the *Wars*. Thus, both works present a similar range of philosophical positions regarding providence; they use similar arguments both for and against those positions; and they eventually choose the same position as the correct one.

Yet, upon closer examination one notices significant differences between the two presentations, differences that can be accounted for by the modes of exposition they employ. Let us look first at the commentary on Job. What one notices in this work is that the biblical text inspires Gersonides to bring out aspects of his deliberations on providence not found in the *Wars*. This is particularly evident in his explication of the discussion between Job and his three friends. The lengthy dialogue between them affords Gersonides the opportunity to come up with a much greater number of arguments both for and against the various viewpoints on providence than those found in the *Wars*.

While there are numerous examples that one could call on to illustrate this point, let us look at one such instance concerning Job's response to Bildad in chapter 10 of Job. In Gersonides' reading, Bildad has just presented his argument that the suffering of the righteous does not impugn God's justice because the evil afflicting the righteous invariably results in a good outcome that may not be immediately foreseen. Job responds with a number of refutations of Bildad's viewpoint. For instance, if Bildad is right, the evils that afflict the righteous and the wicked would have different final causes and therefore should be different in species as well. However, this is not the case, for these evils are, in fact, of the same species. Job also argues that if Bildad is correct, the evil that affects the righteous is potentially worse than that which affects the wicked. The wicked may die from their suffering and will therefore be put out of their misery before they have suffered extensively, but the righteous will be kept alive so as to receive the ultimate benefit from their suffering and will therefore suffer for a longer period of time than the wicked.[113]

What is important for our purposes is that these arguments do not appear in the *Wars*. The exercise of composing a commentary on Job, it would seem, inspires Gersonides to come up with arguments against Bildad's view absent from his philosophical treatment in the *Wars*.

Even more significant is that the exegetical exercise in the commentary on Job seems to bring out an aspect of Gersonides' own position on providence, one not found in the *Wars*. In his explication of Elihu's speech, Gersonides suggests that the two major forms of providence—prophecy and providential suffering—not only save an individual from harm, they also teach him to repent, which in philosophical terms means abandoning one's attachment to material pleasure and pursuing intellectual perfection. This educational benefit of providence is obvious with respect to providential suffering in its second manifestation since it is endemic in its very purpose. In this manifestation of providence, once a righteous individual has begun to stray from the path of intellectual perfection he is caused to suffer so that he will be guided back to that path.[114] Yet, in his commentary on Elihu's address, Gersonides makes clear that the other forms of providence exhibit a similar feature as well. A person who receives a prophecy about oncoming danger not only is given the opportunity to save himself from physical harm, but his experience encourages him to take stock of his life and improve his conduct:

> God will open men's understanding [through prophecy] to the afflictions and chastisements that are determined by the constellations to come upon them so that they will be saved from them by taking account of it [i.e., prophecy]; for free will can gain dominance over this [natural] order as explained earlier. It will also *cause them to fear God more and repent to Him with* [*all their*] *might*.[115]

Providential suffering in its first form has a similar effect on the recipient. An individual who is caused to suffer and then realizes that he has been saved from greater physical harm will be inspired to repent of his sins:

> At the end of the affair [i.e., providential suffering], he will be healed and will be more fresh and vigorous than he was in his youth. . . . An added benefit to this is that during his illness he will put his heart into praying to God and will have desire for Him. God will pay attention to this prayer and outcry, since he is attempting to cleave to God and repent to Him.[116]

What is striking about the mention of the educational value of providence alluded to in these passages is that it finds no parallel in the *Wars*. There Gersonides depicts providence as a force that serves a direct practical function. Its primary purpose is simply to save a person from physical harm. It is the reward for one's intellectual accomplishments, not the cause.[117] Therefore, in his commentary on Job, Gersonides inserts a new element into his theory on providence. This is not to say that Gersonides has entirely changed his position. In the commentary on Job the practical function of providence is still dominant. The educational benefits, it would seem, are only a desirable by-product of providence. Nonetheless, the presence of this element imparts a new spin to Gersonides' thinking on providence mostly absent from his major philosophical work.

It is the biblical text that appears to have inspired Gersonides to come up with the notion that there are added educational benefits in experiencing providence. Regarding the benefits of prophecy, Gersonides is prompted by Elihu's suggestion that God speaks to men "in a dream, a night vision," and "by disciplining them leaves His signature" (Job 33:16). The reference to discipline here invites Gersonides to propose that prophecy is designed to improve our conduct, not just to save us from harm. A similar purpose is imputed by Gersonides to providential suffering because of Elihu's remark that the person who suffers but is eventually saved from his afflictions "prays to God" and confesses to other men that "I have sinned" (Job 33:26–27). Gersonides seems to have concluded from Elihu's statement that if a person is inspired by providential suffering to pray and repent, he has received more benefit from it than physical well-being alone.[118]

Another element in Gersonides' commentary on Job that is absent from the *Wars* is an emphasis on the limitations of human knowledge regarding God's providential activity. Thus, we are told on a number of occasions in Gersonides' commentary that if we are unable to make sense of events in the world, we should sooner blame our own deficiencies than attribute any lack of power to God. This idea crops up in Gersonides' interpretation of the addresses of both Elihu and God. Gersonides paraphrases Elihu's thoughts on this matter:

> It is evident that God does not want wickedness or iniquity, and when we find that He does not maintain justice and uprightness regarding the goods and evils affecting individual people, it is proper that we investigate how this is possible without attributing to God wickedness and iniquity. But if we cannot grasp this, it is proper that we attribute it to our [intellectual] limitations.[119]

An even stronger statement is found in Gersonides' interpretation of God's address. In Gersonides' paraphrase of one section of that address, God says to Job:

> Do you have the power of God . . . such that you can conceive of the meaning of His power and say that He is limited and weak? In fact, "power" is attributed to you and God by equivocation only. Therefore, you cannot conceive of the power of God and His might. . . . Rather, all the other existent beings are inferior to Him, and their power emanates from His power. Therefore, there is no relation between the power of the other existent beings and the power of God, because God's power belongs to His essence, while the power of the other existent beings comes to them from outside them.[120]

Here Gersonides casts his thoughts about the limitations of human knowledge in terms of his theory of divine attributes. There is no relationship between our power and divine power because the term "power" is equivocal when applied to God and to us. God's power is part of His essence, while our power comes from outside us since it is nothing but a manifestation of His power. Therefore, Job should not question God's capacity as a providential Deity.[121]

While these statements are certainly not inconsistent with Gersonides' discussion of providence in the *Wars*, there is no suggestion in the *Wars* that the limitations of human knowledge and the equivocal nature of divine attributes are factors in how we approach the question of providence. There Gersonides seems quite confident that an understanding of providence is well within our grasp. Moreover, these sorts of arguments never enter into Gersonides' attempt to refute Aristotle's view, which Job represents, as they do in the commentary.

It would appear that once again it is the exegetical format of the Job commentary that furnishes Gersonides with the opportunity to bring out ideas that his philosophical presentation in the *Wars* does not. The speeches of Elihu and God, which extol the glories of nature at great length, prompt Gersonides to emphasize that human beings are unable to entirely fathom God's providential activity.

If the commentary on Job provides insights not found in the *Wars*, the reverse is also true. The format of systematic philosophical argumentation allows Gersonides to delve into issues not dealt with in his exegetical work because here he is freed from the constraints of the biblical text, which in large measure dictate what he will talk about in his commentary. Therefore, in the *Wars* Gersonides exhibits a freedom of inquiry that is not evident in the Job commentary.

An important illustration of this point is that in the *Wars* Gersonides has the opportunity to give a more rigorous defense of his own theory of providence than he does in his commentary.[122] For instance, as part of this defense, Gersonides grapples with a number of philosophical challenges from the rabbinic position, according to which individual providence cares for all human beings.[123] There is no such discussion by Gersonides in his commentary on Job because there is no opportunity for it. According to the biblical text, Elihu responds only to Job, whose situation and deliberations about suffering inspire the entire dialogue. At no point does Elihu engage in any discussion with Job's three friends regarding these issues.[124] Thus, the biblical text presents Gersonides with an opportunity to defend his theory of providence only against Aristotle, whom Job represents, but not against the rabbis, whose position is supported by Job's friends. We should add that in the *Wars* Gersonides also responds to a number of philosophical challenges to his own theory that are identified as belonging to none of the major positions on providence represented in the Book of Job. It goes without saying that the Job commentary does not present Gersonides with an opportunity to grapple with these objections either.[125]

Another example of philosophical material found in the *Wars* but absent from the Job commentary is Gersonides' justification of his theory of providence in light of his impersonal conception of God. As I noted at the beginning of this chapter, the central pillar of Gersonides' philosophical system is his Aristotelian-Averroist conception of God, according to which God has limited knowledge of the world below, cannot change His will, and therefore cannot interact directly in human affairs. Gersonides must therefore find a way to show that such a God can provide providential help through prophecy and providential suffering, forms of assistance that seem more appropriate for a personal Deity. As we have seen, Gersonides solves this difficulty in the *Wars* by arguing that in one way or another all providential activity in which God appears to be reaching out to us is really activity in which we reach out to Him.[126]

Actually, Gersonides does allude to these difficulties in his commentary as well. One of Job's arguments against the positions of Eliphaz, Bildad, and Zophar is that since God cannot possibly know particulars, there can be no individual providence.[127] The same issue is no less of a challenge for Elihu, for he too believes in individual providence, at least for select people. Therefore, Gersonides must have Elihu address this problem. In the passage in which Gersonides informs us of Elihu's response, it is interesting to see what he says:

> Regarding that which Job argued against his friends who said[128] that God punishes man for his deeds and has cognizance of him, and [regarding that which Job] explained [when he said] that this was impossible both from the standpoint of sense-perception and philosophy (*'iyyun*), as explained earlier—it is evident that this doubt has been solved as Elihu has posited in this inquiry; namely, that he [i.e., Elihu] does not posit that God knows these particular things in the sense that they are particulars. Therefore, he said, "But insignificant things, God does not hear" (Job 35:13). Yet, [God] does know all of them in another sense, as we have fully explained in the book, *The Wars of the Lord*. And with this knowledge which He has of them, knowledge of these particulars will reach the prophets by means of the faculty of imagination before their advent.[129]

Notice how brief these remarks are in addressing the issue at hand. Gersonides' reading of Elihu addresses the philosophical problems raised only by prophecy, not by providential suffering, and what Gersonides says about these problems is rather meager. Indeed, he alludes to his theory that God does not know particulars as particulars and that in the process of prophecy the general information in the Divine Mind becomes concretized in the prophet's imagination—all essential ingredients in Gersonides' solution to the apparent conflict between individual providence and divine knowledge. Yet, these bits of information do not really add up to an explanation. Most telling is that Gersonides refers his reader to the *Wars*, as if to admit that he has not fully dealt with the issue here.

The brevity of Gersonides' remarks can again be explained by the constraints of the exegetical medium. Elihu's comments on the issue of divine knowledge are contained in one solitary verse: "But insignificant things God does not hear, / And Shaddai does not see" (Job 34:13).[130] Gersonides therefore has little opportunity here to elaborate fully on a philosophical explanation and must refer his readers to the *Wars.*

It is rather ironic that the philosophical format of the *Wars* allows Gersonides to conduct a discussion of the suffering of the righteous that is in some respects more comprehensive than that found in the commentary on Job. While the discussion of this issue in the *Wars* is not nearly as lengthy as it is in his commentary, Gersonides presents a number of reasons for the suffering of the righteous that are not found in the commentary.[131] Here again we can explain the difference between the *Wars* and the commentary by the constraints the biblical text imposes on Gersonides in his role as exegete. In the commentary, Gersonides is forced to talk about the suffering of the righteous as it pertains to Job's specific situation if he is not to digress too much from the biblical text. In the *Wars* there is no such limitation. Thus, in the latter work, Gersonides can entertain explanations for the suffering of the righteous that he cannot in his exposition on Job.

Another element entirely missing from Gersonides' commentary on Job but present in the *Wars* is the philosophical identities of the various opinions found in the Book of Job. It is, in fact, only in the *Wars* that we learn that Job represents the view of Aristotle, that Eliphaz, Bildad, and Zophar represent in several variations the standard Jewish view, and that Elihu's view represents the elite opinion of thinkers such as Maimonides.[132] It is not clear why in the Job commentary Gersonides would fail to correlate the opinions in the dialogue with their respective philosophical schools. One possibility is that because the biblical text does not mention them, Gersonides does not see any reason to refer to them either. However, in other biblical commentaries, Gersonides is not averse to mentioning the names of philosophical thinkers whose views accord with the biblical text, and one would have thought it a simple matter to do so here.

The answer to this question may lie in remarks made by Gersonides at the end of his commentary. As I noted in my summary, Gersonides justifies God's praise of Job in the final chapter of the book by arguing that Job's position was closer to the truth than the views of his three friends. Job's friends argued in bad faith in that they took positions they knew were untrue in order to vindicate God. While Job questioned God's justice, he was at least sincere in the position he presented. Moreover, Job argued on the basis of sense experience, while his friends did not. Finally, Job's view was at least correct with respect to those who do not experience providence, since the latter are in fact abandoned by individual providence.[133] There are important implications in these remarks when one is made aware that Job is representative of Aristotle and his friends are representative of the followers of the Torah. What Gersonides is implying, by favoring Job's view over those of his three friends, is that

Aristotle's view is, in fact, superior to that of the rabbis. The favoring of Aristotle's view is striking, since nowhere is this partiality expressed in Gersonides' discussion of providence in the *Wars*.

All this may suggest that Gersonides does not correlate the views of the figures in Job with the philosophers they represent in order to conceal his preference for Aristotle. That preference adds a more radical edge to Gersonides' theory of providence than he may have wanted to reveal. Gersonides therefore makes no reference to the identity of the viewpoints in Job, on the assumption that only the astute reader familiar with his discussion in the *Wars* would know that he, in fact, favors Aristotle's position over that of the rabbis.

We should be cautious about drawing such a conclusion, given that, as I have noted, Gersonides does not engage in esoteric discourse and that in other places he tends to be quite open about views that may be offensive to the traditional reader. Yet, it could be argued that here Gersonides may have been more fearful than usual in expressing his true views, for in this instance he impugns the very integrity of the Jewish position. He claims, after all, that not only is that view incorrect, but that it is put forth in bad faith by basing itself on a misplaced desire to vindicate God. While Gersonides often favors Aristotelian thinking over that of the rabbis, to my knowledge he never offers elsewhere so harsh a critique, essentially attacking the very foundation of their views.

The foregoing analysis does not exhaust all that one can glean from a comparison of Gersonides' *Wars* and his commentary on Job. A full examination of this issue could be a study in its own right. Nonetheless, on the basis of my analysis, some preliminary conclusions can be drawn regarding the relationship between the two works. The *Wars* and the commentary on Job, while covering similar ground, seem to serve a complementary function. What pure philosophical argumentation does not accomplish in the *Wars* is fulfilled by exegesis in his commentary on Job, and vice versa. Each medium brings out insights and emphases not contained in the other. It would seem that Gersonides expected his audience to read both works in order to gain a full understanding of his views on providence. It is perhaps for this reason that in each of these works, he makes sure to frequently cite the other.[134]

Gersonides' commentary on Job is the most original reading of the book in medieval Jewish philosophy since Maimonides, and its richness has been evident on every level of our analysis. This is not to say that antecedent influences are absent. Maimonides' presence pervades Gersonides' commentary in both its content and its structure. Ibn Tibbon also seems to have had an impact on the commentary, particularly his interpretation of Job 33. Yet, Gersonides departs from his two predecessors in a number of significant ways. First, he interprets the Book of Job through a new and original conception of providence, one that is not merely grafted from Maimonides, as was the case with Ibn Tibbon and Zeraḥiah Ḥen. Most striking is the conservative thrust that Gersonides brings to the Book of Job. He seems determined to interpret the book as a philosophical defense of the biblical-rabbinic notion that there is individual providence in this world and that it protects our physical and material well-being. In this endeavor Gersonides appears to be deliberately opposing the radical Tibbonian reading of Job, which argued that there is no individual providence in this world and that the truest manifestation of providence is immortality. We speculated that Gersonides' reading may be explained by his intellectual historical context. With the widespread controversy that thinkers such as Ibn Tibbon engendered, and their radical interpretation of Maimonidean philosophy, Gersonides seems to have attempted to shore up the traditional notion of providence, but without abandoning Aristotelian philosophy.

As an exegete, Gersonides confronts the major challenges presented by the biblical text in a manner that is also unmistakably Maimonidean; yet, here too his originality comes through. His solutions to those challenges are ultimately very much his own and in some respects more sophisticated than those of Maimonides. Most impressive is the way Gersonides deals with the ambiguities in the figure of Job. He adopts Maimonides' view that Job is intellectually deficient, but he paints a far more nuanced and subtle portrait of Job than Maimonides did, so that he is able to better explain the conflicting signals in the biblical text regarding his character.

In my analysis of the relationship between Gersonides' reading of Job and his systematic treatment of providence in the *Wars*, the richness of Gersonides' thought was again evident. No thinker in medieval Jewish philosophy produced as extensive a body of material on providence in both the systematic and exegetical modes as Gersonides did with these two works, and they therefore serve as an ideal focus for investigating the relationship between philosophy and exegesis in medieval Jewish philosophy. We discovered that the *Wars* and the commentary on Job cover similar ground and ultimately support the same position on providence. Yet, with a close reading, it became clear that there are important differences between them, and that those differences can be explained as emanating from their respective modes of discourse. Each mode allows Gersonides to bring out elements in his thinking on providence not present in the other.

We will see that Gersonides' reading of Job represents an important transition in the interpretation of this text in medieval Jewish philosophy. With this reading, Aristotelianism still reigns supreme as the thought system for interpreting Job; yet, a conservative step has been taken away from the most radical type of Aristotelian reading found in Ibn Tibbon. As we approach the fifteenth century, the conservative element introduced by Gersonides will only gain strength. The next thinker in my study will exemplify that tendency.

7

Simon ben Ẓemaḥ Duran

The last figure in my study is R. Simon ben Ẓemaḥ Duran (1361–1444), a noted rabbinic authority and philosopher. Duran spent the first thirty years of his life in Majorca, where he worked as a physician and also established himself as an esteemed rabbinic scholar. In 1391 Duran narrowly escaped death when violent riots broke out against the Jewish community in Spain and spread to Majorca. He was forced to flee to Algiers, where he spent the rest of his life. There he was unable to find employment as a physician because the practice of medicine in his new homeland was based more on superstition than on up-to-date science, and there was thus little use for his professional expertise. Consequently, Duran was forced to take a salaried position with the Jewish community as a rabbi. He was eventually appointed chief rabbi of Algiers.[1]

Duran is best known as one of the leading halakhists of his era. He left behind a number of halakhic works, the most important of which is his collected responsa, *Tashbeẓ* (*Teshuvot Shimon ben Ẓemaḥ*). He is less known as a philosopher, but his contributions in this area are nonetheless substantial. His two major philosophical works are *Magen Avot* (*Defender of the Fathers*) and *Ohev Mishpat* (*Lover of Justice*). The first work is a commentary on tractate *Avot*, but the majority of it is actually a lengthy three-part introduction dealing with the basic beliefs of Judaism.[2] *Ohev Mishpat* is a commentary on the Book of Job.[3] Both works show a remarkable range of erudition not just in Jewish but in non-Jewish learning as well. Duran demonstrates a familiarity with mathematics, logic, astronomy, history, philosophy, and grammar. He was also able to read Arabic and Latin.[4]

There has been little modern scholarship on Duran's philosophy. The only comprehensive studies of his thought are a lengthy article by Jakob Guttmann written in several parts in 1908 and 1909 and a more recent dissertation by Naḥum Arieli.[5] The one area of Duran's thought that has received significant scholarly attention is his attempt to establish a Jewish creed, an issue that preoccupied Jewish philosophers in Duran's era as Jews were increasingly pressured to justify their beliefs in the face of Christian polemics. Duran is recognized as having made important contributions in this area.[6]

Despite the little that has been written on Duran, the general character of his thought is well known. Duran is one of the first representatives of a traditional backlash in medieval Jewish philosophy against Maimonides, Gersonides, and Jewish Aristotelianism in general, which began at the end of the fourteenth century and gained momentum through the fifteenth. The other representatives of that backlash were also Spanish figures for the most part, notably Joseph Albo and Ḥasdai Crescas. These thinkers can be classified as rationalists, but they adhered to a rationalism that tended to support an understanding of Judaism more closely wedded to the literal reading of biblical and rabbinic sources than did their philosophical predecessors.[7] Duran is also representative of a trend in medieval Jewish thought that combined philosophical speculation with Kabbalah. In fifteenth-century Jewish thought, syncretism between philosophy and Kabbalah was very much in vogue.[8]

It is Duran's commentary on Job, *Ohev Mishpat*, that will be the focus of my concerns here. This work rivals Gersonides' commentary in its length. It contains an introduction of thirty-five chapters and then a line-by-line commentary on the biblical text. It was composed in 1405 and published in Venice in 1590 along with *Mishpat Ẓedek*, a commentary on Job written by Obadiah ben Jacob Seforno (c. 1470–c. 1550).[9]

The general neglect of Duran's philosophical thought is especially evident in the paucity of scholarship on *Ohev Mishpat*. Arieli's dissertation, while purporting to be a study of Duran's thought as a whole, is based almost exclusively on *Magen Avot* and makes little mention of *Ohev Mishpat*.[10] The only published study of *Ohev Mishpat* is an article written a number of years ago by J. David Bleich.[11] Bleich's discussion focuses for the most part on Duran's views on providence as they are developed in that work, and he deals only tangentially with his interpretation of Job. Much of my analysis will therefore be an attempt to explore territory that is mostly uncharted.

The structure of my discussion will be similar to that adopted for the other thinkers in this study, but with one major difference. Because Duran presents his systematic views on providence in his introduction to the commentary on Job, I will deal with Duran's thinking on this issue as part of my summary of the commentary, rather than in a separate section, as I did with Maimonides and Gersonides. My analysis as a whole will be aided by the fact that Duran's philosophical thought is in many respects a reaction against Maimonides, and he therefore does not adopt esoteric discourse. Thus, his commentary on Job is relatively clear and straightforward.

The Commentary on Job

Let me begin by summarizing the content of Duran's commentary. Duran opens his introduction to this work with a number of preliminary thoughts regarding the Book of Job and the type of commentary he intends to write on it.[12] First, he argues for the centrality of providence as a principle of Jewish belief. The importance of that doctrine lies in its connection to the observance of the divine commandments. It is concerned with the issue of reward and punishment and is therefore the prime incentive for obeying God's word.[13]

Duran goes on to explain that the philosophers have had a great deal of difficulty with the principle of providence, and for good reason. There are three types of philosophical issues: those that can be demonstrated by reason, such as the existence of God; those that cannot be demonstrated by reason, such as creation; and those that can be demonstrated by reason but the senses disprove, such as providence. Providence is in this last category because reason can show that there is a providential God, but the senses contradict that finding because we constantly witness the suffering of the righteous and the prospering of the wicked. The suffering of the righteous is a particularly strong challenge to the doctrine of providence, especially when the victim is sure in his own heart that he is innocent, as was the case with Job. In fact, so great is the perplexity posed by the suffering of the righteous that the greatest of the sages and prophets in Israel have been consistently preoccupied with it. It is therefore no surprise that the philosophers should have difficulty with this issue as well.[14]

Duran concludes that one needs the guidance of revelation in order to establish the proper view of providence and to address the challenge of the suffering of the righteous, and that it is for these very purposes that Moses composed the Book of Job.[15] Thus, for Duran, Job deals with the entire problem of providence in both its positive and negative aspects. On the one hand, it provides rational proof that there is divine providence. On the other, the Book of Job addresses the major difficulty with the doctrine of providence, which is the suffering of the righteous.[16]

Duran notes, however, that the Book of Job is itself problematic. It is obscure both in the meaning of its words and verses and in its overall message. Duran goes on to explain that this is the reason different approaches have been used to unlock the meaning of Job. One group of commentators has attempted to make sense of the plain meaning of the book, while another group has interpreted it from a philosophical standpoint, which entails trying to define the positions represented by the various participants in the dialogue.[17] Duran declares that his own commentary will function as an anthology of these various readings of Job, the motivation here being convenience. The interpretations of previous commentators are "scattered here and there," and therefore Duran has decided to compose a commentary "so that the issues will be ordered, and I, and those like me, will be assisted in not having to expend effort searching the issues in many books."[18]

Duran goes on to say that he has also composed an introduction to the commentary designed to help clarify the overall meaning of the book and the issue of providence in general. In this portion of the commentary, Duran adds, he has "deviated in some respects" from what others have said and asks his readers not to be critical of him, since such disagreements are common among Torah scholars, particularly with respect to the meaning of Job. Duran thus hints that his commentary will contain some original thinking.[19]

Once Duran shares these preliminary thoughts, he spends a good deal of energy providing proofs for the existence of providence and demonstrating how those proofs are found in the dialogue in Job. He declares that there are two proofs for divine providence: that which is based on the concept of God's perfection, and that which is based on God's actions in the world.

The proof from God's perfection goes as follows: A perfect master does not ignore his servants and will not desist from giving them their proper due in accordance with their actions. Given that man is the most exalted of His creatures, it is therefore appropriate that God provide providential care by rewarding and punishing him for his actions.[20]

The second proof, based on God's actions in the world, is really a series of arguments in three categories: arguments based on God's actions in the world as a whole; arguments based on God's actions in the animal kingdom; and arguments based on God's actions vis-à-vis human beings.

Regarding God's actions in the world as a whole, there are two arguments. The first has to do with God's actions at the beginning of the world. A person who creates something perfect will want that thing to persist in its perfection afterward. It thus stands to reason that God, who has created a perfect world, will want the world to remain perfect. Given that man is the most exalted of God's creatures, it is therefore fitting that God provide providential guidance for him to achieve perfection through reward and punishment. The second proof involving God's actions in the world as a whole concerns His actions *after* creation. This proof essentially relies on a detailed description of the many wonders of nature. Duran is especially impressed by the phenomenon of rain, which provides water to living beings at the correct times and in the exact quantities. Duran concludes that if God's guidance of nature is evident throughout nature, it is fitting that He should exercise providence over human beings through reward and punishment.[21]

The proof of providence from God's actions in the animal and plant kingdoms is a variation on this last proof. Here, too, Duran offers a lengthy list of the wonders of nature, this time with a focus on how nature provides for the needs of many different animal species. Again the conclusion is drawn that human beings should receive the greatest of divine care, given their exalted status, and that they therefore deserve to be guided by reward and punishment for their actions.[22]

Finally, Duran provides a series of proofs for providence from God's actions in the world involving human beings. Divine providence is evident in several phenomena:

1. God's creation of the human body, with its many wonders, in particular its capacity for reason.
2. God's giving of commandments to human beings for their improvement.
3. The relative paucity of evil in the world, despite the number of evil people wishing to do harm to others.
4. The frequency of instances in which the wicked prosper despite their deserving to be punished.
5. The occurrence of veridical dreams, which warn people against oncoming evil.
6. The frequency of instances in which the wicked suffer according to the principle of measure for measure.[23]

As Bleich has already noted, in these arguments Duran tends not to distinguish between general providence and individual providence. Thus, God's governance of the natural order and His care for the various species of animals is proof for Duran of the existence of individual providence over human beings as well. Previous philosophers in the Maimonidean school, however, tend to draw a sharp distinction between the two.[24]

In Duran's discussion of the proofs for the existence of providence, philosophy and exegesis are tightly integrated. All the arguments adduced thus far in favor of providence are supported by Duran with verses in the Book of Job uttered by the various participants in the dialogue. This book is significant here because all the figures of the dialogue support the doctrine of providence—including Job himself, who, as we shall see, never doubts the principle of providence.

Now that Duran has established the existence of divine providence, he moves on to discuss its mechanism. Duran first summarizes the views of Maimonides and Gersonides on providence, which tie God's providential care to the perfection of the intellect, but he goes on to reject that approach in favor of an explanation that he identifies with Kabbalah. It is the human soul as a whole that is responsible for providence being attached to human beings. The soul is a separate form that has existed from the beginning of creation and, despite its high degree of perfection, comes into the body in order to perfect itself further. That perfection is achieved by the observance of the divine commandments and results in providence, which consists of rewards and punishments in this life. The correctness of this position is confirmed by the biblical text, which testifies constantly to the connection between the observance of the commandments and providence.[25]

Duran emphasizes that punishment comes directly from God by first intention and does not consist in the abandonment of human beings to chance events, as the philosophers claim.[26] He also endorses Naḥmanides' theory of "hidden miracles" (*nes nistar*), whereby an individual is rescued from harm by divine providence acting in concert with natural laws.[27] Finally, as part of his discussion about providence, Duran rejects all philosophical attempts to interpret the figure of Satan symbolically. Duran adopts the rabbinic view that Satan is an actual angel who aids in the implementation of providence by prosecuting human beings for their sins and punishing them.[28]

In the next phase of his discussion, Duran tackles the question of the suffering of the righteous, which is the primary obstacle for believing in divine providence and is the subject matter of Job. The direction of the first part of this discussion is not entirely clear, but it would seem that Duran begins with a series of deliberations about what actually constitutes unjust suffering. He argues that not all instances of the suffering of the righteous are problematic from a philosophical standpoint. In particular, we should not be troubled when righteous individuals experience misfortune caused by natural disasters, because the natural order is generally a good one and calamities caused by it are few and far between. The suffering of the righteous is a problem only when it seems to have come from "individual providence." Duran appears to be saying that the suffering of the righteous becomes a philosophical difficulty only when a righteous individual seems to have been targeted for misfortune *as* an individual; but when misfortunes come from natural disasters, we cannot object, since they emanate from processes that are in essence benevolent and they kill the innocent with the guilty unintentionally. Duran provides no criteria for how precisely to distinguish between the two types of misfortune.

Duran also discusses another series of considerations that further limit the definition of unjust suffering. The general thrust here is that our judgment of whether or not an event is evil is relative to the circumstances of the victim. Thus, for instance, a king who has been forced to become a merchant has experienced evil, while a slave who has become even a lowly tailor has experienced good. Alternatively, a person who dies young in a region where the climate and water are of poor quality has not experienced evil, since a short lifespan is expected in such places, whereas the same person has experienced evil when he dies young in a region where the climate and air quality are good.[29]

After these preliminary considerations, Duran then offers the following explanations for the suffering of the righteous, most of which are not original to him:

1. The righteous may suffer on account of natural processes of generation and corruption, an explanation that essentially repeats Duran's earlier point that sometimes the righteous are victims of natural disasters.
2. The righteous are perhaps being punished for the little evil they have done in this world so that they can enjoy eternal bliss in the world to come.
3. The righteous may be undergoing a divine test that provides them the opportunity to earn extra reward for bearing their suffering with fortitude; this type of suffering is what the rabbis call *yisurin shel ahavah,* or "sufferings of love."
4. The suffering of the righteous may be not be true evil in that what is deemed evil at present may turn out to have positive consequences in the long run.

5. It may be that the righteous are being punished on account of the sins of others in their generation that they have made no effort to correct.
6. The righteous sometimes suffer on account of their forefathers who have sinned and were punished. Thus for example, the Jews are in a state of humiliation and exile because their forefathers worshipped idols, and even though they may now be righteous, they will continue to suffer from the punishment meted out to their forefathers until they have reached a sufficient level of righteousness to merit redemption.
7. Sometimes the righteous are punished along with a wicked generation because in such instances God may make no effort to differentiate between the righteous and the wicked.[30]

In the course of this discussion, Duran explicitly equates the third explanation—suffering as a test—with the suffering of Job, and he devotes considerable energy to an explanation of that position. I would like to leave Duran's explanation aside for the time being, since it will make more sense once we have looked at his reading of the opening chapters of Job.

At the beginning of his commentary on the story of Job, Duran provides a number of critical details about Job and his background. First, Duran debates the question whether or not Job existed, citing evidence for both positions already adduced by previous thinkers in our study, and concludes unequivocally that Job was a historical individual. As for Job's national origin, Duran claims on the basis of rabbinic sources that Job was a non-Jew who lived either before or around the time that the Torah was given.[31] Duran surmises that Job was most likely descended from Abraham through Esau, since, according to one biblical source, the land of Uz, where Job lived, was occupied by Edom, and Edom is the nation identified with Esau's progeny.[32] Duran also believes that all the other participants in the dialogue were descended from Abraham.[33]

Duran's evaluation of Job's character is extremely positive. Because Job was a descendant of the Patriarchs, he believed in God through received tradition and worshipped Him by means of those commandments that are universal and rational. Duran's view here is based on the notion, originating in rabbinic literature and adopted widely in medieval Jewish philosophy, that God imparted commandments and esoteric knowledge to mankind before the revelation at Mount Sinai. Duran's proof for Job's righteousness is found in the first verse of the story, in which he is described as one who is "blameless and upright . . . feared God and shunned evil." Duran rejects Maimonides' suggestion that because these verses describe Job's ethical qualities they are evidence of Job's intellectual deficiency and that it was for this reason that he suffered. Duran counters that the biblical text mentions these qualities because they are the only ones that truly matter in evaluating a person's character. Moreover, it is only because Job is a righteous figure that his suffering is perplexing and deserves discussion. If he were a deficient individual, as Maimonides suggests, then there would be no enigma here whatsoever, and the book would have no point.[34] Duran also argues, contrary to Maimonides, that Job is in fact very accomplished intellectually—even if this quality is not essential for judging Job's level of virtue. This is evident from the knowledge Job displays throughout the dialogue regarding nature and God. Duran also notes that Job experiences prophecy at the end of the story, which generally does not occur to someone who is deficient in knowledge.[35]

Duran points out that a good number of medieval commentators accuse Job of adopting heretical views in reaction to his many afflictions. Job has been found guilty of adhering to at least three incorrect opinions: that all human events are predetermined by the stars, that God does not know particulars, and that God has knowledge of human deeds but denies human beings providence because of His contempt for them. Duran never specifies who these commentators are, but the first two views are attributed to Job by Gersonides, while the third is attributed to him by Maimonides.[36] Duran adheres to his positive assessment of Job and rejects all three criticisms. Job maintains his belief in divine providence even after his afflictions and at no point adopts heretical views. Duran finds proof for his position in the fact that Elihu finds fault with Job only for accusing God of injustice (Job 32:2). Had Job been guilty of the heresies imputed to him, surely Elihu would have also found fault with Job's defense of his own innocence throughout the dialogue.[37]

Why, then, does Job suffer? According to Duran, all the participants in the dialogue agree that he has experienced his afflictions as a result of sin. Even Job himself acknowledges this, for he recognizes that no person is completely guiltless, even an individual as righteous as he. Nonetheless, Job protests his suffering because he feels God has treated him unjustly. As Job would have it, God should have punished him incrementally over an extended period of time but instead has waited for his sins to accumulate in order to exact punishment for all his sins at once. Job also argues that God's actions are unbecoming of Him, since He appears to be acting like human beings, who often cannot punish their enemies when they want and therefore bide their time until the opportunity arises to exact revenge with one severe blow. Another objection that Job has is that even if God has in fact delayed his punishment, he cannot comprehend why God would bring afflictions upon him one after another with hardly a break in between. In short, Job accepts the notion that he is deserving of divine punishment but complains throughout the dialogue that he cannot accept the way in which that punishment has been administered, in terms of both its timing and its severity.[38]

As for Satan, Duran reiterates his support for the rabbinic view that this figure is an angel responsible for prosecuting and punishing human beings who have sinned. He also presents a critique of the views of previous medieval Jewish philosophers regarding Satan, in particular the Maimonidean position that Satan is an allegorical representation of natural forces.[39] According to Duran, Satan afflicts Job because he is being punished for sinful conduct—though Job's complaints about the timing and severity of that punishment have yet to be addressed.

In his explication of the dialogue between Job and his three friends, Duran tells us that the explanation Eliphaz gives for Job's suffering is close to the truth. The special status of Eliphaz is attested to by the fact that at the end of the story God addresses him and not the other two companions.[40] Eliphaz's position is that Job is righteous, but he argues that since it is impossible for a person to be completely free of sin, Job is being punished by God for whatever minor sins he may have committed. But Eliphaz emphasizes that because Job's sins were minor, the suffering caused by his afflictions is intended as full penitence for his misdemeanors. That is, Job need not go through any formal procedures of repentance to make amends with God, since in the case of minor sins, suffering is all that is needed to accomplish that purpose. According to Duran, suffering of this sort is what the rabbis called "sufferings of love" (*yisurin shel ahavah*).[41]

Nevertheless, Duran concludes that in the end Eliphaz is not able to provide Job with a satisfactory explanation for his ordeal. First, Eliphaz's position, while on the right track, is not as comprehensive as it should have been—a judgment that is clarified only when Duran deals with Elihu. Moreover, Eliphaz changes his position as the dialogue proceeds and ends up with a view that is entirely incorrect. This occurs in the second round of responses to Job on account of the latter's stubborn resistance to Eliphaz's explanation. Eliphaz is particularly offended by Job's angry and strident statements, which appear to impugn God's justice. These statements, Eliphaz concludes, indicate that Job has, in fact, been thoroughly wicked all along and that his suffering must be full-fledged punishment for his sins. Eliphaz's negative assessment of Job is strengthened by his realization that his first theory cannot explain why so many afflictions have come upon Job all at once.[42]

Bildad, who speaks to Job after Eliphaz, is inclined to take Eliphaz's view that Job has suffered on account of minor offenses, but because Job reacts with such anger in his rejection of Eliphaz's argument, Bildad wonders whether Job's sins were of a more serious nature. Bildad thus differs from Eliphaz in that he begins his address to Job already suspecting that Job is an inveterate sinner, and he is ultimately convinced of that position—much as Eliphaz was—on account of Job's aggressive tone as the dialogue proceeds. Zophar, as the last to respond to Job, begins his own address completely convinced that Job has been wicked all along as a result of listening to Job's angry responses to the other two friends.[43]

In short, Duran envisions the dialogue as one of escalating tension between Job and his friends. It begins with his friends positively disposed toward him and attempting to explain his suffering as a means for him to make amends for minor offenses. Job's angry responses gradually convince his friends that he is in fact a wicked individual and that his suffering must be divine punishment for past sins.

It is Elihu who in Duran's opinion offers the correct explanation of Job's suffering, a view that has been unanimous among the thinkers in this study. As noted earlier, Duran believes that Elihu's answer was anticipated by Eliphaz but that his explanation was not sufficiently comprehensive. Therefore, Duran's description of Elihu's position will be in part familiar to us.

Duran's first attempt to explain Elihu's viewpoint in fact occurs in his introduction to the commentary, well before he discusses Eliphaz's position. As we saw earlier, Duran identifies Job's suffering as a test in a discussion laying out a series of explanations for the suffering of the righteous. Let us now take a closer look at what he says there:

> The third [explanation for the suffering of the righteous] has been written by the Geonim, may their memory be blessed. It is that God brings afflictions upon the righteous in order to add to their reward in the world to come. These are sufferings of love (*yisurin shel ahavah*) which the Sages, may their memory be blessed, have noted.
>
> This is the meaning of the test: God tests the righteous as it is written, "in order to test you by hardships only to benefit you in the end" (Deut. 8:16). If it is a tradition which they [i.e., the Geonim] possess, we will accept it, for from the standpoint of inference (*sevara*), it is not a proper judgment that God should bring suffering upon a righteous person without any sin whatsoever; our Sages have already said, "there is no suffering without sin."[44] . . .
>
> The meaning of sufferings of love is not that they occur without any sin whatsoever, for they surely come on account of some sins; rather those sufferings come in the manner of love as a father chastises his son, as it says, "for whom the Lord loves, He rebukes" (Prov. 3:12). This is the love with which he inspects him [i.e., the righteous individual] every morning and examines him every day,[45] so that his sins will not multiply and his punishment for them will not grow. . . . It is impossible that the meaning of the test not be for some sort of sin because of which God brings that righteous person to a test. Our Sages, may their memory be blessed, have said, "What is meant by 'after' (Gen. 22:1)? After the words of Satan."[46] It is known that Satan does not prosecute unless there is some sort of sin. Naḥmanides has already expanded on the notion of sufferings of love and tests in his book, *Torat ha-Adam*.[47]

Duran's explanation here is not entirely clear. He begins by citing the Geonim, who believe that God causes the righteous to suffer in order to test them and give them opportunity to earn extra reward in the world to come. This type of test is identified with the Talmudic doctrine of sufferings of love. Duran has clearly adopted the view of Saadiah Gaon regarding trials that we saw earlier, and it is obvious that it is to him that Duran is making reference when he cites the "Geonim." Yet, Duran also appears to be uncomfortable with the notion that God can cause suffering for no sin whatsoever because the sages seem to deny that possibility. Nonetheless, he recommends accepting the doctrine of sufferings of love since it is a long-established tradition. But almost immediately Duran goes on to argue that God could not possibly cause someone to suffer who is completely guiltless, and therefore sufferings of love must involve sinful conduct. Duran concludes that sufferings of love are a chastisement to ensure that a righteous individual's sins do not accumulate and warrant greater punishment at some point in the future. To illustrate his idea, Duran cites the example of Abraham. According to the Talmudic source to which Duran alludes, Abraham is tested by God with the binding of Isaac after Satan accuses him of not having shown sufficient gratitude to God for all that He has done for him. In Duran's reading, the idea here is that Abraham, having sinned by failing to acknowledge God's kindness, must make amends for his misconduct by being tested. This example demonstrates that divine trials are indeed a consequence of sin.

There is thus some inconsistency in Duran's presentation as he struggles to determine whether or not sufferings of love are the result of previous sin. At first, he appears to identify this type of suffering with Saadiah's conception of trials, according to which no sin need be involved for God to test a righteous individual, seeing as it is an opportunity for that person to earn reward. Duran, however, goes on to reject that view with the claim that some sin must be involved. Another difficulty in understanding Duran is that if divine trials are indeed an appropriate remedy for sinful conduct, Duran does not sufficiently explain why that is the case.

These problems are cleared up when Duran gives a detailed explanation of Elihu's position later on in the introduction to his commentary:

> Elihu knew the truth regarding Job's afflictions, that they were by way of chastisement for a few minor transgressions which he committed. For we know that God, may He be blessed, allowed Satan to cause him harm, and it is known that Satan does not have permission to cause harm except to one who sins. . . . When God wants the good for those who love Him and sees that sometimes they have stumbled into transgressions accidentally and are deserving of punishment—for the Torah requires a sacrifice for one who commits a sin accidentally—He gives permission to Satan to prosecute him and to bring him to a test in order to elicit his good intention in action and atone for his accidental sin through the pain of the test. This was [the meaning of the] trial of Abraham our father according to one who says that it [i.e., Abraham's trial] was through Satan. They said, "What is meant by 'after' (Gen. 22: 1)? After the words of Satan."[48] He [i.e., Satan] prosecuted [Abraham by saying] that he had offered not a single sacrifice in all those banquets. Abraham our father committed this [sin of negligence] accidentally and was like one who acts insolently[49] due to the abundant goodness [of God] and forgets the Lord his maker, and [thus] he did not sacrifice before Him offerings of thanksgiving for the birth of Isaac. Therefore, for that very sin he was tested [by being asked] to sacrifice before Him Isaac his son. And when he withstood his test, he was forgiven for that sin, for he revealed that it [i.e., his sin] was not rebellion nor treachery. God said to him, "For now I know that you fear God" (Gen. 22: 12). Since Job lived in a state of comfort (*be-shalvato*), it is impossible that he should not commit minor sins occasionally. God is compas-

> sionate and is forgiving of iniquity, and in order to cleanse (*le-marek*) those sins, he gave Satan permission to prosecute him and said, "Have you noticed My servant Job?" (Job 1: 8). Satan charged that Job worshipped God and feared Him on account of his state of comfort; however, if his circumstances were to change for the worse, he would rebel. God gave him permission to test him with respect to his possessions and his children.[50]

Here Duran reiterates the notion that the righteous experience divine trials as a consequence of sinful conduct, but what is important is that Duran clarifies that trials are meant to make amends for sinful conduct of a specific sort: transgressions committed accidentally or carelessly. Duran's logic seems to be—and this is confirmed throughout his discussion—that minor transgressions of this nature do not require full-fledged repentance or punishment. Still, they are sins, as confirmed by the fact that according to the Torah one must bring a sacrifice when they are committed. Therefore, God will sometimes deal with the accidental sins of the righteous by requiring a test that, if passed, is sufficient to cleanse them of their misdeeds. Duran finds confirmation of this concept once again in the rabbinic Abraham, whom we encountered above. Abraham sinned unintentionally by not offering sacrifices to God for all the good He had shown him—especially the birth of Isaac. Abraham's omission was mere oversight, and yet it required some sort of correction. Abraham was therefore subjected to the trial of being asked to sacrifice his son. The same principle explains Job's suffering. Duran notes that Job, like Abraham, lived a life of ease—an obvious reference to Job's wealth and large family, described at the beginning of the story. Duran therefore presumes that Job must have committed accidental transgressions once in a while due to the complacency his comfortable circumstances engendered. Satan is therefore permitted to test Job so that he can make amends for those transgressions.

There is one ambiguity in Duran's understanding of Job's trial. In the passage just cited, Duran at one point suggests that it is simply the "pain of the trial" that atones for accidental sins. Yet, in the same passage, he also implies that trials make amends for such sins because they are an opportunity for an individual to show his devotion to God by enduring the trial with patience. That is, the trial allows the righteous person to regain God's favor by demonstrating that his accidental sins were no reflection of his level of commitment to God. This second interpretation comes out particularly in the example of Abraham, who, in passing the test, convinces God that his accidental sins were not an act of rebellion. Here it is not the pain of the trial that makes up for past misconduct, but the demeanor of the person while in the throes of his trial.

It is possible that Duran saw both explanations as correct. Yet, it would seem that the first explanation is perhaps more appropriate for Job. As noted earlier, Duran acknowledges Job's protests about his condition throughout the dialogue and explains that they emanate from his perplexity regarding the timing and severity of the punishment meted out against him. Thus, in

Duran's thinking, Job clearly does not accept his suffering with absolute devotion and patience, and it would seem, therefore, that it is the pain of the trial that makes amends for Job's accidental sins.[51]

We have yet to see how Elihu answers Job's questions, which, according to Duran, are posed at the beginning of the dialogue and prompt the discussion between Job and his friends. As I have noted, in Duran's thinking, Job believes at the outset that he deserves punishment for his sins, but what he cannot understand is, first, why God allowed those sins to accumulate without warning of his eventual punishment, and second, why, once God decides to act against him, his afflictions have not been more spread out. Elihu has at least begun to address Job's perplexity by explaining to him that his afflictions are not punishment but a test, but the questions Job has asked regarding the timing and severity of his afflictions still need to be dealt with.

Duran finds the answers to these queries in Job 33, the chapter that all the philosophers in this study identify as key to the entire book. Elihu begins his response to Job by arguing that God allows the accidental sins of the righteous to accumulate with no action taken, in order to allow them time to correct their behavior. Moreover, God does in fact warn the righteous, through prophetic dreams, of the afflictions that await them if they do not change their ways. These thoughts are extracted from the following verses, which are by now familiar to us:

> For God speaks once,
> And not a second time,
> In a dream, a night vision,
> When deep sleep falls upon men,
> While they slumber on their beds,
> Then He opens men's understanding
> And delays their affliction. (Job 33: 14–15)[52]

As Duran puts it, God "does not punish them immediately, for through the revelation that He reveals to them, they may repent."[53]

Duran also argues that Job in fact experienced prophetic dreams warning him of his impending afflictions but did not heed them. Duran finds evidence for this in the following verses, which Job utters at the end of his first speech:

> For what I have feared has overtaken me;
> What I dreaded has come upon me.
> I had no repose, no quiet, no rest,
> And trouble came. (Job 3: 25–26)

According to Duran, Job's sense of impending doom could have come only from prophetic dreams, and it is to those very dreams that Elihu alludes in his remarks about God speaking to human beings in "a dream, a night vision."[54]

Elihu goes on to explain that if the righteous do not correct their behavior after they have been warned, then God has no choice but to allow Satan to test them with afflictions. These thoughts, according to Duran, are found in the continuation of Job 33, which deals with the sick man:

He is reproved by pains on his bed . . .
He comes close to the Pit,
His life [verges] on death. (Job 33: 19–22)

Elihu goes on to explain that Satan has no right to bring death in such situations since the person being tested is righteous despite his accidental sins, and his past good deeds will protect him from the ultimate punishment. These ideas are brought out from the next verses in the passage:

If he has an angel,[55]
One advocate against a thousand
To declare the man's uprightness,
Then He has mercy on him and decrees,
"Redeem him from descending to the Pit,
For I have obtained his ransom;
Let his flesh be healthier than in his youth;
Let him return to younger days." (Job 33: 23–24)

Like Saadiah, Duran adopts the reading of a Talmudic source that interprets the angel here as a metaphor for an individual's good deeds, which act as "ransom" to spare a righteous person's life.[56] As Duran puts it, these deeds act as "defending attorneys" for him so that he is not killed.[57]

Elihu has therefore effectively addressed Job's first question, which is why God allowed his sins to accumulate so that his afflictions would, in the end, be more severe. God was giving him time to correct his ways and even warned him through prophetic dreams of the consequences of failing to act.

Duran goes on to argue that in the verses just cited regarding the angel, Elihu has also implicitly dealt with Job's other question, which is why his afflictions had to come all at once and were not more spread out after God had finally decided to punish him. Duran reasons that there is no danger of Job's life being taken because the angel, or Job's past good deeds, will protect him from death, and therefore it is better that he experience all his afflictions at once rather than in piecemeal fashion, since the latter alternative would result in a slow and painful decay of the body. As Duran explains, "It was good for him that his sin be cleansed all at once given that his body would remain in existence protected from death and that he would not gradually waste away."[58]

According to Duran, Elihu wraps up his remarks in Job 33 by telling Job that once the righteous endure their trials, they will pray to God and thank Him for cleansing them of their sins. They will also thank Him for giving them the opportunity to go to heaven and not to hell (*gehinom*) once they reach the afterlife. These ideas are read out of the verses in the passage that follow from my last citation:

He prays to God and is accepted by Him;
He enters His presence with shouts of joy,
For He requites a man for his righteousness.
He declares to men,

> "I have sinned; I have perverted what was right;
> But I was not paid back for it."
> He redeemed him from passing into the Pit;
> He will enjoy the light.
> Truly God does all these things
> Two or three times to man,
> To bring him back from the Pit,
> That he may bask in the light of life. (Job 33: 26–30)

Duran interprets Elihu's reference to the reward of "the light of life" as an allusion to recompense in the afterlife.[59]

Toward the end of his discussion of Elihu's views, Duran informs us that the rest of Elihu's address in subsequent chapters is a chastisement of Job for having spoken insolently to God. Duran also comments on God's address to Job but has relatively little to say about it. According to Duran, it too is a chastisement of Job.[60]

In his comments on the final chapter of the Book of Job, Duran explains why it is that despite His chastisements of Job, God praises Job as His "servant" and is "incensed" at his friends.[61] Duran explains that God is angered at Job's friends because they took the positions they did only in order to please Him, and God does not sanction the unjust condemnation of the righteous even if the intention is to declare Him just. Duran also states emphatically that one should never condemn an individual for wickedness when that person is certain of his own righteousness, and that is precisely what Eliphaz, Bildad, and Zophar did to Job. By contrast, God is pleased with Job because even though he protested against God, he did so in a sincere search for the truth. He honestly did not know why his afflictions were so severe, and it was for this reason that he complained.[62]

Yet, Duran's assessment of Job's friends is not entirely negative. Duran follows the rabbinic opinion that Eliphaz, Bildad, and Zophar are prophets.[63] He also argues that the views of all three of Job's friends are valuable for us: even if they are incorrect in explaining Job's particular predicament, they nonetheless provide insight into the suffering of the righteous and the prospering of the wicked. They also provide proofs for the existence of divine providence, which were summarized earlier. Duran also reminds his readers at the end of the introduction to his commentary that Eliphaz is to be commended because his position was closest to that of Elihu. It is just that Eliphaz was unable to provide the kind of comprehensive explanation for Job's suffering that Elihu did.[64]

Antecedents

As we begin to explore the first interface and examine the relationship between Duran's commentary on Job and previous readings of Job in medieval Jewish philosophy, the first question we must ask is whether Duran's commentary even belongs to this school of thought. In his treatment of providence, Duran rejects the Maimonidean connection between intellectual perfection and providence in favor of the more traditional, biblical-rabbinic notion that God personally rewards and punishes individual human beings for their actions. Duran also fashions his theory of providence with the help of kabbalistic ideas.

Duran's reading of the actual Book of Job betrays a similar traditional reaction against Maimonidean thinking. He rejects Maimonides' notion that Satan is merely an allegorical figure in favor of the rabbinic view that Satan is an angel who prosecutes and punishes human beings for their sins. In fact, Duran is the only thinker in this study to think of Satan in these literal terms. Even Saadiah, our most conservative commentator thus far, could not tolerate such an idea.

Duran's treatment of Job's suffering displays a similar traditional bent. He explicitly opposes Maimonides' suggestion that Job is intellectually deficient and that this is the reason for his suffering. Furthermore, according to Duran, all the participants in the dialogue—including Job himself—agree on the biblical-rabbinic notion that God personally rewards and punishes individuals for their actions and that Job is deserving of punishment for his past sins. The only question that divides them is the extent of Job's wickedness and whether his suffering is proportionate to his misdeeds. This observation applies no less to Elihu, whose answers to Job's questions about the timing and severity of his afflictions reflect the same basic view of reward and punishment. Duran's reading of the dialogue is quite striking because it is the only one in this study that sees complete unity among the participants around a traditional concept of providence. Not even Saadiah proposes such unity, for in his reading, Job temporarily loses faith in that conception of providence once he experiences his suffering.

Yet, a closer examination of Duran's commentary will reveal that despite these observations, his reading of Job is very much indebted to the philosophical tradition. It is just that Duran has combined his philosophical ideas with concepts drawn from sources with a more traditional orientation, with the result that the philosophical dimension of the commentary is quite conservative. In some sense, this is reflective of Duran's philosophical corpus as a whole, which, as noted in the beginning of this chapter, displays a high degree of syncretism and a conservative philosophical sensibility.

These characteristics are evident in Duran's handling of the issue of providence, which occupies a large portion of his introduction to his commentary on Job. In fact, Duran's arguments for the existence of providence are openly philosophical. He begins his introduction with the claim that providence can be proven through "reason"—even though the senses disprove it—and then proceeds to provide a series of lengthy proofs in the discussion that follows.[65] It is only when Duran moves from the question of the existence of providence to the question of its actual mechanism that he appears to abandon philosophical argumentation and relies instead on kabbalistic tradition.[66]

Yet, we should be careful when we speak of the "rational" and "kabbalistic" elements in Duran's thinking. In his arguments for the justification of providence according to the principle of "reason," Duran's proofs are sometimes dependent on concepts that derive explicitly from revealed tradition. Thus, for instance, we have seen that one of Duran's arguments for the existence of providence is based on the notion that God created the world in a perfect state and will therefore want it to persist in that state.[67] Duran openly admits here that this idea is acceptable only to those who believe that the world was created *ex nihilo*, a principle that Duran concedes can be known only through revelation. Duran is well aware of the difficulty in including a revealed principle in an ostensibly rational argument but explains that "our words are for those who have completely accepted the opinions of revealed religion (*de'ot ha-emunah ha-toranit*) and are in doubt only about this question alone [i.e., providence], such as Job."[68] Duran therefore acknowledges that his argument is not based on purely rational principles.[69] A similar example can found in another proof for providence in which Duran argues for the existence of providence on the basis of the notion that God has shown His beneficence to human beings by giving them commandments. Here again Duran appears to have no difficulty using revealed tradition as a basis for his argument.[70]

All this indicates that when Duran declares his intention to prove the doctrine of providence on the basis of "reason," the type of reason he has in mind is not the purely scientific rationalism that we find in the Aristotelianism of Maimonides. In some respects, it resembles the more conservative and dialectical type of rationalism that we find in Saadiah. In fact, Duran's arguments in favor of providence are at times stylistically similar to those used by Saadiah. Thus, for instance, Duran makes arguments in favor of providence on the basis of analogies between God and human beings, on the one hand, and a master and his servants, on the other. That type of reasoning is common in Saadiah's *Beliefs and Opinions*.[71]

If Duran does not seem wholeheartedly philosophical in justifying the existence of providence, he is also not entirely kabbalistic when dealing with its mechanism. While Duran cites Kabbalah as his source for the mechanism of providence, there is nothing distinctly kabbalistic about his views. Absent is any reference to the standard symbolism of Kabbalah, such as the tripartite division of the soul and the relationship of its parts to one or another of the *sefirot*.[72] Nor is any kabbalistic text cited. Instead, Duran cites sources from Judah Halevi and Naḥmanides, and while the latter figure is certainly a kabbalist, the texts borrowed from him are not overtly kabbalistic. Most important, the notion central to Duran's discussion of the mechanism of providence is that the human soul exists from the time of creation and enters into the body in order to perfect itself, and this concept is more broadly Neoplatonic than kabbalistic per se.[73] Thus, Duran's understanding of the mechanism of providence is perhaps not as kabbalistic as he indicates. In sum, the impression one gets here is that in his deliberations on providence, Duran is a thinker who stands between philosophical, kabbalistic, and rabbinic schools of thought, with no desire to commit himself wholeheartedly to any one of them.

The same eclecticism is evident in his interpretation of the Book of Job. In his interpretation of Job's trial, we see not only Duran's tendency to combine sources from different schools, but also his talent in reworking those sources for his own ends. Here again the philosophical influence is evident. As I have already noted, in formulating his view that Job's suffering is a trial, Duran explicitly mentions his dependence on the Geonim, a reference that is clearly an allusion to Saadiah. Yet, Duran does not accept Saadiah's position without modification, because he is uncomfortable with the notion that Job is caused to suffer for no sin whatsoever.[74] Duran therefore settles on the position that Job is being tested, but the test is meant to give him an opportunity to cleanse himself of accidental sins and is not really punishment in the normal sense.[75]

In a passage cited earlier, Duran also mentions Naḥmanides' essay *Torat ha-Adam* as inspiration for his conception of Job's trial.[76] Here too Duran creatively reworks his sources. Indeed, in *Torat ha-Adam* Naḥmanides argues that sufferings of love are to be understood as atonement for prior accidental sins and this is a concept Duran adopts.[77] In the same essay, however, Naḥmanides has a discussion about divine trials in which he takes the position that God can inflict suffering on a wholly righteous individual in order to give him an opportunity to earn future reward. This position is in line with Saadiah's thinking but very much at odds with Duran's in that he explicitly rejects divine trials for those innocent of wrongdoing.[78] Thus, Duran draws from Naḥmanides the notion that sufferings of love are for prior accidental sin, but he extends that notion to divine trials in a manner Naḥmanides does not. Duran also deliberately overlooks Naḥmanides' understanding of Job's trial, which is tied to his theory of reincarnation—an issue to which I will return shortly. Duran has therefore read Naḥmanides selectively and creatively in order to formulate his viewpoint.

The same use of sources is evident in the way Duran incorporates the figure of Abraham into his conception of Job's trial. We saw that Duran sees a commonality between Job's trial and the binding of Isaac—a connection that, I argued, is implied by Saadiah as well. However, Duran imparts a new twist to the rabbinic Abraham with the notion that he is tested because he has sinned. The full citation of the source upon which Duran draws will make the point clear:

> *After these things,*[79] *God put Abraham to the test* (Gen. 22: 1): What is meant by "after"? After the words of Satan. As it is written, "The child grew up and was weaned, [and Abraham held a great feast on the day that Isaac was weaned]" (Gen. 21: 8). Satan said to the Almighty: "Sovereign of the universe! To this old man you have graciously given the fruit of the womb at the age of a hundred. Yet, from the entire banquet he prepared, he did not have one turtledove or pigeon to sacrifice before You!" [Satan] said: "Did he not do [it—i.e., the banquet] only for his son?!" [God replied]: "If I were to say to him, 'sacrifice your son before Me,' he would sacrifice him." Straightaway, "God put Abraham to the test."[80]

In this passage God never suggests that Satan is correct and that Abraham has somehow sinned by not bringing Him a sacrifice. In fact, on the contrary; it would seem that God wants to prove to Satan that his judgment of Abraham is wrong. But Duran assumes that Satan's accusations are not without foundation. Thus, Duran has interpreted this source for his own purposes. Duran's understanding of Job's trial is therefore shaped by harmonizing and reinterpreting sources that come from Saadiah, Naḥmanides, and rabbinic midrash.

The eclectic nature of Duran's reading of Job is also evident in the way he approaches Job 33. As I have already noted, Duran finds a message in this chapter that is very much at odds with the thinking of the Aristotelian interpreters of Job. I would argue that this school of thought nonetheless exerts a significant influence because Duran imposes a structure upon Job 33 very much reminiscent of that found in Gersonides. Both Duran and Gersonides interpret Job 33 as speaking about two types of providence: prophetic dreams, which warn us of impending suffering, and physical suffering, which is designed to correct bad conduct. Both thinkers identify the latter with the rabbinic doctrine of sufferings of love. They are also united in dividing the chapter in precisely the same manner, in that verse 33: 19, which initiates the description of the sick person—"He is reproved by pains on his bed"—marks the transition from Elihu's description of the first type of providence to the second. The difference between them is that Duran has, of course, recast the content of Job 33 by replacing Gersonides' Aristotelian reading with an entirely traditional one in which there is a personal God who interacts with human beings.[81]

Also telling in Duran's reading of Job 33 is the way he deals with Naḥmanides' interpretation of this chapter. Naḥmanides takes the position that Elihu finds the solution to Job's suffering in the kabbalistic doctrine of *gilgul* or reincarnation. The righteous suffer as atonement for sins committed in a previous lifetime, and that is why a guiltless individual such as Job can experience such terrible afflictions.[82] Duran comments on Naḥmanides' theory in his interpretation of Job 33:15–17, in which Elihu states that God speaks to human beings "in a dream, a night vision," so as "to turn man away from an action, to suppress pride in man." In explicating this passage, Duran notes that "Naḥmanides, may his memory be blessed, interprets this with a deep interpretation; it is well known to all people that his view has to do with the issue of reincarnation."[83]

Yet, Duran never fully explicates Naḥmanides' reading and goes on to give his own interpretation of the verses. Furthermore, when Duran comes to the verses in Job 33 that are critical for Naḥmanides' theory of *gilgul*, Duran makes no mention of him. I am referring to Job 33:29–30, in which Elihu states:

> Truly God does all these things
> Two or three times to man,
> To bring him back from the Pit,
> That he may bask in the light of life.

For Naḥmanides, the notion that God acts "two or three times" in order "bring him back from the Pit" is the key reference in the Book of Job to the process of reincarnation. Duran interprets these verses without any allusion to Naḥmanides.[84] Finally, in a passage that appears somewhat later on in his commentary, Duran again states that Naḥmanides' doctrine of reincarnation is "a deep matter pertaining to the secret of creation that the masters of Kabbalah use to answer the two queries [that Job put forth regarding his suffering]; I have already made some allusion to it in [my] interpretation of the verses." Yet, once again, Duran goes on to repeat his own interpretation of Elihu's position, with no reference to Naḥmanides.[85]

Thus, while Duran shows respect for Naḥmanides' theory of reincarnation, he stops short of actually adopting it. What is difficult to explain is that Duran seems to accept Naḥmanides' theory of reincarnation quite explicitly in a passage in *Magen Avot*. Moreover, Duran even cites the verses in Job 33: 29–30 as proof of this theory, verses that were key for Naḥmanides in his reading of the Book of Job but that Duran seems to have understood differently in *Ohev Mishpat*.[86] Complicating matters further is that in another passage in *Magen Avot* Duran gives a summary of his reading of the Book of Job as explicated in *Ohev Mishpat*.[87] Therefore, while in *Ohev Mishpat* Duran prefers his own reading of Job over that of Naḥmanides, in *Magen Avot* he appears to support both simultaneously!

No attempt will be made here to explain why Duran's views in *Magen Avot* are different from those in *Ohev Mishpat*. A proper investigation of this issue would require an examination of the overall relationship between the two works, and that is beyond the scope of my discussion and, to my knowledge, has not been broached by scholars.[88] But we can at least draw conclusions regarding Duran's attitude to Naḥmanides in *Ohev Mishpat*. In this work, it makes sense that Duran would feel ambivalent toward Naḥmanides' theory of reincarnation, seeing as it is very much at odds with some of the most basic premises of Duran's reading of Job. Naḥmanides' understanding of the book is predicated on the notion that the righteous can suffer even if they are entirely guiltless because they are being punished for sins of a previous lifetime. By contrast, Duran's understanding is based on the belief that there are no guiltless individuals and that suffering is always due to sin committed within one's present lifetime. Thus, Duran is willing to pay respect to Naḥmanides' position but cannot adopt it as his own. It would overturn his entire interpretation of Job.

What is most important for our concerns is that these observations about Duran's treatment of Naḥmanides highlight the complexity of his intellectual orientation in his reading of Job. Duran's commitment to a philosophical interpretation of Job, albeit of a conservative kind, seems to preclude an embrace of Naḥmanides on the issue of reincarnation. Yet, he seems unable to reject Naḥmanides unequivocally. Thus, what Duran has done here is similar to what we saw in his discussion of the mechanism of providence; he seems interested in kabbalistic ideas but does not seem willing to commit himself to them entirely.[89]

Two other instances indicate evidence of influence from philosophical sources on Duran's reading of Job. The first is Duran's interpretation of the dialogue between Job, Eliphaz, Bildad, and Zophar. This reading bears a striking resemblance to that of Joseph ibn Kaspi, a philosophical writer whose commentaries on Job are not examined in this study. Duran, however, never mentions Kaspi as a source of his interpretation.[90] We should also note that Duran follows Gersonides in his explanation of the critical exchange in the final chapter of the book, in which God praises Job as His "servant" and scolds Eliphaz, Bildad, and Zophar. Duran follows Gersonides in his view that God finds favor in Job because he spoke with sincerity throughout the dialogue—even if his views were in error—and God criticizes Job's friends because they took the positions they did only in order to vindicate God.[91]

A good way to appreciate Duran's contribution to the reading of Job in medieval Jewish philosophy is to see it as a further step in the traditional direction initiated by Gersonides. Maimonides, Ibn Tibbon, and Zeraḥiah Ḥen tended to radicalize the message of Job by spiritualizing it. For these thinkers, Job learned that true providence was equated either with an inner psychological immunity from suffering or with immortality of the soul. Gersonides' reading took a deliberate, traditional turn away from that approach when he argued that the central message of Job was that providence is individual and that it protects us from physical harm, as the Bible tells us. Gersonides, however, justified his view on the basis of Aristotelian premises, which assumed that God is an impersonal Deity and that providence is consequent upon intellectual perfection. Duran, in effect, completes the traditional turn away from Maimonides. He reads Job as supporting the biblical-rabbinic conception of providence, as Gersonides does, but goes one step further in stripping it of its Aristotelianism. For Duran the Book of Job teaches us that providence is individual and physical, but he assumes the existence of a personal God who rewards individuals not for their intellectual achievements but for their actions.

Yet, Duran is still very much connected to the philosophical tradition in his interpretation of Job. For despite his differences with the philosophers, his reading of Job is still largely rationalistic in its method, and in his interpretation of its content he borrows a good deal from his philosophical predecessors. In fact, Duran has brought us full circle. His understanding of Job is similar to that of our first thinker, Saadiah, who also reads the book in light of a conservative rationalism. Moreover, Duran seems to bear the direct influence of Saadiah in viewing Job's suffering as a divine trial.

Exegesis

With respect to the second interface, Duran's reading of Job clearly exhibits sensitivity to the major exegetical challenges that the book presents. First, Duran follows suit with previous medieval Jewish philosophers in the Maimonidean school in displaying a keen interest in the question of whether or not Job is an allegory, and he devotes a substantive discussion to this issue, in which he weighs the evidence for both positions. His conclusion differs from that of the Maimonidean philosophers in that he firmly supports the position that Job and his story are historical, a position that should occasion no surprise given Duran's traditional orientation.

Duran's interest in the larger exegetical issues in Job is most evident in his handling of the dialogue between Job and his friends. Duran is able to make sense of the long and rambling discussion with an intriguing combination of philosophical and literary insight. He brings coherence to the dialogue by giving all the figures participating in it a role in imparting important philosophical truths. Elihu, of course, makes the greatest contribution by providing the correct explanation for Job's suffering. Eliphaz, Bildad, and Zophar also make important contributions to the dialogue, for even though they turn out to be wrong with respect to Job's situation, they play a vital role in providing arguments supporting the existence of providence and in giving insight into the problem of the suffering of the righteous and the prospering of the wicked. Duran also makes sense of the flow of the dialogue with a sensitive literary reading of the escalating tension between Job and his friends—though, as I noted, here Duran appears to be influenced heavily by Kaspi.

Somewhat perplexing is the little that Duran says about God's role in the dialogue. Besides chastising Job, God seems not to contribute much to the philosophical content of the book. Duran is therefore like Ibn Tibbon and Zeraḥiah Ḥen in placing all the focus on Elihu as the figure who explains Job's suffering.

Duran's exegetical sensitivities are also evident in his handling of the figure of Job. Duran resembles Gersonides in that he is able to navigate the contradictions in the biblical text regarding Job by portraying him as a figure of great virtue but possessing one critical flaw. The particulars of Job's intellectual journey, however, are ultimately very different in Duran than they were in Gersonides. According to Duran, the biblical text is fully justified in describing Job in superlative terms in its opening verse because Job is indeed a figure with both ethical and intellectual virtue. Yet, the first verses of the story also clue us in to Job's major flaw when they describe his great wealth. Job's easy circumstances have bred in him a certain degree of complacency, which in turn has caused him to commit accidental sins. This is the reason Job is made to suffer. His sins do not require repentance in the normal sense because they are accidental. Nonetheless, he must experience afflictions in order to be cleansed of them.

Duran's depiction of Job also accounts for his protests throughout the dialogue. Even though Job acknowledges that he has committed sins and is deserving of some form of punishment, he honestly does not understand why God has delayed his punishment and why it has been so severe. With this reading, Duran is able to blunt the sting of Job's challenges. He is not objecting to his suffering, only the way it has been administered. Moreover, as we have surmised, it would seem that in Duran's view it is the pain of the trial that cleanses Job of his sins, not the devotion he demonstrates toward God in the course of the trial. Therefore, that Job challenges God is no great problem. The fact that he simply endures his trial is sufficient for him to be cleansed of his sins.

Finally, when Elihu arrives, Job's questions are answered. He learns that his punishment has been delayed because God gives the righteous a chance to repent and warns them of their punishment through prophetic dreams. Job therefore had the opportunity to avoid his suffering. He had, in fact, experienced prophetic dreams warning him of punishment but had not heeded them. Job also learns from Elihu that his suffering has been severe because God has no interest in killing him for sins that are only accidental and therefore he might as well be cleansed of them all at once.

Duran's reading explains why by the end of the story God can still refer to Job as His "servant." Job was never so sinful to begin with, and even when he protested against God, it was out of genuine ignorance of the reason for his suffering. He is therefore to be praised above his friends, who have misrepresented the truth for the sake of vindicating God.

One issue Duran does not explain is why Job repents at the end of the story if he was being as truthful as he could be throughout the dialogue.[92] Apparently, Duran feels that even though Job's protests are expressed out of honesty, Job still needs to repent in the end because of his ignorance regarding the nature of his suffering, an oversight all the more serious because of the prophetic warnings he received regarding his punishment. This reasoning, however, is not explicitly stated by Duran.

Did Duran have any thoughts about the audience of the Book of Job? Like many of the other philosophers in this study, Duran at no point declares a position on this question, but there are clues that indicate what his feelings are. First, in his acknowledgement that Job and his friends are non-Jews, Duran seems to support the view that the book has a universal quality to it. The problems that Job deals with are therefore clearly applicable outside the Jewish sphere.

The question, then, is whether Duran also saw Job as having a message for the Jewish people in particular. There is no doubt that this is the case, since the book deals with the subject matter of providence, which, as Duran tells us at the very beginning of his commentary, is an issue that Jews must understand properly in order to have incentive for observing the commandments and a proper understanding of their relationship with God.[93] What seems to be lacking in Duran's reading of Job is any suggestion that Job's predicament is somehow reflective of the corporate suffering of the Jewish people, as we have seen in Saadiah and Gersonides. The relevance of Job to the Jewish people is more prescriptive than it is descriptive. By clarifying the issue of providence, it encourages Jews to obey God, but it does not seem to directly confront the past experience of the Jewish people in exile.

Exegesis and Philosophy

As we proceed to the third interface, which concerns the relationship between Duran's interpretation of Job and his systematic thinking on providence, it should be clear from our discussion that there is little to say about this issue.[94] Duran's systematic treatment of providence makes up the greater part of the introduction to *Ohev Mishpat* and is therefore separate to some degree from the actual exegesis of the biblical text. But in the course of his introduction Duran also lays out his entire reading of Job, along with an in-depth exegesis of key passages. Indeed much of my analysis of Duran's reading of Job has been based on his introduction to the commentary. The tight relationship between philosophy and exegesis here is predicated on Duran's assumption that all the arguments for providence are contained in the addresses of the participants in the dialogue in Job. Consequently, each of Duran's philosophical proofs for providence is supported by verses in Job. Systematic philosophy and biblical exegesis are, in this instance, tightly intertwined; if there is a relationship between the two, it is one of near identity.

The seamlessness of the relationship between Duran's treatment of providence and his reading of Job is unique in our study. Maimonides is the only other thinker we have examined who provides a reading of Job in the same work in which he offers a systematic discussion of providence. His exposition on Job is embedded in a section of the *Guide* that, broadly speaking, is concerned with providence and the problem of evil. Yet, as I noted in my treatment of Maimonides, the relationship between the two is not entirely clear. In Duran there is no ambiguity. His systematic discussion of providence and his reading of Job lead to precisely the same conclusions.

Duran's Job and Duran's Biography

I would like to share one more series of observations that I believe will throw much light on Duran's commentary on Job. As we have seen, Duran claims at the beginning of his introduction to his commentary that his work is mostly an anthology of interpretations found in previous thinkers. He does indeed add that his introduction will include insights of his own; however, the overall impression he gives us is that his commentary will have relatively little to offer that is original.[95] From my analysis, it is obvious that Duran has been exceedingly modest. Certainly, he cites a wide array of thinkers in his commentary and incorporates them into this own reading of Job, as I have shown.[96] It is equally clear that he provides much more than just an anthology of the views of others, and that he formulates a reading of Job that is in some respects unique. In particular, his notion of Job's ordeal, which combines the idea of punishment for sin with Saadiah's conception of divine trials, is unlike that of any of interpreter examined here.[97]

Yet, if Duran's reading is highly original, it is also in some sense highly peculiar in that he understands the Book of Job as dealing with a very specific and distinctive situation. Job is an individual who is righteous but guilty of committing the kind of accidental sins that all people commit, and he believes he is worthy of punishment for those sins. His only difficulty is with the timing and severity of his punishment, and it is for this reason that he protests. Only when Elihu appears does Job come to understand that even accidental sins can bring severe punishment from God if they are allowed to accumulate. Thus, even though Duran tells us that the purpose of the Book of Job is to prove the existence of providence and address the problem of the suffering of the righteous, Duran's actual reading of the book indicates that its focus is far more narrow. The major point of contention in the dialogue is not really the issue of providence, for, as Duran informs us, all the participants in the dialogue are in agreement on this issue. Nor, in Duran's reading, does the Book of Job really provide a comprehensive answer to the problem of the suffering of the righteous, for he offers six reasons for the suffering of the righteous, and yet, in his exegesis of the Book of Job itself, he deals only with the one that applies to Job. In short, for Duran, the Book of Job is mostly about Job's specific predicament.

One wonders what Duran intended us to learn from his interpretation of Job. While the readings I have analyzed up to this point of the study seem to deal with general philosophical questions of providence and theodicy, Duran's interpretation seems too specific to serve in that role. It could be that Duran is simply reading the biblical text as best he can. We have seen, after all, that Duran is sensitive to the exegetical challenges the Book of Job presents and that his construction of the story attempts to respond to those challenges. However, my suspicion is that the peculiar nature of Duran's reading of Job has a better explanation, one that can be found in his biography.

As I noted at the beginning of this chapter, Duran was forced to flee the violence that rocked the Jewish community in Spain in 1391, and he spent the rest of his life in Algiers. The tragedy for the Duran family was magnified by the fact that it had a great deal of wealth that was entirely lost when it went into exile.[98] One can only imagine the hardship Duran endured, arriving penniless in Algiers and adjusting to a far more modest lifestyle in exile. Might it be, then, that Duran composed a commentary on Job in order to grapple with his own ordeal?

This connection is certainly possible given that the commentary was written in 1405, not quite fifteen years after the upheavals in Duran's life. It is noteworthy that, of his many works, *Ohev Mishpat* is to our knowledge the only commentary that Duran composed on a book of the Bible. Duran's personal difficulties would certainly explain why he chose to focus on this one text. These difficulties would also explain the care and thoroughness with which he attacks the issues of providence and the suffering of the righteous, for there are few discussions in medieval Jewish philosophy about these subjects that are as extensive as Duran's.

There may also be evidence in *Ohev Mishpat* itself that Duran was grappling with his own misfortunes. Significant in this regard is Duran's discussion in the introduction to his commentary attempting to show that what is identified as true suffering is relative to one's circumstances. I mentioned this discussion earlier but will now look at it in greater detail.[99] Duran illustrates his point with a number of different examples, which can be summarized as follows:[100]

1. *Evil is relative to the social status of the individual.* A king who is deposed and becomes a merchant has experienced evil because of his loss of prestige—even if he becomes a wealthy merchant. However, a slave who graduates to become a lowly tailor has experienced good, even if he does not become wealthy.

2. *Evil is relative to the quality of climate, water, and air where a person lives.* If a person lives in a region where these are of low quality and dies young, we do not consider it evil since that is the norm for everyone in that region. But if a person dies young in a region where these are of high quality, we consider it evil.
3. *Evil is relative to the nation to which one belongs.* If a person belongs to a nation that has always experienced oppression and humiliation, and that individual experiences those burdens along with his fellow countryman, we do not consider it evil. However, if one belongs to a nation that experiences oppression and humiliation but somehow manages to avoid those burdens, then that person has experienced good even if his circumstances are still worse than those of others in more successful nations.
4. *Evil is relative to family status.* If someone comes from a family of kings and becomes a lowly officer, he has experienced evil. But if someone is a lowly villager and becomes an army officer, it is considered good.
5. *Evil is relative to one's bodily constitution.* If a person with a strong bodily constitution becomes sick, it is evil. If someone with a weak constitution becomes sick, we do not consider it evil.[101]

With these examples Duran is clearly anticipating his discussion of the Book of Job. Most significant are those dealing with a sudden loss of wealth and status, since that is precisely what happened to Job. Duran is therefore arguing implicitly that Job's afflictions do indeed qualify as true suffering.[102] What is also significant is that the same line of reasoning could just as easily apply to Duran himself, since his misfortunes involved a sudden loss of wealth and status as well. Duran's insights raise the prospect that Duran's Job is none other than a projection of Duran himself.

If this theory is correct, it would shed interesting light on other aspects of Duran's commentary. Most significant, it would suggest that Duran considered his explanation for Job's suffering to be an explanation for his own tragedy as well. That is, Duran felt that he, like Job, was an individual of great prestige and wealth, whose easy circumstances had bred a sense of complacency, which had in turn led to accidental sins, sins that had to be rectified. Thus, in his commentary on Job, Duran might have been expressing, even unconsciously, a sense of guilt that in Spain he was lacking in proper piety due to his comfortable life and high social standing and that it was for this reason that God caused him to suffer.[103]

A passage in Duran's commentary that I mentioned earlier is perhaps illuminated by the biographical connection as well. We saw that, according to Duran, the suffering of the righteous is most problematic when an individual is sure in his own heart that he is righteous, as is the case with Job.[104] Duran also goes on to make the startling claim that the prophets of Israel complained to God mostly about their own suffering and not that of others. Since it is the certainty of one's own innocence in the face of suffering that brings the greatest perplexity regarding divine justice, the prophets were moved to protest only about their own difficulties.[105] Duran's view here can only give one pause, since the prophets are traditionally understood to be pleading on behalf of the Jewish people. Yet, one wonders whether Duran is once again talking about himself. Perhaps Duran is relaying to us the sentiment that he himself initially felt upon experiencing his own suffering, which was the feeling that he did not deserve the misfortunes that had befallen him. And what better way to justify that sentiment than by linking his own claims of innocence not just with Job but with all the prophets of Israel, who, as it turns out, were also worried about their own suffering and not that of others.

Admittedly, the readings of these texts are speculative, because we are delving into psychological matters that do not lend themselves to easy confirmation. Even so, the fact that Duran's commentary on Job is the only commentary he composed on a biblical book and that he invested such energy into the issue of the suffering of the righteous is reason to suspect that Duran composed his work from deeply personal motives.[106] Even more important, the biographical connection would provide an answer to our original question, which is why Duran would construct a reading of Job that deals with a figure in so distinctive a situation. In truth, Duran may not have been concerned as much with the larger questions of providence as he was with the suffering in his own life.

An important corollary here is that we now have confirmation for my earlier surmise that Duran saw little connection between Job's suffering and the historical experience of suffering of the Jewish people in exile. In his reading of Job, it is his own suffering that seems to occupy his attention. Another piece of evidence for this conclusion is found in Duran's list of six explanations for the suffering of the righteous in his introduction to the commentary on Job. As we have already noted, the third explanation, involving the notion of divine trials, becomes the basis for Duran's interpretation of Job's suffering. Yet, it is the sixth explanation that is used to account for the suffering of the Jewish people. According to that explanation, which is borrowed from Gersonides, the Jewish people must endure the suffering of exile because their forefathers had sinned, and even though subsequent generations are not accountable for what their forefathers have done, the situation of exile nonetheless persists until the Jews are sufficiently righteous to merit redemption.[107] Thus, Job's suffering and that of Jewish people are given completely different explanations in the very same discussion.

These observations introduce another consideration into the investigation of medieval Jewish interpretations of Job that we have not yet encountered, which is that medieval Jewish commentators on Job may have been grappling not just with the suffering of the Jewish people as a whole through their readings of this book, but with their own personal troubles. I will close this portion of my discussion by mentioning an instance of this phenomenon that is more obscure than Duran's but more unambiguous. Judah ben Joseph Alcorsono was a fourteenth-century Moroccan Jew who was put in prison for unknown reasons. While incarcerated he composed *Aron ha-'Edut* (*The Ark of Testimony*), a lengthy treatise that is found in numerous manuscripts but has yet to be examined by scholars. In that work, Alcorsono attempts to find a reason for his suffering, and he does so quite consciously by writing an extensive commentary on the Book of Job.[108] While Alcorsono declares his intention to follow Maimonides and Ibn Ezra in his reading of the book, it becomes clear in the course of his treatise that Maimonides is the primary influence. In the final chapters, Alcorsono lays out his most important speculations and concludes that Job suffered because he failed to perfect his intellect and therefore did not experience providence. He also comes to the conclusion that his own imprisonment occurred for a similar reason.[109] Here we have a wonderful example of how a medieval Jewish figure with philosophical interests found solace in the Book of Job for his own personal troubles.[110]

Duran's commentary on Job presents us with yet another rich and original interpretation of the book. While his exposition is dependent on previous philosophical readings of Job—particularly Saadiah's—Duran's commentary also betrays the strong influence of non-philosophical sources in rabbinic midrash and Kabbalah, and these influences result in a reading of Job that is very conservative in orientation. The traditional turn initiated by Gersonides is completed in Duran. What we have here is a reading of Job that is "rationalistic" in the broad sense of the term, but one that has abandoned Aristotelianism and its concomitant radicalism.

Duran displays his talents as an exegete in confronting the major difficulties in the Book of Job, particularly in the way he deals with the figure of Job. As with Gersonides, Duran sees Job as an individual with many virtues but also with one critical flaw that explains his difficulties. Yet, Duran goes in his own direction by proposing that Job's flaw consists of accidental sins generated by the complacency his wealth has brought. Duran also stands out among our thinkers with respect to the nature of the synthesis he creates between exegesis and philosophy in his reading of Job. The two spheres are more closely integrated in his commentary than in any of the other commentaries examined in this study.

Finally, Duran's commentary introduces a new element not seen before in this study, and that is the prospect that medieval Jewish thinkers composed commentaries on Job in order to grapple with troubles in their own lives. Historical context has certainly been important in this study all along, for we have seen a number of thinkers use the Book of Job to understand the suffering of the Jewish people. We have now discovered that in some instances the historical context influencing the reading of Job is immediate and highly personal.

8

Medieval Jewish Philosophy and the Exegesis of Job

In this study, we have examined a complex and diverse body of material. Our six readings of Job span five centuries; they originate in geographical locations as far apart as Baghdad and Provence; they reflect a wide range of philosophical orientations and perspectives; and they contain numerous insights about every aspect of Job. As we proceed to the final phase of the study, we face the challenge of formulating general conclusions about this material. For this purpose, we will be greatly aided by the scheme of three interfaces around which this study has been organized. We will look at these interfaces once again in order to draw general conclusions about these readings of Job as a collective. We will also discuss the implications of these conclusions for the field of medieval Jewish philosophy as a whole.

A Tradition of Commentaries?

Let me begin with the first interface, which is concerned with the relationship between the readings of Job examined in our study and their antecedent sources. In chapter 1, the major question I posed with respect to this interface was the extent to which the antecedent sources of our commentaries were to be found within medieval Jewish philosophy itself. In particular, I was interested in exploring whether these commentaries were a series of isolated works having little to do with one another or constituted an actual tradition of interpretation of Job in the sense that they formed a school of interpretation that gradually evolved over an extended period of time.

The evidence in this study strongly supports the second alternative; there does appear to be a tradition of interpretation on the Book of Job in medieval Jewish philosophy. Every philosopher I examined formulates his understanding of Job by absorbing insights from the readings of Job of earlier philosophers and utilizing those insights to fashion a new understanding of the book—even though such engagement with earlier readings is not always explicitly acknowledged. Thus, Maimonides is clearly influenced by the approach that Saadiah takes toward Job in understanding the dialogue in Job as a philosophical debate, in identifying Elihu as the figure who provides the correct understanding of Job's suffering, and in focusing on Elihu's remarks in Job 33 as the chapter revealing the key elements of his position, particularly Elihu's mention of the angel in Job 33:29. At the same time, Maimonides moves in his own original direction by using Aristotelian philosophy to formulate a reading of Job that is far more radical than that of Saadiah.

The same balance of absorption and innovation is found in other thinkers in this study. Ibn Tibbon and Zeraḥiah Ḥen accept all the basic premises of Maimonides' reading, but each imparts his own spin to it. Thus, Ibn Tibbon shifts the focus of Job to immortality, a theme only hinted at in Maimonides' reading, while Zeraḥiah accentuates Maimonides' elitism, so that in important respects his reading of the book is different from that of his predecessor. Gersonides interprets Job with the help of elements adopted from Maimonides and Ibn Tibbon, but his interpretation ultimately takes a traditional turn away from theirs by bringing the focus of Job back to a notion of providence that protects our physical and material well-being in this world. The conservative turn is then completed in Duran, who absorbs elements of the readings of Maimonides and Gersonides but departs from them in abandoning Aristotelianism almost entirely and in adopting an understanding of Job reminiscent of Saadiah's.[1]

The evolution of views from one thinker to the next varies in its mode. Sometimes it is philosophical, sometimes exegetical. Thus, for instance, Maimonides differs from Saadiah in adopting an entirely different philosophical paradigm for interpreting the Book of Job than that of his predecessor, while Ibn Tibbon differs from Maimonides primarily on exegetical matters.

The case for a tradition of Joban interpretation in medieval Jewish philosophy is strengthened by the fact that there are common threads that run through all our thinkers. Perhaps the most basic factor uniting them is their respect for rationalism as a means of unlocking the meaning of Job. More important, these writers display a remarkable unanimity regarding a number of issues in Job itself. All the philosophers in this study believe that the dialogue in Job is a philosophical discussion; they all take the position that the central message of the book is contained in the address of Elihu; and they all believe that chapter 33 is the most important section of Elihu's speech. Moreover, there is a great deal of commonality among the philosophers regarding the details of Job 33. Many of them approach the chapter in a similar manner, even if they differ as to its meaning. For instance, all the writers regard the angel in Job 33:29 as the key concept in that chapter. One could say, in fact, that the tradition of Joban interpretation in medieval Jewish philosophy can be largely understood as an evolution of views regarding Job 33 and Elihu's angel.

There appears to be a tradition of Joban interpretation among the writers in this study despite the fact that there are wide differences among them with respect to philosophical orientation. That is, the unanimity displayed by the philosophers regarding the issues in Job overcomes the divide between more conservative and more radical thinkers. Maimonides' radical reading of Job may be entirely different from Saadiah's conservative reading in terms of content. Yet, Maimonides shows the unmistakable imprint of Saadiah's commentary in viewing the dialogue in Job as a philosophical discussion, in the interest he displays in Elihu's speech, in his focus on Job 33, and in the emphasis he places on Elihu's angel. Duran's conservative understanding of the Book of Job is in many respects an explicit rejection of the more radical readings of Maimonides and Gersonides, but once again Duran's interpretation has much in common with the expositions of these two philosophers, for he too sees the book as a philosophical discussion and believes that the central message of the book is to be found in Job 33. There is also reason to suspect that Duran's reading of Job 33 is influenced by Gersonides not just in terms of its framework, but even in terms of content. Duran organizes the chapter around the issues of prophecy and providential suffering much as Gersonides did, though he denudes them of their Aristotelian meaning.

At the center of the tradition of Joban interpretation in medieval Jewish philosophy is Maimonides, a fact that is not surprising given that he is the most influential of medieval Jewish philosophers. It is his reading of Job that sets the agenda for all the interpretations in our study—with the obvious exception of that of Saadiah, who precedes him—and the fact that our writers hark back to Maimonides is an important factor in explaining the commonalities found among their readings of Job.

Yet, a significant conclusion that emerges from this study is that Ibn Tibbon's reading of Job is almost as important in medieval Jewish philosophy as that of Maimonides. Ibn Tibbon shapes Maimonides' hints and clues regarding Job 33 into a comprehensive reading of that chapter, and it becomes clear from this study that it is that reading that guides the interpretations of the same chapter in Jewish philosophical commentators on Job who come after him. That influence extends to such figures as Immanuel of Rome, Elijah ben Eliezer ha-Yerushalmi, Isaac Arundi, and perhaps Zeraḥiah Ḥen. There is also good reason to suspect that it extends to Gersonides, whose reading of Job 33 also appears to bear the imprint of Ibn Tibbon.[2]

One could argue that I am overstating Ibn Tibbon's influence here seeing as his impact concerns only one chapter of Job. Nevertheless, as I have noted, Job 33 holds the key to the Book of Job in all the writers I have examined, and therefore Ibn Tibbon's influence on the interpretation of this chapter makes him a pivotal figure in shaping the tradition of Joban interpretation in medieval Jewish philosophy. My study therefore confirms the growing appreciation of Ibn Tibbon's role in the development of Jewish philosophical exegesis in the medieval period, which has been the subject of recent scholarship.[3]

In ascertaining the existence of a tradition of interpretation on Job in medieval Jewish philosophy, I certainly cannot speak for all medieval Jewish philosophers because I have analyzed only some of them in this study. However, the philosophers I have examined are among the most important in that school, and therefore it is significant that they are linked in a tradition. Only further research will determine whether the other figures not examined are connected to that tradition as well.

The Medieval Jewish Philosophers as Exegetes of Job

The second interface concerns the philosophers in our study as pure exegetes. The question here was whether the philosophers displayed sensitivity to the major exegetical challenges the Book of Job presents and whether they responded to those challenges. I think that we can answer both questions firmly in the affirmative. The philosophers in this study consistently exhibited an understanding of the exegetical difficulties in Job and provided solutions to them that were often striking in their originality. This dimension of their thinking can easily be missed, since it is often camouflaged by their philosophical deliberations.

In the introductory chapter I listed a number of exegetical issues that commentators on Job have commonly confronted, and one can show how effective these philosophers have been as exegetes by reviewing those issues and seeing how the thinkers have dealt with them. The first concerned the historicity of the Book of Job, and I noted that commentators have been divided over whether the book represents actual historical events or is mere fiction. The thinkers in this study are divided on this issue as well. Saadiah, Duran, and perhaps Gersonides believe that the story is historically true, while Maimonides, Ibn Tibbon, and Zeraḥiah Ḥen claim that it is fiction.

But what is significant is that most of the thinkers in this study provide cogent and sometimes detailed arguments for their positions on this issue, arguments based on clues in the biblical text both from the Book of Job itself and from other parts of the Bible. Most impressive in this regard is Zeraḥiah Ḥen's lengthy discussion justifying his position that Job is an allegory. The thinkers in this study who did not support their positions with explicit argumentation were Maimonides and Ibn Tibbon. In all fairness, though, Maimonides' notion that Job is fiction is justified implicitly by his entire approach to the biblical text in the *Guide*, according to which there are whole sections of scripture that are allegorical. Ibn Tibbon can be excused for not providing arguments for his position because his discussion is focused mainly on Elihu and he does not discuss the character of the Book of Job as a whole.

I also noted the key exegetical role played by the allegorical understanding of the figure of Satan in Maimonides, Ibn Tibbon, Zeraḥiah Ḥen, and Gersonides. For these thinkers, Satan is a symbol of privation or matter, which is the cause of Job's suffering, and this truth is finally imparted to Job toward the end of the dialogue when Elihu gives him the correct explanation for his afflictions. Thus, through their understanding of Satan, these philosophers define the relationship between the dialogue and the prologue in the Book of Job, a relationship that has often been a source of perplexity for biblical commentators. Elihu's address, in effect, reveals to Job the philosophical truths of the prologue that have already been made known to the reader. The allegorical understanding of Satan in these thinkers is therefore critical for bringing unity and coherence to the entire book.

A central difficulty that all interpreters have faced in reading the Book of Job is the ambiguities and contradictory signals in the biblical text regarding the figure of Job himself—particularly his level of virtue. On this question as well, the commentators studied here have proven themselves to be skillful exegetes. Saadiah Gaon's handling of this issue is the weakest among these thinkers. He understands Job as a figure who is highly virtuous but must be tested in order to quell the slander that his jealous contemporaries have uttered against him. Saadiah is therefore able to explain the praise that Job receives from the narrator at the beginning of the book and from God in the closing chapters, but he is unable to explain in a satisfactory manner how Job's virtue squares with his protests against God throughout the dialogue.

Maimonides handles the ambiguities in Job's character with much greater skill by taking advantage of his esoteric method of reading the biblical text. The praise of Job in the opening verse of the story masks a deeper truth, which is that Job is intellectually deficient and therefore deserving of suffering. Maimonides is then able to explain the inconsistencies regarding Job throughout the rest of the story as a reflection of different phases in his pedagogic journey to intellectual perfection and the experience of providence. Thus, Job protests his afflictions in the dialogue because his intellectual deficiency does not yet allow him to understand why he has suffered, but at the end of the story he still earns praise from God because by this point in the story he has achieved intellectual perfection and a philosophical understanding of his ordeal, accomplishments that in turn inspire him to recant his protests.

The material on the figure of Job in Ibn Tibbon's exposition is not as substantive as it is for the other thinkers in this study because his focus is mainly on Elihu's address in Job 33. Yet, it is clear that Ibn Tibbon's depiction of Job departs from that of Maimonides in one important respect: he does not envision Job achieving intellectual perfection by the end of the story, only an understanding of its benefits.

Zeraḥiah Ḥen utilizes Maimonides' esoteric method to deal with the figure of Job, but in a manner significantly different from that of his predecessor. While Maimonides hinges his understanding of the figure of Job on an esoteric reading of the first verse of the book alone, Zeraḥiah applies the esoteric method to the depiction of Job throughout the entire story. According to the exoteric reading, Job bears his suffering with patience and composure throughout the dialogue, and he protests his afflictions only because of genuine curiosity about why he has suffered. He is ultimately informed by Elihu and God that a true understanding of providence is beyond the capacity of human beings and that an explanation for his suffering is therefore not possible. Job dutifully accepts his limitations, and it is for this reason that he recants his protests. The message to the masses, therefore, is that like Job, they too must exhibit patience and composure in the face of suffering and recognize that an understanding of providence is beyond their ken. However, the esoteric message of the Book of Job is quite different. Providence is tied to intellectual perfection and manifests itself in prophecy and immortality; Job is unable to learn these truths because of his intellectual deficiencies.

Gersonides handles the figure of Job in a manner that is more nuanced and subtle than that of any other philosopher in this study. For him, Job is a figure who is mostly perfect in ethics and intellect but has one critical flaw, which is his lack of understanding of providence, and it is for this reason that he suffers. Thus, the positive and negative signals in the biblical text regarding Job can be explained on the basis of which aspect of Job's character predominates at a given point in the dialogue. When Job protests his suffering, it is because his flaw has got the better of him and he loses faith in God's governance. But he is able to achieve a proper understanding of providence once Elihu speaks to him because his intellectual qualities again come to the fore. Ultimately, God praises Job above his friends because those intellectual qualities had been evident throughout the dialogue, for even though Job's viewpoint was incorrect, it was closer to the truth than that of his friends.

Duran deals with Job in a manner similar to Gersonides. He too believes that Job has a high degree of virtue but possesses one flaw that is key to understanding his suffering. Yet, Duran's view of that flaw is much different from that of Gersonides. For Duran, Job acknowledges that he is suffering because of accidental sins that have been inspired by a wealthy lifestyle and the complacency it has encouraged, but he does not understand why the punishment has been so severe. It is only when Elihu addresses Job that he comes to understand that his accidental sins have accumulated over a lengthy period of time and that he has failed to heed divine warnings that he would be punished for them. Thus, Job's protests throughout the dialogue do not compromise his essential goodness because, first, he has already admitted wrongdoing, and second, his protests emanate from a genuine lack of understanding of why his suffering has been so severe. God's praise of Job at the end of the story is warranted for these same reasons.

The exegetical skill of these medieval philosophers was especially evident in their treatment of the dialogue in Job, which commentators have recognized is long, disorganized, and sometimes contradictory. Saadiah organizes the discussion by finding three positions in it: that of Job, who believes his suffering is evidence of God's arbitrary power; that of Eliphaz, Bildad, and Zophar, who believe it is evidence that Job has sinned and is therefore being punished; and that of Elihu, who believes that Job is being tested. Saadiah also gives meaning to the dialogue by claiming that the viewpoint of Eliphaz, Bildad, and Zophar has an important place in the discussion, even if it is incorrect with regard to Job's particular situation. These figures support the notion of retributive justice, of which the reader must be reminded since it too explains a good deal of human suffering. Finally, Saadiah expends substantial effort attempting to show how the addresses of each of the participants are a response to previous addresses, so that every element of the dialogue is accounted for and serves some purpose.

Maimonides, Ibn Tibbon, and Zeraḥiah Ḥen organize the dialogue between Job and his three friends by maintaining that each of the participants represents the viewpoint of a defined philosophical or theological school.[4] Maimonides acknowledges that according to a plain reading of the biblical text, the participants all make statements that do not seem to correspond to their respective viewpoints, but he is able to deal with this problem by arguing that such statements are part of the exoteric reading of the text and are designed to conceal its esoteric content. It is only the skilled philosopher who is able to recognize which verses uttered by the participants in the dialogue reveal their true viewpoints.

Gersonides strives more than any other exegete to bring coherence to the dialogue in Job. He adopts Maimonides' view that the participants each represent different philosophical viewpoints, but he goes further than Maimonides in bringing cohesiveness to the dialogue by indicating that Job and his friends, despite being superseded by Elihu, all express truths that contribute to the correct position on providence. Gersonides also introduces a certain symmetry into the dialogue. Job begins the story confused about whether there is individual providence. In the wake of Job's afflictions, he and his three friends take positions at opposite extremes, with Job denying individual providence and his friends supporting it. When Elihu resolves the matter, he formulates a view that is a synthesis of these two opposing points of view.

Duran also attempts to bring order to the dialogue. According to him, there are three positions: that of Job, who believes he is being punished for accidental sins; that of Eliphaz, Bildad, and Zophar, who hold that Job is being punished because he is thoroughly wicked; and that of Elihu, who supports Job's claim but is able to explain to him the timing and severity of his punishment. Duran is similar to Saadiah in arguing that there is significance in the opinions of Eliphaz, Bildad, and Zophar, even though they are proven wrong. They still make a valuable contribution to the dialogue in furnishing proofs for the existence of providence and in providing reasons for the suffering of the righteous. Duran also attempts to bring coherence to the dialogue in a more literary fashion by showing how the dialogue between Job and his friends is one of escalating tension. Job's friends become more extreme toward him and more hardened as he consistently and vociferously rejects their explanations for his suffering.

One of the more surprising features of the interpretations of Job examined in this study is their unanimous position that it is Elihu who provides Job with the correct explanation for his suffering. So central is Elihu's role for the commentators that most of them either relegate God to a role that is secondary to that of Elihu or give Him no substantive role whatsoever. This is remarkable, given that God enters the dialogue in the final chapters in such dramatic fashion, that He also has the last word, and that He is, after all—God!

Of all the philosophers in the study, Maimonides is the one who seems to give God the most significant role. God supplements Elihu's remarks about the workings of providence with important information about the limits of human knowledge in comprehending God's ways, so that Job recognizes in the final chapter that his only escape from suffering is to achieve intellectual perfection and a psychological immunity from suffering. Other commentators are not as generous with God. Gersonides suggests that God's address to Job is meant to teach him about the prospering of the wicked, since that issue had not been dealt with by Elihu, whose focus was the suffering of the righteous. Yet, while in Gersonides' thinking the question of the prospering of the wicked is certainly one that must be answered if a full theory of providence is to emerge from the Book of Job, it is a problem that he clearly considers tangential to the more central issues of providence dealt with by Elihu several chapters earlier. Moreover, the question of the prospering of the wicked does not bear directly on Job's specific situation, which is the central theme in the book.

Even more intriguing are those thinkers in this study who do not believe that God's address adds anything at all to what Elihu has said. Saadiah openly embraces this position—though in his case it fits in with his interpretation of the story. God deliberately provides no information to Job about his suffering because if He did, it would spoil the meaning of the test, which is predicated on Job's ignorance of the reasons for his afflictions. Ibn Tibbon takes the position that God does not even speak to Job, at least not directly. The tempest is merely a metaphor for the lessons Job has learned via his suffering. Zeraḥiah Ḥen also finds little value in God's words, for according to him they merely extend the lesson already taught by Elihu, which is that Job should accept his ignorance regarding the workings of divine providence. Moreover, this lesson is only for the masses, who have not achieved intellectual enlightenment. Therefore, for Zeraḥiah God's lesson adds nothing that has not been said by Elihu, and it imparts wisdom with no esoteric value. Duran is most open about his lack of interest in God's address. He states explicitly and unabashedly that God's words add nothing new to the dialogue but merely reinforce what has already been said by Elihu.

Why do most of the thinkers in this study give the central role in the dialogue to Elihu while pushing God off to the side? Some provide explicit reasons for their favoring of Elihu. For instance, Saadiah points out that Elihu is the only figure not rebuked by God at the end of the dialogue. He also notes that Elihu declares that he will rebut the arguments of all the other participants in the dialogue, a statement that none of the other participants make.[5]

There may also be other factors at play here. First, that the philosophers favor Elihu's address over that of God may reflect the fact that in the biblical text Elihu's address has more content than God's, which is, after all, heavily rhetorical and very repetitive. Elihu's address therefore presents the philosophers with more of an opportunity than God's for finding a substantive answer to the problem posed by Job's situation. It is also possible that because of their methodology, the commentators in this study were intent on choosing a human being for providing the correct explanation for Job's suffering. After all, the hallmark of medieval philosophy is its respect for human reason as a faculty capable of grappling with ultimate questions. The ultimate answer to Job therefore has to come from a human being, not from God.[6]

Another question raised in the introduction as an exegetical consideration was whether the medieval Jewish philosophers gave any thought to the audience to which the Book of Job was directed. Did they see it as a book addressed only to the Jewish people? Or did they also appreciate its universal meaning? Might they have considered the possibility that the book speaks on *both* levels?

One of the significant conclusions to emerge from this study is that all the thinkers seem to have appreciated the universal meaning of Job. Some are more explicit about this than others. Saadiah states openly that Job deals with issues that are of importance to all of humanity. In Maimonides, an appreciation for the universal meaning of the Book of Job is not stated openly but is certainly implied. First, he envisions the dialogue in Job as a debate between representatives of different philosophical and religious viewpoints both inside and outside Judaism, with the viewpoint of the Torah being only one of these positions. Second, and perhaps more important, in Maimonides' reading the central lesson of the Book of Job is theoretically applicable to all people, not just Jews, since any individual should be able to achieve intellectual perfection and experience providence in the manner Maimonides describes. Ibn Tibbon and Zeraḥiah Ḥen follow Maimonides in this regard by viewing the dialogue in a similar manner. Gersonides also follows Maimonides on this issue, though in his reading the dialogue in Job is not quite as ecumenical as it is in Maimonides. Duran seems to appreciate the universality of the Book of Job in arguing that Job is a non-Jew who lived at the time of the giving of the Torah.

Yet, alongside this recognition of the universal meaning of Job is the belief of many of these commentators that the Book of Job is directed to Jews. In Saadiah there are strong hints that Job represents the Jewish people and that his suffering is paradigmatic of their experience in exile. That position becomes most explicit in Gersonides, who, in a critical passage in his commentary, links Job's story to that of the Jewish people. These thinkers seem to have had no qualms about having a non-Jew serve as a representative of the Jewish people.[7]

For Maimonides the Book of Job is directed to the Jews not as a people but as individuals. Maimonides clearly uses Job as a model for the transformation that Jews unenlightened in philosophical wisdom should themselves undergo. Thus, in his reading, Job had an erroneous belief in providence because of his attachment to "traditional stories" but was able to come to a true understanding of providence once he became philosophically enlightened. Maimonides' position is largely duplicated by Ibn Tibbon and Zeraḥiah Ḥen—though, as noted, these thinkers do not consider Job to be a model of intellectual enlightenment quite in the same way Maimonides does. Duran seems to be an exceptional case in that his reading of Job, while having some applicability to Jews, seems more concerned with coming to terms with his own personal experience of suffering in the wake of the disturbances in Spain and Majorca in 1391.

One more issue that should be mentioned in this portion of the discussion is how these thinkers dealt with the question of the authorship of Job. On this point they are unanimous: they all accept the rabbinic notion that Moses is the author of Job. In agreeing on this position, the medieval Jewish philosophers do not distinguish themselves from other medieval Jewish exegetes, most of whom also believed that Moses was the author of Job.[8] The only figure in this study who offers original ideas on this matter is Zeraḥiah Ḥen, who, as we saw, has a good deal to say about the authorship of Job and why it is not mentioned in the biblical text itself. As part of his discussion, Zeraḥiah also shares his radical view that the Book of Job is not the product of revelation but was composed entirely from human wisdom.

I stated in my introduction that my concern would be with how these thinkers confronted the broad exegetical challenges of the Book of Job, and that I could not dwell on how they dealt with the minutiae of the biblical text. Nonetheless, we did have the opportunity to see how they handled specific sections of Job—most notably Job 33—and it is evident that they were not lacking in exegetical skills when it came to the details of the biblical text. In many instances they were seriously engaged with philology, syntax, grammar, and interpretation through context. However, a thorough examination of this aspect of the commentaries must be left for another occasion.

The Exegesis of Job and Systematic Thought in Medieval Jewish Philosophy

I now proceed to the third and final interface, which concerns the relationship between exegesis and systematic philosophy. The question here was the nature of the association between the readings of Job and the systematic discussions of providence and theodicy in medieval Jewish philosophy. Did the interpretations of Job by medieval philosophers merely confirm what was found in the systematic treatments of these issues, or did they have anything to add to them?

There is ample evidence for the first tendency: it is clear that the philosophers in this study often come to the biblical text with an idea of what they want to find in it. We could call upon many examples to illustrate this point. For instance, almost all the philosophers do not accept a literal understanding of the figure of Satan and his interactions with God in the prologue of Job. Saadiah insists that Satan is a human being bent on slandering Job, while Maimonides, Ibn Tibbon, Zeraḥiah Ḥen, and Gersonides understand Satan as an allegorical figure representing either matter or privation. Duran stands alone in accepting the biblical text at face value when he upholds the view that Satan is an angel whose job it is to prosecute and punish sinners. That the figure of Satan should invite a series of nonliteral interpretations from the thinkers in this study is no surprise, given the philosophical difficulties that Satan raises. At the very least, the conversations between God and Satan seem to compromise God's wisdom and omnipotence by implying that Satan convinces God to make Job suffer against His better judgment. Maimonides, Ibn Tibbon, Zeraḥiah Ḥen, and Gersonides have the added philosophical problem that they cannot accept the notion that Satan is an angel as described literally in the biblical text, because according to their metaphysics angels are not personal beings. Thus, most of the philosophers in this study reinterpret the figure of Satan in a manner that conforms to prior philosophical assumptions.

Further evidence that philosophy influences exegesis in these thinkers is that we find many instances in which their exegetical insights reflect their general philosophical orientations. I am referring here to the division between radical and conservative philosophical approaches that scholars commonly use to classify medieval Jewish philosophers and of which I have made use as well. Maimonides, Ibn Tibbon, and Zeraḥiah Ḥen have been placed in the radical camp; Saadiah and Duran, in the conservative camp; and Gersonides has been located somewhere in the middle of the two.[9] The thinkers studied here take predictable positions on a wide range of issues in Job depending on the philosophical camps to which they belong.

This is an issue that should be explored in some detail. Let us begin with the subject of allegory. It is no surprise that Maimonides, Ibn Tibbon, and Zeraḥiah adopt the view that Job is an allegory, because they represent the more radical wing of medieval Jewish philosophy, for which allegory was a common hermeneutic technique. Allegory allowed these philosophers to divide the message of the biblical text into esoteric and exoteric layers and to identify their radical philosophical doctrines with the esoteric layer. Saadiah and Duran predictably opt for the view that the Book of Job is historically true because their more conservative orientation generally brings with it a more literal approach to the biblical text. Duran's insistence on a literal reading of Job is no doubt connected with a deliberate backlash against the use of allegory in biblical interpretation, a backlash that is fairly common among conservative Jewish philosophers after Maimonides. Thus, when it comes to the issue of allegory, there is no question that philosophical orientation helps shape exegesis.

The division between radical and conservative philosophical orientations is reflected in other exegetical decisions made by these thinkers. It is no surprise that two of the more conservative philosophers in our study, Saadiah and Gersonides, hold the view that the Book of Job is relevant to the historical suffering of the Jewish people. In medieval Jewish philosophy, a conservative philosophical orientation went hand in hand with a concern for Jewish history and the uniqueness of the Jewish people.[10] For more radical thinkers such as Maimonides, Ibn Tibbon, and Zeraḥiah, the important demarcation was not so much between Jew and non-Jew but between philosopher and non-philosopher. Therefore, it is to be expected that according to these thinkers there is no connection between Job's suffering and that of the Jewish people as a whole. Instead, Job represents individual Jews who suffer because of intellectual inadequacies but with effort can achieve intellectual perfection and experience the protection of providence.

Most significant is how the philosophical orientations of the thinkers in this study affect their respective understandings of the central message of Job. The more radical thinkers—Maimonides, Ibn Tibbon, and Zeraḥiah—need little comment, for it is obvious that when it comes to the central message of

Job, these thinkers impose meaning on the biblical text that supports their philosophical agenda. For these philosophers, the Book of Job relays esoteric truths about the doctrine of providence, understood in Aristotelian terms. For the more conservative thinkers—Saadiah and Duran—philosophical orientation is equally determinative in their understanding of the central message of Job in that both thinkers rely on the notion of divine trials as an explanation of Job's ordeal, an explanation that is well grounded in rabbinic sources and a traditional rabbinic worldview.[11] The contrast between the two groups can be brought into sharper focus by noting that the more radical thinkers in this study could never accept the notion that God tests Job—or anyone, for that matter—because their metaphysics does not allow for a God who is personally involved in human affairs.[12] The conservatives are free of these constraints, and thus for them the notion of a test is not only plausible, but the preferred explanation of Job's suffering.[13]

These observations about the respective approaches of the radical and conservative thinkers toward the central message of Job help explain another distinction between them concerning the place of Job in the Bible. According to the radicals, Job is the central book of the Bible for informing us about the subject of providence, for in presenting the true esoteric doctrine on providence, this book also determines how providence is to be understood in the rest of scripture as well. This is true even with respect to the Torah, for it too must be reread esoterically through the message that emerges in Job. This position is reflected in the way in which the radical philosophers conceive of Job's pedagogic process. Job initially adheres to a material view of providence that is congruent with a literal reading of Torah, but once he achieves philosophical enlightenment, he comes to understand that providence is consequent upon intellectual perfection. Job's intellectual development therefore underscores the privileging of the message of his own book over that of Torah. While this understanding of Job is initiated by Maimonides, it is actually most pronounced in Ibn Tibbon, who explicitly argues that the later books of the Bible reveal doctrines that are not found, or are only hinted at, in the earlier books.[14]

The conservatives take an approach on this issue that is practically the opposite of that of the radicals. The view that Job's suffering is a test allows the conservatives to read the Book of Job against the background of the Torah, rather than the reverse. This is exemplified by the fact that both the conservative thinkers in this study—Saadiah and Duran—attempt to understand Job's suffering in light of Abraham's test, for in drawing this connection, the conservatives allow the Torah to maintain its preeminent position. Another advantage of this perspective is that the philosophers understand Job by reference to a story in the Torah that highlights the personal involvement of God with the affairs of human beings and that therefore supports their conservative approach to providence. Thus, by reading the Book of Job in light of the Torah, the conservatives also manage to suppress any potential radicalism in the Book of Job—particularly in its final chapters.

Yet, it would be a mistake to assume that the readings of Job examined here only mirror the systematic dimension of medieval Jewish philosophy. We have seen consistently that these texts also contribute to that dimension. This contribution has emerged in a number of variations. First, we have encountered several instances in which a thinker produces both an interpretation of Job and a separate systematic discussion regarding providence or theodicy, and in all such instances the interpretation of Job in one way or another plays a critical role in the presentation of that thinker's view on the systematic dimension of his thought.

Saadiah provides a good example of this phenomenon, for in his case the major treatment of the problem of theodicy is, in fact, found in his commentary on Job—not in his systematic treatise *Beliefs and Opinions*. Saadiah's commentary on Job is the earlier of the two works, and I demonstrated that the discussion of theodicy in *Beliefs and Opinions* is a summary of the ideas already dealt with in the commentary. It is for this reason that in his discussion of theodicy in *Beliefs and Opinions* Saadiah assumes his reader's familiarity with the Job commentary. It is also for this reason that in his commentary on Job he renames the Book of Job *The Book of Theodicy*.

In my treatment of Maimonides, it was not possible to conduct a comprehensive assessment of the relationship between his reading of Job and his views on providence because the latter would require a lengthy discussion in its own right. Nonetheless, it was clear from my analysis that Maimonides' reading of Job serves an important function in the presentation of his philosophical ideas on providence. Most significant, it is in his exposition on Job that Maimonides introduces his central conception with respect to providence, which is that the highest form of providence consists of a psychological immunity from suffering.

In Gersonides we found a sterling example of how exegesis contributes to systematic philosophy. There is a great deal of overlap between Gersonides' commentary on Job and his systematic discussion of providence in the *Wars*, and there is evidence that each continued to be edited in light of the other after their completion. We also discovered a number of instances in which the systematic discussion in the *Wars* contributes insights on providence not found in the Job commentary. Yet, the reverse is also true; the commentary on Job provides philosophical information not found in the *Wars*. In the Job commentary Gersonides introduces the notion that the primary manifestations of providence—prophecies about future harmful events and providential suffering—encourage "repentance," or the striving for intellectual perfection, and that these forms of providence are therefore designed to do more than just to save one from physical harm, as is argued in the *Wars*. It is also in the commentary on Job that Gersonides emphasizes the limitations of human knowledge in comprehending divine providence, a conception absent from the *Wars*.

There were thinkers in this study for whom the interpretation of Job was essential for the presentation of their views on providence, because they produced no systematic discussion of this issue. The most significant thinker in this category was Ibn Tibbon. Moreover, the views Ibn Tibbon expresses about providence in his reading of Job are picked up by a series of thirteenth- and fourteenth-century Jewish philosopher-exegetes who incorporate them into their own commentaries on Job. These are Immanuel of Rome, Elijah ben Eliezer ha-Yerushalmi, Isaac Arundi, and perhaps Zeraḥiah Ḥen—all of whom are similar to Ibn Tibbon in expressing their views on providence in an exegetical mode. In Ibn Tibbon and his followers, we therefore have a striking example of how the exegesis of Job contributes to the dialogue in medieval Jewish philosophy about the nature and scope of providence.

Duran presents us with yet another variation on how the exegesis of Job plays a central role in the formulation of philosophical views on providence. Duran's systematic speculations on providence are found in his commentary on Job itself, because in his opinion all philosophical proofs for the existence of providence are represented in the dialogue between Job and his friends. Here exegesis and philosophical reflection are so tightly intertwined that one cannot easily distinguish between them.

The case should not be overstated here. I have shown that the philosophers in this study valued exegesis as a genre of literature for presenting their philosophical ideas. I have not demonstrated that they saw exegesis as an actual hermeneutic tool for producing those ideas. It is possible that they regarded an exegetical format only as the preferred medium to express philosophical ideas, but that those ideas had been derived from prior philosophical speculation that they had not yet shared in writing.

There is reason to suspect that this was the case with many of the thinkers studied here. For instance, although Maimonides, Ibn Tibbon, and Zeraḥiah Ḥen all use their readings of Job to introduce philosophical ideas about providence, one gets the impression that those ideas were not discovered through the actual interpretation of the biblical text but through prior systematic reflection that was then applied to the text. Thus, in his reading of Job Maimonides presents the notion that providence consists of psychological immunity from suffering; but it seems likely that this idea was derived through prior philosophical reflection, since this conception seems to follow from his systematic discussion on providence, in which he concludes that providence is consequent on the perfection of the intellect. Through his exegesis of Job, Ibn Tibbon introduces the notion that the highest form of providence is immortality of the intellect, but I argued that he viewed this conception as one that Maimonides had already deduced from philosophical reflection.

Yet, with some of the thinkers, exegesis does seem to function as more than just a convenient format for expressing philosophical conceptions. We saw that both Gersonides and Duran look to the biblical text to derive philosophical ideas regarding providence. Gersonides' notion that the experience of providence inspires one to achieve a higher degree of intellectual perfection appears to be derived from specific statements in Elihu's address in Job 33. Duran's proofs for providence are all supported by prooftexts in Job that are liberally intermingled with his philosophical reasoning. Therefore, with these thinkers exegesis serves as a tool for the actual production of philosophical ideas.

Still, we should not lose sight of the central point here. Even if many of these philosophers used their readings of Job to express ideas about providence that had already been worked out through prior systematic reflection, this does not take away from the importance of these works as a valuable repository for ideas about providence in medieval Jewish philosophy. Thus, regardless of how the medieval philosophers derived their ideas about providence, we cannot afford to ignore the exegetical literature of these thinkers in any serious discussion of this subject.

This is especially the case for thinkers such as Ibn Tibbon, who presents his views on providence exclusively in an exegetical format. One who does not consult the exegetical literature on Job in medieval Jewish philosophy will be unaware of Ibn Tibbon's notion that the highest form of providence is the immortality of the intellect, and this is a serious oversight; for while Maimonides had tied providence to the perfection of the intellect, Ibn Tibbon was the first medieval Jewish philosopher to emphasize immortality as the most important manifestation of that perfection. Without the exegetical literature, one would also miss the fact that Ibn Tibbon's notion of providence is highly influential on subsequent philosopher-exegetes in medieval Judaism. What I am saying here is borne out by a perusal of the scholarship in medieval Jewish philosophy. When scholars discuss the issue of providence in this school, they generally make no mention of Ibn Tibbon and his followers, and that is because their analysis of this issue is almost always based on the systematic treatises of the philosophers, not their exegetical literature.[15]

Each of the three interfaces highlights in its own way the importance of the commentaries on Job that we have examined. From my exploration of the first interface, we have learned that the readings of Job of the medieval Jewish philosophers were not just an unrelated collection of texts, but a body of commentaries linked in a coherent and evolving tradition of interpretation of a single biblical book. My examination of the second interface has shown that the commentaries on Job by medieval Jewish philosophers have to be regarded as works of serious exegesis that grapple with the meaning of the biblical text. From the third interface, we have discovered that the exegesis of Job in medieval Jewish philosophy is essential for understanding how medieval Jewish philosophers dealt with the subject of providence from a systematic standpoint.

Implications for the Study of Medieval Jewish Philosophy

The conclusions drawn here have implications that take us beyond the Book of Job in medieval Jewish philosophy. First, we can dispel the common notion that medieval Jewish philosophers are not true exegetes because they merely impose their philosophical readings on the biblical text. There is no doubt that these philosophers understood the biblical text through the lens of philosophical systems that were current in their period, but to view their exegetical enterprise only in this manner is to have an inadequate and incomplete understanding of it. I have shown in my examination of the first interface that all the medieval Jewish philosophers in this study were sensitive to the purely exegetical challenges that the biblical text presented, and often, when they impose their philosophical views on the biblical text, they are at the same time confronting those challenges. We have also seen in my examination of the third interface that there are instances in which the philosophers will draw philosophical meaning out of the biblical text.

The exegesis of the medieval Jewish philosophers therefore functions on at least three levels: it reads philosophical ideas into the biblical text, it draws philosophical ideas out the biblical text, and it grapples with the basic exegetical challenge of making sense of the biblical text. I am not arguing that these three levels of interpretation are equally manifest in all the thinkers in this study. Gersonides and Duran are more inclined to read philosophical ideas out of the biblical text than are the other thinkers in this study. We have also seen that some thinkers in this study are more sensitive than others to the purely exegetical difficulties of Job. Moreover, I am not arguing that all exegesis in medieval Jewish philosophy can be characterized by the three levels described here. After all, in this study I have analyzed only one sample of texts. But I have shown that the exegesis of the medieval Jewish philosophers is a far more complex and fruitful venture than scholars have assumed, and they cannot be dismissed as genuine biblical interpreters.

In addition to the implications our discussion has for the study of the medieval Jewish philosophers as exegetes, it also has implications for the field of medieval Jewish philosophy as a whole. I noted in the introduction that modern scholars of medieval Jewish philosophy have tended to organize their studies almost exclusively around philosophical concepts, such as divine attributes, creation, and providence. Interest has focused primarily on a "history of ideas" approach, in which the views of medieval Jewish philosophers on these major philosophical themes are analyzed in terms of prior influences both from inside and outside the Jewish sphere. Put in other terms, scholars of medieval Jewish philosophy have generally been interested in the tradition of interpretation that has evolved around these central concepts. This method has had remarkable longevity, dominating the scholarly study of medieval Jewish philosophy since the field's inception in the nineteenth century.

Our study suggests that there is another angle from which to approach the field of medieval Jewish philosophy, one in which the literature in this school is organized not around philosophical categories but around exegetical ones, for, as I have shown, one can just as easily demonstrate the existence of a tradition of interpretation regarding the exegesis of Job as one can regarding such issues as divine attributes. It is not that I have ignored the systematic treatises of the medieval Jewish philosophers; these works have been an important part of this study. Rather, I have attempted to examine those systematic works in a new light by studying them in tandem with the exegetical literature of the philosophers and by placing the exegetical questions at the center of the study, rather than on the periphery, to which scholars have generally confined them.

The notion that the literature of medieval Jewish philosophy can be analyzed along exegetical lines opens up new directions for research beyond the present study. First, much exegetical literature was produced by medieval Jewish philosophers on books of the Bible other than Job, in both published texts and unpublished manuscripts. If there is a tradition of interpretation of Job in medieval Jewish philosophy, should we not expect to find similar traditions for these other books as well? Some scholars have already begun exploring whether there is a tradition of interpretation in medieval Jewish philosophy on the Song of Songs.[16] Numerous commentaries were also written by medieval Jewish philosophers on other books of the Bible, such as Proverbs and Ecclesiastes, and these have yet to be explored. There are also portions of biblical books that attracted much attention in medieval Jewish philosophy, such as the first three chapters of Genesis and the first chapter of Ezekiel, and on these texts as well there are numerous unexplored commentaries.

There are exegetical categories in medieval Jewish philosophy concerning hermeneutics that need to be investigated as well. Almost no examination has been conducted on the exegetical techniques employed by medieval Jewish philosophers. While I have had a good deal to say about this issue in my own study, it has only scratched the surface of a much larger subject. For instance, medieval Jewish philosophers made extensive use of allegory in their interpretation of the biblical text, but little work has been done on their use of this interpretive technique.[17] Moreover, medieval Jewish philosophers were often interested in such exegetical categories as *peshat* and *derash*, terms that have been virtually ignored in the scholarship in medieval Jewish philosophy.[18] How, then, did medieval Jewish philosophers relate to these hermeneutic categories? Did traditions develop regarding the use of these methods in medieval Jewish philosophy? And how did these techniques affect the development of philosophical ideas? These questions should also arouse the interest of scholars outside medieval Jewish philosophy, in particular scholars of medieval Jewish exegesis, who have thus far shown little interest in the philosophers as exegetes. The exegesis of Maimonides and Gersonides should be of no less significance in understanding how medieval Jewish thinkers interpreted the Bible than the exegesis of Rashi or Rashbam.

I must emphasize that the study of exegetical literature in medieval Jewish philosophy is not just for gaining insight into medieval Jewish exegesis. It should help us better understand how medieval Jewish philosophers approached philosophical concepts that have been the traditional focus of scholarly research. That is because the distinction between what is philosophical and what is exegetical in medieval Jewish philosophy is not always an easy one to make, given that the philosophers draw on both disciplines for developing their ideas. In my own study, I have shown that a history of approaches to the question of providence in medieval Jewish philosophy would, in fact, be incomplete without an exploration of interpretations of Job in this school, because entire viewpoints on this subject would be lost, most notably that of Ibn Tibbon. My study therefore underscores that it is imperative to consult the exegetical literature of the medieval Jewish philosophers in order to better understand their thinking on issues that are at the heart of systematic philosophy.

I would again like to emphasize as I did in my introduction that I am in no way denigrating the way medieval Jewish philosophy has been studied, nor am I calling into question the value of the scholarship that has defined the field up to this point. There is no question that a primary task in the study of medieval Jewish philosophy is to trace the historical development of ideas regarding basic philosophical concepts, such as divine attributes and creation. All I am arguing is that there are axes in the exegetical sphere of medieval Jewish philosophy that also need to be explored in order to have a comprehensive understanding of the field, and that an investigation of these can only enrich our understanding of the systematic dimension of this school.

9

Job Medieval, Job Modern

I conclude this study by exploring whether there is any commonality between the medieval readings of Job I have examined and the readings of Job in the modern period. A legitimate question one may ask here is what value there is in making such a comparison. The readings of Job that I have explored stand as fine examples of exegetical literature even if they share nothing in common with those of modern writers. However, one cannot avoid being curious about such a comparison, especially if the readings of Job in this study are as sophisticated as I have argued. Does that sophistication manifest itself in insights that are valid beyond the confines of the medieval period? We can also turn the issue around and say that if there is commonality between the readings of Job in our study and those of modern interpreters, it would certainly bolster my claim about the sophistication of our material, since it would indicate that the insights of our medieval thinkers transcend their place, time, and intellectual culture.[1]

Before even beginning to discuss this matter, I should note the problems involved in making a comparison between the readings of Job in this study and those in the modern period. We have encountered a considerable variety of interpretations of Job in medieval Jewish philosophy, and it is therefore difficult to formulate generalizations about those interpretations so as to facilitate a comparison with modern views. With the modern views themselves, we come up against the same difficulty multiplied a hundredfold; here the sheer volume of material is overwhelming. In fact, few books of the Bible have elicited as much commentary in the modern period as Job.

This last point deserves some elaboration. In the past two centuries, scores of interpretations have appeared that deal with Job from many different perspectives and with a wide range of methodologies. The academic world alone has produced an enormous number of studies on Job. The style of scholarship on Job with the longest history is represented by scholars such as Marvin H. Pope, Georg Fohrer, and Harold H. Rowley, who have written on Job from the perspective of the historical-critical method. These scholars are primarily interested in the history of the composition of the text, its parallels and sources in ancient Near Eastern literature, its date and author, and its linguistic features.[2] Another academic approach that has been popular in the last half century is one that is more focused on theological issues. Representatives of this method include Samuel Terrien, Robert Gordis, and Matitiahu Tsevat.[3] We should also include in this group Norman C. Habel and Edwin M. Good, who have taken a literary approach to Job, because these writers are interested in theological issues as well.[4] There are also modern readings of Job outside the academic sphere that are, in effect, *re*readings of the book, such as those found in Archibald MacLeish, Franz Kafka, and Robert Frost—writers who use the story of Job as a basis for the composition of original literature.[5]

In order to facilitate an intelligible comparison between the medieval interpretations of Job in this study and those found in the modern period, it is necessary to be selective about which modern interpreters will be discussed. I have thus chosen to limit myself to those academic thinkers who are primarily interested in the theological message of Job—in particular Terrien, Gordis, Tsevat, Habel, and Good, who I believe are the best representatives of this approach. I have chosen this group of interpreters because their theological agenda seems closest to that of the medieval thinkers in our study. I will also cite some of the scholars of the historical-critical method whose observations are relevant to our deliberations. However, I will not engage the modern literary rereadings of Job of thinkers such as MacLeish and Kafka, since their agenda, it would seem, is rather distant from that of the philosophers in this study, who see themselves primarily as commentators on the biblical text rather than creative literary writers.[6]

One can find any number of insights about Job in medieval Jewish philosophy that are congruent with those in the modern period. However, in many cases that congruence is of limited significance, since it involves only an isolated opinion or a minority view among the modern interpreters. Thus, for instance, we have seen that all the medieval Jewish philosophers in our study look to Elihu as the figure who provides the answer to Job's challenge. That same view is, in fact, argued by a number of significant early twentieth-century interpreters of Job, including Karl Budde, Carl Cornill, and Yehezkel Kauffmann. Like the medievals, these modern writers see Elihu, not God, as the figure who articulates the central message of the book.[7] Yet, most modern scholars do not take this position. Not only do they not believe that Elihu's address contains the central message of the book, but most of them insist that his speeches are a later interpolation into the original dialogue.[8]

Of much greater interest are instances in which the insights of the thinkers in this study are congruent with those in the modern period that have found widespread acceptance. For instance, the notion set forth by Maimonides, Ibn Tibbon, and Zeraḥiah Ḥen that Job is fiction is very much in line with modern interpreters. It was Zeraḥiah Ḥen who provided the most thorough, sophisticated, and insightful justification for this approach, and I have already noted that his observations on this matter foreshadow some of those offered by Habel.[9] Habel is not the only modern interpreter who believes that Job is fiction. Most modern scholars argue that the story of Job was originally a folk tale in the prologue and epilogue, to which the lengthy intervening dialogue was later added.[10] Nonetheless, the notion that Job is fiction receives its strongest support—at least implicitly—in the readings of such analysts as Habel and Good, whose literary approach to Job assumes that it is an artfully constructed work.

It is significant that in entertaining the notion that Job is fiction, the medieval Jewish philosophers bear a greater resemblance to the moderns than to their medieval Christian counterparts. Christian interpreters, from the earliest Patristic interpreters to the end of the Middle Ages, almost without exception read Job as a record of true historical events. That is because the figure of Job was valuable to Christian thinkers as a living example of a righteous gentile justified in God's eyes before the giving of the Law at Mount Sinai. To have read Job as fiction would have denuded it of its polemical value.[11] Since the medieval Jewish philosophers obviously did not share these concerns, many of them had no qualms about accepting the view already expressed in early rabbinic literature that the Book of Job was fiction.

Medieval Jewish philosophers and modern scholars have different motivations for understanding Job as fiction. For the first group, the urge to fictionalize Job is connected to a larger program of reading key portions of the biblical text as allegory in order to find within it esoteric philosophical truths. For the moderns, there is no such scheme. Job is read as fiction on the basis of contemporary findings about ancient Near Eastern culture, the nature of its literature, and its transmission of folk-tale traditions.

The medieval Jewish interpreters in this study also anticipate modern views of Job in their appreciation of the book's universal message. As already noted, every thinker in this study either states explicitly or at least implies this position. That very same view is assumed by practically all modern interpreters of Job.[12] On this point, the medieval Jewish philosophers are not unique, in that they take a position very much similar to that of their medieval Christian counterparts. As noted earlier, all medieval Christian commentators saw Job as having universal meaning. However, for the medieval Jewish philosophers the universalizing of the message of Job was a more daring move than it was for the Christians, given the traditional belief that the Hebrew Bible was a revelation directed to the Jewish people. Of course, some of our medieval thinkers also saw Job as a figure representing the suffering of the Jewish people, and the particularistic element is therefore present in their thinking as well. It is nonetheless striking that all the thinkers in this study—even the most conservative among them—appreciated the universality of the message in Job.[13]

Commonality between the medieval Jewish philosophers and the modern interpreters can also be found with respect to the interpretation of Job's viewpoint during the dialogue with his friends. Susan Schreiner has already noted that Maimonides, Thomas Aquinas, and John Calvin anticipate the modern understanding of the figure of Job as an individual who loses faith in the moral order of the universe once he has experienced his suffering and before he has received his revelation from God. As Schreiner notes, this is an interpretation that contrasts sharply with early Christian readings in which Job is the paragon of faith and patience throughout the entire book.[14] Yet, the same conclusion can also be drawn regarding all the medieval Jewish philosophers in my study—not just Maimonides, who is the only Jewish commentator with whom Schreiner deals. All of them paint a picture of a disillusioned Job who in some measure has lost faith in God's providential order as a result of his suffering. Saadiah's interpretation of Job is particularly significant in foreshadowing modern interpretations. He depicts Job as a figure who in the wake of his suffering becomes convinced that God relates to human beings through arbitrary power, not justice. This interpretation of Job's attitude is one that is found in such modern interpreters as Terrien and Good.[15]

We can even go a step further with Saadiah by noting that his understanding of the entire disagreement between Job, on the one hand, and Eliphaz, Bildad, and Zophar, on the other, mostly anticipates modern readings. According to Saadiah, the debate is about the suffering of the righteous, with Job's friends representing the traditional view of retributive justice and Job rejecting that view in favor of the belief that God can bring suffering as an act of arbitrary power. That is precisely the way many modern scholars read the dialogue.[16] Where Saadiah's view is different from that of the moderns is in his belief that the position of Job's friends supporting retributive justice, while inapplicable to Job's specific situation, is nonetheless valid in other instances and therefore constitutes an important part of the book's message. Job did not suffer as a result of sin, but his three friends nonetheless remind us that this explanation for suffering is at times correct. By contrast, modern interpreters generally feel that the Book of Job stands entirely in opposition to the doctrine of retributive justice and that Job's friends are therefore viewed by its author as holding an opinion that is completely incorrect.[17]

How do the medieval thinkers in this study compare with the moderns with respect to the central message of the Book of Job? The two most conservative thinkers, Saadiah and Duran, certainly display some commonality with modern interpreters of Job, for it is not unusual for the latter to assume that Job's suffering is a test.[18] However, the similarity here between the two groups of commentators is at best superficial. Both Saadiah and Duran propose interpretations of Job's test that find no analogue in the modern writers—at least those I have examined. Saadiah believes that Job's test is designed, at least in part, to prove his righteousness to his contemporaries, an interpretation predicated on his unique and novel interpretation that Satan is, in fact, a human being and the ringleader of Job's enemies. Duran's reading of Job's test is idiosyncratic in proposing an elaborate theory according to which Job's suffering is part trial and part punishment to cleanse him of accidental sins.

It is a different story with the more radical philosophers in this study—

Maimonides, Ibn Tibbon, and Zeraḥiah Ḥen—because these thinkers propose an understanding of the central message of Job that in some respects displays a remarkable resonance with the readings of modern interpreters. First, these philosophers anticipate the modern understanding of Job with the claim that Job undermines the traditional notion of retributive justice represented in the Torah. That reading is first proposed by Maimonides and is faithfully supported by Ibn Tibbon and Zeraḥiah Ḥen. As noted above, it is a reading that is also accepted by many modern scholars.[19]

Yet, this commonality between the radical philosophers and the moderns is limited to a viewpoint that the Book of Job eventually rejects. When it comes to identifying the positive position on undeserved suffering that the book offers in place of retributive justice—what is, in effect, the book's central message—the two groups of thinkers seem rather far apart.

The radical philosophers in this study believe that the Book of Job is essentially a philosophical text that grapples with theodicy by engaging the more general question of providence. Moreover, they agree that the suffering of the righteous, like all human suffering, is due to matter or privation but can be overcome through intellectual perfection. In Maimonides, that perfection brings with it the capacity to experience psychological immunity to suffering, while for Ibn Tibbon and Zeraḥiah Ḥen it results in immortality.

Among modern interpreters there is a wider range of views regarding the central message of Job. Some, such as Matitiahu Tsevat, are similar to the medieval thinkers in arguing that the Book of Job offers a theodicy. According to Tsevat, what Job discovers is that God is neither just nor unjust; He is just God. Thus, God is not responsible for the type of suffering Job experiences, and the only justice to be found in the world is that which human beings create.[20]

But most modern thinkers reject the notion that the Book of Job offers a theodicy of any sort. The elusive nature of God's address from the tempest would suggest that there is no rational explanation for suffering proposed here. This position, in turn, takes a number of forms. A common view is that the Book of Job instructs us not in how we should understand undeserved suffering, but in how we should react to it. For instance, according to Pope, Job receives no explanation for his suffering but learns that the only proper response to his ordeal is to have faith in God. By implication, all individuals who experience undeserved suffering should react in the same manner.[21] Gordis argues for a more elaborate version of this theory. According to him, Job learns from the voice in the tempest that the natural order and the moral order of the universe are similar because in both realms there are things we understand and things we cannot. That is, Gordis insists that there is some positive content to the knowledge that God provides in his final speech to Job, even if no theodicy emerges here. Job should therefore express joy in that which he does comprehend about the order of the universe and from that sentiment be inspired to believe that there is also meaning in his suffering, which he does not comprehend.[22] Finally, there are a number of interpreters who take an existentialist approach to Job, including Buber, Terrien, Habel, Rowley, and Fohrer.

These commentators all argue a variation on the same theme, which is that the answer Job receives from God is the very experience of God's presence and that it is this experience that provides comfort, given that no theodicy is possible. Here there is no cognitive content to God's final address to Job but rather the experience of closeness to God, which is all that human beings can hope for.[23]

The medieval commentators in this study offer a far more positive and optimistic assessment of the central message of Job than do the moderns. While the medievals propose that the book teaches a theodicy that solves the problem of the suffering of the righteous, the moderns are more inclined to conclude that no rational explanation for this problem is forthcoming and that one must find comfort in some other experience, whether it be faith or a feeling of closeness to God.

Upon closer examination, however, we find that there is greater affinity between the two groups of interpreters than may be evident. Most significant in this respect is Maimonides, for although Maimonides solves the problem of Job's suffering in philosophical fashion by identifying privation as the cause of his afflictions and by claiming that intellectual perfection overcomes them, when it comes to explaining God's role in this process, Maimonides refers us to the notion of an unknowable God whose providential activity transcends the realm of the rational. According to Maimonides, one can explain only the natural mechanism of Job's suffering, but not how that mechanism squares with God's providence and justice. Regarding the latter issue, Maimonides states emphatically that God's providence is entirely unlike our providence and that we must therefore be satisfied with our ignorance on this matter. Thus, Maimonides displays a remarkable similarity to the moderns in claiming that the Book of Job places the critical question of divine justice beyond the limits of human reason and that we must achieve comfort in our suffering despite our inability to understand God's ways.

One may argue that Maimonides still remains very much a medieval thinker, since he places more confidence in reason than the moderns would, for in his view Job learns to appreciate the "otherness" of God's providential activity only through philosophical speculation, which leads him ultimately to a recognition of the equivocal nature of divine attributes. Yet, in his approach, Maimonides is not all that far from a thinker such as Robert Gordis. As I have noted, according to Gordis, Job learns that we must exult in what we know about the glories of the natural world and use that perception as a springboard for having faith in God regarding that which we cannot fathom—most notably, the suffering of the righteous. Maimonides therefore anticipates Gordis in claiming that what we know about the world through our limited intellects allows us to come to terms with its mysteries—in particular, the suffering of the innocent.[24]

We should not minimize the differences between Maimonides and the modern interpreters. The major premises of Aristotelianism that inform Maimonides' reading are obviously absent from modern interpretations. Thus, no modern interpreter is interested in Job's intellectual perfection in the same way as Maimonides is. Furthermore, Maimonides believes that the Book of Job teaches us that there are pedagogic benefits to undeserved suffering. Suffering allows Job to appreciate the distinction between God's ways and ours and thus allows him to understand the equivocality of divine attributes. Modern interpreters perhaps acknowledge implicitly that the Book of Job is meant to teach us that the experience of undeserved suffering has benefits, since, however one reads the story, it is hard to get around the fact that Job becomes enlightened in some way or another through his afflictions. Yet, modern interpreters are reluctant to say that the Book of Job posits a notion of suffering that is positive.[25]

The observations I have made about Maimonides and his foreshadowing of the moderns do not apply to his followers, Ibn Tibbon and Zeraḥiah Ḥen. These thinkers solve Job's problem through the notion of the immortality of the intellect and do not invoke the concept of an unknowable God whose attributes are equivocal.[26] Thus, for them there is no sense in which the solution to Job's problem transcends the rational, as it does for Maimonides and the moderns. Even so, both Ibn Tibbon and Zeraḥiah exhibit significant commonality with modern scholars in their belief that the Book of Job is firmly at odds with the retributive justice of the Torah. Of all the radical thinkers in our study, it is Ibn Tibbon who most strongly makes a case for that opposition.

In sum, it would seem that with respect to the central message of Job, Maimonides is alone among the philosophers in this study in anticipating the modern view that Job never penetrates the mysteries of God's providential activity. Still, Ibn Tibbon and Zeraḥiah Ḥen join Maimonides in anticipating the modern notion that the Book of Job is meant to subvert the doctrine of retributive justice.

In reading the Book of Job as a rejection of retributive justice, the more radical medieval Jewish philosophers in this study exhibit an intriguing affinity with medieval Christian commentators. Christian interpreters also believed that a central theme in Job was the undermining of the notion of retributive justice in the Hebrew Bible, specifically as it related to the observance of the Law. As already noted, medieval Christian interpreters generally held up the figure of Job as the model gentile who was vindicated by God despite the fact that he did not observe the Law. This Christian reading has a particular affinity with that of Maimonides, who, of all the thinkers in our study, most explicitly questions the relationship between the observance of the divine commandments, on the one hand, and physical and material well-being, on the other. According to Maimonides, Job's initial mistake was his faith in that relationship.

There is no need to posit a direct historical connection to explain the similarity between the two groups of interpreters. It is best accounted for by their common belief in a hidden layer of meaning in the Hebrew Bible that differs from its literal sense. For the Jewish philosophers, that layer contains esoteric philosophical truths, while for the Christians, it anticipates the truths of Christianity. Yet, while the hidden layer reflects different truths for each group, it allows them both to appreciate for their own respective purposes the radical element in Job, which throws into question the literal layer of the Hebrew Bible and its espousal of a relationship between observance of the divine commandments and material well-being. Thus, there is a convergence of interpretations due to a similar outlook on the biblical text as a whole.[27]

We can go a step further by noting that on one level the Christian reading of Job is from a Jewish perspective more radical than that of Maimonides and his followers. While the latter group may have used the Book of Job to reject the traditional notion that the observance of the commandments brings direct reward from God, they nevertheless saw the commandments as having value both for the social welfare of the masses and for training the elite to achieve intellectual perfection. The Christian commentators, by contrast, saw the Book of Job as an opportunity to press home their point that the biblical commandments are not needed.

However, in another respect, Maimonides and his followers are more radical than the Christians, for unlike the Christians, these Jewish interpreters were willing to entertain the notion that the God who speaks to Job out of the tempest at the end of the book is not a personal Being. That point was made most explicitly and forcefully by Ibn Tibbon. No major Christian commentator, to my knowledge, entertained such a notion, and for good reason: radical Aristotelianism never penetrated into medieval Christian philosophy in the way that it did medieval Jewish philosophy.[28]

One other point of convergence between the radical philosophers in our study and the modern interpreters is deserving of comment. A basic premise of the radical approach to Job in medieval Jewish philosophy is the notion that the book is an esoteric text that contains different messages directed simultaneously to different audiences: the masses and the elite. We saw how Maimonides, Ibn Tibbon, and Zeraḥiah Ḥen utilize this premise in different ways in their respective interpretations. The same approach has been entertained by modern scholars as well. Kember Fullerton, an early-twentieth-century scholar, constructs an elaborate theory of this kind. According to his reading, the central message of the Book of Job is in chapters 3–19, in which Job protests against his suffering. What the author of these chapters wants to tell us through Job's protests is that there is no divine justice in this world. The author, however, appreciated the radical nature of this message and therefore sought to conceal it from the traditionalists while making it available to critical thinkers. The conclusion of the book was therefore composed in deliberately ambiguous fashion in order to speak to both audiences at once. The rhetorical questions in God's speech were directed to the critical thinker in order to reinforce the correct view that Job's earlier protests were justified and that divine justice is not manifest in the world, while Job's recantation of his protests was inserted to appease the traditionalists, who believe in divine justice.[29]

If Fullerton's theory were the only one of its kind, it would not be noteworthy. Yet, two recent and important interpreters of Job go in a direction similar to his. One of these is Matitiahu Tsevat, who presents an esoteric reading of Job far less elaborate than Fullerton's. As I noted above, the central message Tsevat sees in the Book of Job is that God's actions are neutral from the standpoint of justice and that the only justice in the world is that which human beings implement. Tsevat contends that it is essentially this point that is made by God in an oblique manner when He speaks to Job out of the tempest. Tsevat goes on to ask why the author of the book did not simply have God state this viewpoint openly. His answer is that it was too radical a position to be revealed explicitly and was therefore presented in concealed fashion. As Tsevat puts it, "The very radicalism of the book's answer, shattering a central biblical doctrine and a belief cherished in ancient Israel, would itself demand the protection of a veil."[30] Further on, Tsevat adds that "the answer of God, presenting a doctrine as radical as it is new, a doctrine in diametrical opposition to the teaching of the tradition, may never have been tolerated or preserved for us but for the protection of its form, its eschewal of the direct, categorical pronouncement."[31] Tsevat's views here are striking in their resonance with the esoteric exegesis of the medieval Jewish philosophers.

Tsevat's position is also endorsed by J. Gerald Janzen, another recent and prominent interpreter of Job. Janzen believes that Tsevat is correct in his esoteric reading of Job but adds that the author's intent was that God should conceal the true meaning of His address not only from the reader but from the figure of Job himself as well.[32] This reading is similar to that of Zeraḥiah Ḥen, who also believed that the esoteric understanding of providence was hidden from Job, not just the reader. We therefore have two significant recent interpreters who adopt an esoteric approach to the Book of Job reminiscent of that proposed by the radical medieval Jewish philosophers in our study.

To summarize my results in this chapter, it would appear that of the thinkers examined in this study, those in the radical camp have the most in common with the modern interpreters of Job. First, they anticipate the moderns by reading Job as fiction. Second, they foreshadow the moderns with the view that the book as a whole stands in opposition to the notion of retributive justice. Maimonides comes closest to the moderns with respect to the central message of Job by understanding the final chapters of the book to be teaching us that God's providential activity is ultimately beyond the comprehension of human beings—even sophisticated philosophers. This emphasis on the mystery of God's ways is one of the most distinctive features of the modern reading of Job. Finally, the radical philosophers in this study read Job as an esoteric text that is conscious of its own radicalism. This view as well has supporters in the modern period. However, the conservative thinkers in this study also display some commonality with the moderns in some respects. Most significant is Saadiah, who reads the dialogue between Job, Eliphaz, Bildad, and Zophar as a battle between Job, who believes that God acts with arbitrary power, and Job's three friends, who defend the notion of retributive justice. This is precisely how most modern commentators read the dialogue.

What we have learned in this final chapter complements what we have discovered with respect to the second interface: the medieval Jewish philosophers were sophisticated biblical interpreters who were sensitive to the exegetical challenges presented by the Book of Job, and they proposed original solutions to those challenges. That sophistication is now more readily apparent. Not only did these thinkers confront the difficulties in Job in an original manner, but sometimes their responses to those difficulties bear striking resemblance to those proposed by modern thinkers.

Certainly we must recognize that medieval and modern thinkers occupy different intellectual universes and that their respective readings of the biblical text reflect that difference. But one of the hallmarks of a great interpreter is the capacity to offer insights about an important work of literature that transcend his or her worldview, and we have seen that the philosophers in this study at times display that very ability. These philosophers should therefore be appreciated not only as interesting thinkers whom we analyze across the chasms of time, place, and intellectual culture, but as interpreters who can speak to us directly about the meaning of the Bible and the eternal questions with which it grapples.

Appendix: A Bibliography of Commentaries on Job in Medieval Jewish Philosophy

The entries below are arranged according to the century in which they were written, but those within each century are arranged alphabetically since, in some cases, we do not know the exact year of composition. For each listing, I have provided the geographical location in which the commentary was written and the editions used in this study. Not all the works listed below are commentaries in the strict sense of the term. Some are discussions of Job found in larger treatises and are included here because of their substantial length or importance. For each entry, I have indicated whether the commentary is a full-length exposition on Job or a discussion in a larger work.

TENTH CENTURY

Saadiah Gaon (Iraq): full-length commentary in Arabic; the subject of chapter 2 of this book; citations from *Iyyov: Targum u-Perush ha-Rasag*, Arabic text with Hebrew translation and notes by Joseph Kafiḥ (Jerusalem: ha-Makor, 1973), and the English translation of Lenn E. Goodman, *The Book of Theodicy: Translation and Commentary on the Book of Job by Saadiah ben Joseph al-Fayyūmī* (New Haven: Yale University Press, 1988).

TWELFTH CENTURY

Maimonides (Egypt): discussion of Job in *Guide of the Perplexed* III:22–23; the subject of chapter 3 of this book; citations from the Arabic text, *Dalālat al-Ḥā'irīn*, ed. I. Joel (Jerusalem: Junovich, 1929), the Hebrew translation found in standard editions of *Moreh Nevukhim*, and the English translation of Shlomo Pines (Chicago: University of Chicago Press, 1963).

THIRTEENTH CENTURY

Ibn Tibbon, Samuel (Provence): discussion of Job in *Ma'amar Yikkavu ha-Mayim*, ed. M. L. Bisliches (Pressburg, 1837), pp. 100–117; the subject of chapter 4 of this book.

Ḥen, Zeraḥiah ben Isaac ben She'alti'iel (Spain and Italy): full-length commentary published in *Tikvat Enosh*, ed. Israel Schwartz (Berlin, 1868; reprint, Jerusalem, 1969), vol. 1, pp. 169–293; the subject of chapter 5 of this book; citations from Schwartz's edition and Ms. Munich 79, fols. 2r–101v.

Levi ben Abraham of Villefranche (Provence): discussion of Job in *Livyat Ḥen, Sha'ar ha-Hashgaḥah,* which survives in manuscript.

Menaḥem ben Solomon ha-Me'iri (Provence): commentary no longer extant, as noted in Gregg Stern, "Menaḥem ha-Meiri and the Second Controversy over Philosophy" (Ph.D. diss., Harvard University, 1995), p. 115.

FOURTEENTH CENTURY

Abba Mari ben Eligdor (Provence): full-length commentary survives in six manuscripts, four of which are complete.

Arundi, Isaac (Spain): full-length commentary survives in four manuscripts, three of which are complete; discussed in chapter 4 of this book; citations from Ms. Milano-Ambrosiana 16 (C300 Inf), fols. 1r–50v.

Elijah ben Eliezer ha-Yerushalmi (Crete): full-length commentary survives in a single manuscript; discussed in chapter 4 of this book; citations from Ms. Vatican 250/8, fols. 104r–132r, and Ms. Vatican 530/30, which contains the last page of the first manuscript.

Immanuel of Rome (Italy): full-length commentary survives in three complete manuscripts, discussed in chapter 4 of this book; citations from Ms. Parma 58.

Gersonides (Provence): full-length commentary has been printed several times; the subject of chapter 6 of this book; citations from standard rabbinic Bibles.

Kaspi, Joseph ibn (Provence): long and short commentary on Job published in *'Asarah Keley Kesef*, ed. Isaac Last (Pressburg: Alkalay, 1905), vol. 1, pp. 135–79.

FIFTEENTH CENTURY

Albo, Joseph (Spain): discussion of the suffering of the righteous, much of which focuses on Job, in *Sefer ha-'Ikkarim*, ed. and trans. Isaac Husik (Philadelphia: Jewish Publication Society of America, 1930), vol. 4, part 1, p. 54ff.

Duran, Simon ben Ẓemaḥ (Spain): full-length commentary on Job, *Ohev Mishpat* (Venice, 1590); the subject of chapter 7 of this book.

Ibn Shem Tov, Joseph ben Shem Tov (Spain): commentary no longer extant, as noted in Shaul Regev, "Theology and Rational Mysticism in the Writings of R. Joseph ben Shem Tob" (in Hebrew) (Ph.D. diss., Hebrew University, 1983), p. 39.

SIXTEENTH CENTURY

'Arama, Meir [son of Isaac 'Arama, author of *'Akeidat Yiẓḥak*] (Spain and Italy): full-length commentary, *Me'ir Iyyov* (Venice, 1567).

Seforno, Obadiah (Italy): full-length commentary in *Kitvey R. 'Ovadiah Seforno*, ed. Zev Gottleib (Jerusalem: Mosad Ha-Rav Kuk, 1987), pp. 258–330.

Notes

CHAPTER I

1. David J. A. Clines has amassed an impressively comprehensive and lengthy bibliography of religious, literary, and scholarly literature on Job from late antiquity to the present day; Clines, *World Biblical Commentary: Job 1–20* (Dallas: Word Books, 1989), pp. lxi–cxv. Thomas F. Dailey and Watson E. Mills also provide a helpful bibliography of writings on Job with an emphasis on modern scholarly research; Watson and Mills, *The Book of Job*, Bibliographies for Biblical Research, Old Testament Series 13 (Lewiston, N.Y.: Edwin Mellen Press, 1997). A number of scholarly studies examine the history of interpretation of the Book of Job. A pioneering work in this area is Nahum N. Glatzer's still useful work *The Dimensions of Job: A Study and Selected Readings* (New York: Schocken Books, 1969). Glatzer provides a series of introductory essays on the history of Joban interpretation in Jewish and Christian thought, followed by edited selections from modern theologians, scholars, and literary figures who have written on Job. C. A. Newsom and Susan E. Schreiner offer a brief but excellent overview of the interpretation of Job in Western thought in their article "Job," in *Dictionary of Biblical Interpretation*, ed. John H. Hayes (Nashville: Abingdon Press, 1999), vol. 1, pp. 587–99. This article also incorporates some Jewish material. Other studies have appeared that are more limited in scope but nonetheless examine the history of Joban interpretation in Western thought across a number of thinkers. Explorations of interpretations of Job in the patristic period can be found in Charles Kannengiesser, "Job chez les Pères," in *Dictionnaire de spiritualité*, ed. Marcel Viller, Charles Baumgartner, and André Rayez (Paris: G. Beauchesne and Sons, 1974), pp. 1218–24; Robert Gillet, "Les sources des 'Morales,' " *Sources chrétiennes* 32 (1975): 82–85; Judith R. Baskin, *Pharaoh's Counsellors: Job, Jethro, and Balaam in Rabbinic and Patristic Tradition* (Chico, Calif.: Scholars Press, 1983), pp. 32–43. An analysis of literary aspects of interpretations of Job in medieval and early modern Christianity is provided in Barbara Kiefer Lewalski, *Milton's Brief Epic: The Genre, Meaning, and Art of*

Paradise Regained (Providence: Brown University Press, 1966), pp. 10–36. Lawrence Besserman analyzes medieval interpretations of Job in Christian theology, liturgy, and literature in *The Legend of Job in the Middle Ages* (Cambridge, Mass.: Harvard University Press, 1979). Leonard Siger examines interpretations of Job in early modern Christianity in "The Image of Job in the Renaissance" (Ph.D. diss., Johns Hopkins University, 1960). An exceptional study is Susan E. Schreiner, *Where Shall Wisdom Be Found? Calvin's Exegesis of Job from Medieval and Modern Perspectives* (Chicago: University of Chicago Press, 1994), which has chapters on Gregory the Great, Maimonides, and Thomas Aquinas, in addition to Calvin. An analysis of how Job is dealt with by eighteenth-century interpreters is provided in Jonathan Lamb, *The Rhetoric of Suffering: Reading the Book of Job in the Eighteenth Century* (Oxford: Clarendon Press, 1995). Relatively little has been written on the interpretation of the Job story in Islam. See J.-F. Legrain, "Variations musulmanes sur le thème de Job," *Bulletins d'études orientales* (1988): 51–114; and Jean-Louis Déclais, *Les premiers musulmans face á la tradition biblique: trois récits sur Job* (Paris: L'Harmattan, 1996). For studies devoted specifically to the history of Jewish interpretation of Job, see nn. 3 and 4 of this chapter.

2. This, of course, does not apply to all places and periods. Christian Hebraism in the medieval period opened up the Hebrew Bible in its original language to Christian thinkers, and certainly with the advent of modern scholarship, non-Jews have grappled with the original text of Job with no less skill than Jewish scholars.

3. There is speculation that an early rabbinic midrash was written on Job entitled *Midrash Iyyov*. Solomon A. Wertheimer attempts a reconstruction of that work on the basis of citations from later medieval commentators in his edition; *Batey Midrashot* (Jerusalem: Ktab Yad Wasepher, 1989), vol. 2, pp. 150–86. However, even if this work existed, it is still a fragmentary treatment of Job. Like most midrashic works, it is an anthology of rabbinic interpretations of individual biblical verses rather than a continuous and coherent commentary. I wish to thank Jason Kalman for bringing this work to my attention.

For examinations of early rabbinic interpretations of Job, see Hermann Eziechel Kauffmann, *Die Anwendung des Buches Hiob in der Rabbinischen Aggadah* (Frankfurt a. M., 1893); Isaak Wjernikowski, *Das Buch Hiob nach der Auffassung der rabbinischen Literatur in den ersten fünf nachchristlichen Jahrhunderten* (Breslau: H. Fleischmann, 1902); Louis Ginzberg, *Legends of the Jews* (Philadelphia: Jewish Publication Society of America, 1909), vol. 2, pp. 223–42, and vol. 5, pp. 381–90 nn.; Baskin, *Pharaoh's Counsellors*, pp. 7–44; Ephraim E. Urbach, *The Sages: Their Concepts and Beliefs*, trans. Israel Abrahams (Cambridge, Mass.: Harvard University Press, 1987), pp. 407–15; Joseph H. Leibowitz, "The Image of Job as Reflected in Rabbinic Writings" (Ph.D. diss., University of California, Berkeley, 1987); Joanna Weinberg, "Job versus Abraham: The Quest for the Perfect God-Fearer in Rabbinic Tradition," in *The Book of Job*, ed. W.A.M. Beuken (Leuven: Leuven University Press, 1994), pp. 281–96.

4. As I mention in my preface, I was privileged to get hold of Talmage's bibliography with the help of Barry Walfish. Medieval Jewish interpretations of Job are examined in Nahum N. Glatzer, "The Book of Job and Its Interpreters," in *Biblical Motifs: Origins and Transformations*, ed. Alexander Altmann (Cambridge, Mass.: Phillip W. Lown Institute of Advanced Judaic Studies, 1966), pp. 197–220. See also the introduction of Herbert Basser and Barry D. Walfish to their critical edition of Moshe Kimḥi, *Commentary on the Book of Job* (Atlanta: Scholars Press, 1992), pp. xi–xii. Rachel Margalioth, *The Original Job: The Problem and Its Solution* (in Hebrew) (Jerusalem: Re'uven Mass, 1988), provides a discussion on Job from the perspective of several medieval Jewish exegetes, including Rashi, Naḥmanides, and Gersonides.

5. Scholars have had difficulty defining precisely what *peshat* is, because the notion that there is a "plain sense" to the biblical text is highly variable and subjective. However, it is best understood as a method of reading the biblical text that developed among Jewish exegetes between the tenth and twelfth centuries and eschewed the often flighty and imaginative method of biblical interpretation found in rabbinic aggadah and midrash in favor of a more disciplined, empirical, and scientific approach. The *peshat* style of medieval Jewish exegesis is dealt with in Moshe H. Segal, *Biblical Exegesis* (in Hebrew) (Jerusalem: Kiryat Sefer, 1952), pp. 60–78. It is also discussed by various scholars in Moshe Greenberg, ed., *Jewish Biblical Exegesis: An Introduction* (in Hebrew) (Jerusalem: Magnes Press, 1983), pp. 15–100. See also Sarah Kamin, *Rashi's Exegetical Categorization in Respect to the Distinction between "Peshat" and "Derash"* (in Hebrew) (Jerusalem: Magnes Press, 1986), pp. 11–22; David Weiss Halivni, *Peshat and Derash: Plain and Applied Meaning in Rabbinic Exegesis* (New York: Oxford University Press, 1991), pp. 3–30, 52–88.

6. In some instances, these interpreters offer comments that have philosophical import. Sara Japhet attempts to make this case with respect to Rashbam; Japhet, *The Commentary of Rabbi Samuel Ben Meir (Rashbam) on the Book of Job* (in Hebrew) (Jerusalem: Magnes Press, 2000), pp. 120–60. However, these commentators almost never offer positions that are truly philosophical in that they are rarely justified on the basis of systematic discussion and rational argument. The philosophical content of these commentaries has to be inferred from their often terse glosses on the biblical text.

7. The division in medieval Jewish exegesis between *peshat*-oriented commentaries on Job and those of a philosophical bent is noted by Simon ben Ẓemaḥ Duran, the last thinker I will be analyzing in my study. See chapter 7. I might also note here that there was interest in Job in Kabbalah, the rival school to philosophy in medieval Judaism. Naḥmanides' commentary on Job is the first and perhaps most important interpretation of Job in this tradition of thought. It appears in Moses Naḥmanides, *Kitvey Ramban*, ed. Chayim D. Chavel (Jerusalem: Mosad ha-Rav Kuk, 1973), vol. 1, pp. 17–128. Baḥya ben Asher provides a reading of Job that is essentially an explication of Naḥmanides' commentary; see Baḥya ben Asher, *Kad ha-Kemaḥ*, ed. Ḥayim Breit (Lemberg, 1880), pp. 68b–73a. There are also speculations on the Book of Job in the *Zohar*. See *Sefer ha-Zohar*, ed. Moshe Margaliyot (Jerusalem: Mosad ha-Rav Kuk, 1978), vol. 2, pp. 33a, 34a; vol. 3, p. 101b; Isaiah Tishby and Fischel Lachower, *The Wisdom of the "Zohar,"* trans. David Goldstein (London: Oxford University Press, 1991), vol. 1, p. 453; vol. 3, p. 1426. An intriguing episode in the history of Joban interpretation in Jewish mysticism is provided by the Sabbatian movement. Nathan of Gaza made extensive use of the figure of Job to explain Shabbetai Ẓevi's bouts of severe depression and to bolster his claims to be the Messiah. See Gershom Scholem, *Sabbatai Ṣevi: The Mystical Messiah, 1626–1676*, trans. R. J. Zwi Werblowsky (Princeton: Princeton University Press, 1973), pp. 308–11. However, the degree of interest in Job in medieval Kabbalah is relatively small compared to that of the *peshat*-oriented exegetes and the philosophers. As we shall later see, kabbalistic readings of Job were either ignored or vilified by medieval Jewish philosophers; however, one of the figures analyzed in this study, Simon ben Ẓemaḥ Duran, displayed much interest in Naḥmanides' reading of Job.

8. Of course, this observation could be applied to most other discussions of philosophical matters in rabbinic literature.

9. This is true even with respect to the *Midrash Iyyov* mentioned in note 3. Leibowitz argues that the rabbis were more interested in the core issues of the Book of

Job than is generally assumed (pp. 381–82). However, the rabbis made no attempt to give a comprehensive and systematic reading of Job of the kind that we find among medieval Jewish philosophers.

10. Surveys of medieval Jewish philosophy include Isaac Husik, *A History of Medieval Jewish Philosophy* (Philadelphia: Jewish Publication Society of America, 1958); Julius Guttmann, *Philosophies of Judaism*, trans. David Silverman, part 2 (New York: Schocken Books, 1973); Colette Sirat, *A History of Jewish Philosophy in the Middle Ages* (Cambridge: Cambridge University Press, 1986); Daniel H. Frank and Oliver Leaman, eds., *A History of Jewish Philosophy*, part 2 (London and New York: Routledge, 1997). Discussion of the controversy engendered by the study of philosophy in medieval Judaism can be found in Joseph Sarachek, *Faith and Reason: The Conflict over the Rationalism of Maimonides* (Williamsport: Bayard Press, 1935); Daniel J. Silver, *Maimonidean Criticism and Maimonidean Controversy, 1180–1240* (Leiden: E. J. Brill, 1965); Bernard Septimus, *Hispano-Jewish Culture in Transition: The Career and Controversies of Ramah* (Cambridge, Mass.: Harvard University Press, 1982).

11. In light of these figures, one can only view with surprise Robert Gordis's statement that few medieval Jewish philosophers were interested in Job: "Only a rare medieval philosopher like Maimonides and Gersonides would turn to Job for ideas bearing on God and the problem of evil" (Gordis, *The Book of God and Man: A Study of Job* [Chicago: University of Chicago Press, 1965], p. 227).

12. A list of these commentaries is found in the appendix. I should note that absent from this list is Abraham ibn Ezra's *Commentary on Job* because his exegesis of Job is almost exclusively concerned with *peshat*. As Glatzer notes, Ibn Ezra's commentary contains not even a single reference to his theory of evil, which is mentioned numerous times elsewhere in his commentaries and should have been relevant to his reading of Job ("The Book of Job and Its Interpreters," p. 205). Ibn Ezra does discuss the philosophical meaning of Job in a short appendix to the commentary, and there are a number of references to esoteric philosophical doctrines in the commentary itself (*Perush 'al Sefer Iyyov*, rabbinic Bibles, on Job 6:1, 23:13, 33:23, 38:36). This material certainly deserves study. Still, my sense is that the philosophical material here is too meager to render the commentary a philosophical one of the kind that I examine in this study. I wish to thank Zev Harvey for bringing to my attention the references to esoteric philosophical doctrines in Ibn Ezra's commentary.

There was interest in the philosophical meaning of Job among Karaite thinkers, who are not examined in this study. We have, for example, Aaron ben Elijah, who lived in Byzantium in the fourteenth century and provided an extensive discussion of Job in his major work, *'Eẓ Ḥayyim*. Moreover, in the course of his discussion on Job, Aaron gives an extensive characterization of the views of the "Karaite scholars" on Job. Daniel Frank speculates that Aaron may have been referring to a commentary on Job written by Aaron ben Joseph, a thirteenth-century Karaite forerunner of Aaron ben Elijah—a work that is no longer extant. Yet, the reference may also suggest the existence of an idiosyncratic Karaite reading of Job that was common to a number of interpreters. See Daniel Frank, "The Religious Philosophy of the Karaite Aaron ben Elijah: The Problem of Divine Justice" (Ph.D. diss., Harvard University, 1991), p. cxiv.

One commentary on Job that might have been included in my list is that of Me'ir Loeb ben Yeḥi'el Mikha'el Malbim. Even though Malbim's commentary was composed in the nineteenth century, it is evident even from a cursory examination of it that Malbim's reading of Job was heavily influenced, both in style and content, by medieval Jewish philosophers—in particular Maimonides and Gersonides. There is, however, a strong admixture of Kantian thinking in Malbim's reading that makes it unmistakably modern in some respects. This commentary is discussed in Noah Rosenblum, *The Malbim: Exegesis, Philosophy, Science, and Mysticism in the Writings of Rabbi Me'ir Leivush Malbim* (in Hebrew) (Jerusalem: Mosad ha-Rav Kuk, 1988), pp. 197–206.

13. Eisen, "Gersonides' *Commentary on the Book of Job*," *Journal of Jewish Thought and Philosophy* 10 (2001): 239–88. This article is the basis for my chapter on Gersonides in the present study. Gersonides' commentary on Job was first printed in Ferrara in 1477.

14. Isaac 'Arama's *'Akeidat Yizḥak* is, technically speaking, not a commentary but a collection *derashot*, or homiletical discourses on the weekly Torah portions. Nonetheless, it must be included in any list of works of philosophical exegesis in medieval Judaism, and it must be studied as philosophical exegesis, because it is no less exegetical than the more formal biblical commentaries of such figures as Gersonides. The same goes for other collections of *derashot* written in a philosophical mode, such as Jacob Anatoli's *Malmad ha-Talmidim*.

15. In recent years, a number of critical editions of exegetical works by medieval Jewish philosophers have appeared. These include Joseph ibn Kaspi, *Shulḥan Kesef*, ed. Hannah Kasher (Jerusalem: Ben Ẓvi Institute, 1996); Nissim ben Moshe, *Ma'aseh Nissim*, ed. Hayim Kreisel (Jerusalem: Mekiẓey Nirdamim, 2000). There have been few book-length studies on the exegesis of the medieval Jewish philosophers. Two fine studies are Sarah Klein-Braslavy, *Maimonides' Interpretation of the Adam Stories in Genesis: A Study in Maimonides' Anthropology* (in Hebrew) (Jerusalem: Re'uven Mas, 1986), and *Maimonides' Interpretation of the Story of Creation* (in Hebrew) (Jerusalem: Re'uven Mas, 1988). There is also my own *Gersonides on Providence, Covenant, and the Chosen People: A Study in Medieval Jewish Philosophy and Biblical Commentary* (Albany: State University of New York Press, 1995). The only attempt at a comprehensive characterization of the exegetical literature in medieval Jewish philosophy is Maurice R. Hayoun, *L'exégèse philosophique dans le judaïsme médiéval* (Tübingen: J.C.B. Mohr [Paul Siebeck], 1992). Several dozen articles have also appeared in recent years dealing with exegetical matters in medieval Jewish philosophy. Most notable is Shalom Rosenberg, "On Biblical Interpretation in *The Guide of the Perplexed*" (in Hebrew), *Jerusalem Studies in Jewish Thought* 1 (1981): 85–157, which called attention to the exegetical aspects of medieval Jewish philosophy's most important treatise.

16. Allegory was at the center of the controversy over Maimonides' writings in the century after his death, particularly at the beginning of the fourteenth century—the phase of the dispute that led to the *ḥerem* of Rashba. A recent attempt to provide a characterization of allegory and its use in medieval Jewish thought is Frank Talmage, "Apples of Gold: The Inner Meaning of Sacred Texts in Medieval Judaism," in *Jewish Spirituality*, ed. Arthur Green (New York: Crossroad, 1988), vol. 1, pp. 313–56. See also Marc Saperstein, *Decoding the Rabbis: A Thirteenth-Century Commentary on the Aggadah* (Cambridge, Mass.: Harvard University Press, 1980), pp. 14–15, 219 n. 62. Mordechai Z. Cohen, *Three Approaches to Biblical Metaphor: From Abraham Ibn Ezra and Maimonides to David Kimḥi* (Leiden: E. J. Brill, 2003), provides important insight into the exegetical uses of allegory in medieval Jewish philosophy.

17. The major exception is Cohen's *Three Approaches to Biblical Metaphor*, cited in the previous note. The medieval Jewish philosophers are discussed by Segal in his survey of the history of Jewish exegesis (pp. 51–60), but Segal characterizes the philosophers as interpreters who merely created "philosophical midrash" on the biblical text (p. 52), a comment that greatly underestimates their sophistication as exegetes. Many of them were interested in such matters as grammar, philology, *peshat*, and *der-*

ash and had much to say about these issues, particularly those who were influenced by Maimonides. Segal dismisses all post-Maimondean exegetes in medieval Jewish philosophy as contributing nothing original to the study of the biblical text (p. 60). The present study will show, I hope, just how far off the mark Segal's statements are. Much more sympathetic to the exegesis of the medieval Jewish philosophers are the various authors in Greenberg, *Jewish Biblical Exegesis*. However, in this work, there is no section devoted to Maimonides, despite the fact that he is the most important philosophical exegete in medieval Judaism.

18. The full citations are Uriel Simon, *Four Approaches to the Book of Psalms: From Saadiah Gaon to Abraham ibn Ezra*, trans. Lenn J. Schramm (Albany: State University of New York Press, 1991) and Barry D. Walfish, *Esther in Medieval Garb: Jewish Interpretation of the Book of Esther in the Middle Ages* (Albany: State University of New York Press, 1993).

19. The tradition of philosophical exegesis on Song of Songs is dealt with in Shalom Rosenberg, "Philosophical Hermeneutics on the Song of Songs: Introductory Remarks" (in Hebrew), *Tarbiẓ* 59 (1990): 133–51; Israel Ravitzky, "R. Immanuel b. Solomon of Rome, *Commentary on the Song of Songs—Philosophical Division*" (in Hebrew) (master's thesis, Hebrew University, 1970). The interest of medieval Jewish philosophers in the Song of Songs stemmed from the fact that they routinely read this book as an allegory for the conjunction of the human intellect with the Active Intellect. The medieval Jewish philosophers' interest in Ecclesiastes and Proverbs is understandable in light of the philosophical character of these books. Proverbs in particular seems to have attracted a great deal of attention from these philosophers. I have yet to compile a list of commentaries written by medieval Jewish philosophers on Proverbs, but my preliminary estimation is that their number is greater than that composed by the philosophers on any other book in the Bible. These works, however, have received virtually no attention from scholars. Medieval Jewish philosophers also produced a great deal of philosophical commentary on the first chapters of Genesis and the first chapter of Ezekiel.

20. Hannah Kasher has also dealt with Kaspi's commentaries on Job; Kasher, "Joseph ibn Kaspi's Aristotelian Interpretation and Fundamentalist Interpretation of the Book of Job" (in Hebrew), *Da'at* 20 (1988): 117–25.

21. *B.T. Bava' Batra'* 15a. In two other sources, Resh Lakish also takes the position that Job "never was, and never existed" (*J.T. Sotah* 20c; *Bereshit Rabbah* 57:4). However, in these sources, another tradition is adduced in which Resh Lakish asserts that Job indeed existed and lived during the time of Abraham. The contradiction is resolved by the conclusion that, according to Resh Lakish, Job in fact existed, but the story about him was fictional.

22. See, for instance, *B.T. Bava' Batra'* 15b. Leibowitz discusses the attitude of early rabbinic Judaism toward Job's national identity, pp. 202–25.

23. Job 42:7.

24. Job 39:34–35, 42:2–6.

25. Job 42:7.

26. Early rabbinic commentators did not provide much discussion about the dialogue in Job. They were far more preoccupied with other questions, such as Job's character and the reasons for his suffering. However, there are some rabbinic sources on this matter. See Leibowitz, pp. 344–58.

27. The early rabbis have surprisingly little to say about God's remarks to Job, which has prompted some modern commentators, such as Glatzer, to conclude that they were not concerned with the core issues of the book. Leibowitz objects to this

assessment and attempts to demonstrate that with a careful reading of rabbinic sources on Job, the concern of the rabbis for the core issues becomes evident (pp. 381–82).

28. *Pesikta de-R. Kahana* 16:6; *Pesikta Rabbati* 26:7.

29. A notable exception is Schreiner's study of Calvin's views on Job, which provides an insightful discussion comparing medieval and modern interpretations of Job (pp. 156–90).

30. The scholar of medieval Jewish and Islamic philosophy who more than anyone else brought this whole issue to the fore in the modern period is Leo Strauss. Chief among his contributions is *Persecution and the Art of Writing* (Glencoe, Ill.: Free Press, 1952). However, there is still debate among scholars about the degree to which the medieval Jewish and Islamic philosophers concealed views at odds with their respective traditions. In medieval Jewish philosophy, most of the debate has revolved around Maimonides, but there has been disagreement about other thinkers as well. For a thorough history of medieval and modern views on Maimonides' esotericism, see Aviezer Ravitzky, "The Secrets of the *Guide of the Perplexed*: From the Thirteenth to the Twentieth Centuries," in *Studies in Maimonides*, ed. Isadore Twersky (Cambridge, Mass.: Harvard University Press, 1990), pp. 159–207.

CHAPTER 2

1. This chapter incorporates material from my article "Job as a Symbol for Israel in the Thought of Saadiah Gaon," *Da'at* 41 (Summer 1998): v–xxv. Much of that material has been revised here.

2. The most comprehensive overview of Saadiah's life and works is still Henry Malter, *Saadia Gaon: His Life and Works* (Philadelphia: Jewish Publication Society of America, 1921).

3. There is an extensive literature on Saadiah's philosophical thought. General surveys include Jakob Guttmann, *Die Religionsphilosophie des Saadia* (Göttingen: Vandenhoeck and Ruprecht, 1882); Moïse Ventura, *La philosophie de Saadia Gaon* (Paris, 1934); Husik, pp. 23–47; Julius Guttmann, pp. 69–83; Sirat, pp. 18–36.

4. There is as yet no comprehensive study of Saadiah's biblical commentaries or exegetical method. Various aspects of Saadiah's biblical commentaries have been dealt with in numerous articles and chapters in larger studies. Of these, the best overall discussion is Moshe Zucker, introduction to Saadiah Gaon, *Perushey R. Sa'adyah Ga'on li-Bre'shit* (New York: Jewish Theological Seminary, 1984), pp. 9–69.

5. Malter provides information on nineteenth-century editions and translations of this commentary (p. 321). They have all been surpassed by that of Yosef Kafiḥ (Jerusalem: ha-Makor, 1973), who bases his edition on manuscripts not available to earlier scholars. Kafiḥ provides the original Arabic text with a translation into modern Hebrew.

6. The full title of Goodman's edition is *The Book of Theodicy: Translation and Commentary on the Book of Job by Saadiah ben Joseph al-Fayyūmī* (New Haven: Yale University Press, 1988). All citations of Saadiah's commentary will be from Goodman's text, henceforth referred to as CJ (for "commentary on Job"). The only other scholarly study of Saadiah's commentary on Job of which I am aware is an article by E.I.J. Rosenthal, "Saadya's Exegesis of the Book of Job," in *Saadya Studies*, ed. E.I.J. Rosenthal (New York: Arno Press, 1980), pp. 177–205. Its content is largely devoted to philological matters in Saadiah's commentary that are not relevant to the present discussion.

7. Saadiah Gaon, *Sefer ha-Nivḥar be-Emunot ve-De'ot* (the Hebrew title of *Beliefs*

and Opinions, henceforth ED), Arabic text with Hebrew translation by Yosef Kafiḥ (Jerusalem: Sura, n.d.) 5:3, pp. 176–77 (hereafter cited as Kafiḥ); for an English translation, see Saadiah Gaon, "Selections of *Beliefs and Opinions,*" ed. and trans. Alexander Altmann, in *Three Jewish Philosophers,* ed. Hans Lewy, Alexander Altmann, and Isaak Heinemann, part 2 (New York: Atheneum, 1969), pp. 137–39 (hereafter cited as Altmann). For English translations of ED, I will be citing Altmann on those portions of ED that are translated by him. For all other sections of ED, I will cite the somewhat less accurate but complete translation by Rosenblatt (Saadiah Gaon, *The Book of Beliefs and Opinions,* trans. Samuel Rosenblatt [New Haven: Yale University Press, 1948]) (hereafter cited as Rosenblatt).

8. ED 5:2, Kafiḥ, p. 174; Altmann, pp. 134–35.

9. ED 5:3, Kafiḥ, p. 176; Altmann, p. 137.

10. Ibid. Divine trials are a basic feature of Saadiah's conception of the relationship between God and human beings. God is constantly testing his creatures to give them an opportunity to earn more reward. See, for instance, Saadiah's statement that one of the reasons the soul is placed in the body is to subject it to trials so that the soul can be purified (ED 6:4, pp. 203–5; Rosenblatt, pp. 246–47). In his commentary on Job, Saadiah even goes as far as saying that "God created human beings in the first place to test them" (CJ introduction, p. 129).

11. ED 5:3, Kafiḥ, p. 176; Altmann, p. 138.

12. The irony here seems to escape Saadiah. Job's wealth is a sign of divine favor, but it is taken away in order to prove that Job is the recipient of divine favor.

13. ED 5:3, Kafiḥ, p. 177; Altmann, p. 138.

14. *B.T. Ta'anit* 11a, *J.T. Pe'ah* 1:1, *J.T. Sanhedrin* 10:1, *Bereshit Rabbah* 33:1.

15. Israel Efros, *Studies in Medieval Jewish Philosophy* (New York: Columbia University Press, 1974), pp. 97–98; Zucker's introduction to *Perushey R. Sa'adyah Ga'on li-Bre'shit,* pp. 398 n. 260, 400 n. 261.

16. CJ, pp. 94–95, 136–37 n. 24; Efros, p. 98. The concept of *yisurin shel ahavah* appears in early rabbinic literature in a number of sources. See, for instance, *B.T. Berakhot* 5ab. For a scholarly discussion of *yisurin shel ahavah,* see Urbach, pp. 444–48.

17. *Bereshit Rabbah* 55:1. The translation is from the Hebrew text in the critical edition of Theodor and Albeck (*Bereshit Rabbah,* ed. with notes by J. Theodor and Ch. Albeck, 3 vols. [Jerusalem: Wahrmann Books, 1965]) and is adapted from the English translation of Freedman (*Midrash Rabbah,* trans. H. Freedman and Maurice Simon [London and New York: Soncino Press, 1983]), vol. 1, p. 482.

18. In parallel midrashic passages, the message is more particularistic in that the *'akeidah* story is understood to teach only about Abraham's worthiness and is not emblematic of the trials endured by righteous people in general. These sources are quite explicit in the suggestion that the audience of Abraham's test is the non-Jewish nations who learn to revere Abraham above all other human beings on account of his willingness to sacrifice his son. See *Tanḥuma,* ed. Solomon Buber (New York, 1946), *Be-Ḥukotay* 7, p. 114, and *Va-Yera'* 43, pp. 110–11. We have other rabbinic sources that explore the public dimension of Abraham's trial but in a different way from the passage cited here. For example, in a discussion in *Bereshit Rabbah* 55:4 that appears shortly after this passage, we have the view that the *'akeidah* was meant to prove Abraham's worthiness to Abraham himself! This passage paints Abraham as a figure plagued with self-doubt who worries that he has received ample blessing from God but has given nothing to God in return. God therefore tests Abraham in order to assure him that he deserves his blessings. According to a second opinion in this passage, Abraham is tested in order to prove his worthiness to the angels. It is they who

challenge God to show that Abraham deserves the blessing he has received. The final opinion in this passage depicts the *'akeidah* as an event meant to test Isaac, who must prove his worthiness in order to ward off a challenge from Ishmael. What all these opinions share in common is that the *'akeidah* does not teach God something He does not already know. Rather, it is a public test designed to establish the worthiness of either Abraham or Isaac in response to anyone who might challenge the special status of either.

19. It is unclear what Saadiah is referring to with this first type of suffering, since suffering for the purpose of "discipline and instruction" appears to overlap with suffering of the second type, which is equated with punishment for sin. There may be some clue in a discussion in ED 4:2, Kafiḥ, pp. 153–54; Rosenblatt, pp. 184–85. There Saadiah explains why it is that God created man with a feeble constitution that is susceptible to disease and the extremes of heat and cold. Saadiah responds that sicknesses are "salutary" for man because "they keep him away from sin, and render him submissive to his Master, and introduce balance into his affairs." Similarly, extremes of heat and cold, along with the poisons from reptiles and animals, are for his benefit since they provide man with an understanding of what pain is so that he will then fear punishment in the afterlife. What is significant here is that Saadiah is attempting to explain suffering without resorting to either the concept of punishment for past sins or trials. Emphasis is placed on the instructive and preemptive value of suffering. It is possible that it is this brand of suffering that Saadiah has in mind when he posits "discipline and instruction" as the first type of suffering in the commentary on Job.

20. CJ introduction, pp. 123–26. Similar programmatic statements about divine trials are to be found in two passages in the recently published fragments of Saadiah's commentary on Exodus. See *Perushey R. Sa'adyah Ga'on le-Sefer Shemot*, ed. Yehudah Ratzaby (in Hebrew and Arabic) (Jerusalem: Mosad ha-Rav Kuk, 1998), pp. 14–15, 217–18.

21. CJ introduction, pp. 127–28.

22. CJ introduction, pp. 128–29.

23. Job 32:1–33:12; CJ introduction, p. 130.

24. CJ introduction, p. 130.

25. CJ introduction, p. 130.

26. CJ introduction, pp. 131–32.

27. CJ introduction, p. 127.

28. CJ 42:13, p. 411.

29. CJ introduction, pp. 127–30.

30. CJ introduction, p. 130.

31. CJ introduction, p. 129. My understanding of Saadiah's thinking here is supported by his views on the general relationship between scripture and reason that is outlined in the first book of *Beliefs and Opinions*. There Saadiah takes the position that reason requires the help of revelation because reason takes an extended time to arrive at truth and is also prone to error. Revelation supplies correct beliefs both as a guide to reason and to ensure that we are not left bereft of those beliefs during the period that reason takes to confirm them. See ED introduction: 6; Kafiḥ, pp. 27–28; Altmann, pp. 45–46. The Book of Job performs this very function for Saadiah since it prevents people from committing the common error of assuming that suffering is only punishment for sin, and it guides them to the realization that the righteous can suffer because God is testing them.

32. CJ 1:1, pp. 151–52.

33. The notion that Job lived during the period of the exodus is mentioned in *B.T. Bava' Batra'* 15a; *J.T. Sotah* 5:6; *Bereshit Rabbah* 57:4. These sources also entertain a wide range of other opinions on when Job lived. He is located as early as the period of Abraham and as late as the period of Esther. Two opinions correspond to Saadiah's view. R. Joshua ben Levi maintains that Job is a contemporary of Moses. R. Johanan and R. Eliezer claim that Job's life span was from the time that the Israelites entered Egypt until the time they left. As for the lineage of Job and his companions, Saadiah bases his connections on biblical evidence found in a number of genealogical passages in Genesis. We find similar attempts to identify the characters in the Book of Job in numerous rabbinic sources. The notion that Moses is the author of Job is found in *B.T. Bava' Batra'* 15a.

34. CJ 1:5, p. 153.

35. CJ 1:6, p. 153; Job 1:6, 2:1.

36. CJ 1:6, pp. 153–60; Job 1:6–12. The very fact that God would address himself to Job's rival requires comment on Saadiah's part, since Saadiah is of the opinion that God does not normally speak to someone who is of no special standing. Saadiah's response is that there are in fact instances in which an ordinary individual is addressed by God if it provides some benefit for the righteous. Thus, for instance, God addresses Abimelech in the interest of Abraham; Laban in the interest of Jacob; and Balaam in the interest of Israel. Here, too, Satan receives prophecy for Job's ultimate benefit (CJ 1:6, p. 159).

37. See earlier in this chapter, section headed "The Philosophical Background."

38. CJ 1:6, pp. 154–55.

39. CJ, p. 167 n. 28.

40. CJ 2:4–6, pp. 173–74; Job 1:13–22, 2:1–10.

41. CJ 1:12, p. 162.

42. CJ 1:12, p. 161.

43. CJ 1:6, pp. 173–74, and Goodman's comments, p. 176 n. 6.

44. This is according to Goodman's translation of Saadiah's rendering in the Arabic (CJ p. 352).

45. This reading is very different from NJPS, which understands the same verses as follows: "He is reproved by pains on his bed, / And the trembling in his bones is constant. / He detests food; / Fine food [is repulsive] to him, / His flesh wastes away till it cannot be seen, / And his bones are rubbed away till they are invisible." In this reading there is no suggestion of God's compensating the individual for his suffering.

46. This is according to Goodman's translation of Saadiah's rendering in Arabic (p. 352). The same verses are translated in NJPS as follows: "He comes close to the Pit, / His life [verges] on death. / If he has a representative, / One advocate against a thousand / To declare the man's uprightness, / Then He has mercy on him."

47. *B.T. Shabbat* 32a.

48. Here I believe Kafiḥ translates Saadiah's Arabic better than Goodman. Compare Kafiḥ, p. 165, with CJ, p. 354. Saadiah's comments here are somewhat perplexing because, according to his thinking, a person who has but one good deed to his credit would not be tested in the first place, because he is not all that righteous and is therefore not deserving of a test.

49. Again, this is according to Goodman's translation of Saadiah's Arabic (CJ, p. 353). The NJPS translates: "To bring him back from the Pit, / That he may bask in the light of life."

50. CJ 33:29, pp. 353–54, 369. Interestingly, these verses are given a somewhat

different reading in Saadiah's introduction to the commentary. See CJ introduction, p. 129.

51. CJ 38, pp. 382–84.

52. CJ 42:2, 42:13, pp. 410–11.

53. CJ, pp. 33–34, 40–43, 103–4, 141 n. 5. Goodman claims that al-Zamakhsharī is the only Islamic figure who provides an exegesis of Job that is similar to that of Saadiah. This is not the case with other Islamic exegetes such as al-Ṭabarī, Ibn Kathīr, al-Maḥallī, and al-Sūyūṭi—nor with the Islamic historians of the prophetic figures such as Ibn 'Asākir, al-Kisā'ī, and al-Maqdisī. In these thinkers one finds a far more literary, imaginative, and creative approach toward the Job story, with the focus on such issues as the wiliness of Satan, the purity of Job, and the role of his wife. For an analysis of some of these thinkers, see sources cited chapter 1, n. 1. Déclais includes in his study a discussion of Saadiah's commentary on Job (pp. 68–77), but it is mostly a summary of the commentary, and any analysis contained therein is generally drawn from Goodman.

54. CJ, pp. 54–56.

55. CJ, pp. 94–95, 136–37 n. 24.

56. See earlier in this chapter, section headed "The Philosophical Background."

57. See *Avot de-R. Natan*, ed. Solomon Schechter (London and Frankfurt, 1887), chapter 7, pp. 33–34; second version, chapter 14, p. 33, in which Abraham is depicted as being more charitable than Job; and *Bereshit Rabbah* 49:9, where it is argued that Abraham debated with God about the fate of Sodom and Gomorrah in a more respectful manner than Job did about his own fate.

58. See *B.T. Sotah* 31a, where R. Meir expresses the view that both Job and Abraham served God out of love. Cf. Mishnah *Sotah* 5:5, the passage upon which R. Meir is commenting.

59. See *B.T. Bava' Batra'* 15b, which records the statement of R. Johanan that Job is to be accorded greater praise than Abraham.

60. *B.T. Sanhedrin* 89b.

61. This interpretation is based on Gen. 22:20–21, which follow immediately after the *'akeidah*. Abraham is informed that Milcah, the wife of Abraham's brother Nahor, has given birth to eight children, including Bethuel, the father of Rebecca. Although the most obvious reason for the biblical text imparting this information is that it introduces Rebecca, who will soon be Isaac's wife, the juxtaposition of this section with the *'akeidah* story leads to a number of other midrashic suggestions. The whole chapter of *Bereshit Rabbah* 57 is in fact devoted to this issue. Most important for our concerns is *Bereshit Rabbah* 57:4, where the inference is made that after the *'akeidah* Abraham expresses fear that he will have to undergo more trials. God responds that Job will now be the recipient of Abraham's trials, an interpretation based on the fact that one of Milcah's children is named Uz, the same name given to the land in which Job lived according to the opening line of the story. Cf. *Tanḥuma*, ed. Buber, *Shelah* 27, p. 37.

62. CJ 35:15, p. 367.

63. CJ introduction, p. 127.

64. According to Goodman's rendering of Saadiah's Arabic translation of Job 42:7, p. 410.

65. Kafiḥ, p. 206.

66. This observation escapes the attention of Goodman, who provides another explanation for Saadiah's reading. See CJ, p. 412 n. 5.

67. Note also that in Saadiah's reading, Eliphaz explains the prospering of the wicked in a manner entirely consistent with a passage in *Beliefs and Opinions*. According to this explanation, the wicked prosper in order for God to delay their punishment, so that He can eventually punish them more harshly than He would have, had He exacted punishment earlier (CJ 22:29, pp. 307–8; ED 5:3, Kafiḥ, pp. 168–69; Rosenblatt, p. 216). Here again is evidence that for Saadiah, the position of Job's three companions is not incorrect from a theoretical standpoint; it is wrong only with respect to Job. Saadiah's favorable view of the opinions of Job's three companions also explains why Saadiah believes that at the end of the story they are rewarded by God just as Job is (CJ 42:13, p. 411).

68. CJ, pp. 93–94.

69. CJ introduction, p. 128.

70. CJ 42:13, p. 411.

71. Job not only appears in the Koran, but his story is the subject of much speculation on the part of medieval Islamic commentators and historians as noted earlier in this chapter, section headed "Antecedents."

72. ED 3:10, Kafiḥ, pp. 148–49; Rosenblatt, p. 179.

73. The translation of this passage is my own, though I have consulted Rosenblatt and Kafiḥ. The emphasis is also mine.

74. A comparison between Job and Israel along the same lines is also mentioned in the introduction to Saadiah's commentary on the book of Exodus; see *Perushey R. Sa'adyah Ga'on li-Bre'shit*, p. 399 n. 261.

75. CJ introduction, p. 130.

76. *B.T. 'Avodah Zarah* 24a.

77. ED 8:6, Kafiḥ, p. 249; Rosenblatt, p. 306.

78. See, for instance, *Pesikta de-R. Kahana* 16:6.

79. Following rabbinic tradition, Saadiah believes that while in the Garden of Eden, Adam and Eve were given a number of divine commandments in addition to the prohibition of eating from the Tree of Knowledge of Good and Evil; see *Perushey R. Sa'adyah Ga'on li-Bre'shit*, p. 62 (Arabic), p. 272 (Hebrew).

80. *Perushey R. Sa'adyah Ga'on li-Bre'shit*, pp. 81–83 (Arabic), pp. 300–302 (Hebrew).

81. Ibid., pp. 108–9 (Arabic), p. 349 (Hebrew).

82. If this interpretation is correct, it would find an interesting parallel in the exegesis of Job of the early Christian exegete Gregory the Great, who believed that the argument between Job and his friends was a foreshadowing of the battle between the early church and the heretics who attacked it (Schreiner, p. 43). Here, too, the dialogue of Job is read as symbolic of later religious polemics. An interesting example of this tendency in early modern Jewish thought is found in a commentary on Job composed by a certain She'alti'el Naḥmias that exists in a single manuscript at the Jewish Theological Seminary (Ms. 1114). Naḥmias understands the dialogue between Job and his friends as a religious disputation in which Job represents the Jewish people defending itself against the attacks of Catholic Christianity, Protestantism, and Islam, which are represented by the other figures in the dialogue. I was able to find no information about Naḥmias—though the family name Naḥmias is well known. He seems to have lived in Europe just after the Protestant Reformation, since he refers to Catholic Christianity simply as "Christianity" and refers to Protestantism as a new religion led by an individual named *Lutir*! The manuscript itself was copied in 1602.

83. In fact, the two levels of exegesis are connected in that Saadiah often makes use of his formidable knowledge of philology and grammar to solve the larger diffi-

culties. We saw this in his clever reading of the dialogue between God and Satan, where Saadiah makes use of his command of philology and grammar to argue for his novel interpretation. Yet, as I noted in chapter 1, we cannot delve into the philological and grammatical insights of our authors in any detail.

84. CJ, p. 27.

85. ED introduction:5; Kafiḥ, p. 16; Rosenblatt, p. 19. My translation here deviates somewhat from that of Rosenblatt. See also Malter, p. 321, who mentions this reference.

86. CJ 15:18–19, pp. 264–65.

87. ED 5:3, Kafiḥ, p. 176; Altmann, p. 138; see earlier in this chapter, section headed "The Philosophical Background."

88. ED 3:10, Kafiḥ, pp. 148–49; Rosenblatt, p. 179; see earlier in this chapter, section headed "The Philosophical Background."

89. See Siger, pp. 7–8; Besserman, pp. 27–30, 160 n. 28; Schreiner, p. 73. Saadiah's notion that Job is being tested in order to prove his worthiness to fellow human beings also finds parallels in Gregory and Thomas Aquinas; see Schreiner, p. 77. An interpretation of the Book of Job similar to that of the first group of Christian exegetes mentioned here is suggested by Aaron ben Elijah in *'Eẓ Ḥayyim*. He too believes that Job suffered a test so that he could be rewarded in the afterlife and that he himself was aware of the test. See Frank, "The Religious Philosophy of the Karaite Aaron ben Elijah," pp. cxiv–cxvi and 137–40. There are also Islamic sources suggesting that Job was well aware of his test; see CJ, p. 91. The only medieval Jewish exegete I have discovered who suggests that Job was aware of his being tested is R. Jacob Tam, as noted in Jacob Tam, *Perush 'al Sefer Iyyov*, ed. Yisra'el Ta-Shema, *Koveẓ 'al Yad* 13 (1996): 196.

90. CJ, pp. 288–89.

91. Ibid.

CHAPTER 3

1. There are too many studies of Maimonides to list here. In n. 6 of this chapter is a list of works on Maimonides' theory of providence and his reading of Job that will be central to our concerns in this chapter.

2. The influences of Greek and Islamic thinkers on Maimonides' philosophy have been well documented in Shlomo Pines, translator's introduction, in *The Guide of the Perplexed* (Chicago: University of Chicago Press, 1963), pp. lvii–cxxxiv.

3. Maimonides, *The Guide of the Perplexed*, trans. Shlomo Pines (Chicago: University of Chicago Press, 1963), introduction, pp. 5–6 (hereafter cited as *Guide*).

4. A vast literature could be cited on this issue since it impinges on every aspect of Maimonides' thought. Let me just note that representatives of the traditional reading of Maimonides include such scholars as Isadore Twersky, *Introduction to the Code of Maimonides (Mishneh Torah)* (New Haven: Yale University Press, 1980), and Marvin Fox, *Interpreting Maimonides* (Chicago: University of Chicago Press, 1990). The radical reading is championed in the many works of Leo Strauss, including *Philosophy and Law*, trans. Fred Baumann (Philadelphia: Jewish Publication Society of America, 1987), and "The Literary Character of the *Guide of the Perplexed*," in *Persecution and the Art of Writing*, pp. 38–94.

5. *Guide* III:22–23, pp. 486–97.

6. The following is a partial list of studies on Maimonides' theory of providence: Alvin Reines, "Maimonides' Concepts of Providence and Theodicy," *Hebrew Union*

College Annual 43 (1972): 169–205; Charles Touati, "Les deux théories de Maïmonide sur la providence," in *Studies in Jewish Religious and Intellectual History*, ed. Siegfried Stein and Raphael Loewe (University, Ala.: University of Alabama Press; London: Institute of Jewish Studies, 1979), pp. 331–40; Avraham Nuriel, "Providence and Governance in *The Guide of the Perplexed*" (in Hebrew), *Tarbiẓ* 49 (Summer 1980): 346–55; Charles M. Raffel, "Providence as Consequent upon the Intellect: Maimonides' Theory of Providence," *AJS Review* 12, no. 1 (Spring 1987): 25–72; Mikha'el Nehoray, "Maimonides and Gersonides: Two Approaches to the Nature of Providence" (in Hebrew), *Da'at* 20 (Winter 1988): 51–64. Substantial discussions of Maimonides' theory of providence are also found in Eliezer Goldman, "The Special Worship of Those Apprehending the True Realities" (in Hebrew), *Bar-Ilan* 6 (1968): 287–313; Howard Kreisel, " 'The Suffering of the Righteous' in Medieval Jewish Philosophy" (in Hebrew), *Da'at* 19 (1987): 17–29, especially pp. 20–26. An extensive bibliography of the secondary literature on Maimonides' theory of providence is provided in Israel Jacob Dienstag, "Providence in the Teaching of Maimonides: A Bibliography" (in Hebrew), *Da'at* 20 (1988): 5–28.

Many of these studies deal with Maimonides' reading of Job as well, but there are a number of others devoted specifically to that topic: Leonard S. Kravitz, "Maimonides on Job: An Enquiry as to the Method of the *Moreh*," *Hebrew Union College Annual* 38 (1968): 149–58; Hannah Kasher, "The Image and Views of Job in the *Guide of the Perplexed*" (in Hebrew), *Da'at* 15 (Summer 1985): 81–89; Warren Zev Harvey, "Maimonides on Job 14:20 and the Story of the Garden of Eden" (in Hebrew), in *Between History and Literature: Essays in Honor of Isaac Barzilay*, ed. Shlomo Nash (Tel Aviv: Ha-Kibbuẓ ha-Me'uḥad, 1997), pp. 143–48; Jacob S. Levinger, "Maimonides' Exegesis of the Book of Job," in *Creative Biblical Exegesis: Christian and Jewish Hermeneutics Throughout the Centuries*, ed. Benjamin Uffenheimer and Henning Graf Reventlow (Sheffield: Sheffield Academic Press, 1988), pp. 81–88; Shalom Rosenberg, "Job as Allegory: Philosophy and Literary Exegesis" (in Hebrew), in *Studies in Bible and Education*, ed. Dov Rafel (Jerusalem: Touro College, 1996), pp. 146–58; Raphael Jospe, "The Book of Job as a Biblical *Guide of the Perplexed*," in *Revelation, Reason, and Faith: Essays in Honor of Truman G. Madsen*, ed. Donald W. Parry, Daniel C. Peterson, and Stephen D. Ricks (Provo, Utah: Brigham Young University Press, 2002), pp. 566–84. Mordechai Z. Cohen provides important insight into Maimonides' reading of Job in his forthcoming article, "*Peshat* Exegesis of a Philosopher: Maimonides' Literary Approach to the Book of Job and Its Place in the History of Biblical Interpretation" (in Hebrew), which will appear in *Shnaton: An Annual for Biblical and Ancient Near Eastern Studies*. However, I saw this article only after this study was completed. A number of studies have been written comparing Maimonides' reading of Job to that of Thomas Aquinas. See Martin D. Yaffe, "Providence in Medieval Aristotelianism: Moses Maimonides and Thomas Aquinas on the Book of Job," *Hebrew Studies* 19–20 (1979–80): 62–74; Avital Wohlman, *Thomas d'Aquin et Maïmonide: un dialogue exemplaire* (Paris: Cerf, 1988), pp. 72–76, 83–97; Idit Dobbs-Weinstein, *Maimonides and St. Thomas on the Limits of Reason* (Albany: State University of New York Press, 1995), pp. 39–60.

7. *Guide* III:17, pp. 464–69. The "Law" refers to the Torah and is Pines's translation of the term *sharī'a*. In Maimonides *sharī'a* can refer to any law, divine or nomic, but in the passages I will be discussing, it always refers to the Torah.

8. *Guide* III:17, pp. 471–74.

9. *Guide* III:17, pp. 471–72, 474.

10. *Guide* III:18, pp. 474–77.

11. A thorough discussion of Maimonides' views on the practical intellect is provided in Howard Kreisel, *Maimonides' Political Thought* (Albany: State University of New York Press, 1999), chapter 5.

12. *Guide* III:22–23, pp. 486–97. My mention of Maimonides' discussion of Job here preempts my analysis of this discussion later on. However, one cannot easily discuss any one section of Maimonides' treatment of providence without mentioning the others.

13. For the sake of making this a manageable summary, I have simplified and conflated the views of a number of medieval and modern commentators, all of whom bring their own emphases and nuances to the possibilities suggested here. I have also left out a number of less popular interpretations. Among the medieval commentators whose views are represented here is Ibn Tibbon, who deals with Maimonides' views on providence in a letter to him published in Z. Diesendruck, "Samuel and Moses ibn Tibbon on Maimonides' Theory of Providence," *Hebrew Union College Annual* 11 (1936): 341–66, especially pp. 355–57; I will be discussing this letter in the next chapter. Also represented here are the views of Moses Narboni, *Perush 'al Moreh Nevukhim [Commentary on the Guide]*, in *Sheloshah Kadmoney Mefarshey ha-Moreh*, ed. Jacob Goldenthal (Jerusalem: Ortsel, 1961), pp. 53b–55a, 59b–61a. I have taken into account a number of modern interpreters as well: Goldman, pp. 299–302; Julius Guttmann, p. 194; Reines, especially pp. 187–94; Touati; Kreisel, "The Suffering of the Righteous," pp. 22–23; Raffel; and Nehoray, p. 56.

14. Most of the commentators mentioned in note 13 take this position in one form or another. Raffel, however, takes another approach, arguing that there is no distinction here between esoteric and exoteric. The naturalistic interpretation of the notion that providence is consequent upon the intellect stays within the bounds of the "fundamental principles of the Torah," which Maimonides delineates as the basis of the Torah's view. Therefore, Raffel argues, the naturalistic conception of providence that Maimonides forwards is in no way inconsistent with the Torah's view; rather, it gives that view a philosophically cogent reading. See Raffel, especially pp. 37–51.

15. Samuel ibn Tibbon makes this claim in his letter to Maimonides; Diesendruck, pp. 355–56. A similar claim is made by Joseph ibn Kaspi, *'Ammudey Kesef*, ed. S. Werbluner, in *Sheloshah Kadmoney Mefarshey ha-Moreh* (Jerusalem: Ortsel, 1961), pp. 126–28. Most interesting is the opinion of Shem Tov ben Joseph ibn Shem Tov, who claims that Maimonides follows Aristotle's theory of providence, though unwittingly, because Maimonides has misunderstood him! Shem Tov is of the opinion that Aristotle, like Maimonides, believes in individual providence. Therefore, the view of Aristotle as depicted by Maimonides in the *Guide* denying that claim is incorrect. See Shem Tov, *Perush 'al Moreh Nevukhim*, standard Hebrew edition, *Guide* III:23, pp. 27b, 35a. Among modern interpreters who identify Maimonides' view on providence with Aristotle, see Pines, translator's introduction, pp. lxv–lxvii—though note that in the same essay he goes on to identify Alfarabi as the source for Maimonides' view on providence (pp. lxxiv–lxxx). Leo Strauss takes another position on this issue, claiming that Maimonides does indeed have an esoteric position on providence, but it is Plato's. See Strauss, "Quelques remarques sur la Science Politique de Maïmonide et de Farabi," *Revue des études juives* 99–100 (1935–36): 1–37; "Der Ort der Vorsehungslehre nach der Ansicht Maimunis," *Monatsschrift für Geschichte und Wissenschaft des Judentums* 81 (1937): 93–105.

16. *Guide* III:51, pp. 624–26.

17. My formulation of the difficulty in this passage is indebted to Ibn Tibbon, who, in his letter on providence to Maimonides, frames the problem in a similar

manner; see Diesendruck, pp. 361–62. Ibn Tibbon entertains a number of interpretations of *Guide* III:51 but finds none satisfactory. He therefore leaves the matter open and awaits Maimonides' reply—though, to the best of our knowledge, none ever came. While I cannot provide a full analysis of the many explanations commentators have proposed for the passage under discussion, here are the major approaches. Some medieval commentators on *Guide* III:51 attempt to show how the perfection of the intellect can, in fact, provide physical protection from harm through a naturalistic mechanism. The provenance of this theory is, for the most part, Neoplatonic. The general approach here is that a perfected intellect causes one to resemble a celestial being, which is impervious to physical harm. See Shem Tov ibn Falaquera's comments in Ya'ir Shiffman, "Rabbi Shem Tov ben Joseph Falaquera's *Moreh ha-Moreh*" (Ph.D. diss., Hebrew University, 1990), vol. 2, pp. 227–28, and Shiffman's comments in vol. 1, pp. 418–19; Narboni, p. 64a–b; Shem Tov, p. 67a–b. However, as Shiffman notes (vol. 1, p. 419), this sort of interpretation is ultimately foreign to Maimonides' way of thinking. Other commentators read Maimonides' remarks in *Guide* III:51 as a figurative depiction of psychological immunity from suffering which is the central message of his reading of Job. See Efodi, *Perush 'al Moreh Nevukhim*, standard Hebrew edition of the *Guide*, p. 67b, who hints at this solution. More explicit in proposing this explanation is Touati, "Les deux théories," pp. 337–40. The problem with this interpretation is that it reads Maimonides nonliterally, a practice that always carries with it the risk of imputing to him ideas that are not his. Julius Guttmann surmises that the passage in *Guide* III:51 is somehow designed to conceal Maimonides' true views, though Guttmann is uncertain about its exact meaning; see Guttmann, p. 502 n. 99. As Raffel notes, pp. 25–26, the confusion in Maimonides' views on providence forces Guttmann into an esoteric interpretation most uncharacteristic of his overall approach toward Maimonides.

18. *Guide* III:22, p. 486. My discussion will not follow the precise order of Maimonides' presentation but will go roughly according to the order of events in the biblical text.

19. *B.T. Bava' Batra'* 15a.

20. Job 1:1.

21. Gen. 22:21.

22. *Guide* III:22, pp. 486–87. The notion that *'Uẓ* is a symbolic term is found in the Talmud (*Bava' Batra'* 15a), but there it is related to the word *'eẓ*, or "tree." Maimonides' interpretation resonates with that of at least one prominent modern interpreter of Job. Norman Habel argues that *'Uẓ* could be a pun on the noun *'eẓah*, meaning "counsel or design," a word also related to the root *'uẓ*, "to reflect" or "to meditate." Habel points out that this association is appropriate since the notion of counsel or design is a common theme in wisdom literature, of which Job is a part. See Norman Habel, *The Book of Job* (London: S.C.M. Press, 1983), p. 86.

23. *Guide* III:22, p. 487. Pines uses italics to distinguish Hebrew terms and phrases from the Judeo-Arabic, the language in which the *Guide* is written. I will preserve this stylistic feature in all my citations from Pines's translation.

24. Job 1:1.

25. *Guide* III:23, pp. 492–93.

26. *Guide* III:22, p. 486. The rabbinic dictum presented here in italics is from a section in the Talmud dealing with Ezekiel's vision in Ez. 1 (*B.T. Ḥagigah* 13a). It is significant that Maimonides cites this source when one considers an insight provided by Steven Harvey. Harvey shows that in the *Guide* Maimonides' definition of *ma'aseh merkavah*—the philosophical doctrines contained in Ez. 1—is not uniform. Although,

at the beginning of the treatise, *ma'aseh merkavah* refers to metaphysics, in the third part of the *Guide* it refers more specifically to the issue of providence (Steven Harvey, "Maimonides in the Sultan's Palace," in *Perspectives on Maimonides*, ed. Joel Kraemer [Oxford: Oxford University Press, 1991], pp. 58–59). Therefore, it is significant that Maimonides uses a rabbinic phrase that comes out of a discussion dealing with Ez. 1 when introducing his discussion about Satan in the Book of Job, a book which in Maimonides' reading deals with providence. This would seem to bolster Harvey's contention that in the later parts of the *Guide*, *ma'aseh merkavah* is indeed synonymous with providence.

27. Here I depart from the NJPS translation of "adversary" for the term *satan*. The transliterated term "Satan" better captures the religious and mythic overtones that a medieval Jewish thinker such as Maimonides would have attached to that term.

28. *Guide* III:22, p. 487.

29. Ibid.

30. *Guide* III:22, p. 488.

31. Efodi, p. 32a; Shem Tov, p. 32a.

32. Maimonides, *Le guide des égarés*, ed. and trans. Solomon Munk (Paris: A. Franck, 1855–66), vol. 3, p. 162 n. 1.

33. Avraham Nuriel, "Toward a Clarification of the Concept of Satan in *The Guide of the Perplexed*" (in Hebrew), *Jerusalem Studies in Jewish Thought* 5 (1986), pp. 85–86.

34. *Guide* I:2, p. 23; I:49, pp. 108–9; II:6, pp. 261–65. The term *elohim* can also refer to "judges," according to Maimonides—though this rendering is not significant here.

35. This is my own inference. Neither Efodi, Shem Tov, nor Munk, who support the identification of Satan with a panoply of natural forces, provides justification for their position.

36. Nuriel, "Toward a Clarification," pp. 85–86. That the "sons" of *elohim* can refer to the production of natural beings—as the term does in all of the interpretations suggested here—is justified by Nuriel, who points out that in Maimonides' lexicon, the verb *yalad*, "to give birth," can be understood figuratively. In a passage in the *Guide*, Maimonides mentions that, in addition to its biological meaning, this verb can allude to "the bringing into existence of natural things" (Nuriel, "Toward a Clarification," pp. 85–86; *Guide* I:7, p. 32).

37. Thus, for instance, an eye that is blind experiences the privation of sight since the eye in its normal state should see but at present lacks that capacity. The concept of privation has its roots in Aristotle. For a discussion of it, see W.K.C. Guthrie, *A History of Greek Philosophy* (Cambridge: Cambridge University Press, 1981), vol. 6, pp. 104, 121–22.

38. The commentators who identify Satan with privation are Efodi, p. 32a; Shem Tov, pp. 32a–33a; Crescas, *Perush 'al Moreh Nevukhim*, standard Hebrew edition of the *Guide*, pp. 32a, 32b–33a; Narboni, on *Guide* III:10, p. 50a; Solomon ben Yuda' ha-Nasi, *Perush 'al Sodot ha-Moreh*, Ms. Cambridge Add. 373/2, fols. 145a, 145b–146a. Crescas and Shem Tov also refer to the identification of Satan with matter without explaining how this squares with the equation of Satan with privation (Crescas, p. 33a; Shem Tov, on *Guide* III:8, p. 10b). The confusion here is due to Maimonides' own mixed signals about where the ultimate source of evil lies, as we shall see later.

39. Munk, vol. 3, pp. 162 n. 1, 165 n. 1; Nehoray, pp. 54–55. It would seem that the same view is also held by Raffel; see pp. 155–57.

40. Levinger, pp. 81–82.

41. Kravitz, pp. 155–57. Cf. Sarah Klein-Braslavy, "Toward an Identification of the Figures of 'Satan' and 'Samael' in Maimonides' Interpretation of the Garden of Eden Story" (in Hebrew), *Da'at* 10 (Winter 1983): 9–18.

42. Reines, p. 202 n. 34.

43. Rosenberg, "On Biblical Interpretation in *The Guide of the Perplexed,*" p. 134. But cf. Rosenberg, "Job as Allegory," pp. 152–53.

44. Nuriel, "Toward a Clarification," pp. 86–91. Many of the opinions regarding Maimonides' interpretation of Satan are cited in Nuriel, "Toward a Clarification," pp. 83–84.

45. *Guide* III:8, pp. 430–31; III:10, pp. 438–40. A similar description of privation is given in *Guide* I:17, pp. 42–43: "When a form is achieved, the particular privation in question, I mean the privation of the form that is achieved, disappears, and another privation is joined with matter; and this goes on forever, as has been made clear in natural science."

46. Undoubtedly, this ambiguity is why some medieval commentators seem unsure as to whether Satan is representative of matter or privation, as pointed out in n. 38 to this chapter. Reines, who sees Satan as representative of both matter and privation together, seems to have responded to the same ambiguity.

47. See earlier in this section.

48. *Guide* III:10, p. 439.

49. *Guide* III:10, pp. 439–40.

50. The subject of this citation is more broadly the issue of "evil" than privation per se. However, the entire discussion of which this passage is part is about privation, and therefore evil can be viewed here as synonymous with privation. This point, in fact, is evident from the second part of the passage cited, where privation becomes the focus of Maimonides' remarks.

51. See earlier in this section.

52. *Guide* III:10, p. 440.

53. See earlier in this section.

54. Here I depart from the NJPS translation, "only spare his life (*nefesh*)." The term *nefesh* here is understood by Maimonides in its medieval sense as "soul."

55. *Guide* III:22, p. 488.

56. Maimonides' views on immortality are difficult to determine, since there are relatively few references to this subject in his writings. There appears to be general agreement that Maimonides follows the views of the Islamic Aristotelians, who believed that immortality was consequent upon the perfection of the intellect. Other details of his thinking on this issue are highly unclear, such as whether there is individual immortality and whether there are gradations of immortality corresponding to the intellectual perfection achieved during one's lifetime. The lack of detail and clarity in Maimonides' references to immortality has even prompted some to question his convictions on this issue, especially Shlomo Pines, who, late in his career, declared Maimonides an agnostic on this question. Most others are unwilling to go this far, even when questioning the firmness of Maimonides' beliefs on immortality. See Harry Blumberg, "The Problem of Immortality in Avicenna, Maimonides, and St. Thomas," in *The Harry Austryn Wolfson Jubilee Volume,* ed. Saul Lieberman (Jerusalem: American Academy for Jewish Research, 1963), vol. 1, pp. 165–85; Shlomo Pines, "The Limitations of Human Knowledge According to Al-Farabi, Ibn Bajja, and Maimonides," in *Studies in Medieval Jewish History and Literature I,* ed. Isadore Twersky (Cambridge, Mass.: Harvard University Press, 1979), pp. 82–109; Alexander Altmann, "Maimonides on the Intellect and the Scope of Metaphysics," in *Von der mittelalterlichen zur*

modernen Aufklärung (Tübingen: J.C.B. Mohr [Paul Siebeck], 1987), pp. 85–91; Herbert Davidson, *Alfarabi, Avicenna, and Averroes on the Intellect* (New York: Oxford University Press, 1992), pp. 202–3; Kreisel, *Maimonides' Political Thought*, pp. 142–43, 149.

57. *B.T. Bava' Batra'* 16a.

58. *Guide* III:22, pp. 488–89.

59. *Guide* III:22, p. 489.

60. *Guide* III:10, p. 439.

61. The association between the imagination and the evil inclination is made in *Guide* II:12, p. 280. The notion that Adam's sin is due to his focusing on matters of the imagination is argued in *Guide* I:2, p. 25. See also *Guide* I:46, p. 98, where Maimonides argues that the masses believe in anthropomorphisms due to the imagination.

62. See *Guide* III:10, pp. 439, 440–41, where ignorance is described by Maimonides as a privation of knowledge. The imagination is not mentioned in these passages, but one can surmise that when there is a privation of knowledge, it is the imagination that becomes dominant, and that this faculty is therefore symbolic of the privation of knowledge.

In his discussion of Resh Lakish's dictum, Maimonides seems particularly intrigued by the equation of Satan with the evil inclination or the imagination. He discusses this association at some length, adducing a number of rabbinic passages that he believes support his interpretation of this conception. This focus on the evil inclination has prompted Kravitz and Levinger to conclude that Satan represents nothing other than the imagination in Maimonides' reading of the Book of Job. However, the evidence would indicate that this is too narrow an interpretation of Maimonides' views on Satan. As we have shown, Maimonides' clues about Satan throughout *Guide* III:22 point in the direction of privation as the referent of Satan. Moreover, in his reading of Resh Lakish's dictum, Maimonides seems to hint quite strongly that Satan, the angel of death, and the evil inclination are all caused by one underlying factor, and privation is the best candidate for linking these three.

63. *Guide* III:23, p. 490; *B.T. Ḥagigah* 16a, *Berakhot* 60b.

64. *Guide* III:12, pp. 443–48. This correspondence is noted by Narboni on *Guide* III:12, p. 50a. The same approach is taken by Solomon ben Yuda' ha-Nasi. See Mikha'el Nehoray, "R. Solomon ben R. Yuda' ha-Nasi and His Commentary on *The Guide of the Perplexed*" (in Hebrew) (Ph.D. diss.: Hebrew University, 1978), pp. 123–24.

65. *Guide*, introduction, p. 10. More accurately, what Maimonides says is that chapters with no "equivocal term" in them are preparatory either for those that contain them or for those that deal with biblical parables.

66. This is also implicit in Leo Strauss's scheme of organization of chapters in the *Guide*, presented in his "How to Begin to Study *The Guide of the Perplexed*," in *Guide*, p. xii.

67. *Guide* III:12, p. 443.

68. Job 1:16, 1:19. It is likely that Maimonides understands the phenomenon of "fire from heaven" as a reference to lightning strikes, which can, on occasion, have deadly consequences.

69. *Guide* III:12, p. 444.

70. Job 1:15, 1:17.

71. *Guide* III:11, pp. 440–41.

72. *Guide* III:12, pp. 445–48.

73. Neither Narboni nor Solomon ben Yuda' ha-Nasi, who develop the correspondences between the three categories of evil and those that afflict Job, take notice of this difficulty. It is possible that Job's illness may be included under the first category in Maimonides' tripartite classification of evils. In discussing the first category, Maimonides mentions that in addition to destructive meteorological phenomena, privation can cause "infirmities and paralytic afflictions." Thus, Maimonides apparently believes that illness is not always caused by one's vices. Complicating matters is a passage in *Guide* I:72, p. 190, in which Maimonides talks about a disease, *al-jutham*, a term translated as *sheḥin* in Kafiḥ's Hebrew translation of the *Guide* (p. 405 n. 67), the same bodily illness that afflicts Job (2:7). The passage is given two widely different interpretations by Klein-Braslavy and Nuriel. Klein-Braslavy (p. 12 n. 6) interprets the passage to mean that *sheḥin* is due to the imagination, since it is this faculty that arouses the appetitive faculty to excess indulgence in food and other pleasures, thereby causing disease. Nuriel (p. 90) reads the same passage differently and draws out the lesson that *sheḥin* is due to natural forces emanating from outside man. It is therefore difficult to determine to which category of evil in *Guide* III:12 this particular disease belongs. Another complication is that many of the evils affect Job's children, an observation that raises the question why it is that they suffer in addition to Job. In fact, they end up dying from the wind that destroys their house. Maimonides never addresses this issue. However, it is interesting to note that Job's children are apparently guilty of indulging in vices of which Job is innocent. We are told at the beginning of the story that Job's children gather every day to eat and drink (Job 1:4–5). Maimonides specifically rails against public gatherings of this sort in his discussion of evil (*Guide* III:8, p. 434). The irony is that Job's children are the ones who should have been stricken with bodily illness, according to Maimonides; yet, it is Job who is afflicted in this manner instead, even though he is the one who has moral virtue.

74. *Guide* III:23, pp. 490–91, 495. While Maimonides does not say so explicitly, the only view of providence not represented in the dialogue in Job is that of Epicurus. Apparently, Maimonides felt that this view did not have to be accounted for because it denied the existence of providence altogether (*Guide* III:17, p. 464).

75. *Guide* III:23, pp. 491–97.

76. *Guide* III:23, pp. 495–96.

77. Some commentators argue that what Job learns here is "negative theology." There is, however, some difficulty in invoking that concept here. The basic position argued in Maimonides' major discussion of negative theology is that we refer to God's perfections only by negating His imperfections (*Guide* I:58–59, pp. 134–43). That position is not really represented here. However, Maimonides' negative theology is certainly founded upon the equivocal nature of divine attributes, because one must refer to those attributes in the negative when one realizes that they mean something totally different when applied to us than when applied to God. That position is very much represented here in the total distinction Maimonides draws between divine and human providence. One can therefore use the phrase "negative theology," here but only in a very loose sense. It is for this reason that I would rather refer to Job's lesson as one that concerns the equivocality of divine attributes, not negative theology.

78. *Guide* III:23, pp. 496–97.

79. I deliberately begin with the modern interpreters of Maimonides here rather than with the medieval ones, because the latter are unhelpful for initiating an analysis of the particular section in the *Guide* with which we are dealing. Some of the medieval commentaries—such as those of Efodi, Crescas, and Kaspi—consist of a series of glosses on select words or phrases in the *Guide*, a format that in this case cannot

provide a comprehensive understanding of Maimonides' presentation. One must not only make sense of the components of Maimonides' reading of the speeches of Elihu and God, but also show how they fit together and form a coherent position. Others, such as Narboni and Solomon ben Yuda' ha-Nasi, provide a running commentary on Maimonides which, it would seem, should furnish the sort of comprehensive interpretation missing in the first approach. However, these commentators often follow the Maimonidean imperative that one must not reveal too much of the truth, and therefore they often obfuscate their true opinions regarding what Maimonides is saying. The difficulty here is that we must first decipher their esoteric interpretation of Maimonides before we decipher that of Maimonides himself. While this challenge is certainly worthwhile, it is one that could easily occupy us for the remainder of this chapter. Shem Tov is perhaps the exception in that he writes a running commentary that is relatively clear. However, Shem Tov does not usually argue his points, but instead provides a paraphrase of Maimonides—a style of writing very common in medieval Judaism, but one that does not clarify how he has arrived at his positions. It must be emphasized that these observations do not mean that the medieval commentators are of no help whatsoever. In fact, their insights will be critical for my discussion. It is just that with the particular type of text in the *Guide* we are examining, it is more fruitful to begin with the modern commentators.

80. See earlier in this chapter, section headed "The Philosophical Background."

81. Kravitz, p. 157.

82. Levinger, p. 85. The notion that Maimonides sees Elihu's angel as the human intellect is also argued by the medieval encyclopedist Levi ben Abraham of Villefranche in his *Livyat Ḥen*, Ms. Munich 58, fols. 103r–104r.

83. Touati never uses the term "practical intellect," but that is effectively the intellectual faculty to which he is referring.

84. Touati, "Les deux théories," pp. 337–40; Raffel, pp. 51–67. A similar reading of Elihu's speech is given by the fourteenth-century rabbi Nissim ben Moshe of Marseilles in *Ma'aseh Nissim*, pp. 194–95. However, the higher level of providence that Job achieves by the end of the book is the capacity for immortality, a reading that, as we shall see, has its source in Samuel ibn Tibbon.

85. Other scholars express support for the notion that Job's ultimate lesson concerns the capacity to achieve a psychological immunity to suffering but do not provide a detailed interpretation of Maimonides' reading of Job. See Goldman, pp. 15–16; Kreisel, " 'The Suffering of the Righteous,' " pp. 20–26; Kreisel, *Maimonides' Political Thought*, pp. 137, 244–45.

86. *Guide* III:23, p. 495.

87. My emphasis.

88. I prefer the translation of "angel" for *mal'akh* over the NJPS translation of "representative," since this better captures Maimonides' understanding of the term.

89. Here too I depart from NJPS, which renders this line "One advocate against a thousand." As I show here, Maimonides clearly goes according to my translation.

90. Efodi, pp. 35b–36a; Shem Tov, p. 35a; Munk, p. 183 n. 1.

91. Efodi, p. 35b.

92. *Guide* III:23, p. 495.

93. Efodi, pp. 35b–36a; *Guide* II:38, pp. 336–37.

94. Here I cite the NJPS translation, which differs somewhat from the old JPS rendering cited by Pines in his translation of Maimonides.

95. *Guide* II:38, pp. 336–37. The problem is that according to this translation, which follows that of the NJPS, the prophetic communication is also meant to some-

how discipline the individual and suppress his pride. It is not clear how this would fit with Maimonides' notion of divination. One of the difficulties here and elsewhere in the *Guide* is that Maimonides does not always provide us with sufficient information to determine how he read the biblical text. This is especially problematic for Maimonides' interpretation of passages in the Book of Job, since this particular book is considered one of the most difficult texts in the biblical canon and is therefore open to a wide range of interpretations. The passage under discussion could, in fact, be read a number of ways, as we shall see throughout this study.

96. *Guide* III:23, pp. 495–96.

97. See earlier in this section.

98. Ibid. A curious element in the passage under discussion is Maimonides' claim that Elihu discusses the "circumstances of animals." What is interesting to note is that the biblical verse he cites to support this notion (Job 34:20) makes no mention of animals whatsoever, nor does the larger passage of which it is a part (Job 34:16–24). Rather, the verse and passage are concerned with human beings. Yet, the fact that Maimonides refers to animals here is not so hard to explain in light of my interpretation. As I have argued, the concern here, according to Maimonides, is with natural processes, which oftentimes guard the welfare of human beings and animals in precisely the same fashion. Therefore, it is likely that Maimonides deliberately refers to animals here, even though the biblical text deals with human beings, in order to bring home the point that with natural processes, the fate of animals and that of human beings is often one and the same.

99. *Guide* III:23, p. 496.

100. Later on in the passage, after a review of some of the "natural matters" that Job learns, Maimonides interjects that "*Elihu* too derives his warnings from the various species of animals," a statement that again reinforces the impression that God's remarks are a continuation of Elihu's.

101. Cf. Ibn Ezra, who also emphasizes the mystery of God's ways in the epilogue to his commentary on Job (rabbinic Bibles).

102. *Guide* I:58–59, pp. 134–43.

103. *Guide* I:31, pp. 65–67; I:58, p. 136; II:3, p. 254; II:12, p. 279. There has been a lively debate in recent years about the extent of the limitations of human knowledge in Maimonides' thought. A number of years ago, Pines introduced the radical thesis that Maimonides was an agnostic on metaphysical matters ("The Limitations of Human Knowledge"). That position has been attacked and qualified by a series of scholars. See Altmann; Warren Zev Harvey, "Maimonides on Human Perfection, Awe, and Politics," in *The Thought of Moses Maimonides,* eds. Ira Robinson, Lawrence Kaplan, and Julian Bauer (Lewiston, N.Y.: Edwin Mellen Press, 1990), pp. 1–15; Tzvi Langermann, "The True Perplexity: *The Guide of the Perplexed,* Part II, Chapter 24," in *Perspectives on Maimonides,* pp. 159–74; Herbert Davidson, "Maimonides on Metaphysical Knowledge," *Maimonidean Studies* 3 (1992–93): 49–103. Interestingly, none of these scholars addresses the issue of Maimonides' views on providence and his interpretation of Job, even though both are important for examining his attitude on the limitations of human knowledge.

104. See the sources in n. 103, especially *Guide* II:3, p. 254.

105. The limitations that Maimonides places on human knowledge here may be even more restrictive. He tells us that Job's lesson is that there is no going beyond "the description" of sublunar phenomena. This would imply that a full understanding of sublunar phenomena is not possible. It would also suggest there are limitations to

human knowledge in the description of celestial phenomena. I wish to thank Zev Harvey for this insight.

Some scholars have compared Maimonides' position on the limitations of knowledge with that of Thomas Aquinas, who also deals with this issue in his commentary on Job. I tend to support Dobbs-Weinstein, who sees much commonality between the two thinkers here and argues against Yaffee and Wohlman, who emphasize the differences between them. See Dobbs-Weinstein, *Maimonides and St. Thomas*, pp. 39–59, 172–77. Schreiner also agrees with Dobbs-Weinstein (Schreiner, pp. 82–83) and cites other examples of overlap between Maimonides and Aquinas in their readings of Job (pp. 57, 70).

106. *Guide* III:23, p. 497.

107. *Guide* III:23, pp. 492–93.

108. For the sake of consistency, I cite Pines's translation of the biblical text, rather than NJPS.

109. Kreisel, *Maimonides' Political Thought*, p. 137.

110. *Guide* III:51, pp. 620–28. Maimonides identifies this form of devotion with the rabbinic concept of "worship of the heart" (*'avodah she-ba-lev*) (*B.T. Ta'anit* 2a).

111. *Guide* III:51, p. 620.

112. *Guide* III:51, pp. 623–24.

113. Kreisel, *Maimonides' Political Thought*, pp. 136–40. Discussions of Maimonides' views on the acquired intellect are also found in Davidson, pp. 201–2, and Altmann, pp. 79–85. For an analysis of the notion that the best of the prophets were able to contemplate God while participating in the affairs of this world, see Lawrence Kaplan, " 'I Sleep, but My Heart Waketh'; Maimonides' Conception of Human Perfection," in *The Thought of Moses Maimonides*, pp. 130–66.

114. Altmann appears to read the passage this way as well. See Altmann, p. 86 n. 202.

115. *Guide* III:23, pp. 492–93. Maimonides' reading of Job 42:6 has been accepted, sometimes unwittingly, by modern scholars of Job. See P. A. H. De Boer, "Does Job Retract?," in *Selected Studies in Old Testament Exegesis*, ed. C. Van Duin (Leiden: E. J. Brill, 1991), pp. 179–95; Dale Patrick, "The Translation of Job XLII 6," *Vetus Testamentum* 26 (1976): 369–71; Lawrence Kaplan, "Maimonides, Dale Patrick, and Job XLII 6," *Vetus Testamentum* 28 (1978): 356–57; E. J. Van Wolde, "Job 42:1–6: The Reversal of Job," in *The Book of Job*, ed. W. A. M. Beuken (Leuven: Leuven University Press, 1994), pp. 223–50.

116. It is paradoxical that the highest form of knowing God is through negative theology, which emphasizes what we do *not* know about Him. One therefore wonders what Job, or anyone else with intellectual perfection, is thinking when contemplating the Divine Being. This paradox is a problem endemic to Maimonides' negative theology in general and therefore cannot preoccupy us here.

117. Here I follow Maimonides' understanding of the love of God as contained in various references in the *Guide*, especially III:51, pp. 618–28. There is a somewhat different understanding in the *Mishneh Torah*. See, for instance, *Mishneh Torah, Laws of the Principles of the Torah* 2:1. There are analyses of Maimonides' conception of love of God in Goldman; Georges Vajda, *L'amour de Dieu dans la théologie juive du Moyen Age* (Paris: J. Vrin, 1956), pp. 118–40; Norman Lamm, "Maimonides on Love of God," *Maimonidean Studies* 3 (1992–93), pp. 131–42; Kreisel, *Maimonides' Political Thought*, chapter 7.

118. I might note here incidentally that Maimonides' understanding of the value

of Job's suffering finds resonance with some early Christian thinkers with whom he was unlikely to have been familiar. The notion that the Book of Job teaches us that suffering is of benefit in that it causes one to detach oneself from material things is expressed by Ambrose and Chrysostom. However, that theme is most developed by Gregory in his *Magna Moralia*, where he argues in a Neoplatonic framework that suffering is meant to turn the individual inward so that he will attach himself to the realm of the eternal and the unchangeable. See Newsom and Schreiner, p. 588; Schreiner, pp. 24–25, 27–31, 33–35. As Schreiner points out, Gregory's ruminations about the value of suffering are part of a much larger and complex reading of Job.

119. *B.T. Yoma'* 23a, *Gittin* 36b.

120. See, for instance, the commentary of Ritva' on this passage in *B.T. Yoma'* 23a and the commentaries of Rif and Maharsha on the same passage in *B.T. Gittin* 36b, all cited in *'Ein Ya'akov*.

121. For a discussion of this motif in Maimonides, see Altmann, p. 122. Altmann notes that this motif originates in Plato's *Republic* but may have become known to Maimonides through Ibn Bajja. See also Barry S. Kogan, "What Can We Know and When Can We Know It? Maimonides on the Active Intelligence and Human Cognition," in *Moses Maimonides in His Time*, ed. Eric L. Ormsby (Washington, D.C.: Catholic University of America, 1991), p. 126.

122. Note also the appropriateness of the rabbinic source for Job's situation in that it deals with the insult that one receives from one's fellow human beings. Throughout the dialogue, Job's sense of insult comes not only from the treatment he receives from God, but also from the opinions expressed by his friends.

123. *Mishneh Torah Laws of Character Traits*, 2:3.

124. David Hartman, *Maimonides: Torah and Philosophical Quest* (Philadelphia: Jewish Publication Society of America, 1976), p. 90f.; Daniel H. Frank, "Humility as a Virtue: A Maimonidean Critique of Aristotle's Ethics," in *Moses Maimonides in His Time*, pp. 89–99; Frank, "Anger as a Vice: A Maimonidean Critique of Aristotelian Ethics," *History of Philosophy Quarterly* 7, no. 3 (July 1990): 274–75; Fox, p. 117; Raymond L. Weiss, *Maimonides' Ethics* (Chicago: University of Chicago Press, 1991), pp. 103–4; Robert Eisen, "*Lifnim mi-Shurat ha-Din* in Maimonides' *Mishneh Torah*," *Jewish Quarterly Review* 89, no. 3–4 (Winter 1999): 294–317, especially pp. 299–302.

125. Any number of passages could be cited here, but note especially Job's protests against God in Job 10:1f. and Job's anger at his friends in Job 30:1f.

126. *Guide* III:23, pp. 487–88.

127. *Guide* III:23, p. 494. Maimonides does not comment on the fact that Job, as a morally perfect individual, should have had control over undesirable character traits. Presumably, Maimonides feels that Job's moral perfection could not hold up in the face of the suffering he experienced.

128. The motif of *imitatio Dei* appears to underlie Maimonides' understanding of Job's transformation. That is, there are indications that, in Maimonides' thinking, Job's intellectual and ethical education brings him to a state of perfection that resembles that of God. As noted, Job's intellectual imitation of God is implied by the rabbinic source, which Maimonides cites at the end of his exposition. The ethical perfection Job achieves also seems to be an instance of *imitatio Dei*. Daniel H. Frank has argued that Maimonides mandates the suppression of anger and pride, and not other character traits, because he holds the suppression of these particular traits to be characteristic of God's own ethical behavior (Frank, "Humility as a Virtue," "Anger as a Vice"; see also Eisen, "*Lifnim mi-Shurat ha-Din*," pp. 299–302).

129. Levinger, p. 86.

130. The exception here is Lenn Goodman, who, in his translation of Saadiah's commentary on Job, notes some parallels. See Goodman's introduction to Saadiah Gaon, *The Book of Theodicy*, pp. 58, 140 n. 42, 141 n. 49.

131. See chapter 2, section headed "The Commentary on Job."

132. See chapter 2, section headed "The Commentary on Job."

133. *Guide* III:17, pp. 470–71.

134. In truth, even here the esoteric truths are concealed in that the addresses of Elihu and God need to be interpreted in order to penetrate to their true meaning. It is just that the truths are not concealed in allegorical images as they are in the prologue.

135. I use the term "allegory" here in the sense in which Maimonides understood it. It is an exegetical device that identifies the inner or philosophical meaning of the biblical text beneath its outer layer.

136. This is a point to which I will return later.

137. Jews, however, may have an advantage over non-Jews, in Maimonides' thinking, because they are in possession of the Torah, which gives them guidance to intellectual perfection in a way that other law systems do not. See *Guide* II:40, pp. 381–85. Maimonides' thinking on universalism and particularism is thoroughly analyzed in Menachem Kellner, *Maimonides on Judaism and the Jewish People* (Albany: State University of New York Press, 1991). Throughout his study Kellner supports the universalistic thrust in Maimonides' thought noted here.

138. One could also argue that Maimonides' depiction of Job is universal in meaning, since his implied criticism of the religion of the masses via the figure of Job could theoretically apply to other religious communities as well. It is well known that Maimonides' views on the distinction between the religion of the masses and that of the philosophical elite are drawn from Islamic philosophers, in particular Alfarabi, and in their deliberations on this matter they speak about that distinction in general terms that make it applicable to any religious community. There is every reason to suspect that Maimonides viewed these matters in a similar way, for when he refers to the distinction between the masses and the elite, he too often speaks about it in general terms that lead one to believe that this is not merely a Jewish issue. Therefore, Maimonides' depiction of Job could be meant as a criticism of ignorant individuals in any religious community who insist on a literal reading of scripture and are uninitiated in a philosophical understanding of religion. However, my sense is that the primary target of his remarks is his fellow Jews.

139. The two medieval commentators who most emphasize the centrality of Maimonides' exegesis of Job in his thinking on providence are Narboni and Solomon ben Yuda' ha-Nasi. Both argue that all the chapters in the *Guide* from the treatment of evil in *Guide* III:8 up to the exposition on Job in *Guide* III:22–23 are preparatory for the latter. This case is argued especially strongly by Solomon ben Yuda' ha-Nasi (Nehoray, "R. Solomon ben R. Yuda' ha-Nasi," pp. 119–30; Nehoray himself expresses agreement with this approach in "Maimonides and Gersonides," p. 53). Neither Narboni nor Solomon ben Yuda' offers a clear interpretation of the relationship between Maimonides' reading of Job and his views on providence, preferring instead to relate their views in an esoteric style. The modern interpreters are far clearer in making this connection. Touati, Raffel, and Goldman are the modern commentators who most emphasize the importance of Maimonides' reading of Job in discerning his views on providence. My own analysis of the relationship between Maimonides' reading of Job and his discussion of providence is much indebted to both the medieval and modern interpreters mentioned here.

140. For the sake of simplicity, I will deliberately avoid discussion of Maimonides' treatment of providence in *Guide* III:51.

141. See earlier in this chapter, section headed "The Philosophical Background."

142. This point has been noticed by commentators from the medieval period onward. See, for instance, Narboni on *Guide* III:17, p. 54a.

143. While I have chosen to include Maimonides' notion of psychological immunity from suffering as an expression of his conception of providence according to the intellect, the two medieval commentators who make the greatest effort to read Maimonides' exposition on Job in light of his discussion on providence are strangely reticent about this connection. Narboni is silent about the issue of psychological immunity to suffering in his commentary on the Job chapters of the *Guide* (pp. 60a–61a). Solomon ben Yuda' ha-Nasi, in his commentary on *Guide* III:17, mentions both the activity of the practical intellect and psychological immunity to suffering as expressions of providence (Nehoray, "R. Solomon ben R. Yuda' ha-Nasi," p. 126); but in his discussion of the Job chapters, he says virtually nothing about the latter form of providence (these chapters are not discussed by Nehoray; see Ms. Cambridge, fol. 148r–v). There is at least one modern interpreter who takes the position that the final lesson of Job regarding psychological immunity from suffering represents the sole manifestation of individual providence in Maimonides' thinking, and that is Goldman, pp. 299–302.

144. See earlier in this chapter, section headed "The Philosophical Background."

145. *Guide* III:23, p. 491.

146. *Guide* III:17, pp. 464–66. Kasher also notes that in another passage Maimonides seems to imply a sharp distinction between the views of Aristotle and Job (*Guide* III:16, p. 462). This provides further evidence that Maimonides did not identify Job's view with that of Aristotle.

147. *Guide* III:23, p. 492.

148. Kasher, pp. 81–89.

149. Jospe goes further in arguing that from a series of close readings and linguistic clues Maimonides regards the Book of Job as a biblical *Guide of the Perplexed* and that Maimonides consciously paints Job in the image of the student, R. Joseph, for whom he composed the *Guide*.

CHAPTER 4

1. Biographical details on Ibn Tibbon are sparse. He lived in the community of Lunel and also spent time in Arles, Marseilles, and Béziers. He appears to have traveled to Toledo and Barcelona and perhaps Alexandria. Information on Ibn Tibbon's life can be found in Sirat, pp. 217–22. The flowering of Jewish culture in Provence during Ibn Tibbon's period is discussed in Richard Emory, *The Jews of Perpignan in the Thirteenth Century* (New York: Columbia University Press, 1959); Isadore Twersky, *Rabad of Posquières* (Cambridge, Mass.: Harvard University Press, 1962), pp. 19–29; Twersky, "Aspects of the Social and Cultural History of Provençal Jewry," in *Jewish Society through the Ages*, ed. Haim Hillel Ben Sasson and Shmu'el Ettinger (New York: Schocken Books, 1971), pp. 185–207; Salo W. Baron, *A Social and Religious History of the Jews* (New York: Columbia University Press, 1958), vol. 10, pp. 82–91.

2. Translation was one of the key activities nurturing the development of intellectual culture in Provence. It made available to the Jews of that region the most sophisticated learning of the period in Islamic science and philosophy. It also made accessible the works of Jewish philosophers who had written in Arabic such as Saadiah

Gaon, Baḥya ibn Pakuda, and Maimonides. For information on Ibn Tibbon's activity as translator, see sources cited in Aviezer Ravitzky, "Samuel ibn Tibbon and the Esoteric Character of the *Guide of the Perplexed*," *AJS Review* 6 (1981): 87 n. 1; Tzvi Langermann, "A New Source for Samuel ibn Tibbon's Translation of the *Guide of the Perplexed* and His Notes on It" (in Hebrew), *Pe'amim* 72 (Summer 1997): 51 n 1.

3. Ibn Tibbon's significance was acknowledged early on by Georges Vajda in his study of Ibn Tibbon's *Ma'amar Yikkavu ha-Mayim* and its refutation by Jacob ben Sheshet; Vajda, *Recherches sur la philosophie et la kabbale dans la pensée juive du Moyen Age* (Paris: Mouton, 1962), pp. 14–31. An abridged English version of this chapter appeared as Vajda, "An Analysis of *Ma'amar yiqqawu ha-Mayim* by Samuel ben Judah Ibn Tibbon," *Journal of Jewish Studies* 10, no. 3–4 (1959): 137–49. Yet, it was Aviezer Ravitzky's pioneering work that brought Ibn Tibbon's contributions in philosophy and exegesis to the fore. See Aviezer Ravitzky, "The Thought of Zeraḥiah ben Isaac ben She'alti'el Ḥen and Maimonidean-Tibbonian Philosophy in the Thirteenth Century" (in Hebrew) (Ph.D. diss., Hebrew University, 1979); A. Ravitzky, "The Possibility of Existence and Its Accidentality in Thirteenth-Century Maimonidean Interpretation" (in Hebrew), *Da'at* 2–3 (1978–79): 67–97; A. Ravitzky, "The Hypostasis of Divine Wisdom in Thirteenth-Century Jewish Thought in Italy" (in Hebrew), *Italia* 3, no. 1–2 (1981): 7–38; A. Ravitzky, "Samuel ibn Tibbon"; A. Ravitzky, "Aristotle's Book of *Meteorology* and the Ways of Maimonidean Exegesis in the Account of Creation" (in Hebrew), *Jerusalem Studies in Jewish Thought* 9 (1990): 225–49. A number of recent studies have further filled out our knowledge of Ibn Tibbon's contributions. James Robinson has edited Ibn Tibbon's *Commentary on Ecclesiastes* in "Philosophy and Exegesis in Ibn Tibbon's *Commentary on Ecclesiastes*" (Ph.D. diss., Harvard University, 2002). See also Carlos Fraenkel, *From Maimonides to Samuel ibn Tibbon: The Method of "The Guide of the Perplexed"* (in Hebrew) (Jerusalem: Magnes Press, forthcoming), which deals with Ibn Tibbon's notes to Maimonides' *Guide*. I wish to thank Zev Harvey for bringing this last reference to my attention.

4. The esoteric orientation of Ibn Tibbon's interpretation of Maimonides is already evident in his early works—epistles, critical notes appended to his translation of the *Guide*, a glossary of philosophical terms, and introductions to his translations of various works of Maimonides—but it is extensively developed in his two later works: his *Commentary on Ecclesiastes* and *Ma'amar Yikkavu ha-Mayim*. Ibn Tibbon saw himself as one of the few interpreters uniquely able to comprehend Maimonides' esoteric doctrines, a claim that finds support in a statement by Abraham Maimuni, Maimonides' son, who testifies that his father considered Ibn Tibbon a great sage and one who understood the secrets of the *Guide*. See *Koveẓ Teshuvot ha-Rambam ve-Iggerotav (Collection of Maimonides' Responsa and Letters)*, ed. A. Lichtenberg (Leipzig, 1859; reprint, Jerusalem, 1967), vol. 3, p. 16. Even though Ibn Tibbon's works were composed before the first major wave of the Maimonidean controversy in the 1230s, he shows awareness of the fact that the Jewish community since Maimonides' lifetime was divided over his writings, and he speculates that his own reading of Maimonides would be criticized. In fact, it was—in particular, by the Kabbalist Jacob ben Sheshet, who attacked Ibn Tibbon in his work *Meshiv Devarim Nekhoḥim*. A comprehensive discussion of Ibn Tibbon's esotericism can be found in "Samuel ibn Tibbon." Jacob ben Sheshet's polemic against Ibn Tibbon is discussed in Vajda, *Recherches*, and Dov Schwartz, "The Debate over the Maimonidean Theory of Providence in Thirteenth-Century Jewish Philosophy," *Jewish Studies Quarterly* 2, no. 2 (1995): 188–91.

5. A. Ravitzky, "Samuel ibn Tibbon," p. 88. Ibn Tibbon may have composed another major philosophical-exegetical treatise, *Ner ha-Ḥofesh*. This work is mentioned

at the beginning of *Ma'amar Yikkavu ha-Mayim* and apparently dealt with passages in the Torah. However, no such work has come down to us. See A. Ravitzky, "The Thought of Zeraḥiah," pp. 16–18. The influence of Ibn Tibbon on European and Italian philosophical exegesis in the thirteenth century is discussed extensively throughout Ravitzky's dissertation.

6. Samuel ibn Tibbon, *Ma'amar Yikkavu ha-Mayim*, ed. M. L. Bisliches (Pressburg, 1837) (hereafter cited as MYH). All citations will be from this edition. As noted, the *Commentary on Ecclesiastes* has been edited in a doctoral dissertation by James Robinson.

7. Job is discussed in chaps. 15–18, pp. 100–117.

8. Ibn Tibbon's often impenetrable, esoteric style of writing perhaps best explains the dearth of studies written on him.

9. Moreover, when at the end of the treatise Ibn Tibbon finally deals with the original problem in physics, his solution is by no means clear. That solution is discussed in MYH, pp. 133–35, 143–46. Neither Vajda nor Ravitzky attempts to tackle this difficult issue, and wisely so; it deserves an independent study of its own. A variety of interpretations of Ibn Tibbon's views on creation can be found in medieval sources and are discussed in A. Ravitzky, "Aristotle's Book of *Meteorology*," pp. 244–50.

10. This letter was written in 1199. For Ibn Tibbon's discussion of the book of Job, see Diesendruck, pp. 355–56. MYH was written no earlier than 1221, according to Moritz Steinschneider, *Die Hebraïsche Übersetzungen des Mittelalters und die Juden als Dolmetscher* (Berlin, 1893), p. 200. It therefore postdates the letter.

11. Much of this chapter draws on my earlier article, "Samuel ibn Tibbon on the Book of Job," *AJS Review* 24, no. 2 (Fall 1999): 263–300. However, a number of substantial revisions have been made in some of its arguments and conclusions.

12. MYH, pp. 100–101. Psalm 73 is given a lengthy treatment in MYH, pp. 70–100. Naḥmanides also sees a connection between Psalm 73 and the Book of Job; see *Kitvey Ramban*, vol. 1, pp. 20–21. The connection between the two has also been the subject of speculation among modern scholars. See Paul Dhorme, *A Commentary on the Book of Job*, trans. Harold Knight (London: Thomas Nelson and Sons, 1967), pp. clxii–clxiv.

13. See MYH, pp. 103, 105, 110–14.

14. See chapter 3, section headed "Maimonides on Job."

15. In his reinterpretation of Satan's two arrivals, Ibn Tibbon has also managed to justify why Job's children die, a philosophical problem that Maimonides ignores. As just noted, they die because of their own sins. Ibn Tibbon never specifies what their sins consisted of, but he may have had in mind their regular feasts of eating and drinking mentioned in Job 1:4. As we saw in chapter 3, Maimonides passes harsh judgment on indulgences of this sort.

16. MYH, p. 101.

17. Ibn Tibbon's *Commentary on Ecclesiastes* is largely concerned with immortality. The notion in Greek and Islamic philosophy that immortality is consequent upon intellectual perfection has been extensively examined. See, for instance, Phillip Merlan, *Monopsychism, Mysticism, and Metaconsciousness* (The Hague: Martinus Nijhoff, 1963), especially pp. 85–113; and Davidson, *Alfarabi, Avicenna, and Averroes*, pp. 34–43, 53–58, 70–73, 106–16.

18. MYH, pp. 101–2.

19. Here I depart from the NJPS translation in order to better capture Ibn Tibbon's understanding of the biblical text. I have made the subject of the second clause

"God" rather than "man" because, as I will explain, Ibn Tibbon understands the verse in this manner. The Hebrew original, in fact, is ambiguous here, since the impersonal subject of the clause is co-opted into the third-person masculine verb *yeshurenah*.

20. MYH, p. 104.

21. Ibid.

22. I depart from the NJPS translation, which places the indefinite article in front of "action." Ibn Tibbon clearly understands the verse to be referring to action in the generic sense.

23. MYH, pp. 104–5. I translate the term *shaḥat* here as "destruction" rather than "Pit," as in the NJPS translation. "Destruction" better signifies the loss of immortality to which Ibn Tibbon is referring here.

24. MYH, p. 105.

25. MYH, p. 106f.

26. I have departed from the NJPS translation by translating *mal'akh* as "angel" rather than "representative," since the former rendering is the way Ibn Tibbon understands the term.

27. MYH, pp. 105–6.

28. *Guide*, introduction, p. 11.

29. See chapter 3, section headed "Maimonides on Job."

30. A reference to an earlier section of Ibn Tibbon's discussion, MYH, p. 106.

31. MYH, p. 108.

32. Standard Hebrew edition of the *Guide*, III:17, p. 23b.

33. Diesendruck, p. 356. I will discuss this issue at greater length later in this chapter.

34. The citations are from the passage under discussion here.

35. MYH, p. 109.

36. Ibn Tibbon seems to understand the notion of basking in the "light of life" in Job 33:30 as a reference to immortality. Interestingly, Saadiah understands that phrase in precisely the same way. While there is little to suggest that Ibn Tibbon was influenced by Saadiah's reading of Job, it is possible that he was acquainted with it from his knowledge of Arabic.

37. See chapter 3, section headed "Maimonides on Job."

38. MYH, pp. 109–10.

39. MYH, pp. 114–15.

40. See earlier in this section.

41. *Guide*, III:17, p. 465.

42. See chapter 3, section headed "Antecedents."

43. MYH, pp. 102–3, cited earlier in this section.

44. I depart from the NJPS "*from* their affliction" and translate "*through* their affliction" in order to capture Ibn Tibbon's understanding of the verse. The difference depends on how one translates the preposition *be-* in the word *be-'onyo*. Ibn Tibbon tells us explicitly that he understands this preposition to mean "by means of" or "through" (MYH, p. 115).

45. MYH, p. 115.

46. MYH, pp. 104–5. How prophetic communication can be impersonal is an issue that cannot preoccupy us here, but it is certainly possible in the type of philosophical system that Ibn Tibbon supports. A thinker such as Gersonides, for instance, provides an instructive example of this possibility since he, like Ibn Tibbon, is influenced both by Maimonides and Averroes. Gersonides argues that prophecy is an im-

personal process by which the prophet's imagination concretizes information that the prophet retrieves from the Divine Mind by virtue of his intellectual perfection. I shall have occasion to discuss Gersonides' view in my chapter on him.

47. MYH, p. 106. The esoteric reading would therefore require that the upper-case "H" in my translation be converted to lower-case. Ibn Tibbon notes that other commentators have opted for the exoteric reading, an observation that is borne out by looking at how Rashi and Ibn Ezra deal with the same passage.

48. The reference here is to one who responds to suffering by prayer or one who has been saved by the angel—i.e., general providence—cases discussed previously by Ibn Tibbon in his exposition of Job 33:14–31.

49. The reference here is to the Separate Intellects.

50. MYH, p. 107.

51. Ibid. The reference to God here as "first cause" of events in the world below, including suffering, also has philosophically suggestive overtones. This phrase calls to mind Aristotle's Prime Mover, who is the impersonal source of all events in the universe.

52. A. Ravitzky, "Samuel ibn Tibbon," pp. 118–19.

53. MYH, p. 117.

54. Ibid.

55. See chapter 2, section headed "Concluding Reflections."

56. See chapter 3, n. 56, for sources on Maimonides' conception of immortality.

57. Diesendruck, pp. 355–56.

58. Diesendruck, p. 357. In proposing this form of providence, Ibn Tibbon ties Maimonides' theory of providence to the practical intellect, as a number of other interpreters have done.

59. See n. 17 of this chapter.

60. See chapter 3, section headed "Maimonides on Job."

61. Another clue in Maimonides that may help explain Ibn Tibbon's interpretation but is not mentioned by him is that, according to Maimonides, Job loses faith in reward in the afterlife on account of his suffering and comes to believe that "there is no hope after death" (*Guide* III:22, p. 492). Ibn Tibbon may have inferred from these remarks that when Job underwent his transformation and graduated to a more sophisticated philosophical awareness at the end of the story, he returned to his belief in the afterlife.

62. Ibn Tibbon never actually declares a position on whether the Book of Job is an allegory or represents actual events. My assumption is that he follows Maimonides' position that it is indeed an allegory, since he accepts Maimonides' basic approach to the book as a whole.

63. If this reading is correct, the lesson Job learns from God in Ibn Tibbon's reading is quite different from that found in Maimonides. In Maimonides, Job learns from God that His ways are unfathomable and that no knowledge of His essential attributes is possible. In Ibn Tibbon, Job discovers that there are differences between God's ways and ours, but the knowledge Job gains about God is quite positive in content in that he is told how God, unlike man, can inflict suffering without our attributing injustice to Him.

64. A similar point is made by Aviezer Ravitzky with respect to Ibn Tibbon's views on creation. Here, too, Ibn Tibbon's differences with Maimonides appear to be exegetical, not philosophical. See A. Ravitzky, "Aristotle's Book of *Meteorology*," pp. 239–44.

65. MYH, pp. 173–75; A. Ravitzky, "Samuel ibn Tibbon," pp. 108–16.

66. MYH, pp. 101, 117. As noted, Ibn Tibbon sees a link between the Book of Job and Psalm 73 in particular. This is borne out in his commentary on the latter in which he argues that the central message of Psalm 73 is that true providence is immortality (MYH, pp. 71, 91–92, 98). The issue of providence in general seems to have been a major preoccupation for Ibn Tibbon. A point Ibn Tibbon makes with great frequency throughout *Ma'amar Yikkavu ha-Mayim* and in different contexts is that the biblical text teaches us that there is providence over human beings despite the fact that God is elevated above the matters of this world. See MYH, pp. 31, 32, 41, 51, 61–63, 66, 172. At one point, Ibn Tibbon even claims that this point is the central message of the Bible as a whole (MYH, p. 63). Note also that Ibn Tibbon's *Commentary on Ecclesiastes* is largely concerned with providence in that it reads Ecclesiastes as a book focused on the theme of immortality, the highest form of providence, in Ibn Tibbon's thinking.

67. Ibn Tibbon may also have influenced a number of other medieval Jewish philosophers in their respective interpretations of Job. Zeraḥiah Ḥen could be included in this group, but as we shall see in the next chapter, which is devoted to Zeraḥiah, the relationship between Zeraḥiah's interpretation of Job and that of Ibn Tibbon is somewhat ambiguous. The fourteenth-century Provençal figure Abba Mari ben Eligdor produced a commentary on Job that has survived in a number of manuscripts, and my tentative assessment is that he is influenced by Ibn Tibbon's reading of Job. A full discussion of this relationship will have to be left for another occasion, because it is difficult to locate the philosophical ideas in his commentary on account of the elusive style in which it is written. Abba Mari provides a detailed paraphrase of Job, and it is only with a careful reading that one discerns his philosophical views. Information on Abba Mari can be found in Ernst Renan and Adolf Neubauer, *Écrivains juifs français du XIVème siècle*, vol. 27 of *Histoire littéraire de la France* (Paris, 1893), pp. 548–52; *Encyclopedia Judaica*, vol. 1, p. 37. See my appendix for information about this commentary.

I may also mention here Nissim ben Moshe of Marseilles. This thirteenth-century figure did not produce a commentary on Job. However, in his commentary on the Torah, *Ma'aseh Nissim*—to which I have referred on occasion—Nissim discusses Job in one lengthy passage and seems to adopt the central notion from Ibn Tibbon that Job learns from Elihu that the immortality of the intellect is the highest form of providence (pp. 194–95). Nissim has been left out of my discussion here because his treatment of Job is not as extensive as that of the three thinkers I have chosen to examine.

I can also mention here that some of the speculations on Job found in the *'Eẓ Ḥayyim* of Aaron ben Elijah, the fourteenth-century Karaite philosopher, are similar to those of Ibn Tibbon. According to Aaron, Job's final lesson includes an appreciation of the notion that true reward is immortality of the soul. Moreover, Aaron treats this as an esoteric philosophical doctrine that must be concealed from the masses. There is, however, no evidence to suggest a direct connection between Aaron and Ibn Tibbon. See Frank, "The Religious Philosophy of the Karaite Aaron ben Elijah," p. 78.

68. Information on Immanuel as a philosopher can be found in Israel Ravitzky, "R. Immanuel ben Solomon of Rome, *Commentary on the Song of Songs: Philosophical Division*" (master's thesis, Hebrew University, 1970); Jaqueline Genot-Bismuth, "Poétique et philosophie dans l'oeuvre d'Immanuel de Rome" (Ph.D. diss., University of Paris, Paris, 1976); Aviezer Ravitzky, "Immanuel of Rome's *Commentary on the Book of Proverbs*: Its Sources" (in Hebrew), *Kiryat Sefer* 56 (1981): 726–39; Deborah Shechterman, "The Philosophy of Immanuel of Rome in Light of His Commentary on the

Book of Genesis" (in Hebrew) (Ph.D. diss., Hebrew University, 1984). The only one of Immanuel's commentaries to be published is his *Perush 'al Sefer Mishley (Commentary on Proverbs)*, ed. and introd. David Goldstein (Jerusalem: Magnes Press, 1980).

69. The commentary exists in three complete manuscripts. Citations will be from Ms. Parma 58.

70. Zeraḥiah Ḥen is the other Maimonidean philosopher-exegete who provides a line-by-line commentary on Job. Zeraḥiah's commentary probably predates that of Immanuel. It was completed in 1290 or 1291, and although we have no date for Immanuel's commentary, it is likely to have been later, given that Immanuel was a younger contemporary of Zeraḥiah. These observations raise the question as to whether there is evidence that Zeraḥiah's commentary influenced that of Immanuel. Scholars are generally agreed that Immanuel probably studied with Zeraḥiah in Rome. Some scholars have also assumed that Immanuel's commentaries bear the influence of Zeraḥiah's teachings. However, Aviezer Ravitzky notes that there is no mention of Zeraḥiah in Immanuel's writings, and that the former's influence on the latter thus cannot be taken for granted. Nonetheless, Ravitzky expresses surprise that Immanuel would make no mention of his teacher and therefore urges that the relationship between the two be subjected to further inquiry. The entire question is discussed in A. Ravitzky, "The Thought of Zeraḥiah," pp. 108–19.

71. Ms. Parma 58, fol. 1v. Immanuel's invocation is composed in poetic verse: "I will follow for the most part the intention of Rabbi Moses ben Maimon / I will be his faithful servant . . . I will draw living waters from his interpretations / I will reveal as needed some of his allusions [to philosophical secrets]": ואמשוך ברוב אחר כוונת רבינו משה בן מימון / ואהיה אצלו אמון . . . ואדלה מים חיים מבאריו / וכפי הצורך אגלה רמיזותיו.

72. Immanuel's overall approach to Job is conveniently laid out in an extensive introduction (ibid., fols. 1v–5v).

73. Immanuel is notorious for not citing his sources. See A. Ravitzky, "Immanuel of Rome's *Commentary on the Book of Proverbs.*" Immanuel certainly knew of Ibn Tibbon's works. Both *Ma'amar Yikkavu ha-Mayim* and Ibn Tibbon's *Commentary on Ecclesiastes* are mentioned in Immanuel's *Maḥbarot.* In Immanuel's other biblical commentaries, passages from Ibn Tibbon are often copied word for word, sometimes with attribution and sometimes without. See A. Ravitzky, "The Thought of Zeraḥiah," pp. 108–11.

74. Immanuel's interpretation of Elihu's address is summarized in his introduction to the commentary (Ms. Parma 58, fol. 5r): "The third purpose of this book is [to inform us about] that which Elihu contributes in his address which is the belief in immortality of the soul and its having spiritual reward and spiritual punishment in the world of souls." הכוונה השלישית הנרמזת בזה הספר היא במה שחדש אליהוא בדבריו והיא אמונת השארות נפש האדם והיות לה גמול רוחני ועונש רוחני אחר המות בעולם הנשמות. Immanuel's exegesis of Elihu's remarks is found in Ms. Parma 58, fol. 94v f., with Job 33 being treated on fols. 98r–101ṛ.

75. Note, for instance, Immanuel's interpretation of Job 33:28, which concludes the description of the salvation that the angel provides for the suffering individual. The verse reads as follows according to Immanuel's understanding: "His *nefesh* is redeemed from destruction, / His life will see light." Commenting on this verse, Immanuel tells us, " 'His *nefesh* is redeemed'—that is, his body—'from destruction' . . . and his intellectual soul, which is his 'life,' will merit the afterworld to bask in the light of God's light, may He be blessed" (Ms. Parma 58, fol. 101v). פדה נפשו והוא גופו מעבור בשחת . . . ונפשו המשכלת אשר היא חיתו תזכה באחרית לאור באור השם ית'. The suffering individual who corrects his ways will experience physical protection in this life,

as indicated by the first half of the verse, while at the same time meriting immortality of the intellect, as indicated in the second half of the verse.

76. *B.T. Shabbat* 32a; chapter 2, section headed "The Commentary on Job."

77. Ms. Parma 58, fol. 101r. Immanuel could be following either Maimonides or Ibn Tibbon with this reading. Even though in my reading neither philosopher identifies the angel with the human intellect, the views of both thinkers regarding the angel are sufficiently murky that both could be interpreted this way.

78. Ibid., fol. 116v.

79. Only a detailed analysis of the entire body of Immanuel's philosophical commentaries will yield answers on this question. Support for an esoteric reading of Immanuel's commentaries has been argued by Shechterman.

80. See earlier in this chapter, section headed "Ibn Tibbon on Job."

81. Ms. Parma 58, fol. 5r–5v.

82. Immanuel's desire to highlight this distinction appears to emerge when he asserts that the issue of immortality is "something which is not mentioned at all, neither in the remarks of Job, nor in the remarks of his three friends" (ibid., fol. 5r): והוא דבר שלא נזכר כלל לא בדברי איוב ולא בדברי שלשת רעיו .

83. What is interesting is not just that Immanuel makes the change in Bildad's view, but the way he does it. In his summary of Bildad's viewpoint, Immanuel cites Maimonides' description verbatim from the *Guide* in Ibn Tibbon's Hebrew translation but changes one key expression. Instead of undeserved suffering leading to reward in "the afterlife" (*'olam ha-ba'*), as Maimonides' original description claims, it leads to reward in "this world" (*'olam ha-zeh*). (See standard Hebrew edition of the *Guide* III:22, p. 35a.) It is only the astute reader who would recognize that Immanuel has made such a change. This may help explain why Immanuel does not identify the views of the participants in the dialogue with the specific schools of thought that Maimonides attributes to them. Rather, he refers to their opinions as belonging collectively "to the sages" (*la-ḥakhamim*) (Ms. Parma, fol. 4r). Immanuel may have felt that he could not support Maimonides' correlation, given the critical change that he makes in Bildad's view, which no longer matches the Mu'tazilite view as described by Maimonides. These observations also lend credence to Shechterman's view that Immanuel often appears to be plagiarizing from other thinkers but in reality makes small but critical changes in the passages he copies in order to indicate that he has his own views on a given matter. Shechterman surmises that this technique has its origin in the *scriptor* mode of exegesis found in Christian biblical commentaries during Immanuel's period. See Shechterman, pp. 28–93.

84. For information on Elijah, see Shalom Rosenberg, "The *Sefer ha-Higayon* of Elijah ben Eliezer ha-Yerushalmi" (in Hebrew), in *Da'at* 1, no. 1 (Winter 1978): 63–64. *Sefer ha-Higayon* is Elijah's work on logic. Besides this work and the Job commentary, Elijah also produced *Aderet Eliyahu*, a work on the principles of faith; *Yesod Mora'*, a commentary on portions of the *Guide*, in particular the section dealing with Ezekiel 1; a commentary on *Sefer ha-Bahir*; and a work entitled *Sefer ha-Shaḥak*. All are preserved in manuscript.

85. This work is preserved in a single manuscript: Ms. Vatican 250/8, fols. 104r–132r. The text is complete except for the last page, which is found in Ms. Vatican 530/30, having apparently become detached from the rest of the text.

86. Elijah's interpretation of the early events in the Book of Job is found primarily in Ms. Vatican 250/8, fols. 109r–119v. Elijah, however, does not follow Maimonides entirely. He rejects Maimonides' view of Satan, which, according to Elijah's reading, equates Satan with matter. Instead, Elijah proposes that Satan is chance

occurrence (Ms. Vatican 250/8, fol. 110r–110v). Elihu's opinion is discussed by Elijah on fols. 128v–132r.

87. The precise meaning of Elijah's interpretation of Elihu's view is obscured somewhat by his esoteric style of writing, but it is not too difficult to discern the connection he draws between perfection of the intellect and immortality. Note, for instance, the following passage, in which Elijah provides an interpretation of the activity of Elihu's angel that saves an individual from illness: "Danger occurs to the intellect when it has any ties with the body. Therefore, if one rejects God, his illness will become worse and 'he will detest food' (Job 33:20). But if he strays from it [i.e., the body], he will be like an ill person who goes from illness to health. He will be saved from death on account of his receiving wisdom which is at the opposite extreme from demise and death. If he is an intellect *in actu* attached perpetually [to God], this danger does not occur. The reason for this danger is his being [only] a potential intellect" (Ms. Vatican 250/8, fol. 130r). והסכנה קרתה לשכל לפי שיש לו שום קשר עם הגוף ולפי' אם יהיה אלהים אחריו יכבד חליו וזהמתו לחם. ואם יטה ממנו יהיה כחולה נעתק מן החולי אל הבריאות וינצל מן המות לקבלו החכמה אשר היא בתכלית מרותק מן האבדון והמות. ואלו היה שכל בפועל מדובק תמיד לא קרה לו זאת הסכנה אבל סבת הסכנה זאת היא להיותו שכל בכח. Elijah appears to treat Elihu's description of an ill person who is saved from death by the angel as an allegory for the salvation of the soul from death through the perfection of the intellect. Although the identity of the angel is hidden by Elijah, in one passage he gives insight about its identity by referring to it as "one of those [beings] that dwells on the first level of the three levels of existence that makes contact with an individual; it is this [being] that imparts to him [i.e., the ill person in Job 33:19f.] the capacity for immortality" (Ms. Vatican 250/8, fol. 129v): אחד מן היושבים במדרגה הראשונה משלשת מדרגות המציאות יציץ על האדם והוא שיעתיק אליו כח ההשארות. Elijah seems to be associating the angel with the Active Intellect, which is found in the world of the Separate Intellects—the first level of being, according to a common demarcation in medieval Jewish philosophy—and imparts immortality to human beings by providing them with the capacity for intellectual perfection.

88. Ibid., fol. 130r–130v.

89. Elijah's interpretation of the end of the story is contained in the lone page of the manuscript in Ms. Vatican 530/8.

90. An esoteric reading of Elijah finds support in a passage in which he presents the argument that, strictly speaking, God cannot "reward" human beings because that would imply that God has benefited from us and therefore owes us something (Ms. Vatican 250/8, fol. 131r). Here Elijah seems to be arguing for a philosophical and hence impersonal conception of God and a view of providence that does not include physical and material reward.

91. Ibid., fol. 118r.

92. Another interesting feature Elijah adds to his commentary on Job that is not found in Maimonides or in Ibn Tibbon is the use of Aristotelian logic to classify the arguments between Job and his friends. According to Elijah, Job and his friends present dialectical arguments that are not convincing, and that is why their discussion is structured as argument and response. Elihu presents superior demonstrative arguments that *are* convincing, and that is why his address receives no response from the others (Ms. Vatican 250/8, fol. 104v).

93. Arundi was probably from Ronda in Spain; hence the name Arundi. He is known to have lived in Italy and perhaps Provence. Besides his commentary on Job, he produced a medical work entitled *Ma'amar bi-Sgulah,* preserved in manuscript.

These details come from a brief unattributed article in *Encyclopedia Judaica*, vol. 3, pp. 663–64.

94. Arundi's commentary exists in a number of complete manuscripts. All citations will be from Ms. Milano-Ambrosiana 16 (C300 Inf), fols. 1r–50v. Arundi's commentary had to have been written sometime in the mid- or late fourteenth century, since it attacks Gersonides' commentary on Job, which was completed in 1325.

95. Ibid., fols. 3r–4r.

96. Ibid., fols. 1r–2r.

97. Elihu's speech is dealt with ibid., fols. 31r–46r. According to Arundi, the ultimate lesson of the Book of Job as described by Elihu is as follows: "It has become clear from everything that we have mentioned that ultimate felicity for a man is in his most respected and divine activity, and that is in the activity of theoretical speculation and the cognition of intelligibles through which a person comes to cognize God, may He be blessed, as much as is possible for him to cognize [God]. [It has also become clear] that individual providence for a human being in its primary meaning is in this activity alone, for it is from this [activity] that he experiences immortality of the soul and eternal life with the greatest of pleasure that is unending" (ibid., fol. 39v). הנה כבר התבאר מכל מה שזכרנו שההצלחה האמיתית לאדם הוא בפעל היותר נכבד והיותר אלהי שבו הוא פעול' העיון וההשגה מהמושכלות שבאמצעותם יגיע האדם להשגת השית' מה שאפשר לו להשיג ושההשגחה הפרטית הראויה לאדם על הכוונה הראשונה היא בזה הפעל לבד לפי שמזה ימשך לו ההשארות הנצחי והחיים התמידיים בתענוג מופלג בלתי כלה.

98. Ibid., fol. 32r. Arundi reads this notion out of the same verses Maimonides and Ibn Tibbon saw as referring to prophecy: "For God speaks time and again /— Though man does not perceive it—/ In a dream, a night vision, / When deep sleep falls upon men, / When they slumber in their beds" (Job 33:14–15). Arundi takes the references to God's communication at night not as an allusion to prophecy, but as theoretical speculation, which, according to Arundi, is best engaged in during the nighttime hours.

99. In Arundi's words: "After Elihu adduced all these arguments against Job and his friends . . . , [Job] was worthy of the first type of communication which Elihu mentioned in his first response" (Ms. Milano-Ambosiana 16, fol. 46a). ואחר שסדר אליהוא כל הטענות כנגד איוב וחבריו . . . הנה היה ראוי לדרך הראשון שזכר אליהוא במענה. Arundi provides two reasons to explain why God's communication to Job is described as coming in a *se'arah* or tempest, an issue that, as we have seen, drew Ibn Tibbon's attention. The first is that the communication was "in the manner of a chastisement." What Arundi appears to be saying is that the storm imagery is symbolic of the fact that the cognitions Job has in the final chapters are in the form of criticism—or, perhaps more accurately, self-criticism. According to the second interpretation, Arundi interprets the tempest as a metaphor for Job's material make-up, which prevents him from having direct cognition of God. Arundi's reasoning for this interpretation is excessively terse, but his argument appears to be based on a passage in Eliphaz's first address to Job, which he cites. In that passage Eliphaz refers to nighttime communications in a manner that resonates with the notion of prophetic dreams mentioned by Elihu (Job 4:12–21). What is apparently most important for Arundi is that the term *se'arah* appears here—though Arundi ignores the fact that it is spelled with the Hebrew letter *sin* instead of *samekh*: "A wind passed by me, / Making the *se'arah* [NJPS 'hair'] of my flesh bristle" (Job 4:15). In his explication of this passage in its original context (Ms. Milano-Ambrosiana 16, fol. 5r), Arundi interprets Eliphaz to be referring to intellectual cognition, not prophetic communication, while the mention of *se'arah*

refers to the material make-up of human beings, which prevents direct perception of God. The parallel between Eliphaz's remarks and those of Elihu therefore establishes that Job did not receive prophetic communication from God, and that the *se'arah* is a metaphor for the material composition of human beings, which makes it impossible to perceive God directly.

100. Like Elijah ben Eliezer ha-Yerushalmi, Arundi also attempts to interpret the different arguments presented in the Book of Job according to Aristotelian logic. See Ms. Milano-Ambrosiana 16, fols. 2r, 4r. A similar attempt to organize the arguments in Job around the principles of logic can be found in the nineteenth-century commentary on Job of Malbim, which, as noted earlier (chapter 1, n. 12), is heavily influenced by medieval Jewish philosophers.

CHAPTER 5

1. A. Ravitzky, "The Thought of Zeraḥiah," pp. 69–75. As Ravitzky points out, Zeraḥiah refers to himself as an old man in 1289–90 in his correspondence with Hillel of Verona. That is about as explicit a statement as we have in Zeraḥiah's writings about anything pertaining to his age. The reverence shown to Zeraḥiah in Rome as a teacher of Maimonides is evidence of a rapid growth of interest in philosophical learning in Italy during his lifetime. Half a century earlier, the philosopher-exegete Jacob Anatoli had been in Italy and lamented the lack of interest in philosophical learning in that country (A. Ravitzky, "The Hypostasis of Divine Wisdom," pp. 7–11).

2. Zeraḥiah's works are discussed in A. Ravitzky, "The Thought of Zeraḥiah," pp. 75–94. Zeraḥiah was also responsible for a number of translations of philosophical and scientific works from Arabic to Hebrew (pp. 91–94). There are a number of works attributed to Zeraḥiah that are either not his or are unlikely to have been his (pp. 84–91).

3. Zeraḥiah's connection to the Tibbonian school is the subject of Aviezer Ravitzky's dissertation. It is also discussed in A. Ravitzky, "The Hypostasis of Divine Wisdom," pp. 11–14. There is evidence that Jacob Anatoli also exerted substantial influence on Zeraḥiah, as argued in Martin L. Gordon, "The Philosophical Rationalism of Jacob Anatoli" (Ph.D. diss., Yeshiva University, 1974), pp. 243–49. Zeraḥiah, however, never refers to Anatoli by name.

4. A. Ravitzky, "The Hypostasis of Divine Wisdom," pp. 8–11. Ravitzky notes that in the thirteenth century Jewish thinkers in Italy who came from other parts of Europe—such as Zeraḥiah, who was originally from Spain—did not absorb the teachings of Christian scholasticism. However, Jewish philosophers who grew up in Italy in the same period did take an interest in Christian thought. In the latter category are such thinkers as Moses of Salerno and Judah Romano. But just because Zeraḥiah was not influenced by Christian philosophy does not mean that he was unaware of its presence. As Ravitzky notes, Zeraḥiah urges his Jewish contemporaries to engage in philosophical thought in order that Christian philosophers not be able to deride them for their philosophical ignorance and their inability to justify their beliefs from a philosophical standpoint.

5. A. Ravitzky, "The Thought of Zeraḥiah," pp. 66–67.

6. I have referred to some of Aviezer Ravitzky's studies in previous notes. For citations of all of Ravitzky's studies, see chapter 4, n. 3.

7. *Tikvat Enosh*, ed. Israel Schwartz (Berlin, 1868; reprint, Jerusalem, 1969), vol. 1, pp. 169–293.

8. Ms. Munich 79, fols. 2r–101v.

9. Steinschneider, *Hebraïsche Bibliographie* 12 (1872): 43–47, especially pp. 46–47. Steinschneider found similar omissions in Schwartz's edition of Zeraḥiah's commentary on Proverbs, which had been published elsewhere.

10. Abraham Geiger also noted similar problems with Schwartz's edition of David Kimḥi's commentary on Job, also published in *Tikvat Enosh.* See Geiger, "Alte Commentare zu Hiob," *Jüdische Zeitschrift* 7 (1869): 142.

11. My citations of the Munich manuscript will be designated by "M," followed by the chapter and verse in the biblical text upon which Zeraḥiah is commenting, and then the folio number. I will also refer to pages in Schwartz's edition in parentheses. In addition, I will provide the Hebrew from the Munich manuscript in those instances in which there is a divergence between it and Schwartz's edition.

12. A discussion of these two versions is contained in my article, "Did Zeraḥiah Ḥen Compose Two Versions of His *Commentary on the Book of Job*?" *Da'at* 48 (Winter 2002): v–xxvi.

13. *Iggeret le-Yehudah ben Shlomoh,* Ms. Cambridge Add. 1235, fols. 91r–97v.

14. Aviezer Ravitzky gives a list of five such passages in "The Thought of Zeraḥiah," p. 83 n. 1. Ravitzky argues convincingly against a number of nineteenth-century scholars who believe that Zeraḥiah's correspondence with Judah ben Solomon was written after his commentary on Job. Ravitzky demonstrates that the correspondence is earlier. We would have been helped in our understanding of Zeraḥiah's reading of Job by his commentary on the *Guide* were it not that the section dealing with Job is lost, along with Zeraḥiah's commentary on most of part 3 of the *Guide.* Nonetheless, we do have access to one portion of that section of the commentary, since Zeraḥiah cites a lengthy passage from it in his correspondence with Judah ben Solomon.

15. M, introduction, fol. 2r (Schwartz, p. 169).

16. M, introduction, fols. 2v–3r (Schwartz, pp. 170–71). Ibn Tibbon's commentary on Ecclesiastes has been edited by James Robinson. See chapter 4, n. 3. Moses ibn Tibbon's commentary on the Song of Songs has also been published; see Moses Ibn Tibbon, *Perush Shir ha-Shirim Me-R. Moshe ibn Tibbon* (Lyck: Mekiẓey Nirdamim, 1874).

17. Zeraḥiah's dependence on Maimonides first emerges toward the end of his introduction, when he explicitly adopts Maimonides' explication of the five opinions of Job and his friends. See M, introduction, fol. 4r (Schwartz, p. 173). See also M, 36: 26, fol. 86v (Schwartz, pp. 236–37).

18. "It is not necessary for me in this commentary to bring in everything that the Rabbi [i.e., Maimonides] stated regarding the introduction to the book of Job, because if I were to do this, it would be superfluous; for my goal is to compose this book for those who know and are sensitized to the words of philosophical wisdom, all the more so to the words of the Rabbi and his intention in the third part of *The Guide of the Perplexed*" (M, introduction, fol. 4v [Schwartz, p. 173]).

19. M, introduction, fol. 4v (Schwartz, p. 173).

20. See, for example, M, introduction, fol. 3r (Schwartz, p. 172), and 3:5, fol. 15v (Schwartz, p. 193–94).

21. See, for example, M, 3:1, fol. 14r (Schwartz, p. 190). Zeraḥiah attacks only Naḥmanides' *peshat* exegesis in the version of the commentary under discussion here. In his earlier version of the commentary, there is also an attack on Naḥmanides' kabbalistic exegesis of Job. Zeraḥiah's opposition to Naḥmanides surfaces in other places. In his correspondence with Hillel of Verona, Zeraḥiah voices strong criticism of Naḥmanides on the question of interpreting narrative passages in the biblical

text as prophetic visions. See R. Kirchheim's edition of the correspondence in *Oẓar Neḥmad* 2 (1857): 124, and A. Ravitzky's discussion of the correspondence in "The Thought of Zeraḥiah," p. 275. Zeraḥiah's attitude toward his exegetical predecessors is summarized in M, 36:26, fol. 86v (Schwartz, pp. 236–37).

22. However, with the Book of Job, Zeraḥiah has the advantage of beginning with a full-length discussion in the *Guide*. In their respective commentaries on Ecclesiastes and the Song of Songs, Samuel ibn Tibbon and his son Moses start off with considerably less in that Maimonides devotes no separate discussion to either of these books.

23. M, introduction, fol. 2r (Schwartz, p. 169).

24. M, 1:15, fol. 11r (Schwartz, p. 185).

25. M, introduction, fol. 2r (Schwartz, p. 169–70). Some commentators are troubled by the fact that Maimonides finds allegorical significance in the name *'Uẓ*, even though it is mentioned as a real location in the biblical text (Lam. 4:21). That such a place actually exists would suggest, contrary to Maimonides' assumptions, that Job was a historical individual. Zeraḥiah seems to have been sensitive to the problem, because he argues that "without a doubt the author [of Job] could have chosen many countries from the countries of the world which exist and are mentioned in books, but this author who composed the book of Job without a doubt intended to mention this name [i.e., *'Uẓ*] which alludes to the issue of insight in order to teach as well that this book was composed and arranged according to insight so as to hint at secrets and intelligent insights worthy for every sage to have acquaintance with." (M, introduction, 2r [Schwartz, p. 170]). Zeraḥiah acknowledges that *'Uẓ* exists, but argues that its existence in no way precludes its being used as an allegorical image in the Book of Job.

26. *B.T. Bava' Batra'* 16a.

27. M, introduction, fol. 3v (Schwartz, p. 172).

28. M, 1:2, fol. 7r–7v (Schwartz, p. 179).

29. M, 1:8, fol. 9v (Schwartz, p. 184).

30. M, 40:14, fol. 97r (Schwartz, p. 289); M, 40:24, fol. 97r (Schwartz, p. 290).

31. M, 1:17–19, fol. 11r (Schwartz, p. 186–87).

32. M, introduction, fol. 3v (Schwartz, p. 173).

33. M, introduction, fol. 3v (Schwartz, p. 172); *Guide* II: introduction, pp. 235–39. Zeraḥiah's interpretation is intriguing given that he criticizes the use of *gematria* in Kabbalah in his correspondence with Hillel of Verona (pp. 132–33). Cf. A. Ravitzky's comments on this issue, "The Thought of Zeraḥiah," pp. 244–46.

34. M, introduction, fol. 3v (Schwartz, p. 173).

35. M, introduction, fol. 3v (Schwartz, p. 172); M, 1:6, fol. 9v (Schwartz, p. 183); M, 1:8, fols. 9v–10r (Schwartz, p. 184); M, 1:11, fol. 10r–10v (Schwartz, pp. 184–85); M, 2:3, fol. 12r (Schwartz, p. 187). Zeraḥiah has to grapple with the mention of Job alongside Noah and Daniel in Ez. 14:14. How is it that Job is a mere fictional character if Ezekiel talks about him in the same breath as two other biblical personalities whose historical existence is beyond question? Zeraḥiah gives three answers. First, Ezekiel may have believed erroneously that Job actually lived. Second, Ezekiel may have referred to Job as a historical individual in order to appeal to the masses but did not himself believe that Job was a historical individual. Third, prophets often speak in allegorical terms without informing the reader, and the mention of Job here may be one such instance (M, introduction, fol. 3r [Schwartz, pp. 171–72]).

36. M, introduction, fol. 2r–2v (Schwartz, p. 170).

37. A similar position is taken by Maimonides, who says that non-Jewish sages

from ancient times onward hide their philosophical secrets from the masses by way of allegory (*Guide* I:17, p. 43).

38. M, 42:5, fol. 100v. This passage is entirely missing in Schwartz's edition: כי המון העם יברחו מן המשלים ואינם רוצים אלא מה שהוא כמשמעו וכפשוטו בכל הענינים.

39. Read with M, אלא.

40. M, introduction, fol. 2v (Schwartz, p. 170).

41. *B.T. Bava' Batra'* 14b, 15a.

42. Read with M, וחובר.

43. Read with M, כשאר.

44. M, introduction, fol. 2v (Schwartz, p. 170).

45. Maimonides, *Guide*, introduction, pp. 8–9. Maimonides actually refers to the divine commandments rather than ethics.

46. M, introduction, fol. 3r (Schwartz, p. 171). This passage is taken almost verbatim from Zeraḥiah's correspondence with Judah ben Solomon (fol. 95r–95v). That Satan and the divine beings relate to matters of natural science will be discussed shortly. Why an acquaintance with providence is prerequisite for understanding divine science is not difficult to figure out. In dealing with providence, one is introduced to the study of God's nature as well as His connection to the world below via the celestial realm. The connection between providence and ethics is less clear. Zeraḥiah seems to be echoing Maimonides' view that human ethics is modeled on God's providential care of the world. See *Guide* I:54, pp. 123–25, where Maimonides tells us that God showed Moses all existent beings so that he would understand how to govern the Israelites (see also *Guide* I:21, pp. 48–49; I:37, p. 86; I:38, p. 87).

47. The notion that the Book of Job exemplifies rational speculation in biblical literature is first suggested in Saadiah Gaon, *The Book of Beliefs and Opinions*, trans. Samuel Rosenblatt, 1:6, p. 27.

48. At the end of the passage under discussion, Zeraḥiah entertains the possibility that the Book of Job came through divine revelation, but this is presented as an afterthought and seems not to have been his primary position. One wonders whether Zeraḥiah inserts this statement as a pious gesture to appease his traditional readers.

49. M, 1:1, fols. 6v–7r (Schwartz, p. 179).

50. M, 1:6, fols. 7v–9v (Schwartz, pp. 180–83). This section is taken from Zeraḥiah's correspondence with Judah ben Solomon (fols. 91r–93r).

51. See chapter 3, section headed "Maimonides on Job." It is possible that Zeraḥiah identifies the divine beings with the natural forms simply because he saw the latter as the most appropriate contrast with matter, which is represented by Satan. After all, matter and form are universally regarded as contrasting entities in Greek and medieval philosophy.

52. See earlier in this section.

53. M, 2:9, fol. 13r (Schwartz, pp. 188–89). The kind of intertextual reading we see here between different portions of the biblical text is not uncommon in medieval Jewish philosophy. See, for instance, Moses ibn Tibbon, *Perush Shir ha-Shirim*, where he reads Song of Songs 3:1 in light of Job 33 (pp. 12b–13b).

54. M, 2:9, fol. 13r (Schwartz, pp. 188–89).

55. According to my own reading of Maimonides (chapter 3, section headed "Maimonides on Job"), Satan is identified with the imagination because Satan is representative of privation and privation characterizes the imagination because an undue emphasis on the latter is synonymous with the privation of knowledge. Since Zeraḥiah identifies Satan with matter and not privation, he does not make this connection. Instead, he finds a commonality between Satan as representative of matter, and

Satan as representative of the imagination on the basis of the notion that the imagination is a physical faculty.

56. See Zeraḥhiah's correspondence, *Iggeret le-Yehudah*, fols. 95v–97v. Zeraḥiah is also clearly influenced by Maimonides' reading of the Garden of Eden story, in which Adam goes from a figure occupied with matters of intellect and rational truths to a figure interested in the imagination and conventional truths (*Guide* I:2, pp. 24–26).

57. M, introduction, fols. 5v–6v (Schwartz, pp. 176–78).

58. M, introduction, fol. 5r (Schwartz, p. 175). The second reason Zeraḥiah gives is that Job repents at the end of the story, and repentance is a major principle of the Torah.

59. The notion that Job's curse is harmless because it is directed only against a duration of time is found in Gregory's *Magna Moralia* (Schreiner, pp. 36–37). Given that Zeraḥiah composed his commentary on Job in a Christian environment, it is not inconceivable that his insight here regarding Job's curse came from an acquaintance with Christian commentaries on Job.

60. M, 1:1, fol. 7r (Schwartz, p. 179).

61. M, 22:5–7, fol. 54r–54v (Schwartz, p. 243); see also M, 22:11, fol. 55r (Schwartz, pp. 244–45). Zeraḥiah appears to base this reading on the verses that follow the passage being explained here (Job 22:9f.), in which Eliphaz emphasizes God's elevation above all His creatures.

62. M, 7:19, fol. 27v (Schwartz, p. 212); 9:18, fol. 31r (Schwartz, pp. 216–17). The notion that Job at times adopts the viewpoints of his friends for the sake of argument is also found in Aquinas (Schreiner, p. 80). Here again is an example of Zeraḥiah providing an interpretation that bears similarity to that of Christian exegetes. As remarked in n. 59, it is not inconceivable that Zeraḥiah was familiar with Christian readings of Job.

63. Read with M, יש בו.

64. The second half of this sentence is missing in Schwartz's edition: ודעתו היה המובחר שבדעות שהרי נאמר בו שהיה חכם ויותר שלם מחבריו.

65. This passage has been censored in the Munich manuscript, and that censorship is reproduced in Schwartz's edition. The censored text reads as follows: והיה נוטה אחר דעת הפ האומ' ב' האומרים בהמ' לכה אלא על צד אחד. The uncensored text can easily be reconstructed from a parallel passage found in Zeraḥiah's correspondence with Judah ben Solomon: והיה נוטה אחר דעת הפילוסופים שאמר בהשגחת המין לא בהשגחת האישים אלא על צד אחד (Ms. Cambridge Add. 1235, fol. 93v). The censor of the Munich manuscript created an acronym out of some of the phrases in the passage in order to conceal its message. He also included a variant reading of one word: האומר or האומרים. The censor seems to have felt that Zeraḥiah's position was too radical because it leans toward the views of the philosophers.

66. This phrase is censored in the Munich manuscript. The acronym הה appears in place of השגחת ה'. Again, the correspondence with Judah ben Solomon helps decipher the text (Ms. Cambridge Add. 1235, fol. 93v).

67. Read with M, המשך.

68. Literally, "the natural thing."

69. Read with M, ענינים רבים טבעיים.

70. I translate the term תמיד here as "common" since it best suites the meaning Zeraḥiah is trying to convey.

71. I have glossed over several lines in which Zeraḥiah attempts to justify Mai-

monides' concealment of such truths since they do not add to the philosophical points being made here.

72. M, 32:2–3, fol. 75v (Schwartz, p. 265). This passage comes out of the correspondence of Judah ben Solomon, fols. 94v–95r.

73. Here again is the NJPS translation of the section of Elihu's speech where the transition is made from the experience of prophecy to physical afflictions (Job 33:15–19):

For God speaks time and again
—Though man does not perceive it—
In a dream, a night vision,
When deep sleep falls upon men,
While they slumber on their beds.
Then He opens men's understanding,
And by disciplining them leaves His signature
To turn man away from an action,
To suppress pride in man.
He spares Him from the Pit,
His person, from perishing by the sword.
He is reproved by pains on his bed,
And the trembling in his bones is constant.

74. This reading is confirmed in Zeraḥiah's subsequent exegesis of the passage. See especially Zeraḥiah's comments on Job 33:18 in M, fol. 78r–78v (Schwartz, p. 268), and on 33:29 in M, fol. 79r (Schwartz, p. 269). One may wonder how Zeraḥiah understands the plain meaning of the passage about the sick person. We find this out later in Zeraḥiah's commentary on the actual verses of the biblical text, where he informs us that according to the plain sense, the passage simply refers to a person who has not obeyed God's will and is therefore being punished for his deeds with physical afflictions.

75. M, 33:15–17, fols. 77v–78r (Schwartz, p. 268). According to Zeraḥiah's understanding, those verses would roughly be translated as follows:

For God speaks time and again
—Though man does not perceive it—
In a dream, a night vision,
When deep sleep falls on men,
While they slumber in their beds.
Then He reveals the intentions of men,
And negates what they intend to do.
He turns man away from action
And from man's schemes which are hidden.

Compare to the NJPS translation in n. 73.

76. The English differentiates between the two readings by means of the upper-case "h" for the "He" that refers to God in the first translation, and the lower-case "h" for the "he" that refers to the prophet in the second translation. In the Hebrew there is no upper- and lower-case, hence the ambiguity.

77. It is also possible that Zeraḥiah constructed his statement in a deliberately obscure manner so that the masses would read the passage according to the first rendering, while the philosophical reader would understand it according to the second.

78. M, 33:31, fol. 79r–79v (Schwartz, pp. 269–70). Schwartz's edition hopelessly butchers this passage. The text should read as follows: הקשב איוב שמע לי אמ' לו שישמעוהו מן הדברים שנשארו לו להודיע לאיוב והם דברי שאר המענים אשר יודיע בהם דברים טבעיים ופעולתם בעולם אחר שזכר הנהגת אנשי העולם ומקריהם וחילוף מעשיהם שכל זה בא מכח השם וחכמתו אשר זולתו לא יוכל עליה ולא ידע ענינה בשום פנים. . . . ורצה לומ' אליהוא בזה שאם יהיה איוב מבין דבריו שידבר באלו הענינים. . . יוכל לדעת דרכי השם והנהגתו וחכמתו בבריותיו ויתבאר לו מהם כי כל טענותיו עם הבורא היו טענות בטלות ושאין לשום אדם לשפוט על דרכי השם ועל הנהגתו ולא לתפוש עליהם כי חכמתו אינה כחכמתנו והנהגתו אינה כהנהגתנו ושאין יחס כלל בין שום דבר שימצא בו לשום דבר שימצא בנו . . . ולכל זה הענין רמז אליהוא לאיוב בזכור לו הענינים המתחדשים באויר ובאותות השמים ופעולתם ותנועתם ולהורות אליו כי הפשיעה היתה מאיוב בהתרעם מן השם והיותו נפלא על מעשיו בזה העולם ועל סדר הנהגתו בבריותיו שלא היתה הולכת על הסדר שלנו ובהצלחת החוטא ומכשלת הצדיק וענינים רבים בזה העולם שיפלא האדם בהם בהיותם הולכים על בלתי הסדר הנהוג אצלינו.

79. The same ideas are repeated in subsequent remarks; see M, 36:26, fols. 86r–87r (Schwartz, pp. 276–77).

80. M, 38:1, fol. 90r–90v (Schwartz, p. 282).

81. Ibid.

82. M, 42:1f., fols. 100r–101v (Schwartz, pp. 292–93); see earlier in this section.

83. I translate according to Zeraḥiah's understanding of the verse. According to the NJPS translation, the passage reads: "Shaddai—we cannot attain Him; / He is great in power and justice / And abundant in righteousness; He does not torment."

84. Again, I have departed from the NJPS translation to capture Zeraḥiah's reading. The former reads: "Therefore, men are in awe of Him / Whom none of the wise perceive."

85. My emphasis. I depart here from the NJPS translation, "It is not the aged who are wise," in order to capture Zeraḥiah's understanding of the verse.

86. M, 37:24, fol. 89v (my emphasis). This passage in Schwartz's edition is missing a number of phrases. The text should read: ש-די לא מצאנהו שגיא כח ומשפט ורב צדקה לא יענה: אחר שכלה אליהוא לדבר דבריו עם איוב והודיע לו שאין דרך לשום אדם לדעת דרכי השם והנהגותיו עם הבריות בזה העולם השפל חתם דבריו עמו ואמ' שדי לא מצאנוהו שגיא כח כלומ' הוא שגיא כח עד שלא תמצא יד שכלנו וחכמתינו להשיגו. . . . לכן יראוהו אנשים לא יראה כל חכמי לב: פירושו כי בעבור שהוא שגיא כח בני אדם יראים ממנו לא יראה כל חכמי לב לא ישיג ענינו כל מי שהוא חכם אלא מעטים מהם כמו שאמ' אליהוא בתחלת דבריו לא רבים יחכמו ואין ספק כי בזה הדבר הוא רומז על מה שאמ' במענה הראשון שלו כי באחת ידבר א-ל ובשתים לא ישורנה ואמ' אם יש עליו מלאך מליץ אחד מני אלף כי כל זה רמז על דעת אליהוא ועל כן חתם דבריו בזה הפסוק ובמה שכיון לבאר בו.

87. This is not to say that Zeraḥiah's departure from Maimonides is deliberate. It is quite possible that in his reading of the final chapters of Job, Zeraḥiah offers what he believes to be Maimonides' genuine position, and that his interpretation of Maimonides is simply different from our own. It is impossible for us to determine whether or not this is the case because Zeraḥiah does not refer to Maimonides here. All we can say is that Zeraḥiah has significantly departed from Maimonides according to the way I have understood the latter in my own analysis.

88. *Mikrim* here is most likely meant in the technical philosophical sense of an accidental chance event.

89. *B.T. Yoma'* 23a, *B.T. Gittin* 36b.

90. M, introduction, fol. 5r (Schwartz, p. 175); see earlier, this section.

91. See earlier, this section.

92. See chapter 3, section headed "Maimonides on Job."

93. Read with M, עד שתבין ענין בני הא-לוהים והשטן ונפש איוב גם כן שהשתתף בזה הענין באמור השם בסוף מעשה הסיפור אך את נפשו שמור.

94. I depart here from the NJPS translation, "only spare his life," to better capture Zeraḥiah's understanding of the text. Zeraḥiah clearly understands the term *nefesh* as referring to the soul, as most medieval Jewish philosophers do. For Zeraḥiah the verse means that God is urging Satan not to rob Job of the opportunity to have his soul survive in the afterlife. As I have noted, Maimonides and Ibn Tibbon understand this clause the same way.

95. Before this statement are inserted the words ויען ה' ("and God answered") which make no sense in the context. The reason for this phrase being placed here can be discerned by noting that the word which immediately follows: וענין ("and the meaning of"). Clearly, there was a variant reading in front of the copyist, with ויען ה' an alternative reading for וענין, and the copyist therefore inserted both. However, it is clear that the correct reading is וענין. There are, in fact, a number of other instances in the Munich manuscript in which the copyist appears to have put variant readings into the text. Another example is mentioned in n. 65.

96. *Guide* III:22, p. 488.

97. Literally, "arranged."

98. M, 1:6, fol. 8v (Schwartz, p. 181). This passage draws almost verbatim from the correspondence with Judah ben Solomon, fol. 92r.

99. In his correspondence with Judah ben Solomon, Zeraḥiah also discusses the theme of immortality and again cites Maimonides' interpretation of God's command to Satan, "only spare his soul" (fol. 97v; cf. fol. 92r). The placement of these remarks in Zeraḥiah's correspondence with Judah ben Solomon is also significant, for they come at the very conclusion of Zeraḥiah's discussion of Job. Zeraḥiah therefore seems to be underscoring the centrality of this theme in his reading of Job.

100. Zeraḥiah's depiction of Job is more consistent than that of Maimonides in one respect. According to Zeraḥiah, Job begins the story with ethical perfection and does not fail to exhibit it even in the face of his suffering. Maimonides tells us that Job is ethically perfect at the beginning of the story, but he does not explain how it is that Job fails in his ethical behavior when he experiences suffering.

101. I have retained Shlomo Pines's translation of the verse as Maimonides understands it, since that is the translation I used in my chapter on Maimonides (see chapter 3, section headed "Maimonides on Job").

102. Ibid.

103. My emphasis.

104. M, 42:6, fol. 100r (Schwartz, p. 292).

105. One tension that Zeraḥiah does not resolve is that between the image of Job as a figure characterized by his simplicity and lack of wisdom and the image of Job as representative of Aristotle's viewpoint. The two seem incompatible, for whatever difficulty one might have with Aristotle's theory of providence, it is nonetheless philosophically sophisticated. It is therefore not clear how Job, who is Aristotle's representative, could also be lacking in all philosophical wisdom. Yet, the problem I am identifying here could just as easily be applied to Maimonides, whose depiction of Job exhibits a similar tension. See chapter 3, section headed "Exegesis and Philosophy," where I discussed this issue with respect to Maimonides.

106. That Zeraḥiah takes such a restrictive view of Job's education may betray the influence of Averroes, who has a relatively harsh view regarding the education of the masses. Averroes is particularly opposed to teaching the masses about the allegor-

ical interpretation of scripture. Maimonides, by contrast, allows for a modicum of education of this sort. Here Zeraḥiah seems more in line with Averroes in ruling out the possibility that Job absorbed philosophical truths regarding providence at the end of the story. A comparison between Maimonides and Averroes on this matter is given in Pines, "The Philosophical Sources of the *Guide of the Perplexed*," in his translation of the *Guide*, pp. cxvii–cxx. For Averroes's position, see Léon Gauthier, *La théorie d'Ibn Rushd (Averroès) sur les rapports de la religion et de la philosophie* (Paris, 1909); George F. Hourani, *Averroes: On the Harmony of Religion and Philosophy* (London: Luzac, 1961), p. 81.

107. See chapter 4, section headed "Ibn Tibbon on Job."

108. See earlier in this section.

109. I.e., additional to that which the other participants in the dialogue have said.

110. M, 33:28, fol. 79r. This passage is entirely absent from Schwartz's edition: ובאלו הפסוקים אשר פרשתי עתה ורמזתי בהם על דעת אליהוא הנוסף לא ראיתי שום מפרש שהרגיש בהם מה שהיה ראוי להרגיש.

111. Zeraḥiah also mentions that even though God's address to Job is a literary device, the biblical text depicts Job's prophecy as coming through a "tempest" (*se'arah*), since prophets often refer to storm imagery in their prophecies (cf. *Guide* III: 9, pp. 436–37). Zeraḥiah cites as proof Ez. 1:4, in which Ezekiel also sees his prophetic vision in the form of a tempest. Interestingly, Ibn Tibbon claims that the term "tempest" is not associated with any other biblical prophecy, and that this is evidence that Job did not experience prophecy at all (see chapter 4, section headed "Ibn Tibbon on Job"). Ibn Tibbon may have differentiated between the respective experiences of Ezekiel and Job on the basis of the fact that with Job the biblical text describes God's address as coming directly from the tempest, while in Ezekiel the tempest merely precedes the vision from which God eventually speaks. Ibn Tibbon may therefore have felt justified in his claim that it is only Job who is addressed by God through a tempest.

112. Zeraḥiah's view is perhaps more internally consistent than that of Ibn Tibbon because Ibn Tibbon never explains how, by the end of the book, Job could understand the workings of providence if he had not achieved intellectual perfection. For Zeraḥiah, there is no such problem because Job achieves no philosophical understanding of providence whatsoever.

113. Siger, p. 6 n. 9, pp. 39–70; Harold H. Rowley, "The Book of Job and Its Meaning," in *From Moses to Qumran: Studies in the Old Testament* (New York: Association Press, 1963), p. 146; Lewalski, p. 12.

114. Moshe Greenberg devotes an article to Zeraḥiah's justifications for allegory in "Did Job Exist or Not? A Discussion in Medieval Exegesis" (in Hebrew), *Sha'arei Talmon: Studies in the Bible, Qumran, and the Ancient Near East, Presented to Shemaryahu Talmon,* eds. Michael Fishbane and Emanuel Tov (Winona Lake, Ind.: Eisenbrauns, 1992), pp. 3–10. Greenberg touches on the material in a cursory manner, since he deals only with Zeraḥiah's introduction to the commentary. Yet, Greenberg appreciates Zeraḥiah's contribution to the literary study of Job and calls his arguments for the allegorical nature of the story "amazing in their boldness" (p. 3). Zeraḥiah's contribution is also noted in Rosenberg, "Job as Allegory," pp. 155–57.

115. These theories are discussed throughout the scholarly literature on Job. See, for instance, Gordis, pp. 13–18, and Habel, pp. 36–37.

116. Habel, p. 85.

117. Ibid., p. 60.

118. *Guide* II:45, pp. 395, 398.
119. See earlier in this chapter, section headed "The Commentary on Job."
120. A. Ravitzky, "The Thought of Zeraḥiah," pp. 242–62, 290–91.
121. Literally, "arranged."
122. See earlier in this chapter, section headed "The Commentary on Job."
123. Ibid.
124. Ibid.
125. Ibid.
126. Ibid.
127. Significant for an investigation of this issue is a passage in Zeraḥiah's commentary on Proverbs in which he gives what appears to be a philosophical reading of the doctrine of providence. There Zeraḥiah takes the position that the righteous are rewarded by God to the extent that they achieve *devekut* ("cleaving" to God), while the wicked are punished by being abandoned to chance events. Therefore, all punishments in the Bible in which God appears to punish the wicked directly are not to be taken literally. Zeraḥiah's remarks are too brief to determine with certainty whether he is assuming the existence of an impersonal God, but they are certainly suggestive of such a position. See his commentary on Proverbs (*Imrey Da'at* [Vienna, 1871], pp. 31–32). One other instance where Zeraḥiah may be engaging in esoteric discourse in his commentary on Job is in the introduction, where he argues that Moses composed Job through rational speculation. We noted that at the end of his statement on this question, Zeraḥiah backpedals on this position and mentions the possibility that the Book of Job was the product of divine revelation. One suspects that Zeraḥiah throws in this last statement in order to appeal to the traditional reader who may be offended by this suggestion that Job is not the product of revelation (see earlier in this chapter, section headed "The Commentary on Job"; see especially n. 57 of this chapter). In this connection, we should also note Zeraḥiah's comments on Job 38:7 (M, fol. 90v [Schwartz, p. 283]), where he seems to come up with a compromise position that the Book of Job was written "from Moses's mind" but that because the Divine Spirit never departed from him, the book was included in scripture. Here too we have mixed signals about the source of Moses's inspiration in composing the Book of Job.

CHAPTER 6

1. Details about Gersonides' life and writings are found in Moritz Steinschneider, "Levi ben Gerson," in *Gesammelte Schriften*, vol. 1, (Berlin: H. Poppelauer, 1925), pp. 233–70; Renan and Neubauer, pp. 240–98 (586–644); Joseph Schatzmiller, "Gersonides and the Jewish Community of Orange in his Day" (in Hebrew), *University of Haifa Studies in the History of the Jewish People and the Land of Israel* 2 (1972): 111–26; Schatzmiller, "Some Further Information about Gersonides and the Orange Jewish Community in his Day" (in Hebrew), *University of Haifa Studies in the History of the Jewish People and the Land of Israel* 3 (1972): 139–43; Schatzmiller, "Gersonide et la société juive de son temps," in *Gersonide en son temps*, ed. Gilbert Dahan (Louvain-Paris: E. Peeters, 1991), pp. 33–43; Touati, *La pensée philosophique et théologique de Gersonide* (Paris: Editions de Minuit, 1973), pp. 33–82; Anne-Marie Weil-Guény, "Gersonide en son temps: un tableau chronologique," in *Studies on Gersonides: A Fourteenth-Century Jewish Philosopher-Scientist*, ed. Gad Freudenthal (Leiden: E. J. Brill, 1992), pp. 355–65.
2. The original Hebrew text of Gersonides' *Wars of the Lord* (*Sefer Milḥamot ha-Shem*) was published in two printings (Riva di Trento, 1560; Leipzig: C. B. Lorck,

1866). The work has been translated into English, with some sections translated more than once by different authors. The most authoritative translation and the only one that covers the entire treatise is *The Wars of the Lord,* trans. Seymour Feldman, 3 vols. (Philadelphia: Jewish Publication Society of America, 1984–99). Citations in this chapter will be from the Leipzig edition (cited as *Wars*) and the Feldman translation (cited as *Wars of the Lord*).

3. Gersonides' commentary was first printed in Ferrara in 1477 and has been printed numerous times thereafter. All citations of this commentary will be from the *Mikra'ot Gedolot.* The first four chapters of the commentary were translated into Latin by a Jewish convert to Christianity, Louis-Henri D'Aquin (Paris, 1623). Chapters 6 and 7 were translated into Latin as part of a thesis by Christophore Altenberger, *RaLBaG h.e. Rabbi Levi ben Gersom, Commentarius Rabbinicus in cap. VI et VII HIOBI cum versione latina et annotationibus* (Leipzig, 1705). The Book of Job was put into poetic verse in accordance with Gersonides' reading in 1364 by Zark Berfet, an Aragonese Jew, and was published as *Perush Iyyov be-Kiẓur Muflag* (Venice, 1544; Cracow, 1574). An English translation was produced by Abraham Lassen, *The Commentary of Levi ben Gershom on the Book of Job* (New York: Bloch, 1946). All English translations of the commentary in this paper will be my own. I am indebted to Charles Touati for some of these bibliographic details. See his *La pensée,* p. 64.

4. It is the third level that will interest us most, because it is there that Gersonides brings in most of his philosophical insights. The only exception to the arrangement outlined here is Gersonides' commentary on the first and last chapters of Job, in which all three levels are effectively combined.

5. Touati, *La pensée,* p. 64.

6. Eisen, "Gersonides' *Commentary on the Book of Job,*" *Journal of Jewish Thought and Philosophy* 10 (2001): 239–88. This article served as a basis for the present chapter.

7. Gersonides' biblical commentaries in general have elicited relatively little scholarly interest. However, in recent years, scholars have begun to explore these works. See Feldman, "Gersonides and Biblical Exegesis," in Gersonides, *Wars of the Lord,* vol. 2, pp. 213–47; Feldman, "The Binding of Isaac: The Test-Case of Divine Omniscience," in *Divine Omniscience and Omnipotence in Medieval Philosophy,* ed. Tamar Rudavsky (Dordrecht: D. Reidel, 1985), pp. 105–35; Feldman, "The Wisdom of Solomon: A Gersonidean Interpretation," in *Gersonide en son temps,* pp. 61–80; Jacob J. Staub, *The Creation of the World According to Gersonides* (Chico, Calif.: Scholars Press, 1982); Eliyahu Freyman, "Le commentaire de Gersonide sur la Pentateuque," in *Gersonide en son temps,* pp. 117–32; Menachem Kellner, "Gersonides' Commentary on Song of Songs: For Whom Was It Written and Why?" in *Gersonide en son temps,* pp. 81–107; Kellner, *Gersonides' Commentary on Song of Songs* (New Haven: Yale University Press, 1998); Amos Funkenstein, "Gersonides' Biblical Commentary: Science, History and Providence," in *Studies on Gersonides: A Fourteenth-Century Jewish Philosopher-Scientist,* ed. Gad Freudenthal (Leiden: E. J. Brill, 1992), pp. 305–15; Eisen, *Gersonides on Providence*; Ruth Ben Me'ir, "The Commentary of Levi ben Gershom on Ecclesiastes" (in Hebrew) (Ph.D. diss., Hebrew University, 1993).

8. Touati, *La pensée,* pp. 93–94, 95–96. Touati is most emphatic in denying any suggestion that Gersonides engages in esoteric discourse. See also Kellner, "Gersonides' Commentary on Song of Songs." A comprehensive discussion of Gersonides' views on esotericism can be found in my *Gersonides on Providence,* pp. 99–113. There I argue that Gersonides was not unaware of the dangers of revealing philosophical secrets to the masses but chose to protect those truths in ways other than concealment.

9. Gersonides' position on providence is examined in the following studies: Moïse Ventura, "Belief in Providence According to Gersonides" (in Hebrew), in *Minḥah le-Avraham* (Jerusalem, 1959), pp. 12–21; Touati, *La pensée*, pp. 361–92; J. David Bleich, introduction to his translation of book 4 of the *Wars* in *Providence and the Philosophy of Gersonides* (New York: Yeshiva University Press, 1973); Menachem Kellner, "Gersonides, Providence, and the Rabbinic Tradition," *Journal of the American Academy of Religion* 42 (1974): 673–85; Nehoray, "Maimonides and Gersonides"; Idit Dobbs-Weinstein, "The Existential Dimension of Providence in the Thought of Gersonides," in *Gersonide en son temps*, pp. 159–78; Eisen, *Gersonides on Providence*; Oliver Leaman, *Evil and Suffering in Jewish Philosophy* (Cambridge: Cambridge University Press, 1995), pp. 102–20.

10. *Wars* II:2, pp. 95–98; IV:6, p. 181; *Wars of the Lord*, vol. 2, pp. 33–37, 200.

11. *Wars* IV:1, p. 150; IV:2, p. 152; *Wars of the Lord*, vol. 2, pp. 155, 157–58.

12. *Wars* IV:1, p. 150; *Wars of the Lord*, vol. 2, p. 155.

13. *Wars* IV:2, pp. 153, 155; *Wars of the Lord*, vol. 2, pp. 159, 160–61.

14. *Wars* IV:2, pp. 153, 155; *Wars of the Lord*, vol. 2, pp. 159, 161.

15. *Wars* IV:2, p. 153–54; *Wars of the Lord*, vol. 2, p. 161.

16. *Wars* IV:1, p. 151; IV:7, pp. 185–87; *Wars of the Lord*, vol. 2, pp. 150, 206–9.

17. *Wars* IV:4, pp. 164–65; IV:5, p. 167; *Wars of the Lord*, vol. 2, pp. 174–75, 178. The subject of prophecy takes up the entirety of book 2 of the *Wars*. Gersonides' views on prophecy have been analyzed in Touati, *La pensée*, pp. 366–75, 451–68; Touati, "Le problème de l'inerrance prophétique dans le théologie juive du Moyen Age," *Revue de l'histoire des religions* 174 (1968): 169–87; David W. Silverman, "The Problem of Prophecy in Gersonides" (Ph.D. diss., Columbia University, 1975); Tamar Rudavsky, "Divine Omniscience, Contingency, and Prophecy in Gersonides," in *Divine Omniscience and Omnipotence*, pp. 161–81; Howard Kreisel, "Veridical Dreams and Prophecy in the Philosophy of Gersonides" (in Hebrew), *Da'at* 22 (1989): 73–84.

18. This illustration is Talmudic in origin. See *B.T. Niddah* 31a.

19. *Wars* V:5, p. 167; IV:6, p. 174; *Wars of the Lord*, vol. 2, pp. 178, 188. The rabbinic doctrine of *yisurin shel ahavah* appears in a number of Talmudic passages. For a discussion of this concept, see Urbach, pp. 444–48.

20. Material concerning Gersonides' conception of God is scattered throughout his *Wars*. Touati devotes the second part of his book to a systematic analysis of this material. See his *La pensée*, pp. 101–60. Key here is Gersonides' theory that God does not know particulars as particulars but only in a general way insofar as they are ordered within the scheme of the Divine Mind. This topic occupies most of book 3 of the *Wars*. For scholarly discussion of this issue, see Norbert Samuelson, "The Problem of Free Will in Maimonides, Gersonides, and Aquinas," *CCAR Journal* 17 (1970): 2–20; Samuelson, "Gersonides' Account of God's Knowledge of Particulars," *Journal of the History of Philosophy* 10 (1972): 399–416; Samuelson, introduction to *Gersonides on God's Knowledge* (Toronto: Pontifical Institute for Mediaeval Studies, 1977); Touati, *La pensée*, pp. 129–60; Rudavsky, "Divine Omniscience and Future Contingents in Gersonides," 513–36; Rudavsky, "Divine Omniscience, Contingency, and Prophecy in Gersonides," in *Divine Omniscience and Omnipotence in Medieval Philosophy*, pp. 161–81; Sarah Klein-Braslavy, "Gersonides on Determinism, Possibility, Choice, and Foreknowledge" (in Hebrew), *Da'at* 22 (1989): 5–53. For discussion of the related problem of divine will, see Touati, *La pensée*, p. 201f.; Menachem Kellner, "Gersonides on the Problem of Volitional Creation," *Hebrew Union College Annual* 51 (1980): 111–28.

21. *Wars* IV:6, p. 169; *Wars of the Lord*, vol. 2, pp. 180–81.

22. *Wars* IV:6, p. 169; *Wars of the Lord*, vol. 2, p. 181. My interpretation of provi-

dential suffering differs from that of Touati. For a discussion of this issue, see my *Gersonides on Providence*, pp. 18–20.

23. Miracles are explained by Gersonides in similar fashion. See my discussion in *Gersonides on Providence*, pp. 22–28.

24. *Wars* IV:6, pp. 169–70; *Wars of the Lord*, vol. 2, pp. 182–83. For a discussion of Gersonides' views on immortality, see Touati, *La pensée*, pp. 434–42.

25. As stated earlier, all citations from Gersonides' commentary will be from the *Mikra'ot Gedolot* and will be designated "CJ," for "Commentary on Job." Citations will specify the chapter and which of the three levels of Gersonides' exegesis we are drawing from. The only exceptions will be the introduction and the first and last chapters of Gersonides' commentary, in which all three levels of exegesis are effectively combined. I will not cite page numbers since pagination varies from edition to edition of the *Mikra'ot Gedolot*.

26. The "fundamental principles of the Torah" (*pinnot ha-torah*) have an important hermeneutic function in Gersonides' philosophical exegesis. See my article "Reason, Revelation, and the Fundamental Principles of the Torah in Gersonides' Thought," *Proceedings of the American Academy for Jewish Research* 57 (1991): 11–34, and my study, *Gersonides on Providence*, pp. 185–96.

27. *B.T. Bava' Batra'* 15a; CJ, introduction.

28. Gersonides specifically refers to Aristotle's *Metaphysics*. The apparent reference is to *Metaphysics* 12:9–10.

29. CJ, introduction. The implication is that Moses' perplexity about the suffering of the righteous caused him to write the Book of Job. Gersonides specifically cites Moses' celebrated question in Ex. 33:13 asking to know God's ways as evidence for his concern for the suffering of the righteous. A full explication of this passage is given by Gersonides in his *Commentary on the Torah* (Venice: D. Bomberg, 1547), pp. 114a–115d. Moses's concern about the suffering of the righteous is also noted in a well-known Talmudic passage (*B.T. Berakhot* 7a). Gersonides' remarks here are no doubt inspired in part by this source. He also notes that other prophets, such as Habakkuk and King David, were perplexed by the same question. Gersonides cites as proof of this perplexity Hab. 1:13: "Why do You countenance treachery, / And stand by idle / While the one in the wrong devours / The one in the right?" and Ps. 73:3: "for I envied the wanton; / I saw the wicked at ease."

30. CJ, introduction.

31. Gersonides seems to have in mind discussions such as that which we find in book 1 of Aristotle's *Metaphysics*. There Aristotle deals extensively with the views of his predecessors on the issue of causation before presenting his own opinion.

32. Ez. 14:14.

33. Gersonides frequently calls upon this sort of argument in his biblical commentaries to explain what seem to be superfluous historical details in the biblical text. See, for example, his *Commentary on the Torah* (Gersonides, *Perush 'al ha-Torah* [Venice: D. Bomberg, 1547], pp. 30c, 205c). Interestingly, Zeraḥiah, as we saw in the last chapter, believes there is a lack of historical detail in Job and therefore comes to the opposite conclusion, which is that the book is an allegory (see chapter 5, section headed "The Commentary on Job").

34. CJ, introduction.

35. This discussion is practically identical to that found in *Wars* IV:3, pp. 160–61; *Wars of the Lord*, vol. 2, pp. 168–70.

36. CJ, introduction. For the notion that matter is the source of evil for bodily illnesses, Gersonides explicitly cites Aristotle's *Meteorologica* IV, the reference being to

378b, 12, and 379a, 11, passages that describe how matter becomes corrupted when its passive qualities gain dominance over its active ones. The notion that our ethical traits are affected by matter is based on the premise that no evil can come from the intellect and that matter must therefore be the culprit. This idea is implied by Aristotle in *On the Soul* III:10, 433a, 26.

37. This idea is developed extensively by Gersonides in *Wars* II:2, p. 96f.; *Wars of the Lord*, vol. 2, p. 30f.

38. CJ, introduction.

39. For instance, CJ, *be'ur ha-millot*, 5:12. That Job predates the Sinai revelation also gives Gersonides justification for defending him against the rabbinic criticism that he denied the resurrection of the dead (*B.T. Bava' Batra'* 16a). In fact, Gersonides tells us, he did not believe in that dogma; but since he lived before the time of the giving of the Torah, there is no reason to expect that he should have (end of chapter 7, *ha-kelal*).

40. CJ, chapter 1.

41. CJ, end of chapter 3, *ha-kelal*.

42. CJ, end of chapter 25, *be'ur divery ha-ma'aneh*; see chapter 2, section headed "Concluding Reflections."

43. CJ, chapters 1–2.

44. Job 3:3f.

45. CJ, end of chapter 3, *ha-kelal*.

46. CJ, end of chapter 14, *ha-kelal*; end of chapter 26, *ha-kelal*.

47. CJ, end of chapter 3, *ha-kelal*. Gersonides is initially unsure as to whether Job believes in immortality in the wake of his suffering. Despite these initial doubts, Gersonides takes this belief for granted throughout the rest of his commentary.

48. See earlier in this chapter, section headed "The Philosophical Background." Gersonides asks why, if Job does not believe in reward and punishment in this world, we are told in the opening verses of the book that he offered regular sacrifices for fear that his sons may have sinned (Job 1:4–5). Gersonides' response is twofold. First, one must keep in mind that Job always believed in immortality, and therefore the sacrifices were needed to appease God even if there is no reward in this world. Second, Job did not deny individual providence before his suffering; he was merely uncertain about its existence. Therefore, he brought sacrifices to cover all bases in case there was in fact individual providence in this world.

49. CJ, chapter 2.

50. Eliphaz's viewpoint is conveniently summarized in CJ, end of chapter 5, *ha-kelal*. That of Bildad is summarized in CJ, end of chapter 8, *ha-kelal*. That of Zophar is summarized in CJ, end of chapter 11, *ha-kelal*.

51. See earlier in this chapter, section headed "The Philosophical Background."

52. Ibid. Elihu's viewpoint is summarized in CJ, end of chapter 33, *ha-kelal*.

53. I have departed from the NJPS translation here to better capture Gersonides' reading. The NJPS reads as follows: "For God speaks time and again /—Though man does not perceive it."

54. CJ, end of chapter 33, *be'ur divrey ha-ma'aneh* and *ha-kelal*.

55. CJ, end of chapter 34, *ha-kelal*.

56. CJ, end of chapter 33, *ha-kelal*; end of chapter 37, *ha-kelal*; end of chapter 39, *ha-kelal*; end of chapter 40, *ha-kelal*. This reading of the contents of God's address is alluded to in *Wars* IV:6, p. 179; *Wars of the Lord*, vol. 2, p. 196.

57. Job 42:7.

58. According to Gersonides, Job himself criticizes Bildad and Zophar during

their earlier discussion because their arguments are not based on sense perception (CJ, end of chapter 14, *ha-kelal*).

59. CJ, chapter 42. The arguments of Job referred to here are summarized in CJ, end of chapter 3, *ha-kelal*. These arguments are similar to ones found in the *Wars*, which Gersonides adduces to show the strengths of Aristotle's viewpoint. See *Wars* III: 2, p. 122; IV:2, p. 152; *Wars of the Lord*, vol. 2, pp. 92–93, 157–58.

60. These would include commentaries from such figures as Rashi, Joseph Kara, and perhaps Ibn Ezra, who addresses the philosophical concerns of Job only in a short section at the end of his commentary.

61. CJ, end of chapter 8, *be'ur divrey ha-ma'aneh*; end of chapter 39, *be'ur divrey ha-ma'aneh*.

62. Job 1:6, 2:1.

63. CJ, chapter 1.

64. See chapter 3, section headed "Maimonides on Job."

65. See earlier in this chapter, section headed "The Philosophical Background."

66. See chapter 3, section headed "Maimonides on Job."

67. *Guide* III:22, p. 489.

68. See chapter 3, section headed "Maimonides on Job."

69. CJ, chapter 1.

70. See chapter 3, section headed "Maimonides on Job."

71. Ibid.

72. My interpretation, however, is different. See ibid.

73. Ibid.

74. The translation I have given here is according to the way Gersonides understands the verse. Ibn Tibbon understands the same verse in a slightly different manner (see chapter 4, section headed "Ibn Tibbon on Job"). However, both see the references to God speaking twice to human beings as an allusion to the two types of providence: prophecy and providential suffering.

75. CJ, end of chapter 33, *be'ur divrey ha-ma'aneh*. See chapter 4, section headed "Ibn Tibbon on Job."

76. Ibn Tibbon's conception of providential suffering matches most closely with the second type of providential suffering identified by Gersonides, according to which a person suffers in order that he be inspired to seek intellectual perfection.

77. I made similar observations with respect to Zeraḥiah's commentary. The difference here is that unlike Zeraḥiah, Gersonides fails to mention Ibn Tibbon not just in his commentary on Job, but in all his works. Doubts about a Tibbonian influence are therefore stronger with Gersonides than they were with Zeraḥiah.

78. CJ, introduction.

79. Ben Me'ir, pp. 115–211. Gersonides also claims in the introduction to his *Commentary on the Torah*, p. 2c, that he will not cite aggadic sources in his explication of the biblical text. Yet, he cites aggadic sources practically on every page, often with a philosophical interpretation, and rarely acknowledges his sources. He frequently does the same with Rashi and Ibn Ezra. This is a recurrent point in my study *Gersonides on Providence*, where I trace the aggadic and medieval sources upon which Gersonides relies for formulating his concept of covenant and Jewish chosenness. Gersonides' reluctance to cite his predecessors does not seem to extend to his non-Jewish philosophical influences. He frequently acknowledges his debt to them in both his philosophical works and his biblical commentaries.

My observations here provide, I believe, a corrective to Menachem Kellner's treatment of the relationship between the respective commentaries of Gersonides and

Moses ibn Tibbon, son of Samuel, on the Song of Songs. In a recent study, Kellner argues that it is unlikely that Moses ibn Tibbon's commentary had an influence on that of Gersonides, even though there is reason to believe it should have. There is substantial overlap between the content of the two works; Gersonides lived in close geographical proximity to Ibn Tibbon; and Gersonides composed his commentary shortly after Ibn Tibbon did. A key argument brought by Kellner to support his conclusion is that Gersonides would not have plagiarized Ibn Tibbon's work because he generally acknowledges his sources. My observations here show that this is not necessarily the case. See Menachem Kellner, "Communication or the Lack Thereof among Thirteenth-Fourteenth Century Provençal Jewish Philosophers: Moses ibn Tibbon and Gersonides on Song of Songs," in *Communication in the Jewish Diaspora*, ed. Sophia Menache (Leiden: E. J. Brill, 1996), pp. 227–45.

80. The contents of this manuscript were published by Gérard E. Weil, *La bibliothèque de Gersonide d'après son catalogue autographe* (Louvain-Paris: E. Peeters, 1991). Gersonides' ownership of *Ma'amar Yikkavu ha-Mayim* is noted by Weil, p. 90. It is possible that Gersonides' failure to mention Ibn Tibbon was the result of reasons similar to those I attributed to Zeraḥiah, who also does not mention Ibn Tibbon despite evidence that he was influenced by him. Gersonides may have adopted some of Ibn Tibbon's ideas but felt that the differences between his reading of Job and that of Ibn Tibbon were too great to give him credit as one of his sources.

81. We may also include Zeraḥiah Ḥen alongside Maimonides and Ibn Tibbon as a figure from whom Gersonides departs here, since Zeraḥiah's reading of Job is so close to theirs. However, I have chosen to focus on Maimonides and Ibn Tibbon, since Gersonides certainly was familiar with Maimonides' reading of Job and was likely to have been familiar with that of Ibn Tibbon as well. But there is no evidence I have found to suggest that he was acquainted with the works of Zeraḥiah.

82. Maimonides also sees Job as learning that there is providence over our physical well-being. As I have argued, this is the major point of Elihu's remarks, according to Maimonides. However, I have also shown that Maimonides regards the achievement of an acquired intellect as the most exalted form of providence and Job's most important lesson, one that Job learns once God has finished speaking to him. See chapter 3, section headed "Maimonides on Job."

83. See earlier in this chapter, section headed "The Philosophical Background."

84. CJ, end of chapter 34, *be'ur divrey ha-ma'aneh*; end of chapter 37, *be'ur divrey ha-ma'aneh*.

85. The vilification of Gersonides by later medieval Jewish thinkers is examined in Touati, *La pensée*, pp. 541–49, and Menachem Kellner, "Gersonides and his Cultured Despisers: Arama and Abravanel," *Journal of Medieval and Renaissance Studies* 6 (1976): 269–99. Gersonides' philosophy was often misunderstood and was not as radical as it was often made out to be. Moreover, he became the object of attack in part because of his stature, not because he was necessarily the most radical of philosophers. In fact, Gersonides is a relatively traditional thinker in comparison with other Jewish Aristotelian thinkers in his period, such as Isaac Albalag, Joseph ibn Kaspi, and Moses Narboni. Charles Manekin sheds valuable light on Gersonides' conservatism in "Conservative Tendencies in Gersonides' Religious Philosophy," in *The Cambridge Companion of Medieval Jewish Philosophy*, eds. Daniel H. Frank and Oliver Leaman (Cambridge: Cambridge University Press, forthcoming).

86. See chapter 4, n. 4. Dov Schwartz has described the contours of the debate over the nature of providence in the thirteenth century in his article "The Debate over the Maimonidean Theory of Providence."

87. It is not clear whether Gersonides is also opposing Maimonides' reading of Job, which spiritualizes the notion of providence as well. This seems unlikely given that in the concluding chapter of book 4 of the *Wars*, Gersonides actually voices approval of Maimonides' theory of providence (*Wars* IV:7, pp. 185–87; *Wars of the Lord*, vol. 2, pp. 206–9). The problem is that Gersonides' discussion is peculiar in that he deals with Maimonides' theory in only the most cursory fashion and seems interested only in citing aspects of Maimonides' doctrine of providence that agree with his own. Moreover, in that discussion Gersonides does not attempt to grapple with Maimonides' reading of Job, which is critical for an understanding of Maimonides' theory of providence. One may be tempted to surmise that Gersonides' strategy is merely to score points with his reader by showing agreement between his theory of providence and that of Maimonides, and that he is well aware of their differences. However, this does not make sense given that in other places in the *Wars*, Gersonides is more than happy to voice loud disagreements with Maimonides. Gersonides' attitude toward Maimonides' theory of providence is therefore ambiguous, and thus it is unclear what it can tell us about his opposition to Maimonides' reading of Job.

88. See earlier in this chapter, section headed "The Commentary on Job."

89. Other examples of Gersonides' use of allegory include his reading of the Garden of Eden episode and his commentary on the Song of Songs. Gersonides' restrictive views on allegory are expressed explicitly in his *Commentary on the Torah*, pp. 16d, 28b. This matter is briefly discussed in Touati, *La pensée*, pp. 30, 483–84.

90. Sarachek, pp. 195–261; Charles Touati, "La controverse de 1303–1306 autour des études philosophiques et scientifiques," *Revue des études juives* 127 (1968): 21–37; Marc Saperstein, "The Conflict over the Rashba's *Ḥerem* on Philosophical Study in Political Perspective," *Jewish History* 1 (1986): 27–38.

91. CJ, end of chapter 8, *ha-kelal*; *Wars* IV:1, p. 152; *Wars of the Lord*, vol. 2, p. 155.

92. CJ, end of chapter 8, *ha-kelal*.

93. Maimonides died in 1204. Ibn Tibbon died sometime around 1232, just about the time that the phase of the Maimonidean conflict involving the resurrection controversy came to a head. Gersonides was born in 1288. The resurrection controversy is discussed in Sarachek, pp. 39–65; Silver, pp. 64–66, 109–35; Septimus, pp. 39–61.

94. See earlier in this chapter, section headed "The Commentary on Job."

95. CJ, introduction.

96. The merits of Eliphaz's view are discussed in CJ, end of chapter 5, *ha-kelal*. However, the most comprehensive statement on the strengths and weaknesses of the arguments presented by Job's friends, including Bildad and Zophar, is found in a summary and assessment of those opinions that Gersonides provides at the end of chapter 11, *ha-kelal*, after the first round of arguments has been presented in the biblical text. With respect to Bildad's view, we note that in the *Wars*, the very same prooftext which Gersonides uses to support his view, Is. 12:1, is cited again to support Gersonides' description of his own doctrine of providential suffering (*Wars* IV:2, pp. 158; IV:5, p. 167; *Wars of the Lord*, vol. 2, pp. 165, 179). This indicates that in Gersonides' thinking the correct view on providence co-opts Bildad's approach.

97. That Gersonides creates a synthesis of all the opinions reflects the philosophical method we see throughout the *Wars*. His final opinion on a given philosophical issue is often an amalgamation of the various views set forth at the beginning of his deliberations. This is true of his discussions on divine knowledge in book 3, providence in book 4, and creation in book 6 of the *Wars*. Gersonides' method may ulti-

mately be based on Aristotelian notions of dialectical argumentation. In the *Eudemian Ethics* Aristotle relates that in this form of argumentation opposing viewpoints are supported by their respective claims, after which one chooses one of two alternatives: one either declares one of the viewpoints as the correct one, or one creates a synthesis between the opposing viewpoints. Gersonides seems to have followed the second path with respect to such topics as providence. See *Eudemian Ethics* VII:2, 1235b, 13–18, and the discussion in J.D.C. Evans, *Aristotle's Concept of Dialectic* (Cambridge: Cambridge University Press, 1977), p. 55ff. Arthur Hyman, to whose scholarship I am indebted for these sources, argues that Aristotle's conception of dialectical argumentation informs Maimonides' approach on a number of issues as well; see Hyman, "Demonstrative, Dialectical, and Sophistic Arguments in the Philosophy of Moses Maimonides," in *Maimonides in His Time*, ed. Eric L. Ormsby (Washington, D.C.: Catholic University Press, 1989), pp. 35–51. Therefore, Maimonides may have also influenced Gersonides in this regard.

98. See earlier in this chapter, section headed "The Commentary on Job." An interesting point to note here is that according to Gersonides' discussion of prophecy in the *Wars*, prophecy serves mostly for the prediction of the future. It rarely furnishes information regarding theoretical matters. Job's revelation from God therefore seems to belong to this rare second category, though Gersonides never explicitly says so. See *Wars* II:4, pp. 101–4; *Wars of the Lord*, vol. 2, pp. 42–47.

99. See earlier in this chapter, section headed "The Commentary on Job." In fact one may even suggest that Gersonides views the initial Job as a projection of Moses himself, who, as author of the Book of Job, depicts a figure with a philosophical difficulty similar to his own.

100. Job says this in a number of places, according to Gersonides. See, for instance, CJ, end of chapter 10, *ha-kelal.*

101. CJ, end of chapter 14, *ha-kelal.*

102. CJ, end of chapter 34, *ha-kelal.*

103. The reference here is to the blessings and curses in Lev. 26 and Deut. 28, traditionally known as the *tokheḥah* or "chastisement" sections of the Torah.

104. *Hoda'ah*, lit. "announcement."

105. I translate here according to Gersonides' understanding of the clause. God is warning the Israelites not to treat their misfortune as accidental but as intended by God. A similar reading is given by Maimonides, *Guide* III:36, pp. 539–40. According to the NJPS translation the clause reads, "And if you remain hostile toward Me."

106. I.e., providential suffering.

107. CJ, end of chapter 33, *ha-kelal.*

108. This is the subject of my study *Gersonides on Providence.* Conspicuously absent from Gersonides' remarks here is any reference to inherited providence, which underlies his doctrine of Jewish chosenness (see Eisen, *Gersonides on Providence*, especially chaps. 3, 4, 7, 8).

109. Touati, *La pensée*, pp. 44–46. In his *Commentary on the Torah* Gersonides makes specific reference to the 1306 expulsion (p. 176b). Other references allude in more general terms to the troubles he witnessed (p. 206b; *Wars*, introduction, p. 3; *Wars of the Lord*, vol. 1, p. 93).

110. For details, see Touati, *La pensée*, pp. 49–53, 63–64.

111. See the introductory section of this chapter.

112. See earlier in this chapter, section headed "The Commentary on Job."

113. CJ, end of chapter 10, *ha-kelal.*

114. See earlier in this chapter, section headed "The Philosophical Background."

115. CJ, end of chapter 33, *be'ur divrey ha-ma'aneh*, my emphasis. There may be some inconsistency in Gersonides' thinking here. Presumably a person who experiences prophecy has both moral and intellectual perfection. He is therefore unlikely to have many "sins" for which he needs to repent.

116. CJ, end of chapter 33, *be'ur divrey ha-ma'aneh*. The anthropomorphic language here is not unusual in Gersonides' writings and does not necessarily compromise his impersonal conception of God. For a discussion of this issue, see my study *Gersonides on Providence*, pp. 157–67.

117. *Wars* IV:4–5, pp. 164–67; *Wars of the Lord*, vol. 2, pp. 174–79. The only exception to the practical emphasis is providential suffering in its second form, which stops a righteous individual from straying away from intellectual perfection. However, this form of providence is not actually mentioned in the central section of book 4 of the *Wars*, which reviews the various forms of individual providence. It is introduced only in a later discussion (*Wars* IV:6, pp. 173–74; *Wars of the Lord*, vol. 2, p. 188).

118. There may be influence from Ibn Tibbon here. As we have already seen, according to Ibn Tibbon, the educational benefits of experiencing providence are the central theme of Elihu's remarks. Elihu informs Job that prophecy and providential suffering both serve the purpose of teaching the recipient about the value of achieving conjunction with God through intellectual perfection. Prophecies about future calamities and physical suffering inspire an individual to understand that the life of material pleasure is of no value and that the life of the intellect is what human beings should strive for. These ideas, it would seem, anticipate the notion that providence has educational value that we find in Gersonides' interpretation of Elihu's speech. Gersonides also sees prophecy and the experience of providential suffering as teaching the recipient about the importance of intellectual perfection. Yet, while these educational benefits are central in Ibn Tibbon's reading of Elihu's address, for Gersonides they are only peripheral. Moreover, for Ibn Tibbon the educational benefits of prophecy and providential suffering consist solely in the individual achieving immortality of the soul, while for Gersonides they result in individual providence in this world as well.

119. CJ, end of chapter 34, *ha-kelal*.

120. CJ, end of chapter 41, *be'ur divrey ha-ma'aneh*. A similar statement is contained in the *ha-kelal* as well. See also CJ, end of chapter 37, *ha-kelal*, for another statement regarding our limitations in comprehending divine providence.

121. It is in book 3 of the *Wars* that Gersonides argues that divine attributes are equivocal. However, he also argues that they are not absolutely equivocal, as Maimonides does. Rather, they are ambiguous terms, which means that while divine attributes greatly differ from ours, there is still some commonality between them. See *Wars* III:3, pp. 132–37; *Wars of the Lord*, vol. 2, pp. 107–15. Gersonides' theory of divine attributes is analyzed in Touati, *La pensée*, pp. 108–28; Harry A. Wolfson, "Maimonides and Gersonides on Divine Attributes as Ambiguous Terms," in *Studies in the History of Philosophy and Religion*, ed. Isadore Twersky and George H. Williams (Cambridge, Mass.: Harvard University Press, 1977), vol. 2, pp. 231–47. If in fact there is some degree of commonality between divine and human attributes, one may wonder why, in the cited passage, Gersonides says that there is no relation between God's power and ours. The solution to this difficulty is that Gersonides is engaging in hyperbole. Evidence for this is that he makes a statement that is just as extreme regarding the distinction between divine and human attributes precisely in the portion of his discussion in the *Wars* where he argues that divine attributes are ambiguous terms (*Wars* III:3, pp. 136–37; *Wars of the Lord*, vol. 2, p. 114).

122. Gersonides devotes a lengthy chapter to this one issue in *Wars* IV:6, pp. 168–85; *Wars of the Lord*, vol. 2, pp. 180–205.

123. *Wars* IV:6, pp. 174–76; *Wars of the Lord*, vol. 2, pp. 189–91.

124. Elihu addresses Job's three friends but only in anger at their failure to respond properly to him (Job 32:3).

125. *Wars* IV:6, pp. 176–79; *Wars of the Lord*, vol. 2, pp. 191–95. In the *Wars*, Gersonides also has the opportunity to entertain challenges to his theory of providence from sources in the biblical text that are quite unconnected to the Book of Job. Toward the end of book 4 he deals with a number of problems of this sort. See *Wars* IV: 6, pp. 181–85; *Wars of the Lord*, vol. 2, pp. 198–205.

126. See earlier in this chapter, section headed "The Philosophical Background."

127. Ibid.

128. Lit., "say."

129. CJ, end of chapter 35, *ha-kelal*. See also *be'ur divrey ha-ma'aneh*, where Gersonides makes a similar but briefer statement.

130. This translation is according to Gersonides' own reading. According to NJPS, the passage reads as follows: "Surely it is false that God does not listen / That Shaddai does not take note of it."

131. *Wars* IV:6, pp. 172–73; *Wars of the Lord*, vol. 2, pp. 186–89.

132. As noted in my discussion of book 4 of the *Wars* (see earlier in this chapter, section headed "The Philosophical Background").

133. Ibid.

134. There is one topic that is relevant to the issue of providence but is not dealt with in the commentary on Job or in book 4 of the *Wars*, and that is the subject of miracles. Gersonides tackles this issue at the very end of book 6 of the *Wars*, which is mostly devoted to creation. Gersonides does not state explicitly what the connection is between miracles and creation, but as Touati notes, Gersonides seems to have followed Maimonides in believing that the two topics were closely related (*La pensée*, p. 477).

CHAPTER 7

1. Biographical details about Duran are contained in the following studies: Heinrich Jaulus, "R. Simeon b. Zemach Duran: Ein Zeit und Lebensbild," *Monatsschrift für Geschichte und Wissenschaft des Judentums* 23 (1874): 241–59, 308–17, 355–66, 398–403, 447–61; Isidore Epstein, *The Responsa of Rabbi Simon b. Ẓemaḥ Duran as a Source of the History of the Jews of North Africa* (New York: Ktav, 1930), pp. 1–43.

2. This work was published in pieces. The lengthy three-part introduction was published in Leghorn, 1785, without the polemical section against Christianity and Islam in the fourth chapter of section 2, and the actual commentary on tractate *Avot*. The polemic against Christianity and Islam appeared separately under the title *Keshet u-Magen* in Leghorn, c. 1750. The commentary on *Avot* appeared in Leghorn, 1763. *Keshet u-Magen* has been critically edited in Prosper Murciano, "Simon ben Ẓemaḥ Duran's *Keshet U-Magen*: A Critical Edition" (Ph.D. diss., New York University, 1975).

3. Duran produced other works outside the realm of Halakhah, most notably *Or ha-Ḥayyim*, a polemical treatise against Ḥasdai Crescas, and *Livyat Ḥen*, a series of glosses on Gersonides' commentary on the Torah. Both are lost.

4. Epstein, pp. 6–8.

5. Jakob Guttmann, "Die Stellung des Simeon ben Zemah Duran in der jüdischen Religionsphilosophie," *Monatsschrift für Geschichte und Wissenschaft des Juden-*

tums 52 (1908): 641–72; 53 (1909): 46–79, 199–228; Naḥum Arieli, "The Philosophy of Rashbaẓ: Shimon ben Ẓemaḥ Duran" (in Hebrew) (Ph.D. diss., Hebrew University, 1976).

6. The most thorough study of Duran's views on dogma is Menachem Kellner, *Dogma in Medieval Jewish Thought* (Oxford: Oxford University Press, 1986), pp. 83–107. Kellner also provides a comprehensive bibliography of the scholarship on this subject on pp. 250–51 n. 3. That Duran's views on dogma have been at the center of the scholarship on his philosophical thought is evidenced by the fact that Julius Guttmann and Colette Sirat deal almost exclusively with this topic in their discussions of Duran in their respective surveys of medieval Jewish philosophy. See Julius Guttmann, pp. 275–82; Sirat, pp. 372–81.

7. In taking this approach, these writers were not entirely innovative. They often drew inspiration from earlier thinkers, such as Naḥmanides and Judah Halevi, who had an intellectual orientation similar to that of Duran.

8. Arieli deals with Duran's overall intellectual orientation in the introductory chapter of his dissertation, pp. 1–22. The common judgment on this era of medieval Jewish philosophy is that it lacked all originality. See, for instance, Julius Guttmann, p. 275. Arieli attempts to counter that judgment, at least with respect to Duran. He finds Duran's originality in his attempt to base a systematic philosophy on rabbinic sources. See Arieli, especially pp. 6–7. Arieli's position is not entirely clear. He goes on to admit that Duran's thought is eclectic in nature and that rabbinic sources constitute only one type of literature upon which Duran draws (p. 11).

9. For the date of composition of *Ohev Mishpat*, see Jaulus, p. 453. The date of composition of *Magen Avot*, is much disputed. The dating of both works is discussed in n. 88.

10. Arieli deals with Duran's views on divine providence in two sections of his dissertation (pp. 58–60, 176–87). But because Arieli focuses almost entirely on *Magen Avot*, those discussions fail to deal with most of Duran's speculations on this topic, found primarily in *Ohev Mishpat*.

11. J. David Bleich, "Duran's View of the Nature of Providence," *Jewish Quarterly Review* 69 (1979): 208–25. Bleich's article is based on a somewhat more extensive treatment of this issue in a chapter in his "Providence in Late Medieval Jewish Philosophy" (Ph.D. diss., New York University, 1974), pp. 155–207.

12. I will be discussing Duran's views roughly in the order in which they are presented by him in *Ohev Mishpat*, though I occasionally deviate from that order to provide a clearer exposition of his thinking.

13. *Ohev Mishpat* (henceforth OM) (Venice, 1590), p. 3b. Creation *ex nihilo* is also identified in this discussion as key for inspiring observance of the commandments, since this doctrine is critical for believing in revelation, which, in turn, is necessary for appreciating the divine origin of the commandments. The importance of creation *ex nihilo* for believing in other basic Jewish doctrines such as miracles and divine reward and punishment is emphasized in Maimonides, *Guide* II:25, pp. 327–30.

14. OM, pp. 7a, 8b–9a. Duran goes on to cite a number of sources to prove his point. His evidence is similar to that adduced by Gersonides who makes a similar point; see chapter 6, section headed "The Commentary on Job."

15. As I have noted a number of times, the Mosaic authorship of Job is an opinion already found in the Talmud (*B.T. Bava' Batra'* 15a). It is also supported by most of the thinkers in our study.

16. OM, pp. 3b, 5a, 7b–8a, 17b–18a, 19b–20a. A question raised by Duran is why

the Torah itself does not subject the question of providence to philosophical discussion if it is rationally demonstrable. Duran answers that the Torah does not cite philosophical proofs for *any* of its positions. Two explanations are given for this. First, reason can deduce these positions without assistance from revelation. Second, the Torah's positions are accepted by all nations as revealed truths so that philosophical demonstrations of those truths are again superfluous (p. 7a–b).

17. OM, p. 5a.
18. OM, p. 5a.
19. OM, p. 5a–b.
20. OM, p. 17a.
21. OM, pp. 18a–19a.
22. OM, pp. 19b–20a.
23. OM, pp. 20b–21a.
24. Bleich, "Duran's View," pp. 216–17.
25. OM, pp. 26a–27a.
26. Duran addresses the objection frequently raised by philosophers that the traditional notion of reward and punishment implies that evil comes directly from God. Duran counters that in punishing human beings for their sins, God is doing precisely that which is good.
27. For a discussion of this doctrine, see David Berger, "Miracles and the Natural Order in Naḥmanides," in *Rabbi Moses Naḥmanides (Ramban): Explorations in His Religious and Literary Virtuosity*, ed. Isadore Twersky (Cambridge, Mass.: Harvard University Press, 1983), pp. 107–28; the critique of Berger by Mikha'el Nehoray, "Naḥmanides' Theory of Miracles and of Nature and Its Connection to R. Judah ha-Levi" (in Hebrew), *Da'at* 17 (1986): 23–31; David Novak, *The Theology of Nahmanides Systematically Presented* (Atlanta: Scholars Press, 1992), pp. 61–75; Tzvi Langermann, "Acceptance and Devaluation: Nahmanides' Attitude toward Science," *Journal of Jewish Thought and Philosophy* 1, no. 2 (1992): 223–45.
28. OM, pp. 27a–29b.
29. OM, pp. 32a–33b.
30. OM, pp. 35a–36a. Reason no. 2 is found in a number of rabbinic sources; see *B.T. Berakhot* 4a, *'Eruvin* 19a, *Bereshit Rabbah* 19:1. Reason no. 3 has roots in Saadiah and will be discussed at length shortly, since it is pivotal to Duran's reading of Job. Reason no. 4 is found in rabbinic sources; see, for instance, *B.T. Berakhot* 60a. Reason no. 5 is found in rabbinic sources: see, for instance, *B.T. Sahnhedrin* 20a, *Shabbat* 55a. Reason no. 6 is from Gersonides, *Wars* IV:6, p. 173. Reason no. 7 is found in rabbinic sources; see, for instance, *B.T. Bava' Kamma'* 92a.
31. The notion that Job lived during the period of the giving of the Torah corresponds to a number of rabbinic sources: see *B.T. Bava' Batra'* 15a; *J.T. Sotah* 5:6; *Bereshit Rabbah* 57:4.
32. Lam. 4:21. In the biblical text, Esau himself is named Edom. See Gen. 25:30, 36:1, 36:8–9.
33. OM, pp. 45b–46a. Duran cites Naḥmanides as the source of his views on these relationships. See Naḥmanides, *Commentary on the Book of Job*, pp. 27–28.
34. Maimonides may respond by arguing that the Book of Job is enigmatic but only on the exoteric level, and it is that perplexity that guides us to an esoteric reading, according to which Job is intellectually deficient and therefore suffers for his sins. Duran has thus been somewhat unfair to Maimonides by using the latter's solution to the problem of Job as evidence that Maimonides negates the meaning of that

book altogether. In truth, one could do the same with Duran's own reading of Job, for he too comes up with a solution to its difficulties that, once understood, calls into question why the book was written in the first place.

35. OM, pp. 45b–46b. Duran supports his positive view of Job by citing rabbinic sources maintaining that Job served God out of love, such as *B.T. Sotah* 27b. One may surmise that Duran is adopting the standard philosophical view that prophecy is consequent upon intellectual perfection. But the connection between knowledge and prophecy can be found in rabbinic sources without any necessary association with philosophical conceptions, and it may be those sources that inspired Duran's view here. See *B.T. Shabbat* 92a.

36. See chapter 3, section headed "Maimonides on Job"; chapter 6, section headed "The Commentary on Job."

37. OM, p. 37a. It is interesting to note that in this discussion Duran does not cite the many rabbinic views that give a negative assessment of Job; he cites only those found in medieval Jewish philosophy. Elsewhere he cites the rabbinic source that criticizes Job for rejecting the doctrine of resurrection, but only in order to refute it (OM, p. 26b).

38. OM, pp. 37b–38b.

39. OM, p. 47b. Duran also explicitly rejects Saadiah's view that Satan was a human being.

40. Job 42:7–10. Duran's high estimation of Eliphaz is shared by some modern commentators. Robert Gordis describes him as "dignified and urbane" and "the profoundest spirit" among the friends (p. 77).

41. OM, p. 38b. See chapter 2, n. 16, for sources regarding this concept.

42. OM, pp. 38b, 39b.

43. OM, p. 39a.

44. *B.T. Shabbat* 55a, 55b.

45. A play on Job 7:18. "You inspect him every morning, / Examine him every minute."

46. *B.T. Sanhedrin* 89b.

47. OM, p. 35a–b.

48. *B.T. Sanhedrin* 89b.

49. Lit. "kicked" (*bo'et*), in accordance with the biblical usage, "So Jeshurun grew fat and kicked" (Deut. 32:15).

50. OM, p. 40a–b.

51. See OM, p. 41b, where Duran explicitly says that Job was cleansed of sin "through the pain of the trial."

52. I translate here according to Duran's rendering of the biblical text. It is in his interpretation of the last lines that Duran imparts his own meaning to the passage. Cf. the NJPS translation, where the last lines are read very differently: "He opens men's understanding, / And by disciplining them leaves His signature."

53. OM, p. 41b.

54. OM, p. 41b; see also Duran's comments on the verses cited here in OM, p. 56b.

55. I have again departed from the NJPS translation of *mal'akh* as "representative" and have instead chosen to translate it as "angel," since that is the way Duran understood the term.

56. *B.T. Shabbat* 32a; see chapter 2, section headed "The Commentary on Job." Immanuel of Rome also adopts this reading, as noted earlier in chapter 4.

57. OM, p. 41b.

58. OM, p. 41b. In OM, p. 160b, Duran also suggests that the quick succession of punishments is designed to arouse repentance in Job.

59. OM, p. 42a.

60. OM, p. 42a.

61. Job 42:7.

62. OM, pp. 16b–17a, 198a.

63. *B.T. Bava' Batra'* 15b.

64. OM, p. 42b.

65. Duran wrote a brief appendix to *Ohev Mishpat* (pp. 200b–204b) interpreting the biblical and rabbinic sources dealing with the Leviathan. He was no doubt inspired by Job's reference to this creature on two occasions (Job 3:8, 40:25). What is noteworthy here is that Duran reads the biblical and rabbinic sources on Leviathan as an allegorical description of the process leading to immortality and his discussion is highly philosophical.

We should also note how respectful Duran is of the philosophers even when he rejects their ideas. This is especially the case when Duran takes up the positions of Gersonides that aroused controversy among traditionalists. See, for instance, Duran's comments on Gersonides' theory of free will in OM, p. 12a, and on Gersonides' theory of creation in OM, p. 15b. The latter reference is part of a larger discussion in which Duran shows great tolerance toward views he considers incorrect. Duran draws a distinction between three principal dogmas that he believes are fundamental to Judaism—the existence of God, revelation of the Torah, and reward and punishment—and other dogmas, which are "branches" of those first three. It is only when an individual rejects one of the basic principles that he is to be branded a heretic. Hence, Gersonides' theory of creation from preexistent matter, while incorrect, does not render him a heretic. Duran also insists that one is not a heretic unless one purposefully rejects one of the dogmas of the Torah, but if one denies one of those dogmas without knowing that it is from the Torah, one is not a heretic. Duran's tolerance in matters of dogma is discussed in Kellner, *Dogma in Medieval Jewish Thought*, pp. 95–103.

66. See earlier in this chapter, section headed "The Commentary on Job."

67. Ibid.

68. OM, p. 18b.

69. OM, p. 18a–b. Duran refers to Job as an adherent of revealed religion on the assumption that he and other Noahides had access to revealed wisdom before the giving of the Torah. Duran's beliefs with respect to this matter have already been noted earlier in this chapter, section headed "The Commentary on Job." Interestingly, in the continuation of the passage, Duran goes on to say that even the philosophers who believe in an eternal universe can accept his argument for providence here. All they have to do is follow the same line of reasoning and replace the concept of creation *ex nihilo* with their notion of continuous creation. This addendum serves only to highlight the complexity of Duran's approach to philosophy. While Duran declares in this passage that he is not addressing the philosophers, in fact he ends up doing just that.

70. OM, pp. 20b–21a; see earlier in this chapter, section headed "The Commentary on Job." Presumably this argument would also work for Noahides, since they too have received commandments through revealed tradition.

71. See, for instance, Saadiah's justification for the divine commandments, *Beliefs and Opinions* 3, ed. Altmann, introduction, p. 93ff.

72. Duran tends to refer to the soul with the term *nefesh*, while in medieval Kabbalah the preponderant theory is that there are three parts to the soul: *nefesh, ruaḥ,* and *neshamah.* Duran therefore makes no attempt even in his terminology to give a

faithful rendering of kabbalistic doctrine. For a discussion of kabbalistic theories of the soul in medieval Kabbalah, see Tishby and Lachower, *The Wisdom of the "Zohar,"* vol. 3, pp. 684–723.

73. We find this view in such figures as Ibn Ezra and Abraham bar Ḥiyya, who were not kabbalists.

74. On this point, he may be echoing a discomfort similar to that which we find in Maimonides, who also denies that suffering can occur as a test to a completely guiltless individual. See *Guide* III:17, pp. 470–71; and earlier in this chapter, section headed "The Commentary on Job."

75. In one passage Duran also notes that Saadiah's view of Job's trial is similar to that found among "non-Jews" (*umot ha-'olam*) (OM, p. 51a). This indicates that Duran was aware of interpretations of Job outside the Jewish sphere. It may also indicate that Duran rejects Saadiah's view in part because of its proximity to those non-Jewish interpretations. The difficulty is in ascertaining which non-Jewish interpretations Duran was acquainted with and to what extent he was familiar with them. Many Christian commentators held the view that Job's suffering was a trial, and therefore Duran's brief comments do not give us much insight into these questions.

76. See earlier in this chapter, section headed "The Commentary on Job."

77. Naḥmanides, *Torat ha-Adam*, in *Kitvey Ramban*, vol. 2, pp. 269–70.

78. Ibid., pp. 272–73.

79. I depart from the NJPS translation, "Some time afterward," in order to better capture the rabbinic understanding of this clause.

80. *B.T. Sanhedrin* 89b; the translation here is mine in consultation with the Soncino Talmud.

81. One may recall that Gersonides' reading of Job 33 is in turn dependent on that of Ibn Tibbon (see chapter 6, section headed "Antecedents"). My assumption is that in his approach to Job 33, Duran is influenced by Gersonides rather than Ibn Tibbon, since Duran cites Gersonides throughout his commentary but makes no reference to Ibn Tibbon.

82. Naḥmanides is the first kabbalist to read the Book of Job in light of the doctrine of *gilgul*, and his position is adopted by all later kabbalistic thinkers who deal with this issue. Naḥmanides never mentions the doctrine explicitly in the commentary, preferring instead to allude to it by innuendo. See Gershom Scholem, *On The Mystical Shape of the Godhead*, trans. Joachim Neurgroschel and Jonathan Chipman (New York: Schocken Books, 1991), p. 208; Scholem, *Kabbalah* (Jerusalem: Keter, 1974), pp. 345–46; Naḥmanides, *Commentary on the Book of Job*, pp. 23, 97, 99, 101. Most medieval Jewish philosophers never address the issue of reincarnation, but those who do, most often reject it, including Saadiah, Abraham ibn Da'ud, and Joseph Albo. Abraham bar Ḥiyya initially accepted the doctrine but later rejected it. See Scholem, *Kabbalah*, p. 345.

83. OM, p. 156b.

84. OM, p. 159b.

85. OM, p. 160a.

86. *Magen Avot*, p. 88a.

87. *Magen Avot*, p. 33b.

88. The distinction I have found between the two works regarding Naḥmanides' theory of reincarnation serves only to highlight the need for such an undertaking. We are not even sure as to the order of composition of these two works, an essential piece of information for making any determination about their relationship. Jaulus (p. 453) notes that *Ohev Mishpat* was composed in 1405 on the basis of a statement in

Duran's *Yavin Shemu'ah* (Leghorn, 1744), p. 44, that informs us that he composed *Ohev Mishpat* thirty-five years earlier. On the basis of statements in the work itself (p. 13b) and in *Tashbeẓ* (Amsterdam, 1741), vol. 2, p. 70b; vol. 3, p. 69b, we know that *Yavin Shemu'ah* was composed in 1440. Other scholars have generally accepted Jaulus's argument. The time of composition of *Magen Avot*, however, has been far more difficult to determine. Jaulus claims that it was written between 1423 and 1425 on the basis of two citations: one in *Keshet u-Magen*, which was originally part of *Magen Avot* (n. 2 above), claiming that 1423 years have passed since the birth of Jesus, and another in *Magen Avot* in which Duran identifies the year in which he is writing as 1425 (Jaulus, p. 499). Epstein, without referring to Jaulus, takes another position. On the basis of a gloss on the flyleaf of a copy of *Magen Avot* found in the British Museum (p. 7), he claims that *Magen Avot* was written when Duran was forty-five years old. That would place its time of composition in the year 1406, one year after the completion of *Ohev Mishpat*. Warren Zev Harvey takes yet a third position, arguing that *Magen Avot* must have been written earlier than *Ohev Mishpat* because the latter work cites the former (*Ohev Mishpat*, pp. 12a, 29b). *Magen Avot* must therefore have been written before 1405. Harvey argues that the dates in *Magen Avot* noted by Jaulus as proof for a later time of composition may have been adjusted by Duran or a scribe years after the composition of this work; see Warren Zev Harvey, "Albo's Discussion of Time," *Jewish Quarterly Review* 70 (1979–80): p. 211 n. 14. Menachem Kellner has countered that Harvey overlooks a citation in *Magen Avot* that refers to *Ohev Mishpat* (p. 2b) and appears to reestablish the order of composition proposed by Jaulus. Kellner also notes that in a passage in *Tashbeẓ* (at the end of vol. 2) in which Duran lists his own works in order of composition, *Ohev Mishpat* is placed before *Magen Avot*. Kellner therefore concludes, but with a good deal of uncertainty, that *Ohev Mishpat* is the earlier work. See Kellner, *Dogma in Medieval Jewish Thought*, p. 253 n. 8. My own hunch is that *Ohev Mishpat* is earlier, since *Magen Avot* seems to demonstrate much greater familiarity with the ideas in *Ohev Mishpat* than vice versa. For example, as I have just noted, there is a passage in *Magen Avot*—overlooked by the scholars cited here—in which Duran makes reference to *Ohev Mishpat* and gives a summary of his understanding of the Book of Job as explained in that work (p. 33b). That *Ohev Mishpat* cites *Magen Avot* could be explained by arguing that Duran inserted references to the latter after the initial composition of *Ohev Mishpat*. These observations are highly tentative. This whole question requires separate study.

89. My observations may point to a distinction between *Magen Avot* and *Ohev Mishpat* in their respective treatments of Kabbalah. My sense is that although in *Ohev Mishpat* Duran handles Kabbalah with reserve, in *Magen Avot* he is far more unequivocal in his support for it and draws its ideas more frequently into his discussion. This may suggest that *Ohev Mishpat* was written at a stage of Duran's life in which he was less enamored of kabbalistic ideas than at the time of his composition of *Magen Avot*. Once again, this is a matter that requires separate study. Duran discusses kabbalistic ideas quite openly in his responsa. This is pointed out in Louis Jacobs, *Theology in the Responsa* (London: Routledge and Kegan Paul, 1975), pp. 88–94.

90. See the long commentary on Job in Joseph ibn Kaspi, *'Asarah Keley Kesef*, ed. Isaac Last (Pressburg: Alkalay, 1905), vol. 1, pp. 145–47. Perhaps Duran does not cite Kaspi because he was uncomfortable referring to a philosopher who was so controversial, but one might then wonder why Duran frequently cites Gersonides by name, for the latter was also a controversial philosopher. The answer may lie in the fact that Gersonides was a far better known and more respected philosopher than Kaspi. Another factor may have been that Duran was related to Gersonides. Duran's

father was Gersonides' nephew (Epstein, p. 4), and Duran may have been reluctant to criticize a sage who was also a family member. Another possibility is that Duran fails to mention Kaspi because he is often careless about citing sources even when they are not from controversial thinkers. In this discussion, we have seen a number of examples in which Duran does not mention the rabbinic sources upon which he draws.

91. See earlier in this chapter, section headed "The Commentary on Job."

92. See OM, p. 197b, where Duran's remarks on this issue are meager.

93. See earlier in this chapter, section headed "The Commentary on Job."

94. As I have already noted, there is a discussion of providence in *Magen Avot* in addition to that found in *Ohev Mishpat*. However, I will not deal with *Magen Avot* here, for, as I have already stated, the overall relationship between it and *Ohev Mishpat* has not yet been properly investigated, and an examination of this question is needed before we can draw conclusions about the nature of Duran's treatment of providence in each one (see earlier in this chapter, section headed "Antecedents"). There is also reason to suspect that Duran considers his discussion of providence in *Ohev Mishpat* to be the more central of the two. In *Magen Avot*, Duran declares that his discussion of providence in that work will be brief, since "I have already dealt with this at length in the book *Ohev Mishpat*" (*Magen Avot*, p. 33b). Indeed, a cursory reading of the ensuing discussion bears out Duran's observation. I will therefore confine my inquiry of the third interface to *Ohev Mishpat*.

95. See earlier in this chapter, section headed "The Commentary on Job."

96. Duran cites non-philosophical commentators frequently, commentators that have not been mentioned in this discussion, such as Rashi and Ibn Ezra.

97. As noted earlier, Julius Guttmann describes Duran's philosophy as initiating a period in medieval Jewish philosophy that was for the most part unoriginal. The originality of Duran's theory of divine trials is perhaps not enough to overturn that judgment. However, it may indicate that a reevaluation of Guttmann's assessment is in order.

98. According to Epstein, Duran's father was a man of great wealth, wealth that had been inherited from his grandfather (p. 4).

99. See earlier in this chapter, section headed "The Commentary on Job."

100. The first two examples here were also summarized earlier. See ibid.

101. OM, pp. 32a–33b.

102. See Duran's remarks OM, p. 46b, where he interprets the description of Job in 1:3 as *gadol mi-kol beney kedem* to mean that Job either had more wealth than anyone (this is how NJPS understands the phrase) or was greater than everyone else in social status (*be-yaḥas ve-mishpaḥah*).

103. An interpretation of Job that goes much further in the direction suggested here by Duran can be found in a commentary on Job written by R. Phinehas of Polotsk, a nineteenth-century figure who is the subject of a study by Allan Nadler, *The Faith of the Mitnadgim* (Baltimore: Johns Hopkins University Press, 1997). Phinehas argues that Job's initial wealth and material comfort were a hindrance to his spirituality, and it was only when Job was stripped of these that he could form a close relationship with God. The central message of the Book of Job is therefore the glorification of suffering and asceticism as spiritual values (p. 96f.). In this interpretation, we see that the critique of Job's wealth implied in Duran's reading has been brought to the fore and made into the central theme of the book. There is no reason to suspect that Phinehas was influenced by Duran's commentary.

Nadler argues that although there is no precedent for Phinehas's reading of Job in Judaism, one finds interpretations of Job of this sort in medieval Christianity

(p. 200 n. 66, chapter 2, n. 118). Nadler is mostly correct in this assessment. Yet, it should be modified somewhat in light of this study. First, the notion that the Book of Job casts doubt on the importance of wealth is found in Duran, as I have just argued. Moreover, as I have shown, there is an ascetic message that is also present in the readings of Job in Maimonides and Ibn Tibbon. Both thinkers learn from Job that suffering is a means by which human beings are encouraged to loosen their attachment to material things. Thus, while Phinehas's reading presents an unusually extreme understanding of the Book of Job as a text that advocates asceticism and suffering, this approach is not entirely unprecedented in Judaism.

104. See earlier in this chapter, section headed "The Commentary on Job."

105. OM, pp. 8b–9a.

106. I may add here that if indeed Duran's commentary on Job is an attempt to explain his own misfortunes, there is evidence to suggest that Duran was not made bitter by it. Duran's commentary displays a remarkably positive attitude toward the world. We have seen that in Duran's view divine providence ensures that the natural order is generally beneficent to human beings. Divine providence also explains why the wicked are often punished "measure for measure" for their deeds, and this is the reason that despite the existence of large numbers of wicked people in the world, they in fact perpetrate relatively little evil.

107. See earlier in this chapter, section headed "The Commentary on Job." Other discussions of divine providence over the Jewish people are found in OM, pp. 20b–21a, 24a–b, 28b. Yet, in none of these passages is there any suggestion of a connection between Job's suffering and that of the Jewish people.

108. Ms. Oxford Bodleian 1632, fol. 10v. There is very little material on Alcorsono in modern scholarship. See the brief article in *Encyclopedia Judaica*, vol. 2, p. 155.

109. See Ms. Oxford Bodleian 1632, chapters 18–22.

110. The same phenomenon can also be found in Christianity. Gregory tells us that his lengthy work on Job was in part inspired by physical illnesses and suffering he personally experienced. See Besserman, pp. 52–53.

CHAPTER 8

1. After Duran, the conservative approach toward Job continued in a number of other medieval Jewish philosophers. Most notable are Joseph Albo, Obadiah Seforno, and Meir 'Arama. Albo provided an extensive series of reflections on Job in *Sefer ha-'Ikkarim*, ed. and trans. Isaac Husik (Philadelphia: Jewish Publication Society of America, 1930), vol. 4, part 1, p. 54ff. Seforno composed a full-length commentary which is found in *Kitvey R. 'Ovadiah Seforno* (in Hebrew), ed. Zev Gottleib (Jerusalem: Mosad ha-Rav Kuk, 1987), pp. 258–330. Seforno's reading of Job is distinguished by the fact that Job in the wake of his suffering becomes a Dualist. Meir 'Arama composed a full-length commentary entitled *Me'ir Iyyov* (Venice, 1567), in which he cites extensively both from rabbinic sources and medieval Jewish philosophical sources. These commentaries are worthy of separate study.

2. One could argue that Ibn Tibbon's influence also extends indirectly to Duran, since Duran seems to have interpreted Job 33 with the help of Gersonides. I should also mention here that Ibn Tibbon's son, Moses ibn Tibbon, provides a reading of Job 33 in his commentary on the Song of Songs that is strikingly similar to that of his father. See Moses ibn Tibbon, pp. 12b–13b.

3. The influence of Ibn Tibbon's view comes through in a most interesting way

in the commentary of Isaac Arundi, whom we have looked at only briefly in our study. Throughout his commentary, Arundi openly attacks Gersonides' views on Job while presenting a reading that is in many respects similar to that of Ibn Tibbon. Thus, in effect, Arundi chooses Ibn Tibbon's reading of Job over that of Gersonides despite the latter's great stature and the popularity of his commentary on Job. A full explication of Arundi's reading and the nature of his attack on Gersonides deserves separate study.

4. Saadiah's reading appears to do something similar in that Job seems to represent the view of the Ash'arites, while the three friends appear to represent the positions of the Mu'tazilites. However, Saadiah never makes this correspondence explicit.

5. The biblical text also insinuates that Elihu has an important role to play in the dialogue, in that he is the only one of Job's friends who does not bring a sacrifice at the end of the story in what seems to be an act of penance. See Job 42:7–10.

6. Norman Habel characterizes Elihu as a figure who "seems to represent the theology of those who believe that God no longer intervenes directly in human lives as in the heroic days of Noah and Abraham" (p. 33; see also p. 64). If Habel's description is correct, it may explain why the radical thinkers in this study, in particular, were so attracted to Elihu. The notion that God does not intervene in human affairs fits nicely with the philosophical orientation of these thinkers.

7. Gregory the Great draws a connection between Job's suffering and the suffering of the early church at the hands of heretics and persecutors (Schreiner, p. 40). We therefore have an example of how a Christian thinker used the figure of Job to make sense of the suffering of Christians as a corporate entity, much as Saadiah and Gersonides did with the Jewish people. We also have the interesting theory of Origen, who believed that Moses, while wandering in the land of Midian, either heard the story of Job or more probably encountered the book written in Syriac, and then proceeded to translate it into Hebrew for the purpose of comforting the Israelites, who were then slaves in Egypt. Origen therefore implicitly acknowledges that Job is a symbol for the suffering of the Jewish people, but in his thinking it relates specifically to their suffering in Egypt! See Lewalski, p. 12.

Job was not the only book in the Bible that inspired medieval Jewish thinkers to reflect on the historical experience of exile. In his study *Esther in Medieval Garb*, Barry Walfish demonstrates that a number of medieval Jewish exegetes used the Book of Esther to grapple with Jewish persecution—though most of the thinkers that Walfish deals with in this study were not philosophers.

8. This view is also found among Christian exegetes. Origen, for instance, believed that Moses was the author of Job. See Lewalski, p. 12. Gordis notes that as late as the early twentieth century, scholars dated the Book of Job to the period of Moses but not to Moses himself. Most modern scholars date Job anywhere between the sixth and second centuries B.C.E. Various theories regarding the sources of Job and its editing are discussed extensively in Rowley, pp. 141–86, and Gordis, pp. 65–75.

9. This division is, of course, somewhat simplistic because there are many variations of philosophical approaches within the camps themselves. There are also thinkers who are not easy to classify, such as Gersonides, because they fall between the camps. Moreover, there is sometimes disagreement among scholars on which camp a given philosopher belongs to. For instance, I have placed Maimonides in the radical camp, but there are some scholars who see him as a conservative. Despite these considerations, the demarcation between conservative and radical is beneficial in helping to organize the material examined in this study.

10. For the purposes of this argument, I classify Gersonides as a conservative

because, as we have seen, he has leanings in that direction of the philosophical spectrum in some respects.

11. Yet, most early rabbinic commentators see Job failing the test, while Saadiah and Duran see him passing it. A full discussion of the rabbinic view that Job's suffering is a test can be found in Leibowitz, pp. 247–75.

12. The radical philosophers must, of course, make sense of the classic test in the Bible, which is the binding of Isaac. These thinkers use a number of approaches that cannot easily be summarized here. Maimonides' discussion of the *'akeidah* is found in *Guide* III:24, pp. 500–502. An approach found in later thinkers that attempts to circumvent many of the philosophical problems with the *'akeidah* is the claim that it took place in a prophetic vision. See Jacob Anatoli, *Malmad ha-Talmidim*, p. 18a, and Zeraḥiah Ḥen's letters to Hillel of Verona (Zeraḥiah, *Iggeret le-Hillel mi-Veronah*, ed. R. Kirchheim, *Oẓar Neḥmad* 2 [1857]: 117–43).

13. The *'akeidah* presents other philosophical problems, such as the question of determinism and divine foreknowledge, that are difficult for conservatives and radicals alike. Seymour Feldman discusses these issues as they pertain to the interpretation of the *'akeidah* in Saadiah, Maimonides, and Gersonides; Feldman, "The Binding of Isaac."

14. This is not to say that according to this approach the Book of Job discusses the true view of providence openly. As we have seen, the radical thinkers are unanimous in reading Job as a text that conceals that view. The truth of providence is made available in the Book of Job in a way that it is not in other parts of the Bible, for it is in that book alone that the correct position on providence is systematically worked out—if one knows how to penetrate its inner meaning.

15. See, for instance, Dov Schwartz's reviews of positions on providence in medieval Jewish philosophy; Schwartz, "The Debate over the Maimonidean Theory of Providence," pp. 188–91, and "The *Mesharet Moshe* of R. Kalonymus" (in Hebrew), *Koveẓ 'al Yad*, n.s. 14, no. 24 (1998): 325–35. In neither of these discussions is there any mention of Ibn Tibbon's notion that the highest form of providence is immortality of the intellect.

16. See Rosenberg, "Philosophical Hermeneutics"; I. Ravitzky, "R. Immanuel b. Solomon." See also Kellner, "Communication or the Lack Thereof," and my qualifying remarks, chapter 6, n. 79.

17. As noted earlier, the most authoritative treatment of this issue in recent years is Talmage, "Apples of Gold."

18. Sources for this observation are too numerous to cite, but I will note some representative examples. Ibn Tibbon's exegesis in *Ma'amar Yikkavu ha-Mayim* is filled with references to philology, grammar, syntax, and context in the biblical text—the hallmarks of *peshat* exegesis. Jacob Anatoli identifies the distinction between the outer and inner meaning of the biblical text with the distinction between *peshat* and *derash* (*Malmad ha-Talmidim*, p. 116b). Gersonides and Kaspi composed an extensive body of commentaries that often focus on *peshat* while downplaying allegory. See, for instance, Gersonides' remarks in the introduction to his commentary on the Torah, where he claims that his interest is in reading the biblical text according to its *peshat* (Gersonides, *Perush 'al ha-Torah*, p. 2c).

CHAPTER 9

1. The only scholar who, to my knowledge, has offered an in-depth comparison between medieval and modern views on Job is Schreiner, pp. 156–90, who provides a

groundbreaking treatment of this issue. The present discussion is very much indebted to Schreiner's work. Even though she focuses primarily on readings of Job in medieval Christianity, she also deals with Maimonides, who is a pivotal figure in the present study. Moreover, her overall framing of the issues has provided valuable guidance for the deliberations presented here.

2. Marvin H. Pope, *Job (Anchor Bible Commentary)* (New York: Doubleday, 1965); Georg Fohrer, *Das Buch Hiob* (Gütersloh: Gerd Mohn, 1963); Rowley, pp. 141–83.

3. Samuel Terrien, *Job: Poet of Existence* (New York: Bobbs-Merrill, 1957); Gordis, *The Book of God and Man*; Matitiahu Tsevat, "The Meaning of the Book of Job," *Hebrew Union College Annual* 37 (1966): 73–106.

4. Habel, *The Book of Job*; Edwin M. Good, *In Turns of Tempest: A Reading of Job with a Translation* (Stanford, Calif.: Stanford University Press, 1990).

5. Archibald MacLeish, *J. B.* (Cambridge, Mass.: Riverside Press, 1958); Franz Kafka, *The Trial*, trans. Douglas Scott and Chris Waller (London: Pan Books, 1977); Robert Frost, "Masque of Reason," in *Selected Poems of Robert Frost* (New York: Holt, Rinehart, and Winston, 1963), pp. 272–88. This is by no means an exhaustive list of the various approaches to Job in modern scholarship, but it does account for many of the major interpreters. The lines of demarcation between the groups described here are not always clear. For instance, scholars of the historical-critical school frequently offer important insights into the theological meaning of Job, while the more theologically oriented commentators often rely on the insights of scholars of the historical-critical method for their theological judgments.

6. In her comparison of medieval and modern readings of Job, Schreiner skillfully works these modern literary writers into her discussion (pp. 169–90). However, my sense is that despite her efforts the agenda of such writers is too distant from the medieval philosophers to make such a comparison. If there is any commonality between the two groups, it is only a general one at best.

7. Karl Budde, *Das Buch Hiob* (Göttingen: Vandenhoek and Ruprecht, 1896), p. xxxv; Carl Cornill, *Introduction to the Canonical Books of the Old Testament*, trans. G. H. Box (New York: G. P. Putnam, 1907), pp. 426ff.; Yehezkel Kauffmann, *The Religion of Israel*, trans. and abridged Moshe Greenberg (Chicago: University of Chicago Press, 1960), pp. 336–38. According to these interpreters, Elihu's viewpoint—and hence the message of the book as a whole—is that undeserved suffering is meant to discipline human beings in order to prevent them from sinning in the future. These commentators find that message in Job 33:14f., the same portion of Elihu's address that drew the attention of our medieval philosophers.

8. The various modern scholarly views on the Elihu speeches are summarized in Rowley, pp. 145–46, and Gordis, pp. 104–10. Gordis's own view is that the Elihu speeches are a later interpolation but by the same author who composed the dialogue. He also contends that the speeches function as a bridge between the dialogue and the final answer given by God (Gordis, pp. 110–16).

9. See chapter 5, section headed "The Commentary on Job."

10. Some, however, hold the view that the story may have been based on a true historical figure. Rowley summarizes the major approaches to this issue (p. 146).

11. That Job was a historical individual, however, did not stop medieval Christian interpreters from attaching allegorical meaning to the book. A ubiquitous theme in medieval Christian readings of Job was that the figure of Job was a prefiguration of the suffering Christ. It was Gregory the Great who was most consistent in applying the allegorical method to Job: much of his *Magna Moralia* is focused on this task. Yet, medieval Christian writers generally believed that the figure of Job was a historical

individual and that the Book of Job reported actual events. There is, however, the interesting case of Theodore, Bishop of Mopsuestia in the fourth century, who believed that Job existed but that the biblical book about him was fiction. From various clues in Job, Theodore concluded that the book was written by a pagan writer who had used the story of Job for his own purposes and had therefore demeaned the revered patriarch. Theodore therefore had the book taken out of the biblical canon. Theodore was later removed from good standing by the Fifth Ecumenical Council. The first medieval Christian thinker to show an awareness of the Talmudic view that the figure of Job never existed is Nicholas of Lyra. Nicholas, however, rejected that view. Several centuries later, the historicity of Job was questioned by Luther because he was not convinced that all its details were true. However, Luther believed that the book was in large part historical. In the late eighteenth century, a major debate erupted about the historicity of Job, with a Christian thinker for the first time defending the view that Job was complete fiction. That thinker was William Warburton, who, in a widely circulated study, argued that the Book of Job was an allegory for the situation of the Jews during their captivity in Babylon. The Hebraist Robert Lowth responded to Warburton and defended the view that Job was indeed historically true. Information about medieval and early modern Christian attitudes to the historicity of Job can be found in Siger, p. 6 n. 9, 39–70; Rowley, p. 146; Lewalski. p. 12. Information about the eighteenth-century debate regarding Job's historicity can be found in Newsom and Schreiner, p. 592, and Lamb, pp. 110–28.

12. Note the characterization of Job in J. Gerald Janzen, *Job* (Atlanta: John Knox Press, 1985), p. 5: "The story of Job is set 'long ago and far away.' It is as though a deliberate effort had been made to pose the problems raised in the book in general human terms, by removing the story from a specifically Israelite setting."

13. Some modern thinkers interpret Job as an allegory for Jewish suffering. Martin Buber argues that the Book of Job and the Suffering Servant imagery in Deutero-Isaiah were both an attempt to grapple with Jewish suffering during the Babylonian exile. Steven Kepnes has also argued that Buber seems to have used Job as means for grappling with the Holocaust. See Kepnes, *The Text as Thou: Martin Buber's Dialogical Hermeneutics and Narrative Theology* (Bloomington: Indiana University Press, 1992), pp. 137–40. A more ambitious, albeit less scholarly, attempt to relate the Book of Job to the suffering of the Jewish people throughout history is that of the German-Jewish essayist and poet Margerete Susman; Susman, *Das Buch Hiob und das Schicksal des jüdischen Volkes* (Zurich, 1946). Susman also connects the suffering of Job to that of the nations as a whole. Glatzer presents an English translation of a selection from Susman's introduction to Kafka's *Gestalten und Kriese* in which she summarizes her views on Job (Glatzer, *Dimensions of Job*, pp. 86–92).

14. Schreiner, pp. 159–60.

15. Terrien, pp. 108–9; Good, p. 229; Schreiner, p. 160.

16. See, for example, Gordis, p. 152; Tsevat, pp. 74–76.

17. Rowley, pp. 170–73; Pope, lxxiii–lxxxiv; Terrien, p. 68; Gordis, pp. 149–56; Tsevat, pp. 98f.; Besserman, pp. 11–17; Habel, p. 65. Isaac Arundi and Meir 'Arama read the dialogue as Saadiah does, and therefore they too anticipate modern readings of Job. As we have seen, the radical philosophers in this study take an entirely different position on the nature of the dialogue, arguing that each of the figures represents a different philosophical school of thought. Modern scholars generally do not accept this view, though there are some who come close to it by attempting to show that each of the figures represents a distinct position. See Besserman, p. 10, and sources cited.

18. See, for instance, the comments of Paul Dhorme, *A Commentary on the Book of Job*, trans. Harold Knight (London: Thomas Nelson and Sons, 1967), p. xci.

19. See n. 17 of this chapter for sources. Some modern interpreters have claimed that in arguing against the notion of retributive justice, the Book of Job is taking a stand against the notion of divine justice in the Hebrew Bible as a whole. Recent scholars have taken a more nuanced position, claiming that even though the Hebrew Bible certainly supports the notion of retributive justice in many places, its views on the subject are far from uniform. Therefore, if the Book of Job is arguing against retributive justice, it is arguing against only one, albeit important, strand in the Hebrew Bible, such as that which permeates the Book of Deuteronomy. That strand may reflect the viewpoint of a wealthy social group in ancient Israel that believed their good fortune was indicative of their righteousness. It also represents a viewpoint that was widespread in Mesopotamian culture well before the composition of the Hebrew Bible. At any rate, the important point for our purposes is that the radical philosophers seem to foreshadow the moderns with the position that the Book of Job is speaking out against the notion of retributive justice found in the Hebrew Bible.

20. Tsevat, p. 96f.

21. Pope, pp. lxxiv–lxxvi.

22. Gordis, p. 133. Gordis, therefore, does not see the Book of Job as banishing rational reflection entirely in grappling with the mystery of the suffering of the righteous, only as limiting its usefulness.

23. Martin Buber, *At the Turning* (New York: Farrar, Strauss, and Giroux, 1952), pp. 61–62; Terrien, p. 16; Habel, p. 68; Rowley, pp. 175–79; Fohrer, p. 549.

24. The affinity between Maimonides and the moderns is noted in Schreiner, pp. 160, 162.

25. A similar observation is made by Schreiner, p. 158, in her comparison of medieval Christian readings of Job with those of modern thinkers.

26. Zeraḥiah does refer, in his reading of the final chapters of Job, to the notion that God's ways are unknowable, but, as I have shown, this interpretation is meant for the masses, not for the elite.

27. Schreiner, in fact, implicitly recognizes this affinity by grouping Maimonides with Aquinas and Calvin as thinkers who share a common approach toward the Book of Job when it comes to the question of retributive justice. See Schreiner, p. 158. One cannot deny altogether a historical connection between medieval Jewish and Christian philosophers with respect to the Book of Job. Maimonides' *Guide* was translated into Latin, and it has been long recognized that his reading of Job influenced a number of Christian philosophical exegetes, including Thomas Aquinas, Albertus Magnus, Cardinal Cajetan, and Oecolampadius. See Beryl Smalley, *The Study of the Bible in the Middle Ages* (Notre Dame: University of Notre Dame Press, 1964), p. 302; Newsom and Schreiner, p. 591. Influences of Christian readings on Jewish readings in medieval philosophy are much more rare. In this study, only Zeraḥiah Ḥen may have absorbed Christian teachings on Job, but the evidence is not conclusive. See chapter 5, n. 59 and n. 62. However, there is no historical connection between Jewish and Christian philosophical exegetes with respect to the specific issues discussed here that concern a hidden layer of meaning in Job. The comparison I have made between the two traditions of exegesis regarding this subject is therefore strictly phenomenological.

28. A discussion of this issue can be found in Georges Vajda, *Isaac Albalag: averroïste juif, tradacteur, et annotateur d'Al-Ghazâlî* (Paris: J. Vrin, 1960), pp. 256–60.

Vajda provides a number of reasons why medieval Jewish philosophers were more willing than their Christian counterparts to adopt radical Aristotelianism.

29. Kember Fullerton, "The Original Conclusion of Job," *Zeitschrift für die Alttestamentliche Wissenschaft* 24 (1924): 116–36; Gordis, pp. 124–25, considers this theory "ingenious" but critically flawed.

30. Tsevat, p. 103.

31. Ibid.

32. Janzen, pp. 226–27.

Works Cited

This bibliography includes all sources cited in this study except for commentaries on Job composed by medieval Jewish philosophers, which are described in the appendix.

MANUSCRIPTS

Alcorsono, Judah. *Aron ha-'Edut.* Ms. Oxford Bodleian 1632.

Ḥen, Zeraḥiah ben Isaac ben She'alti'el. *Iggeret le-Yehudah ben Shlomoh.* Ms. Cambridge Addenauer 1235, fols. 91r–97v.

Levi ben Abraham of Villefranche. *Livyat Ḥen.* Ms. Munich 58.

Solomon ben Yuda' ha-Nasi. *Perush 'al Sodot ha-Moreh.* Ms. Cambridge Addenauer 373/2.

PRIMARY SOURCES

Anatoli, Jacob. *Malmad ha-Talmidim.* Lyck: Mekiẓey Nirdamim, 1866.

Aristotle. *The Works of Aristotle.* Translated under the editorship of W. D. Ross. 10 vols. Oxford: Clarendon Press, 1908–31.

Avot de-R. Natan. Edited by Solomon Schechter. London and Frankfurt, 1887.

Babylonian Talmud. Standard edition.

Baḥya ben Asher. *Kad ha-Kemaḥ.* Edited by Ḥayim Breit. Lemberg, 1880.

Bereshit Rabbah. Edited with notes by J. Theodor and Ch. Albeck. 3 vols. Jerusalem: Wahrmann Books, 1965.

Bleich, J. David. *Providence and the Philosophy of Gersonides.* Translation and notes, book 4 of *The Wars of the Lord.* New York: Yeshiva University Press, 1973.

Crescas, Asher. *Perush 'al Moreh Nevukhim.* Standard Hebrew edition of the *Guide.*

Duran, Simon ben Ẓemaḥ. *Magen Avot.* Leghorn, 1763.

———. *Tashbeẓ*. Amsterdam, 1741.

———. *Yavin Shemu'ah*. Leghorn, 1744.

Efodi (Profiat Duran). *Perush 'al Moreh Nevukhim*. Standard Hebrew edition of the *Guide*.

Ein Ya'akov. Standard edition.

Gersonides. *Perush 'al ha-Torah*. Venice: D. Bomberg, 1547.

———. *Sefer Milḥamot ha-Shem*. Riva di Trento, 1560.

———. *Sefer Milḥamot ha-Shem*. Leipzig: C. B. Lorck, 1866.

———. *The Wars of the Lord*. Translated by Seymour Feldman. 3 vols. Philadelphia: Jewish Publication Society of America, 1984–99.

Ḥen, Zeraḥiah ben Isaac ben She'alti'el. *Iggeret le-Hillel mi-Veronah*. Edited by R. Kirchheim. *Oẓar Neḥmad* 2 (1857): 124–43.

———. *Imrey Da'at*. Edited by Israel Schwartz. Vienna, 1871.

Ibn Ezra, Abraham. *Perush 'al Sefer Iyyov*. Standard rabbinic Bibles.

Ibn Tibbon, Moses. *Perush Shir ha-Shirim Me-R. Moshe ibn Tibbon*. Lyck: Mekiẓey Nirdamim, 1874.

Ibn Tibbon, Samuel. *Ma'amar Yikkavu ha-Mayim*. Edited by M. L. Bisliches. Pressburg, 1837.

Immanuel of Rome. *Perush 'al Sefer Mishley*. Edited by David Goldstein. Jerusalem: Magnes Press, 1980.

Jerusalem Talmud. Standard edition.

Kaspi, Joseph ibn. *'Ammudey Kesef*. Edited by S. Werbluner. In *Sheloshah Kadmoney Mefarshey ha-Moreh*, ed. Jacob Goldenthal. Jerusalem: Ortsel, 1961.

———. *Shulḥan Kesef*. Edited by Hannah Kasher. Jerusalem: Ben Ẓvi Institute, 1996.

Kimḥi, Moshe. *Commentary on the Book of Job*. Edited by Herbert Basser and Barry D. Walfish. Atlanta: Scholars Press, 1992.

Lassen, Abraham. *The Commentary of Levi ben Gershom on the Book of Job*. New York: Bloch, 1946.

Midrash Iyyov. Edited by Solomon A. Wertheimer. In *Batey Midrashot*, vol. 2, pp. 150–86. Jerusalem: Ktab Yad Wasepher, 1989.

Midrash Rabbah. 2 vols. Vilna, 1878; reprint, Jerusalem, 1975.

———. Translated by H. Freedman and Maurice Simon. 10 vols. London and New York: Soncino Press, 1983.

Maimonides, Moses. *Le guide des égarés*. Edited and translated by Solomon Munk. Paris: A. Franck, 1855–66.

———. *The Guide of the Perplexed*. Translated by Shlomo Pines. Chicago: University of Chicago Press, 1963.

———. *Koveẓ Teshuvot ha-Rambam ve-Iggerotav*. Edited by A. Lichtenberg. 3 vols. Leipzig, 1859.

———. *Mishneh Torah*. Standard edition.

———. *Moreh Nevukhim*. Standard edition.

Murciano, Prosper. "Simon ben Ẓemaḥ Duran's *Keshet U-Magen*: A Critical Edition." Ph.D. diss., New York University, 1975.

Naḥmanides, Moses. *Kitvey Ramban*. Edited by Chayim D. Chavel. 2 vols. Jerusalem: Mosad ha-Rav Kuk, 1973.

Narboni, Moses. *Perush 'al Moreh Nevukhim*. Edited by Jacob Goldenthal. In *Sheloshah Kadmoney Mefarshey ha-Moreh*. Jerusalem: Ortsel, 1961.

Nissim ben Moshe of Marseilles. *Ma'aseh Nissim*. Edited by Howard (Ḥayim) Kreisel. Jerusalem: Mekiẓey Nirdamim, 2000.

Pesikta de-R. Kahana. Edited by Bernard Mandelbaum. New York: Jewish Theological Seminary, 1987.
Pesikta Rabbati. Edited by Rivka Ulmer. Atlanta: Scholars Press, 1997.
Rashi. *Perush 'al Sefer Iyyov.* Standard rabbinic Bibles.
Saadiah Gaon. *The Book of Beliefs and Opinions.* Translated by Samuel Rosenblatt. New Haven: Yale University Press, 1948.
______. *Perushey R. Saadi'ah Ga'on li-Bre'shit.* Arabic text with Hebrew translation by Moshe Zucker. New York: Jewish Theological Seminary, 1984.
______. *Perushey R. Sa'adiah Ga'on le-Sefer Shemot.* Arabic text with Hebrew translation by Yehudah Ratzaby. Jerusalem: Mosad ha-Rav Kuk, 1998.
______. *Sefer ha-Nivḥar be-Emunot ve-De'ot.* Arabic text with Hebrew translation by Joseph Kafiḥ. Jerusalem: Sura, n.d.
______. "Selections of *Beliefs and Opinions.*" Edited and translated by Alexander Altmann. In *Three Jewish Philosophers,* eds. Hans Lewy, Alexander Altmann, and Isaak Heinemann, part 2. New York: Atheneum, 1969.
Samuelson, Norbert M. *Gersonides on God's Knowledge.* Translation and notes, book 3 of *The Wars of the Lord.* Toronto: Pontifical Institute for Mediaeval Studies, 1977.
Sefer ha-Zohar. Edited by Moshe Margaliyot. 3 vols. Jerusalem: Mosad ha-Rav Kuk, 1978.
Shem Tov ben Joseph ibn Shem Tov. *Perush 'al Moreh Nevukhim.* Standard Hebrew edition.
Tam, Jacob. *Perush 'al Sefer Iyyov.* Edited by Yisra'el Ta-Shema. *Kovez̩ 'al Yad* 13 (1996): 191–233.
Tanḥuma. Edited by Solomon Buber. 2 vols. New York: Sefer, 1946.

SECONDARY SOURCES

Altenberger, Christophore. *RaLBaG h.e. Rabbi Levi ben Gersom, Commentarius Rabbinicus in cap. VI et VII HIOBI cum versione latina et annotationibus.* Leipzig, 1705.
Altmann, Alexander. "Maimonides on the Intellect and the Scope of Metaphysics." In *Von der mittelalterlichen zur modernen Aufklärung,* pp. 61–129. Tübingen: J.C.B. Mohr (Paul Siebeck), 1987.
Arieli, Nahum. "The Philosophy of Rashbaz̩: Simon ben Z̩emaḥ Duran" (in Hebrew). Ph.D. diss., Hebrew University, 1976.
Baron, Salo W. *A Social and Religious History of the Jews.* New York: Columbia University Press, 1958.
Baskin, Judith R. *Pharaoh's Counsellors: Job, Jethro, and Balaam in Rabbinic and Patristic Tradition.* Chico, Calif.: Scholars Press, 1983.
Ben Me'ir, Ruth. "The Commentary of Levi ben Gershom on Ecclesiastes" (in Hebrew). Ph.D. diss., Hebrew University, 1993.
Berfet, Zark. *Perush Iyyov be-Kiz̩ur Muflag.* Venice, 1544; Cracow, 1574.
Berger, David. "Miracles and the Natural Order in Naḥmanides." In *Rabbi Moses Naḥmanides (Ramban): Explorations in His Religious and Literary Virtuosity,* ed. Isadore Twersky, pp. 107–28. Cambridge, Mass.: Harvard University Press, 1983.
Besserman, Lawrence, *The Legend of Job in the Middle Ages.* Cambridge, Mass.: Harvard University Press, 1979.
Bleich, J. David. "Duran's View of the Nature of Providence." *Jewish Quarterly Review* 69 (1979): 208–25.
______. "Providence in Late Medieval Jewish Philosophy." Ph.D. diss., New York University, 1974.

Blumberg, Harry. "The Problem of Immortality in Avicenna, Maimonides, and St. Thomas." In *The Harry Austryn Wolfson Jubilee Volume,* ed. Saul Leiberman, vol. 1, pp. 165–85. Jerusalem: American Academy for Jewish Research, 1963.

Buber, Martin. *At the Turning.* New York: Farrar, Straus, and Giroux, 1952.

Budde, Karl. *Das Buch Hiob.* Göttingen: Vandenhoek and Ruprecht, 1896.

Clines, David J. A. *World Biblical Commentary: Job 1–20.* Dallas: Word Books, 1989.

Cohen, Mordechai Z. "*Peshat* Exegesis of a Philosopher: Maimonides' Literary Approach to the Book of Job and Its Place in the History of Biblical Interpretation" (in Hebrew). In *Shnaton: An Annual for Biblical and Ancient Near Eastern Studies,* forthcoming.

———. *Three Approaches to Biblical Metaphor: From Abraham Ibn Ezra and Maimonides to David Kimḥi.* Leiden: E. J. Brill, 2003.

Cornill, Carl. *Introduction to the Canonical Books of the Old Testament.* Translated by G. H. Box. New York: G. P. Putnam, 1907.

Dailey, Thomas F., and Watson E. Mills. *The Book of Job.* Bibliographies for Biblical Research, Old Testament Series 13. Lewiston, N.Y.: Edwin Mellen Press, 1997.

Davidson, Herbert. *Alfarabi, Avicenna, and Averroes on the Intellect.* New York: Oxford University Press, 1992.

———. "Maimonides on Metaphysical Knowledge." *Maimonidean Studies* 3 (1992–93): 49–103.

De Boer, P.A.H. "Does Job Retract?" In *Selected Studies in Old Testament Exegesis,* ed. C. Van Duin, pp. 179–95. Leiden: E. J. Brill, 1991.

Déclais, Jean-Louis. *Les premiers musulmans face á la tradition biblique: trois récits sur Job.* Paris: L'Harmattan, 1996.

Dhorme, Paul. *A Commentary on the Book of Job.* Translated by Harold Knight. London: Thomas Nelson and Sons, 1967.

Dienstag, Israel Jacob. "Providence in the Teaching of Maimonides: A Bibliography" (in Hebrew). *Da'at* 20 (1988): 5–28.

Diesendruck, Z. "Samuel and Moses ibn Tibbon on Maimonides' Theory of Providence." *Hebrew Union College Annual* 11 (1936): 341–66.

Dobbs-Weinstein, Idit. "The Existential Dimension of Providence in the Thought of Gersonides." In *Gersonide en son temps,* ed. Gilbert Dahan, pp. 159–78. Louvain-Paris: E. Peeters, 1991.

———. *Maimonides and St. Thomas on the Limits of Reason.* Albany: State University of New York Press, 1995.

Driver, Samuel R., and Gray, George B. *A Critical and Exegetical Commentary on the Book of Job.* Edinburgh: T. and T. Clark, 1921.

Efros, Israel. *Studies in Medieval Jewish Philosophy.* New York: Columbia University Press, 1974.

Eisen, Robert. "Did Zeraḥiah Ḥen Compose Two Versions of His *Commentary on the Book of Job?*" *Da'at* 48 (Winter 2002): v–xxvi.

———. "Gersonides' *Commentary on the Book of Job.*" *Journal of Jewish Thought and Philosophy* 10 (2001): 239–88.

———. *Gersonides on Providence, Covenant, and the Chosen People: A Study in Medieval Jewish Philosophy and Biblical Commentary.* Albany: State University of New York Press, 1995.

———. "Job as a Symbol for Israel in the Thought of Saadiah Gaon." *Da'at* 41 (Summer 1998): v–xxv.

———. "*Lifnim mi-Shurat ha-Din* in Maimonides' *Mishneh Torah.*" *Jewish Quarterly Review* 89, no. 3–4 (Winter 1999): 294–317.

______. "Reason, Revelation, and the Fundamental Principles of the Torah in Gersonides' Thought." *Proceedings of the American Academy for Jewish Research* 57 (1991): 11–34.

______. "Samuel ibn Tibbon on the Book of Job." *AJS Review* 24:2 (Fall 1999): 263–300.

Emory, Richard. *The Jews of Perpignan in the Thirteenth Century.* New York: Columbia University Press, 1959.

Encyclopedia Judaica. Jerusalem: Keter, 1972.

Epstein, Isidore. *The Responsa of Rabbi Simon b. Ẓemaḥ Duran as a Source of the History of the Jews of North Africa.* New York: Ktav, 1930.

Evans, J.D.C. *Aristotle's Concept of Dialectic.* Cambridge: Cambridge University Press, 1977.

Feldman, Seymour. "The Binding of Isaac: The Test-Case of Divine Omniscience." In *Divine Omniscience and Omnipotence in Medieval Philosophy*, ed. Tamar Rudavsky, pp. 105–35. Dordrecht: D. Reidel, 1985.

______. "Gersonides and Biblical Exegesis." Appendix to *The Wars of the Lord*, vol. 2, pp. 213–47. Philadelphia: Jewish Publication Society of America, 1987.

______. "The Wisdom of Solomon: A Gersonidean Interpretation." In *Gersonide en son temps*, ed. Gilbert Dahan, pp. 61–80. Louvain-Paris: E. Peeters, 1991.

Fohrer, Georg. *Das Buch Hiob.* Gütersloh: Gerd Mohn, 1963.

Fox, Marvin. *Interpreting Maimonides.* Chicago: University of Chicago Press, 1990.

Fraenkel, Carlos. *From Maimonides to Samuel ibn Tibbon: The Method of "The Guide of the Perplexed"* (in Hebrew). Jerusalem: Magnes Press, forthcoming.

Frank, Daniel. "The Religious Philosophy of the Karaite Aaron ben Elijah: The Problem of Divine Justice." Ph.D. diss., Harvard University, 1991.

Frank, Daniel H. "Anger as a Vice: A Maimonidean Critique of Aristotelian Ethics." *History of Philosophy Quarterly* 7, no. 3 (July 1990): 269–81.

______. "Humility as a Virtue: A Maimonidean Critique of Aristotle's Ethics." In *Moses Maimonides in His Time*, ed. Eric L. Ormsby, pp. 88–99. Washington, D.C.: Catholic University of America, 1991.

Frank, Daniel H., and Oliver Leaman, eds. *A History of Jewish Philosophy.* London and New York: Routledge, 1997.

Freyman, Eliyahu. "Le commentaire de Gersonide sur la Pentateuque." In *Gersonide en son temps*, ed. Gilbert Dahan, pp. 117–32. Louvain-Paris: E. Peeters, 1991.

Frost, Robert. "Masque of Reason." In *Selected Poems of Robert Frost*, pp. 272–88. New York: Holt, Rinehart, and Winston, 1963.

Fullerton, Kember. "The Original Conclusion of Job." *Zeitschrift für die Alttestamentliche Wissenschaft* 24 (1924): 116–36.

Funkenstein, Amos. "Gersonides' Biblical Commentary: Science, History and Providence." In *Studies on Gersonides: A Fourteenth-Century Jewish Philosopher-Scientist*, ed. Gad Freudenthal, pp. 305–15. Leiden: E. J. Brill, 1992.

Gauthier, Léon. *La théorie d'Ibn Rushd (Averroès) sur les rapports de la religion et de la philosophie.* Paris, 1909.

Geiger, Abraham. "Alte Commentare zu Hiob." *Jüdische Zeitschrift* 7 (1869): 141–50.

Genot-Bismuth, Jaqueline. "Poétique et philosophie dans l'oeuvre d'Immanuel de Rome." Ph.D. diss., University of Paris, 1976.

Gillet, Robert. "Les sources des 'Morales.' " *Sources chrétiennes* 32 (1975): 82–85.

Ginzberg, Louis. *Legends of the Jews.* 7 vols. Philadelphia: Jewish Publication Society of America, 1909.

Glatzer, Nahum N. "The Book of Job and Its Interpreters." In *Biblical Motifs: Origins and Transformations,* ed. Alexander Altmann, pp. 197–220. Cambridge, Mass.: Phillip W. Lown Institute of Advanced Judaic Studies, 1966.

———. *The Dimensions of Job: A Study and Selected Readings.* New York: Schocken Books, 1969.

Goldman, Eliezer. "The Special Worship of Those Apprehending the True Realities" (in Hebrew). *Bar-Ilan* 6 (1968): 287–313.

Good, Edwin M. *In Turns of Tempest: A Reading of Job with a Translation.* Stanford, Calif.: Stanford University Press, 1990

Gordis, Robert. *The Book of God and Man: A Study of Job.* Chicago: University of Chicago Press, 1965.

Gordon, Martin L. "The Philosophical Rationalism of Jacob Anatoli." Ph.D. diss., Yeshiva University, 1974.

Greenberg, Moshe. "Did Job Exist or Not? A Discussion in Medieval Exegesis" (in Hebrew). In *Sha'arei Talmon: Studies in the Bible, Qumran, and the Ancient Near East, Presented to Shemaryahu Talmon,* ed. Michael Fishbane and Emanuel Tov, pp. 3–10. Winona Lake, Ind.: Eisenbrauns, 1992.

Greenberg, Moshe, ed. *Jewish Biblical Exegesis: An Introduction* (in Hebrew). Jerusalem: Magnes Press, 1983.

Guthrie, W.K.C. *A History of Greek Philosophy.* 6 vols. Cambridge: Cambridge University Press, 1981.

Guttmann, Jakob. *Die Religionsphilosophie des Saadia.* Göttingen: Vandenhoeck and Ruprecht, 1882.

———. "Die Stellung des Simeon ben Zemah Duran in der jüdischen Religionsphilosophie." *Monatsschrift für Geschichte und Wissenschaft des Judentums* 52 (1908): 641–72; 53 (1909): 46–79, 199–228.

Guttmann, Julius. *Philosophies of Judaism.* Translated by David Silverman. New York: Schocken Books, 1973.

Habel, Norman C. *The Book of Job.* London: S.C.M. Press, 1983.

Halivni, David Weiss. *Peshat and Derash: Plain and Applied Meaning in Rabbinic Exegesis.* New York: Oxford University Press, 1991.

Hartman, David. *Maimonides: Torah and Philosophical Quest.* Philadelphia: Jewish Publication Society of America, 1976.

Harvey, Steven. "Maimonides in the Sultan's Palace." In *Perspectives on Maimonides,* ed. Joel Kraemer, pp. 47–76. Oxford: Oxford University Press, 1991.

Harvey, Warren Zev. "Albo's Discussion of Time." *Jewish Quarterly Review* 70 (1979–80): 210–30.

———. "Maimonides on Human Perfection, Awe, and Politics." In *The Thought of Moses Maimonides,* ed. Ira Robinson, Lawrence Kaplan, and Julian Bauer, pp. 1–15. Lewiston, N.Y.: Edwin Mellen Press, 1990.

———. "Maimonides on Job 14:20 and the Story of the Garden of Eden" (in Hebrew). In *Between History and Literature: Essays in Honor of Isaac Barzilay,* ed. Shlomo Nash, pp. 143–48. Tel Aviv: Ha-Kibbuẓ ha-Me'uḥad, 1997.

Hayoun, Maurice R. *L'exégèse philosophique dans le judaïsme médiéval.* Tübingen: J.C.B. Mohr (Paul Siebeck), 1992.

Hourani, George F. *Averroes: On the Harmony of Religion and Philosophy.* London: Luzac, 1961.

Husik, Isaac. *A History of Medieval Jewish Philosophy.* Philadelphia: Jewish Publication Society of America, 1958.

Hyman, Arthur. "Demonstrative, Dialectical, and Sophistic Arguments in the Philosophy of Moses Maimonides." In *Maimonides in His Time,* ed. Eric L. Ormsby, pp. 35–51. Washington, D.C.: Catholic University Press, 1989.

Jacobs, Louis. *Theology in the Responsa.* London: Routledge and Kegan Paul, 1975.

Janzen, J. Gerald. *Job.* Atlanta: John Knox Press, 1985.

Japhet, Sara. *The Commentary of Rabbi Samuel Ben Meir (Rashbam) on the Book of Job* (in Hebrew). Jerusalem: Magnes Press, 2000.

Jaulus, Heinrich. "R. Simeon b. Zemach Duran: Ein Zeit und Lebensbild." *Monatsschrift für Geschichte und Wissenschaft des Judentums* 23 (1874): 241–59, 308–17, 355–66, 398–403, 447–61.

Jospe, Raphael. "The Book of Job as a Biblical *Guide of the Perplexed.*" In *Revelation, Reason, and Faith: Essays in Honor of Truman G. Madsen,* eds. Donald W. Parry, Daniel C. Peterson, and Stephen D. Ricks, pp. 566–84. Provo, Utah: Brigham Young University Press, 2002.

Kafka, Franz. *The Trial.* Translated by Douglas Scott and Chris Waller. London: Pan Books, 1977.

Kamin, Sarah. *Rashi's Exegetical Categorization in Respect to the Distinction between "Peshat" and "Derash"* (in Hebrew). Jerusalem: Magnes Press, 1983.

Kannengiesser, Charles. "Job chez les Pères." In *Dictionnaire de spiritualité,* eds. Marcel Viller, Charles Baumgartner, and André Rayez, pp. 1218–24. Paris: G. Beauchesne and Sons, 1974.

Kaplan, Lawrence. " 'I Sleep, but My Heart Waketh;' Maimonides' Conception of Human Perfection." In *The Thought of Moses Maimonides,* eds. Ira Robinson, Lawrence Kaplan, and Julian Bauer, pp. 130–66. Lewiston, N.Y.: Edwin Mellen Press, 1990.

———. "Maimonides, Dale Patrick, and Job XLII 6." *Vetus Testamentum* 28 (1978): 356–57.

Kasher, Hannah. "The Image and Views of Job in the *Guide of the Perplexed*" (in Hebrew). *Da'at* 15 (Summer 1985): 81–89.

———. "Joseph ibn Kaspi's Aristotelian Interpretation and Fundamentalist Interpretation of the Book of Job" (in Hebrew). *Da'at* 20 (1988): 117–25.

Kauffmann, Hermann Eziechel. *Die Anwendung des Buches Hiob in der Rabbinischen Aggadah.* Frankfurt a. M., 1893.

Kauffmann, Yehezkel. *The Religion of Israel.* Translated and abridged by Moshe Greenberg. Chicago: University of Chicago Press, 1960.

Kellner, Menachem. "Communication or the Lack Thereof among Thirteenth-Fourteenth Century Provençal Jewish Philosophers: Moses ibn Tibbon and Gersonides on Song of Songs." In *Communication in the Jewish Diaspora,* ed. Sophia Menache, pp. 227–45. Leiden: E. J. Brill, 1996.

———. *Dogma in Medieval Jewish Thought.* Oxford: Oxford University Press, 1986.

———. "Gersonides and his Cultured Despisers: Arama and Abravanel." *Journal of Medieval and Renaissance Studies* 6 (1976): 269–96.

———. *Gersonides' Commentary on Song of Songs.* New Haven: Yale University Press, 1998.

———. "Gersonides' Commentary on Song of Songs: For Whom Was It Written and Why?" In *Gersonide en son temps,* ed. Gilbert Dahan, pp. 81–107. Louvain-Paris: E. Peeters, 1991.

———. "Gersonides on the Problem of Volitional Creation." *Hebrew Union College Annual* 51 (1980): 111–28.

———. "Gersonides, Providence, and the Rabbinic Tradition." *Journal of the American Academy of Religion* 42 (1974): 673–85.

———. *Maimonides on Judaism and the Jewish People.* Albany: State University of New York Press, 1991.

Kepnes, Steven. *The Text as Thou: Martin Buber's Dialogical Hermeneutics and Narrative Theology.* Bloomington: Indiana University Press, 1992.

Klein-Braslavy, Sarah. "Gersonides on Determinism, Possibility, Choice, and Foreknowledge" (in Hebrew). *Da'at* 22 (1989): 5–53.

———. *Maimonides' Interpretation of the Adam Stories in Genesis: A Study in Maimonides' Anthropology* (in Hebrew). Jerusalem: Re'uven Mas, 1986.

———. *Maimonides' Interpretation of the Story of Creation* (in Hebrew). Jerusalem: Re'uven Mas, 1988.

———. "Toward an Identification of the Figures of 'Satan' and 'Samael' in Maimonides' Interpretation of the Garden of Eden Story" (in Hebrew). *Da'at* 10 (Winter 1983): 9–18.

Kogan, Barry S. "What Can We Know and When Can We Know It? Maimonides on the Active Intelligence and Human Cognition." In *Moses Maimonides in His Time,* ed. Eric L. Ormsby, pp. 121–37. Washington, D.C.: Catholic University of America, 1991.

Kravitz, Leonard S. "Maimonides on Job: An Enquiry as to the Method of the *Moreh.*" *Hebrew Union College Annual* 38 (1968): 149–58.

Kreisel, Howard. *Maimonides' Political Thought.* Albany: State University of New York Press, 1999.

———. " 'The Suffering of the Righteous' in Medieval Jewish Philosophy" (in Hebrew). *Da'at* 19 (1987): 17–29.

———. "Veridical Dreams and Prophecy in the Philosophy of Gersonides" (in Hebrew). *Da'at* 22 (1989): 73–84.

Lamb, Jonathan. *The Rhetoric of Suffering: Reading the Book of Job in the Eighteenth Century.* Oxford: Clarendon Press, 1995.

Lamm, Norman. "Maimonides on Love of God." *Maimonidean Studies* 3 (1992–93): 131–42.

Langermann, Tzvi. "Acceptance and Devaluation: Nahmanides' Attitude toward Science." *Journal of Jewish Thought and Philosophy* 1, no. 2 (1992): 223–45.

———. "A New Source for Samuel ibn Tibbon's Translation of the *Guide of the Perplexed* and His Notes on It" (in Hebrew). *Pe'amim* 72 (Summer 1997): 51–74.

———. "The True Perplexity: *The Guide of the Perplexed,* Part II, Chapter 24." In *Perspectives on Maimonides,* ed. Joel Kraemer, pp. 159–74. Oxford: Oxford University Press, 1991.

Leaman, Oliver. *Evil and Suffering in Jewish Philosophy.* Cambridge: Cambridge University Press, 1995.

Legrain, J.-F. "Variations musulmanes sur le thème de Job." *Bulletins d'études orientales* (1988): 51–114.

Leibowitz, Joseph H. "The Image of Job as Reflected in Rabbinic Writings." Ph.D. diss., University of California, Berkeley, 1987.

Levinger, Jacob S. "Maimonides' Exegesis of the Book of Job." In *Creative Biblical Exegesis: Christian and Jewish Hermeneutics Throughout the Centuries,* eds. Benjamin Uffenheimer and Henning Graf Reventlow, pp. 81–88. Sheffield: Sheffield Academic Press, 1988.

Lewalski, Barbara Kiefer. *Milton's Brief Epic: The Genre, Meaning, and Art of Paradise Regained.* Providence: Brown University Press, 1966.

MacLeish, Archibald. *J. B.* Cambridge, Mas.: Riverside Press, 1958.

Malter, Henry. *Saadia Gaon: His Life and Works.* Philadelphia: Jewish Publication Society of America, 1921.
Manekin, Charles. "Conservative Tendencies in Gersonides' Religious Philosophy." In *The Cambridge Companion to Medieval Jewish Philosophy,* eds. Daniel H. Frank and Oliver Leaman. Cambridge: Cambridge University Press, forthcoming.
Margalioth, Rachel. *The Original Job: The Problem and Its Solution* (in Hebrew). Jerusalem: Re'uven Mas, 1988.
Merlan, Phillip. *Monopsychism, Mysticism, and Metaconsciousness.* The Hague: Martinus Nijhoff, 1963.
Nadler, Allan. *The Faith of the Mitnadgim.* Baltimore: Johns Hopkins University Press, 1997.
Nehoray, Mikha'el. "Maimonides and Gersonides: Two Approaches to the Nature of Providence" (in Hebrew). *Da'at* 20 (Winter 1988): 51–64.
______. "Naḥmanides' Theory of Miracles and of Nature and Its Connection to R. Judah ha-Levi" (in Hebrew). *Da'at* 17 (1986): 23–31.
______. "R. Solomon ben R. Yuda' ha-Nasi and His Commentary on *The Guide of the Perplexed*" (in Hebrew). Ph.D. diss., Hebrew University, 1978.
Newsom, C. A., and Susan E. Schreiner. "Job." In *Dictionary of Biblical Interpretation,* ed. John H. Hayes, vol. 1, pp. 587–99. Nashville: Abingdon Press, 1999.
Novak, David. *The Theology of Nahmanides Systematically Presented.* Atlanta: Scholars Press, 1992.
Nuriel, Avraham. "Providence and Governance in *The Guide of the Perplexed*" (in Hebrew). *Tarbiẓ* 49 (Summer 1980): 346–55.
______. "Toward a Clarification of the Concept of Satan in *The Guide of the Perplexed*" (in Hebrew). *Jerusalem Studies in Jewish Thought* 5 (1986): 83–91.
Patrick, Dale. "The Translation of Job XLII 6." *Vetus Testamentum* 26 (1976): 369–71.
Pines, Shlomo. "The Limitations of Human Knowledge According to Al-Farabi, Ibn Bajja, and Maimonides." In *Studies in Medieval Jewish History and Literature I,* ed. Isadore Twersky, pp. 82–109. Cambridge, Mass.: Harvard University Press, 1979.
______. Translator's introduction. In Moses Maimonides, *The Guide of the Perplexed,* pp. lvii–cxxxiv. Chicago: University of Chicago Press, 1963.
Pope, Marvin H. *Job (Anchor Bible Commentary).* New York: Doubleday, 1965.
Raffel, Charles M. "Providence as Consequent upon the Intellect: Maimonides' Theory of Providence." *AJS Review* 12, no. 1 (Spring 1987): 25–72.
Ravitzky, Aviezer. "Aristotle's Book of *Meteorology* and the Ways of Maimonidean Exegesis in the Account of Creation" (in Hebrew). *Jerusalem Studies in Jewish Thought* 9 (1990): 225–49.
______. "The Hypostasis of Divine Wisdom in Thirteenth-Century Jewish Thought in Italy" (in Hebrew). *Italia* 3, no. 1–2 (1981): 7–38.
______. "Immanuel of Rome's *Commentary on the Book of Proverbs*: Its Sources" (in Hebrew). *Kiryat Sefer* 56 (1981): 726–39.
______. "The Possibility of Existence and Its Accidentality in Thirteenth-Century Maimonidean Interpretation" (in Hebrew). *Da'at* 2–3 (1978–79): 67–97.
______. "Samuel ibn Tibbon and the Esoteric Character of the *Guide of the Perplexed.*" *AJS Review* 6 (1981): 88–123.
______. "The Secrets of the *Guide of the Perplexed*: From the Thirteenth to the Twentieth Centuries." In *Studies in Maimonides,* ed. Isadore Twersky, pp. 159–207. Cambridge, Mass.: Harvard University Press, 1990.
______. "The Thought of Zeraḥiah ben Isaac ben She'altiel Ḥen and Maimonidean-

Tibbonian Philosophy in the Thirteenth Century" (in Hebrew). Ph.D. diss., Hebrew University, 1979.

Ravitzky, Israel. "R. Immanuel b. Solomon of Rome, *Commentary on the Song of Songs: Philosophical Division*" (in Hebrew). Master's thesis, Hebrew University, 1970.

Regev, Shaul. "Theology and Rational Mysticism in the Writings of R. Joseph ben Shem Tob" (in Hebrew). Ph.D. diss., Hebrew University, 1983.

Reines, Alvin. "Maimonides' Concepts of Providence and Theodicy." *Hebrew Union College Annual* 43 (1972): 169–205.

Renan, Ernst, and Adolf Neubauer. *Écrivains juifs français du XIVème siècle*. Vol. 27 of *Histoire littéraire de la France*. Paris, 1893.

Robinson, James. "Philosophy and Exegesis in Ibn Tibbon's *Commentary on Ecclesiastes*." Ph.D. diss., Harvard University, 2002.

Rosenberg, Shalom. "Job as Allegory: Philosophy and Literary Exegesis" (in Hebrew). In *Studies in Bible and Education*, ed. Dov Rafel, pp. 146–58. Jerusalem: Touro College, 1996.

______. "On Biblical Interpretation in *The Guide of the Perplexed*" (in Hebrew). *Jerusalem Studies in Jewish Thought* 1 (1981): 85–157.

______. "Philosophical Hermeneutics on the Song of Songs: Introductory Remarks" (in Hebrew). *Tarbiẓ* 59 (1990): 133–51.

______. "The *Sefer ha-Higayon* of Elijah ben Eliezer ha-Yerushalmi" (in Hebrew). *Da'at* 1, no. 1 (Winter 1978): 63–71.

Rosenblum, Noah. *The Malbim: Exegesis, Philosophy, Science, and Mysticism in the Writings of Rabbi Me'ir Leivush Malbim* (in Hebrew). Jerusalem: Mosad ha-Rav Kuk, 1988.

Rosenthal, E.I.J. "Saadya's Exegesis of the Book of Job." In *Saadya Studies*, ed. E.I.J. Rosenthal, pp. 177–205. New York: Arno Press, 1980.

Rowley, Harold H. "The Book of Job and Its Meaning." In *From Moses to Qumran: Studies in the Old Testament*, pp. 141–86. New York: Association Press, 1963.

Rudavsky, Tamar. "Divine Omniscience and Future Contingents in Gersonides." *Journal of the History of Philosophy* 21 (October 1983): 513–36.

______. "Divine Omniscience, Contingency, and Prophecy in Gersonides." In *Divine Omniscience and Omnipotence in Medieval Philosophy*, ed. Tamar Rudavsky, pp. 161–81. Dordrecht: D. Reidel, 1985.

Samuelson, Norbert. "Gersonides' Account of God's Knowledge of Particulars." *Journal of the History of Philosophy* 10 (1972): 399–416.

______. "The Problem of Free Will in Maimonides, Gersonides, and Aquinas." *CCAR Journal* 17 (1970): 2–20.

Saperstein, Marc. "The Conflict over the Rashba's *Ḥerem* on Philosophical Study in Political Perspective." *Jewish History* 1 (1986): 27–38.

______. *Decoding the Rabbis: A Thirteenth-Century Commentary on the Aggadah*. Cambridge, Mass.: Harvard University Press, 1980.

Sarachek, Joseph. *Faith and Reason: The Conflict over the Rationalism of Maimonides*. Williamsport: Bayard Press, 1935.

Schatzmiller, Joseph. "Gersonides and the Jewish Community of Orange in his Day" (in Hebrew). *University of Haifa Studies in the History of the Jewish People and the Land of Israel* 2 (1972): 111–26.

______. "Gersonide et la société juive de son temps." In *Gersonide en son temps*, ed. Gilbert Dahan, pp. 33–43. Louvain-Paris: E. Peeters, 1991.

______. "Some Further Information about Gersonides and the Orange Jewish Community in his Day" (in Hebrew). *University of Haifa Studies in the History of the Jewish People and the Land of Israel* 3 (1972): 139–43.

———. "Suggestions and Addenda to *Gallia Judaica*" (in Hebrew). *Kiryat Sefer* 45 (September 1970): 607–10.

Scholem, Gershom. *Kabbalah.* Jerusalem: Keter, 1974.

———. *On The Mystical Shape of the Godhead.* Translated by Joachim Neurgroschel and Jonathan Chipman. New York: Schocken Books, 1991.

———. *Sabbatai Ṣevi: The Mystical Messiah, 1626–1676.* Translated by R. J. Zwi Werblowsky. Princeton: Princeton University Press, 1973.

Schreiner, Susan E. *Where Shall Wisdom Be Found? Calvin's Exegesis of Job from Medieval and Modern Perspectives.* Chicago: University of Chicago Press, 1994.

Schwartz, Dov. "The Debate over the Maimonidean Theory of Providence in Thirteenth-Century Jewish Philosophy." *Jewish Studies Quarterly* 2, no. 2 (1995): 185–96.

———. "The *Mesharet Moshe* of R. Kalonymus" (in Hebrew). *Kovez̧ 'al Yad,* n.s. 14, no. 24 (1998): 297–394.

Segal, Moshe H. *Biblical Exegesis* (in Hebrew). Jerusalem: Kiryat Sefer, 1952.

Septimus, Bernard. *Hispano-Jewish Culture in Transition: The Career and Controversies of Ramah.* Cambridge, Mass.: Harvard University Press, 1982.

Shechterman, Deborah. "The Philosophy of Immanuel of Rome in Light of His Commentary on the Book of Genesis" (in Hebrew). Ph.D. diss., Hebrew University, 1984.

Shiffman, Ya'ir. "Rabbi Shem Tov ben Joseph Falaquera's *Moreh ha-Moreh.*" 2 vols. Ph.D. diss., Hebrew University, 1990.

Siger, Leonard. "The Image of Job in the Renaissance." Ph.D. diss., Johns Hopkins University, 1960.

Silver, Daniel J. *Maimonidean Criticism and Maimonidean Controversy, 1180–1240.* Leiden: E. J. Brill, 1965.

Silverman, David W. "The Problem of Prophecy in Gersonides." Ph.D. diss., Columbia University, 1975.

Simon, Uriel. *Four Approaches to the Book of Psalms: From Saadiah Gaon to Abraham ibn Ezra.* Translated by Lenn J. Schramm. Albany: State University of New York Press, 1991.

Sirat, Colette. *A History of Jewish Philosophy in the Middle Ages.* Cambridge: Cambridge University Press, 1986.

Smalley, Beryl. *The Study of the Bible in the Middle Ages.* Notre Dame: University of Notre Dame Press, 1964.

Staub, Jacob J. *The Creation of the World According to Gersonides.* Chico, Calif.: Scholars Press, 1982.

Steinschneider, Moritz. *Die Hebraïsche Übersetzungen des Mittelalters und die Juden als Dolmetscher.* Berlin, 1893.

———. "Levi ben Gerson." In *Gesammelte Schriften,* vol. 1, pp. 233–70. Berlin: H. Poppelauer, 1925.

Stern, Gregg. "Menaḥem ha-Meiri and the Second Controversy over Philosophy." Ph.D. diss., Harvard University, 1995.

Strauss, Leo. "How to Begin to Study *The Guide of the Perplexed.*" In *The Guide of the Perplexed,* trans. Shlomo Pines, pp. xi–lvi. Chicago: University of Chicago Press, 1963.

———. "The Literary Character of the *Guide of the Perplexed.*" In *Persecution and the Art of Writing,* pp. 38–94. Glencoe, Ill.: Free Press, 1952.

———. "Der Ort der Vorsehungslehre nach der Ansicht Maimunis." *Monatsschrift für Geschichte und Wissenschaft des Judentums* 81 (1937): 93–105.

———. *Persecution and the Art of Writing*. Glencoe, Ill.: Free Press, 1952.

———. *Philosophy and Law*. Translated by Fred Baumann. Philadelphia: Jewish Publication Society of America, 1987.

———. "Quelques remarques sur la Science Politique de Maïmonide et de Farabi." *Revue des études juives* 99–100 (1935–36): 1–37.

Susman, Margerete. *Das Buch Hiob und das Schicksal des jüdischen Volkes*. Zurich, 1946.

Talmage, Frank. "Apples of Gold: The Inner Meaning of Sacred Texts in Medieval Judaism." In *Jewish Spirituality*, vol. 1, ed. Arthur Green, pp. 313–56. New York: Crossroad, 1988.

Terrien, Samuel. *Job: Poet of Existence*. New York: Bobbs-Merrill, 1957.

Tishby, Isaiah, and Fischel Lachower, eds. *The Wisdom of the Zohar: An Anthology of Texts*. Translated by David Goldstein. 3 vols. London: Oxford University Press, 1991.

Touati, Charles. "La controverse de 1303–1306 autour des études philosophiques et scientifiques." *Revue des études juives* 127 (1968): 21–37.

———. "Les deux théories de Maïmonide sur la providence." In *Studies in Jewish Religious and Intellectual History*, ed. Siegfried Stein and Raphael Loewe, pp. 331–40. University, Ala.: University of Alabama Press; London: Institute of Jewish Studies, 1979.

———. *La pensée philosophique et théologique de Gersonide*. Paris: Editions de Minuit, 1973.

———. "Le problème de l'inerrance prophétique dans le théologie juive du Moyen Age." *Revue de l'histoire des religions* 174 (1968): 169–87.

Tsevat, Matitiahu. "The Meaning of the Book of Job." *Hebrew Union College Annual* 37 (1966): 73–106.

Twersky, Isadore. "Aspects of the Social and Cultural History of Provençal Jewry." In *Jewish Society Through the Ages*, ed. Haim Hillel Ben Sasson and Shmu'el Ettinger, pp. 185–207. New York: Schocken Books, 1971.

———. *Introduction to the Code of Maimonides (Mishneh Torah)*. New Haven: Yale University Press, 1980.

———. *Rabad of Posquières*. Cambridge, Mass.: Harvard University Press, 1962.

Urbach, Ephraim E. *The Sages: Their Concepts and Beliefs*. Translated by Israel Abrahams. Cambridge, Mass.: Harvard University Press, 1987.

Van Wolde, E. J. "Job 42:1–6: The Reversal of Job." In *The Book of Job*, ed. W.A.M. Beuken, pp. 223–50. Leuven: Leuven University Press, 1994.

Vajda, Georges. *L'amour de Dieu dans la théologie juive du Moyen Age*. Paris: J. Vrin, 1956.

———. "An Analysis of *Ma'amar yiqqawu ha-Mayim* by Samuel ben Judah ibn Tibbon." *Journal of Jewish Studies* 10, no. 3–4 (1959): 137–49.

———. *Isaac Albalag: averroïste juif, tradacteur, et annotateur d'Al-Ghazâlî*. Paris: J. Vrin, 1960.

———. *Recherches sur la philosophie et la kabbale dans la pensée juive du Moyen Age*. Paris: Mouton, 1962.

Ventura, Moïse. "Belief in Providence According to Gersonides" (in Hebrew). In *Minḥah le-Avraham*, pp. 12–21. Jerusalem, 1959.

———. *La philosophie de Saadia Gaon*. Paris, 1934.

Walfish, Barry D. *Esther in Medieval Garb: Jewish Interpretation of the Book of Esther in the Middle Ages.* Albany: State University of New York Press, 1993.

Weil, Gérard E. *La bibliothèque de Gersonide d'après son catalogue autograph.* Louvain-Paris: E. Peeters, 1991.

Weil-Guény, Anne-Marie. "Gersonide en son temps: un tableau chronologique." In *Studies on Gersonides: A Fourteenth-Century Jewish Philosopher-Scientist,* ed. Gad Freudenthal, pp. 355–65. Leiden: E. J. Brill, 1992.

Weinberg, Joanna. "Job versus Abraham: The Quest for the Perfect God-Fearer in Rabbinic Tradition." In *The Book of Job,* ed. W.A.M. Beuken, pp. 281–96. Leuven: Leuven University Press, 1994.

Weiss, Raymond L. *Maimonides' Ethics.* Chicago: University of Chicago Press, 1991.

Wjernikowski, Isaak. *Das Buch Hiob nach der Auffassung der rabbinischen Literatur in den ersten fünf nachchristlichen Jahrhunderten.* Breslau: H. Fleischmann, 1902.

Wohlman, Avital. *Thomas d'Aquin et Maïmonide: un dialogue exemplaire.* Paris: Cerf, 1988.

Wolfson, Harry A. "Maimonides and Gersonides on Divine Attributes as Ambiguous Terms." In *Studies in the History of Philosophy and Religion,* ed. Isadore Twersky and George H. Williams, vol. 2, pp. 231–47. Cambridge, Mass.: Harvard University Press, 1977.

Yaffe, Martin D. "Providence in Medieval Aristotelianism: Moses Maimonides and Thomas Aquinas on the Book of Job." *Hebrew Studies* 19–20 (1979–80): 62–74.

Index

Aaron ben Elijah, 238n12, 265n67
Aaron ben Joseph, 238n12
Abba Mari ben Eligdor, 265n66
Abraham, 23, 181. *See also* Binding of Isaac
Active Intellect, 47, 58, 59, 64, 89, 123, 124, 150, 153, 192–93, 268n87
Afterlife, 26, 40–41, 97, 188, 264n61. *See also* Immortality
Aggadah, 284n79
'Akeidah. See Binding of Isaac
Albalag, Isaac, 285n85
Albo, Joseph, 176, 297n1
Alcorsano, Judah ben Joseph, 201–2
Alfarabi, 249n15, 259n138
Allegory, 206–7, 219, 239n16
  Christian thinkers' use of, 300n11
  Duran on, 195, 293n65
  Elijah ben Eliezer ha-Yerushalmi on, 268n87
  Gersonides on, 148, 152–53, 157–58, 160
  Ibn Tibbon on, 101–2, 264n62
  Maimonides on, 49, 73, 101–2, 272n25, 272n38
  Zeraḥiah Ḥen on, 114–17, 125–26, 131, 135, 136, 138, 141
Al-Zamakhshari, 245n53
Ambrose, 40, 258n118
Anatoli, Jacob, 239n14, 270n1, 299n18
Angel of death, 53, 120, 252n62
Angels, 243n18
  Elihu, on intercession of, 56, 57, 58–60, 61, 88–90, 92–93, 106, 123, 124, 150–51, 188, 204, 212–13, 267n87
  Maimonides on, 50–51
  Saadiah on, 24
Aquinas, Thomas, 40, 224, 247n89, 257n105, 274n62, 302n27
'Arama, Isaac, 7, 239n12
'Arama, Meir, 9, 297n1, 301n17
Arieli, Naḥum, 176, 290n8, 290n10
Aristotelianism, 5, 43, 144, 157, 176, 191, 193, 195, 225
Aristotle, 45, 46, 145, 148, 156, 158
  on evil, 282n36
  and Ibn Tibbon's theory of providence, 90–92, 99
  Job as representative of, 56, 121, 122, 169, 171, 277n105
  and logic, 268n92, 270n100, 286n97
  and Maimonides' theory of providence, 75–6, 90, 99, 249n15
Arundi, Isaac, 108–9, 205, 216, 297n3, 301n17

Ash'arites, 28, 45, 56, 71, 93, 158
Averroes, 144, 263n36, 277n106

Beney elohim. *See* Divine Beings
Bildad, 93, 107, 108, 146, 158, 166, 267n83. *See also* Job, Book of: dialogue in
Binding of Isaac (*'akeidah*), 19–20, 29–30, 185, 214, 299n12
Bleich, J. David, 176
Buber, Martin, 225, 301n13
Budde, Karl, 222

Calvin, John, 224
Cassiodorus, 40
Chance occurrence. *See* Evil: caused by chance occurrence
Christian scholasticism, 270n4
Christianity, 246n82. *See also* Job, Book of: Christian commentators
Chrysostom, John, 40, 258n118
Commandments, 177, 179, 181, 228, 246n79
Conventional truths, 120
Cornill, Carl, 222
Crescas, Asher, 255n79
Crescas, Ḥasdai, 7, 176

Daniel, 272n35
Derash, 219, 239n17
Divination, 60–61, 70
Divine beings (*beney elohim*), 24, 50–51, 53–54, 62, 119–20, 152–53, 273n51
Divine spirit, 139
Dobbs-Weinstein, Idit, 257n105
Duran, Simon ben Ẓemaḥ, 204, 175–202, 204f., 224, 237n7

Ecclesiastes, Book of, 8, 113, 154, 219, 240n19
Edom, 181
Efodi, 50, 60
Elihu, 11, 204, 209–10
  Duran's interpretation of, 182, 184–90, 196
  Gersonides' interpretation of, 146, 150–51, 153–54, 160, 162, 170
  Ibn Tibbon's interpretation of, 81, 83f., 98, 104–5, 106
  Maimonides' interpretation of, 56–62, 75
  modern interpretations of, 222
  Saadiah's interpretation of, 21, 26–27
  Zeraḥiah Ḥen's interpretation of, 122–25, 127–28
  See also Angels, Elihu on intercession of; Job, Book of: dialogue in
Elijah ben Eliezer ha-Yerushalmi, 107–8, 205, 216
Eliphaz, 75, 121–22, 145, 246n67, 269n99. *See also* Job, Book of: dialogue in
Emanation, 69
Epicurus, 45
Esau, 181
Esoteric discourse, 214, 223, 227, 228–29
  Duran and, 177
  Gersonides and, 144–45, 166, 172, 280n8
  Ibn Tibbon and, 79–81, 91, 95, 99, 103–4, 261n4
  Immanuel of Rome and, 267n79, 267n83
  Maimonides and, 44, 47, 55–6, 75, 249n14, 249n15, 261n4
  Zeraḥiah Ḥen and, 113, 115–16, 117, 122, 127–30, 133–34, 136–37, 140–41
Evil, 51–55, 148–49, 149–50, 153, 254n73, 282n36, 291n26
  caused by chance occurrence, 82, 84, 87, 149
  caused by matter, 51, 82, 84, 106, 108, 119–20, 149, 206–7, 212
  caused by privation, 51–55, 62, 82, 206–7, 212
  See also Suffering; Theodicy
Evil inclination, 53, 54, 120, 252n60
Ezekiel
  first chapter in Book of, 219, 240n19, 250n26, 278n111
  the prophet, 148, 272n35

Fohrer, Georg, 222
Frank, Daniel H., 258n128
Frost, Robert, 222, 225
Fullerton, Kember, 228

Garden of Eden, 36, 119, 120, 246n79, 286n89
Geiger, Abraham, 112
Genesis, first three chapters of, 219, 240n19
Gersonides, 6, 108, 143–73, 182, 193, 196, 197, 204f., 293n65, 295n90, 297n3, 298n9, 298n10, 299n18
Glatzer, Nahum, 238n12, 240n27
God
  address to Job, 11, 32, 56–57, 62–64, 75, 94, 102, 104–5, 106, 116, 125–26, 134, 151, 160–61, 196, 210–11, 225, 240n27, 269n99
  attributes of, 56, 64, 68, 169, 254n73, 264n63, 288n121
  contemplation of, 46–47, 57, 66–68 (*see also* Knowledge: of God)
  divine knowledge, 13, 49, 146, 170, 281n20
  impersonal character of, 94–95, 96, 108, 122, 140–41, 146–7, 170–71, 214
  justice of, 21, 22, 83–84, 97, 145–46, 182, 224, 225
  love of, 57, 65, 68
  will of, 146, 170
Goldman, Jacob, 259n139
Good, Edwin M., 222, 223, 224
Goodman, Lenn E., 18, 24, 28, 32, 245n53, 259n130
Gordis, Robert, 222, 225, 226, 238n9, 292n40
Greenberg, Moshe, 240n17, 278n114
Gregory the Great, 40, 246n82, 247n89, 258n118, 274n59, 297n110, 298n7
Guttmann, Jakob, 176
Guttmann, Julius, 7, 250n17, 290n8, 296n97

Habel, Norman C., 138, 222, 223, 225, 250n22, 298n6
Halevi, Judah, 191
Harvey, Steven, 250n26
Harvey, Warren Zev, 238n12, 257n105
Ḥen, Zeraḥiah, 13, 14, 111–42, 196, 204f., 223, 225, 226, 228, 229, 265n67, 266n70, 284n77, 285n81
Hillel of Verona, 111, 271n21
Husik, Isaac, 7

Ibn Bajja, 258n121
Ibn Ezra, Abraham, 114, 238n12, 284n60, 284n79, 294n73, 296n96
Ibn Tibbon, Moses, 113, 285n79, 297n2
Ibn Tibbon, Samuel, 13, 14, 79–110, 204f., 299n18
  and Duran, 196, 294n81
  and Gersonides, 153–54, 288n118
  and Immanuel of Rome, 266n73
  and Maimonides, 82–83, 91–92, 98f., 113, 249n17, 262n63, 264n58, 264n61, 264n62
  and modern interpreters of Job, 225, 226, 228, 229
  and Nissim ben Moshe of Marseilles, 255n84
  and Zeraḥiah Ḥen, 111, 132, 278n111, 278n112
Imagination, 51, 53, 120, 131, 253n62, 273n55
Imitatio Dei, 258n128
Immanuel of Rome, 106–7, 205, 216, 266n70, 266n73
Immortality, 204, 265n67
  Duran on, 293n65
  Elijah ben Eliezer ha-Yerushalmi on, 268n87
  Gersonides on, 140, 141, 147, 149, 151, 155, 157
  Ibn Tibbon on, 83f., 255n84, 262n17
  Maimonides on, 53, 67, 252n56
  Zeraḥiah Ḥen on, 98–101, 105, 107, 108, 124, 127, 131–32, 134, 135
  See also Afterlife
Intellect, 46–47, 48, 54, 57, 58, 83, 99, 107, 120, 123–24, 131
  acquired intellect, 66–67, 68, 69, 70
  and cognition, 109
  practical intellect, 46, 57f., 264n58
Intelligibles, 120
Isaac, 243n19
Ishmael, 243n18
Islam. *See* Job (the person): Islamic views of

Janzen, J. Gerald, 229
Japhet, Sara, 237n6
Jewish people. *See* Job (the person): as representative of the Jewish people

Job (the person)
afflictions of, 54–55, 61, 115–16, 140–41, 149–50, 254n73, 258n122
anger and pride of, 69–70, 258n128
assessment of, 10–11, 23–24, 31–32, 72–73, 115, 119, 121, 130, 132–34, 139, 149, 157, 161–62, 181–82, 190, 196, 207–8, 210–11, 224, 258n127, 277n100
background of, 10, 23, 114, 149, 181, 223, 240n21, 244n33
children of, 55, 82, 115, 254n73, 262n15
Islamic views of, 19, 28, 245n53
praised by God, 31–32, 67, 162, 189, 196
and prophecy, 101–2, 125–26, 179, 182, 183, 269n99, 278n111
protests of, 72–73, 121, 160, 196, 207, 208
recantation of, 27, 65–67, 133, 151–52, 161, 196
representative of humanity, 12, 32, 197, 259n138
representative of the Jewish people, 12, 32–36, 163–65, 197, 201, 210–11, 213, 298n7
representative of personal suffering, 199–202
rewards of, 71, 108, 117, 126, 132, 162–63
sacrifices offered by, 283n48
wealth of, 200, 242n12, 296n103
wife of, 119, 245n53
Job, Book of
authorship of, 23, 117–19, 138, 139, 148, 177, 211–12, 279n127, 282n29, 298n7
Christian commentators on, 11, 32, 39–41, 97, 138, 223, 224, 227–26, 236n2, 258n118, 267n83, 274n59, 274n62, 294n75, 300n11, 302n27
dialogue in, 11, 21, 23, 32, 36, 55–56, 71, 74, 108, 116, 119, 120–21, 131, 152, 158, 159, 160–61, 166, 171–72, 179, 182–83, 190, 194–95, 195–96, 204, 208–9, 224, 246n82
exemplifies rational speculation, 273n47
historical-critical approaches to, 222
historical veracity of 10, 31, 48, 114–17, 148, 157, 195, 206–7, 222–23, 300n11 (*see also* Allegory)
intended audience of, 11–12, 32–33, 73–74, 159, 163–65, 197, 210–11, 223
literary character of, 116, 138, 278n114
modern readings of, 221–30
name of, 121
peshat commentaries on, 4
rabbinic interpretation of, 4, 5, 28, 29–30, 236n3, 238n8, 240n26, 240n27
relationship of prologue and epilogue, 73, 160, 207
and the Torah, 104, 119, 214, 225
See also God: address to Job
Jospe, Raphael, 260n149
Judah ben Solomon, 111, 112, 120, 271n14, 277n99

Kabbalah, 176, 179, 190–91, 237n7
Kafka, Franz, 222
Karaites, 238n12
Kasher, Hannah, 76
Kaspi, Joseph ibn, 7, 8, 194–95, 285n85, 299n18
Kauffmann, Yehezkel, 222
Kellner, Menachem, 259n137, 284n79
Kimḥi, David, 114, 271n10
Knowledge
of God, 66, 225 (*see also* God: contemplation of)
limitations of, 64, 65, 168–69, 256n105
Kravitz, Leonard, 51, 57, 252n62
Kreisel, Howard, 66

Leibowitz, Joseph H., 240n27
Levi ben Abraham of Villefranche, 255n82
Leviathan, 293n65
Levinger, Jacob, 57, 71, 252n62
Logic. *See* Aristotle: and logic
Lowth, Robert, 301n11
Luther, Martin, 301n11, 246n82

MacLeish, Archibald, 222
Magen Avot, date of composition, 294n88
Maimonides, 5, 6, 7, 13, 14, 15, 31, 43–77, 204f., 240n17

controversy over writings of, 156–57, 158, 159
and Duran, 182, 190, 198, 202
and Elijah ben Eliezer ha-Yerushalmi, 267n86
and Gersonides, 144, 152, 154f.
and Ibn Tibbon, 82–83, 91–92, 98f., 113, 249n17, 262n63, 264n58, 264n61, 264n62
and Immanuel of Rome, 267n83
and modern interpreters of Job, 224, 225, 226, 228, 229
and Saadiah, 204, 205
and Zeraḥiah Ḥen, 111, 113, 114, 115, 119, 122, 126–27, 128, 130, 131–34, 137, 146, 276n87, 277n100
Malbim, 238n12
Matter. *See* Evil: caused by matter
Medieval Jewish philosophy, 5–6
conservative vs. radical, 5–6, 140–41, 205, 213–14, 225
controversial nature of, 5
in the fifteenth century, 290n8, 296n97
in Italy, 270n4
scholarship on, 6–7, 217–19
Midrash, 2329n17
Midrash Iyyov, 236n3
Miracles, 179, 289n134
Moral virtue, 46, 48–49, 55, 150
Moses, 23, 117, 119, 138, 148, 161, 177, 279n127, 282n29, 287n99, 298n7
Munk, Solomon, 50, 59
Mu'tazilites, 19, 28, 45, 56, 71, 93–94, 107, 121, 130, 158

Nadler, Allan, 296n103
Naḥmanides, 114, 179, 191, 192, 193–94, 237n7, 271n21
Naḥmias, She'alti'el, 246n82
Narboni, Moses, 254n73, 255n79, 259n139, 260n143, 285n85
Nathan of Gaza, 237n7
Natural science, 126, 149
Nature, 178–79
Nicholas of Lyra, 300n11
Nissim ben Moshe of Marseilles, 255n84, 265n67
Noah, 262n35
Nuriel, Avraham, 50, 54

Ohev Mishpat, date of composition, 294n88
Origen, 298n7, 298n8

Peshat, 4, 5, 13, 113, 114, 152, 219, 237n5, 237n7, 271n21
Philosophical exegesis
neglect of in modern scholarship, 7–8, 144
and systematic philosophy, 13–14, 38–39, 74–76, 105, 139–41, 165–72, 197–98, 212–17
Phineas of Polotsk, 296n103
Pines, Shlomo, 252n56
Plato, 249n15, 258n121
Political philosophy, 151
Pope, Marvin H., 222, 225
Privation. *See* Evil: caused by privation
Prophecy
Duran on, 292n35
Gersonides on, 146, 147, 150, 153, 167–68, 263n46, 287n98
Ibn Tibbon on, 85–86, 94–95, 98, 106, 107, 263n46, 288n118
Maimonides on, 56, 57, 60, 263n46
Saadiah on, 244n36
Zeraḥiah Ḥen on, 123, 124, 131–32, 135, 139, 141
See also Job (the person): and prophecy
Proverbs, Book of, 8, 111, 113, 219, 240n19, 279n127
Providence
Duran on, 177, 178–80, 190–91, 297n106
general providence, 56, 92–93, 150
Gersonides on, 145–47, 151–52
Ibn Tibbon on, 83f., 265n66, 288n118
individual providence, 45–48, 122–24, 146, 148, 149, 150, 155, 160, 163, 180
Maimonides on, 45–48, 56, 57, 63, 74–76, 249n14, 286n87
Zeraḥiah Ḥen on, 122–25, 127, 133, 273n46
See also Suffering: as providential

Raffel, Charles, 58, 60, 65, 249n14, 250n17, 259n139
Rashbam, 219, 237
Rashi, 219, 284n60, 284n79, 296n96

Ravitzky, Aviezer, 96, 103, 112, 261n3, 262n9, 266n70, 270n4, 271n14
Reincarnation, 192, 193–94
Reines, Alvin, 51
Resurrection of the dead, 282n39, 292n37
Reward and punishment
  Duran on, 177, 179, 182, 183, 187–89, 190, 291n26
  Elijah ben Eliezer ha-Yerushalmi on, 108
  Immanuel of Rome on, 107
  of Jewish people, 35, 164
  Job's view of, 47, 49, 66
  Saadiah on, 18, 21–22, 23, 35
Rosenberg, Shalom, 51
Rowely, Harold H., 222, 225

Saadiah Gaon, 5, 17–41, 204f., 273n46
  and Duran, 190, 191, 192, 197, 198, 294n75
  and Gersonides, 163
  and Ibn Tibbon, 97, 106, 263n36
  and Maimonides, 43, 44, 59, 71–72, 77
  and modern interpreters of Job, 224
Satan, 207, 212–13, 245n53
  Duran on, 179–80, 182, 185, 186, 190, 192
  Elijah ben Eliezer ha-Yerushalmi on, 267n86
  Gersonides on, 152–53
  Ibn Tibbon on, 82–83, 84, 106, 108
  Maimonides on, 49, 50–55, 62, 67, 252n62
  Saadiah Gaon on, 24–25, 224, 244n36
  Zeraḥiah Ḥen on, 116, 119–20, 131, 273n55
Schreiner, Susan E., 224, 241n29, 299n1, 300n6, 302n27
Schwartz, Israel, 112
Scriptor, 267n83
Seforno, Obadiah, 9, 297n1
Segal, Moshe, 239n17
Separate Intellects, 50, 64, 66
Shabbetai Ẓevi, 237n7
Shechterman, Deborah, 267n79, 267n83
Sheḥin, 254n73
Shem Tov ben Joseph ibn Shem Tov, 50, 249n15, 255n79
Simon, Uriel, 8
Solomon ben Yuda' ha-Nasi, 254n73, 255n79, 259n139, 260n143
Song of Songs, 8, 113, 219, 240n19, 286n89
Soul, 53, 67, 70, 179, 191
Steinschneider, Moritz, 112
Strauss, Leo, 241n30, 249n15
Suffering
  definition of, 199–200
  as providential, 84–87, 108–9, 146, 147, 154, 167, 183, 227, 284n76
  of the righteous, 18–21, 166, 171, 177, 180–81, 243n19
  as a test, 18–19, 21–22, 23, 24, 25, 26–27, 35, 72, 181, 184–88, 191, 196, 198, 214, 224, 242n10
Sufferings of love (*yisurin shel ahavah*), 19, 29, 146, 183, 184, 192, 193
Susman, Margerete, 301n13

Tam, Jacob, 247n89
Terrien, Samuel, 222, 224, 225
Tests, divine. *See* Suffering: as a test
Theodicy, 39, 225. *See also* Evil; Suffering
Theodore, Bishop of Mopsuestia, 300n11
Tokheḥah, 287n103
Touati, Charles, 57, 58, 60, 65, 259n139
Trials, divine. *See* Suffering: as a test
Tsevat, Matitiahu, 222, 225, 228–29

Uz, land of, 48, 115, 245n61, 250n22, 272n25

Vajda, Georges, 261n 3, 262n9

Walfish, Barry, 8, 298n7
Warburton, William, 301n11
Wohlman, Avital, 257n105
Wolfson, Harry A., 6
World to come, 18, 56, 130, 184

Yaffee, Martin, 257n105

Zophar, 146, 158. *See also* Job, Book of: dialogue in